Driven from Home

Driven from Home

Protecting the Rights of Forced Migrants

David Hollenbach, Editor

Georgetown University Press ▪ Washington, D.C.

Chapter 7, "Closed Borders, Human Rights, and Democratic Legitimation," by Arash Abizadeh, draws on his chapter "Citizenship, Immigration, and Boundaries," in *Ethics and World Politics,* ed. D. S. A. Bell (Oxford: Oxford University Press, forthcoming).

The image for the cover is from "Refugees Waiting" by Betty LaDuke, 2000. The original painting is 44″ by 32″ acrylic on canvas. The artist's website is www.bettyladuke.com.
The photograph of the painting was done by Robert Jaffe, rob@robjaffe.com.

Library of Congress Cataloging-in-Publication Data

Driven from home : protecting the rights of forced migrants / David Hollenbach, editor.
    p. cm.
  This book is the second phase of an ongoing project on the human rights of refugees and forcibly displaced persons conducted by the Center for Human Rights and International Justice at Boston College . . . of which a second conference is the outcome.
  Includes bibliographical references and index.
  ISBN 978-1-58901-646-0 (pbk. : alk. paper)
1. Refugees. 2. Forced migration. 3. Human rights. I. Hollenbach, David. II. Boston College. Center for Human Rights and International Justice.
  HV640.D74 2010
  323.3′2914—dc22

             2009026932

15 14 13 12 11 10   9 8 7 6 5 4 3 2
First printing

Printed in the United States of America

Contents

Acknowledgments   vii

Introduction: *Human Rights and New Challenges of Protecting Forced Migrants*   1
   David Hollenbach

Part I
New Realities of Protection in a Human Rights Framework

   1   Rethinking the International Refugee Regime in Light of Human Rights and the Global Common Good   15
   Susan F. Martin

Part II
Normative Responses: *Religion, Human Rights, Gender, and Culture*

   2   Justice for the Displaced: *The Challenge of a Christian Understanding*   37
   Agbonkhianmeghe E. Orobator

   3   Human Rights as a Framework for Advocacy on Behalf of the Displaced: *The Approach of the Catholic Church*   55
   Silvano Tomasi

   4   No Easy Road to Freedom: *Engendering and Enculturating Forced Migration*   71
   M. Brinton Lykes

Part III
Protecting Rights at the Border: *Denial of Asylum and Systemic Responses*

   5   Human Rights as a Challenge to National Policies That Exclude Refugees: *Two Case Studies from Southeast Asia*   97
   Frank Brennan

6 Loving Humanity while Accepting Real People: A *Critique and a Cautious Affirmation of the "Political" in U.S. Asylum and Refugee Law* 115
   Daniel Kanstroom

7 Closed Borders, Human Rights, and Democratic Legitimation 147
   Arash Abizadeh

Part IV
Protection in the Face of Conflict and War

8 The Experience of Displacement by Conflict: *The Plight of Iraqi Refugees* 169
   Maryanne Loughry

9 The Ethics and Policy of War in Light of Displacement 185
   J. Bryan Hehir

10 Reinserting "Never" into "Never Again": *Political Innovations and the Responsibility to Protect* 207
   Thomas G. Weiss

Part V
Protection in Response to Economic Need and Environmental Crises

11 Economic and Environmental Displacement: *Implications for Durable Solutions* 231
   Mary M. DeLorey

12 Refugees or Economic Migrants: *Catholic Thought on the Moral Roots of the Distinction* 249
   Christopher Llanos

Contributors 271
Index 275

Acknowledgments

This book is the second phase of an ongoing project on the human rights of refugees and forcibly displaced persons conducted by the Center for Human Rights and International Justice at Boston College. The key element in the first phase of the project was a conference held in Nairobi, Kenya. The Nairobi conference led to an earlier publication: *Refugee Rights: Ethics, Advocacy, and Africa,* published by Georgetown University Press in 2008. The present book is the outcome of a second conference that again drew together both scholars and practitioners working with and on behalf of forcibly displaced persons. Once again, the endeavor was supported both by the Jesuit Refugee Service (JRS), which works with refugees in fifty countries around the world, and by Catholic Relief Services (CRS), which works on humanitarian assistance and development worldwide.

I am particularly grateful to Daisy Francis of CRS, who made many valuable suggestions on whom to invite to the conference as presenters and respondents. She has helped me appreciate more fully the importance of interaction between practical and academic approaches to the questions we addressed. Ken Hackett, president of CRS, was most gracious in once again providing financial support from his organization. Peter Balleis and Elias Lopez, respectively international director and assistant international director of JRS, were also of great help. Lopez helped refine ideas about the direction of the project, and Balleis suggested bringing the ten regional directors of JRS from around the world to the conference table. Their participation was most valuable.

I am also grateful to Anjani Datla, the assistant director of the Center for Human Rights and International Justice, for making the conference run smoothly and for her skillful help with the editing. Latisha Cansler provided excellent support for the conference and Dorothy E. Rimmelin was a great help with details of all sorts, especially in the editing process. The former assistant director of the Center, Elizabeth King, was also of much assistance in the early phases of developing the project. I want to thank all the others, including Bethany Garrison, who provided additional assistance.

I am grateful to Richard Brown of Georgetown University Press for his confidence in the work of the Boston College Center for Human Rights and International Justice and his support in bringing this book to the public. Again I express my heartfelt thanks for financial support to an international foundation that prefers to remain anonymous.

Introduction

Human Rights and New Challenges of Protecting Forced Migrants

David Hollenbach

People have been driven from their homes by wars, unjust treatment, earthquakes, and hurricanes throughout human history. The reality of forced migration is not new. Nor is awareness of the suffering of the displaced a recent discovery. How to protect and assist those who have been forced from their homes, however, is under serious reconsideration today. This book aims to advance that discussion by addressing questions raised by the growing number of persons who have been driven from their homes and by our increased awareness of their suffering.

A high level of migration is one of the dramatic characteristics of the growing interdependence of today's global situation. One of the most notable manifestations of growing global interconnections is the extraordinary movement of people across the borders of nation-states. Today about 200 million people live in countries where they are not citizens. Many of these people have moved voluntarily in pursuit of better lives for themselves or because of links with family. Many others have moved involuntarily. The United Nations High Commissioner for Refugees (UNHCR) estimated that at the end of 2007 there were a total of 67 million persons in the world who had been forcibly displaced from their homes. These include more than 16 million people who are refugees as officially defined by the 1951 United Nations (UN) Convention Relating to the Status of Refugees—persons who have had to flee across an international border because of "well-founded fear of being persecuted for reasons of race, religion, nationality, membership of a particular social group or political opinion."[1] Often the source of this persecution is the government of their own country. The responsibility to protect these refugees remains a central legal and moral duty in our time.

We have recently become newly aware of older forms of displacement that go beyond that of refugees as defined by the 1951 Convention, and new kinds of displacement have been developing in recent years. These raise additional questions about the scope of responsibilities toward displaced people. Many people are on the move because of conflicts and wars brought about by intergroup and intrastate conflicts. Some of these conflicts are due to struggles over political power or economic resources. Others are, at least in part, cultural in nature. Resistance by traditional

1

and non-Western cultures to the global spread of Western values and lifestyles has been one of the stimuli for the growth of some forms of religious fundamentalism and even terrorism. Among those displaced by conflict there are many who do not fall under the Convention definition of a refugee. These include 26 million people internally displaced within their own countries by war. Another 25 million have been internally displaced by human rights abuses or natural disasters.[2]

Much additional migration is brought about by economic pressures that lead many to move in search of work that will provide a better life for themselves and their children. While it is true that the economic aspects of growing global inter-dependence and economic integration have been accompanied by a decline in the percentage of humanity living in poverty, there continue to be very large numbers of extremely poor people in the world. The most recently updated figures from the World Bank tell us that in 2005 there were 1.4 billion people living in extreme poverty (on less than $1.25 per day). This is down from 1.9 billion in 1981, which is progress, to be sure. But more than half the people of the African continent are still living in extreme poverty, no lower than in 1981.[3] Where poverty exists at this level it is hardly surprising that people leave home in search of a better life. Whether such migration should be called voluntary can be questioned. Extreme economic pressures such as malnutrition and the threat of starvation can drive people to migrate as surely as political and military threats.

Further, increasing numbers of people are driven from home by environmental pressures such as the growth of deserts, rising sea levels, and destructive weather. These environmental changes are in significant part caused by human actions such as the cutting of forests, the use of fossil fuels, and development-oriented projects.[4] People displaced by environmental change, like those forced from home by conflict or economic need, do not fall under the internationally accepted definition of refu-gees. The multiple causes that drive people from their homes are often interwoven and mutually reinforcing. This makes it more difficult to identify the cause of dis-placement and thus to determine who bears the responsibilities to work to alleviate it under the accepted standards of international behavior.[5]

In addition, the fact that so many people are seeking to move across borders for many reasons has led to a growing resistance to admitting them. Concerns about national security have increased in the aftermath of September 11, 2001, and these fears mean refugees often face resistance in their efforts to obtain asylum. People moving for economic reasons are often seen as threats to the jobs and wages of people in the countries they seek to enter. Legitimate asylum seekers are sometimes seen as actually in pursuit of economic advancement and thus not really owed the protection due to refugees. For these reasons, United Nations High Commissioner for Refugees António Guterres has observed that we face a paradox today: "We have more and more people on the move and more and more barriers to their move-ment."[6] This paradox calls for new ways of envisioning response to the needs of forced migrants.

The fact that so many millions of people have been driven from home in today's world raises very basic questions about the nature and scope of our responsibility to protect the forcibly displaced. It has led the high commissioner to call for a "new humanitarian-protection compact" that will respond more adequately to the suffering of the victims of humanitarian crises, the effects of war and conflict, economic desperation, and displacement caused by environmental and climate change.[7] The high commissioner recognizes that forging such a compact will not be simple. He suggests, however, that in the face of the newly emerging challenges, there is a need "to promote a serious discussion on new forms of forced displacement, the protection gaps that are emerging and possible forms of collective response."[8]

The chapters in this book are contributions to this discussion. They are grounded in the belief that the protection of forced migrants should be defined in terms of the human rights of persons who have been forced from their homes. This approach is in line with the position advanced by the Executive Committee of the office of the UNHCR when it noted that "the fundamentally humanitarian, human rights and people-oriented rationale of the 1951 Convention is evident in its preamble."[9] It echoes the UNHCR's Cluster Working Group on Protection, which recently defined protection as "all activities aimed at ensuring full respect for the rights of the individual in accordance with the letter and the spirit of the relevant bodies of law (i.e., human rights law, international humanitarian law, and refugee law.)"[10]

It is evident, of course, that one of the most basic rights all persons have is the right *not* to be driven from their homes. Put positively, people have the right to remain at home. However, when persons have in fact been compelled to leave their homes involuntarily, they have other human rights that must be protected. Humanitarian protection should be understood in light of these rights.

This definition, of course, sets a very broad agenda before us. The 1951 Refugee Convention clearly envisions a narrower set of rights than this broad definition of protection envisions. The Refugee Convention itself does not address the full scope of human rights issues facing persons driven from their homes by conflict, economic deprivation, or environmental causes. Nor does it deal with the rights of those displaced internally within their own countries. Nevertheless, it should also be clear that genuine protection of the fundamental human dignity and well-being of displaced persons cannot be limited to the issues governed by the Refugee Convention alone. Protection of forced migrants, therefore, must include forms of protection called for by the Refugee Convention and response to other equally serious human rights concerns that are not governed by the Refugee Convention as such. The essays in this book seek to advance our understanding how to do so.

In part I, Susan Martin provides a broad overview of challenges raised by a human rights–based response to the multiple forms of displacement occurring today. She argues that limiting the responsibility to protect forced migrants to protecting refugees as defined by the Convention is no longer adequate. In fact, the international refugee regime has developed in notable ways through the twentieth century in response to changing political and international realities. For example, it moved from focus on the displaced of Europe following World War II to a global refugee protection agenda in more recent decades. Thus the regime can be developed further today. Martin argues that the international community, as represented by UNHCR, should take up the responsibility of protecting those driven from home by conflict, natural disasters, and environmental changes, whether they have crossed a national border or not. UNHCR should seek to protect this larger group of dis-placed persons whenever their own governments are unable or unwilling to protect them. Martin thus effectively calls for extending the responsibility of UNHCR to protection of people whose own governments either are persecuting them or are unable or unwilling to protect them from persecution, conflict, or natural disaster. This sets the agenda for further consideration of the meaning and scope of protec-tion in the following chapters.

Determining whom we have a duty to protect, what these duties are, and how to fulfill them depends in significant part on knowing why such responsibilities are affirmed. In part II, Agbonkhianmeghe Orobator and Silvano Tomasi approach the question of why there is an international responsibility toward forced migrants in light of both Christian religious convictions and human rights norms. Oroba-tor notes that religious traditions, including Christianity, have too often regrettably contributed to the conflicts and injustices that have driven people from home. But it is it also clear that the formative traditions of the major religious communities offer strong grounds for providing hospitality and protection to migrants. Recognition of the existence of this responsibility is as ancient as the Hebrew Bible's call to show special concern for the aliens and strangers in the midst of the people of Israel. The Christian tradition sees the followers of Jesus as pilgrims within history, with no permanent home in human cities, and thus as called to solidarity with migrants and refugees. The Muslim community understands itself as beginning from the date of Muhammad's migration (*al-hijra*) from Mecca to Medina. Thus faith-based agen-cies are strongly represented among the organizations working for the protection and assistance of the displaced.

In particular, Orobator shows that the Christian tradition provides theological and ethical reasons why Christians should extend hospitality to forced migrants and work to establish the political structures and international institutions that can better protect them. He also argues that the Catholic tradition's religious and ethi-cal orientation calls not only for charitable assistance to the displaced but also for efforts to alleviate root causes of displacement. Such efforts arise from recognition that the human rights of forced migrants should not be so dependent on changing social circumstances that they are not really rights are all. The dignity and rights of displaced persons call for the development of international institutions and policies that work to prevent displacement and help respond to it more effectively.

Silvano Tomasi points to the convergence of the Catholic tradition with what he calls a global humanitarianism founded on the universal human rights that reach across religious traditions, cultures, and national borders. Agreement that these rights are the basis for protection of forced migrants enables the Catholic commu-nity to form strong alliances with human rights–oriented intergovernmental and nongovernmental organizations. Forced migration is not primarily a political or administrative problem to be addressed in a way that protects state interest, but a humanitarian affair that calls for the protection of human beings and their dignity.

This global humanitarianism implies that the borders that have defined nation-states of the modern era subsequent to the Peace of Westphalia (1648) must be-come increasingly porous and that protection of forced migrants must reach across borders. Tomasi also argues that both in contemporary Catholic thought and in the emerging global human rights ethos, the protection due to migrants should respond to multiple kinds of uprootedness, including refugees, internally displaced persons (IDPs), environmentally displaced persons, and economic migrants. In all these forms of movement, human rights must be protected. This calls for a careful balancing of the rights of the persons, families, and communities who are on the move with the common good of receiving communities, including the common good of receiving nation-states. Roman Catholicism, like current international standards, recognizes that neither the rights of individual migrants nor the common good of the receiving state can be adequately defined apart from each other, for neither is absolute. Nevertheless, the contemporary tendency to limit hospitality and protection to fellow citizens is directly challenged by the human rights standards of both global humanitarianism and Christian theology and ethics.

In a similar way, respect for the dignity of forced migrants has important implications for how issues of gender and culture should be dealt with. Gender and culture can cause forced migration, as when people are compelled to flee gender-based violence or ethnic conflict. There can be significant gender gaps in protection, such as toleration of gender-based violence in camps. M. Brinton Lykes argues that protection must strongly support the active agency of those who have been displaced. Protection based on human rights is not a matter of active protectors coming to the aid of passive victims. Women driven from their homes very often continue to possess strength, resilience, and freedom even under the very difficult conditions they face. Protection, therefore, must not be paternalistic but should support and sustain the active agency of those who have been displaced. Active participation by displaced women in shaping the conditions in camps and other places of refuge, and in the formulation of overall policies toward the displaced, is essential. Such participation is not, of course, a panacea for the challenges raised by gender and culture among forced migrants. For example, there can sometimes be considerable tension between active support for the agency of women and respect for some aspects of the traditional culture of a displaced group. Also larger, macro-level issues such as economic inequality and war have effects on women and cultural groups that need to be addressed in their own right. But the experience of displaced women reveals that protection based on commitment to the full humanity of those driven from home requires the participation and empowerment of the displaced themselves.

Part III addresses ways that human rights call governments to be ready to grant asylum or resettlement to persons driven from home by persecution or other grave threats to their life, freedom, and dignity. The chapters by Frank Brennan and Daniel Kanstroom argue that appeals to human rights at the border can help shape governmental response to the displaced. Brennan explores the influence of human rights appeals on asylum and resettlement in two Southeast Asian contexts—Australia and Cambodia. Kanstroom considers the post–September 11, 2001, response to displaced persons by the United States. Both authors are convinced that universal human rights appropriately challenge exclusivist propensities of national communities. Human rights discourse can thus help shape a more humane response to displaced people and, where necessary, critique and help redefine governmental policy. At the same time, both authors acknowledge that governments have a legitimate concern for the well-being of their own citizens. Brennan therefore observes that human rights can lose effectiveness in influencing policy if they are invoked too often. Practical savvy or prudence rooted in experience and knowledge of the local political situation is thus important in determining when and how to play the universal human rights card in the face of narrower national interests.

Kanstroom notes that U.S. asylum policy has long been a blend of universal humanitarian concerns with strategic political considerations. Sometimes such political considerations can work for the good of the displaced, as when the recognition that the regime that displaced them is in fact engaged in persecution or some other form of tyrannical behavior. On the other hand, political motivations can also arise from unjust preferences based on race, ideological considerations that have little to do with human rights, or excessively narrow considerations of national security. Thus, Kanstroom calls for working to purge the inevitably present political dimensions of asylum and refugee policy of illegitimate forms of bias while accepting the legitimately political aspects of such policy.

Arash Abizadeh presents a philosophical argument for why nation-state borders should be considerably more open to refugees and other forced migrants than is the norm today. He grounds this argument in a liberal egalitarian political theory of human rights. Making sharp distinctions between citizens and noncitizens by granting the former the freedom to come and go and denying this freedom to the latter effectively denies their fundamental equality as persons. This will lead all who hold an egalitarian understanding of human rights to a strong bias toward open borders. Abizadeh reinforces this conclusion by appealing to the principle of democratic legitimacy, which maintains that people whose lives are touched by political institutions should be able to participate in shaping those institutions. As medieval canon law put it, "quod omnes tanget, ab omnibus approbari debet" (what touches all should be approved by all).[11] Clearly, the location and degree of openness of the borders of a state affect not only the citizens of that state but also those of neighboring or even distant nations. Indeed, people facing persecution, the effects of war, grave poverty, and natural disasters can be more profoundly affected by how open or closed nearby borders are than are the citizens within those borders. Thus the norms of democratic political legitimacy require that asylum seekers and potential migrants have at least some say in shaping the institutions that admit or exclude them.

The hard question, of course, remains how much openness is required in light of the prudence rooted in local knowledge, the appropriate balance of universal and particularist values, and the broad democratic legitimacy advocated by Brennan, Kanstroom, and Abizadeh, respectively. In my judgment, neither totally open nor totally closed borders are adequate to the claims of human rights. Not every country in the world can be responsible to assist and protect every group of forced migrants in the world. I would propose that existing special relationships and interactions across borders can give individual nations particular responsibilities to other particular groups. For example, Michael Walzer has argued that an ideological, ethnic, or religious affinity of the people of a nation for another group of potential migrants can give rise to special obligations to admit and/or protect. Walzer also maintains that a country has special responsibilities to admit refugees whose displacement it has caused.[12] So, for example, the United States rightly felt a duty toward the Vietnamese boat people who fled their country following what the Vietnamese call the American war. Though the mass displacement of Iraqis today has not been caused solely by U.S. military action in that country, the initiation of the Iraq conflict by U.S. intervention gives rise to special obligations toward displaced Iraqis. Similarly, a history of colonial and exploitative involvement in Africa by European countries such as France and Britain gives rise to special relationships that generate special duties. The economic benefits to the United States from its trade and investment with Mexico and the rest of Latin America, sometimes backed by military force, can generate relationships that lead to special duties of protection, asylum, and re-settlement.[13] In addition, when migrants have served as guest workers for extended periods, their contributions to the economy of the host country generate legitimate claims to be granted citizenship.[14]

Special relationships like these mediate between the undifferentiated universalism of human rights and the particularities of a people's identity and history. Such special historical, political, economic, cultural, or geographical relationships can generate particular responsibilities to protect outsiders. They can lead to moral duties to protect and assist persons who have migrated because of pressures, sometimes coercive, arising from the military, political, or economic interaction of one country or region with another. Since borders are already penetrated by political, economic, and cultural forces in this way, the responsibility to protect the rights of forced migrants is not simply a free-floating obligation of the whole human race. The duty to protect will be greater for a country or people whose history and politics have linked it with that of the country generating migrants. This will be especially true if the country from which the displaced are seeking protection has gained economic, political, or other benefits from the home country of the displaced or has contributed to the causes of their migration.

Part IV examines the protection of people forced from home by war and conflict. War has always been one of the chief forces driving people from their homes. The realities of interstate and intrastate conflicts today, however, have raised new questions about the human rights of forced migrants. Maryanne Loughry examines the situation of those forcibly displaced by the current conflict in Iraq. Iraq is the source of the single largest number of persons who are of concern to the UNHCR. By mid-2008, approximately 4.3 million Iraqis (15 percent of the Iraqi population) had been forcibly displaced. This included 2.8 million internally displaced persons. A sizeable number of these people were fleeing attacks on their lives and freedoms due to their religious identity or political viewpoints. Determining whether they have been displaced by persecution or some other form of conflict is not easy. In addition, many of these displaced are living in urban areas in neighboring Jordan and Syria rather than in camps. Like many other urban refugees, they often fall through the cracks of the existing protection system. Urban refugees are hard to distinguish from other slum dwellers and from poor economic migrants. Thus, Loughry concludes that the protection being provided to displaced Iraqis falls considerably short of what human rights norms would require. This is in part due to the fact that the Convention definition of refugees does not fit the realities of their displacement. The Iraq situation clearly suggests the need to expand the definition of protection beyond existing official norms.

The way war forces many people from home also suggests that we need to assess the moral and legal reality of warfare itself in light of the experience of the displaced. J. Bryan Hehir shows how the ethical and legal standards for assessing the use of armed force known as the just war ethic have developed through history as the forms and consequences of warfare have changed. He asks whether the way contemporary war causes massive displacement calls for a revision in the ethics and policy of warfare today. Though he concludes that the just war ethic remains a valid approach, he warns against justifying conflict too readily because of the harm it does to so many, including the harm of displacement. In addition, protecting refugees and IDPs themselves might in some limited circumstances be grounds for the use of military force to protect them. Nevertheless, the experience of displacement caused by conflicts such as that in Kosovo should put us on guard against moving to protect people through military means too quickly. The suffering of the displaced should receive considerably more attention than it does in both ethical and policy discussions about the use of force. It should lead us first of all to seek to prevent the injustices and conflicts that drive people from their homes. Though use of armed force to protect the displaced may sometimes be justified, it should only be a last resort. The disproportionate suffering caused by war, even in a just cause, itself often drives people from home.

The "responsibility to protect" (R2P) has become a term of art in recent international policy discussion. First proposed in 2001 in the aftermath of the ethnic cleansing in the former Yugoslavia and the genocide in Rwanda and subsequently affirmed by the 2005 World Summit session of the UN General Assembly, it refers to the responsibility to protect people from the worst forms of human rights violation, such as genocide, war crimes, ethnic cleansing, and crimes against humanity. It has since become a point of intense debate. Thomas Weiss explores aspects of this discussion that are particularly relevant to the protection of refugees and internally displaced people. It is essential to recognize that the responsibility to protect people from conscience-shocking abuses like genocide rests first and foremost with their own government. Only when a government fails to protect its own citizens from such grave crimes does the responsibility to protect move to the larger international community. Thus R2P affirms state sovereignty even while it denies that sovereignty is an absolute. Also, it is not an all-purpose responsibility but is focused on the gravest mass atrocities. The developing world should not see R2P is a reprise of the *mission civilisatrice*, by which colonial powers sought to justify their dominance.

The most important way that people can be protected from truly grave abuses will be through prevention. This calls for action before mass atrocity begins. Weiss wants to keep the understanding of prevention sharply focused on action that will prevent atrocities that are genuinely imminent, not other kinds of action that respond to abuses less serious than genocide, crimes against humanity, or war crimes. Nonetheless, there is clearly a continuum ranging from crises in which mass atrocity is imminent to serious cases where the present or projected harm is serious but falls short of genocide or war crimes. For example, Weiss sees the R2P as a call for regional or global international agencies to help rebuild failed or weak states that are often the context for grave atrocity. Moving in this direction will help prevent forced migration as well.

The responsibility to protect as affirmed by the UN, therefore, is distinct from but clearly related to other types of action called for in response to forced migration. It points toward international responsibilities to aid war victims, to support peace building, and to address the economic causes of displacement. Distinguishing these other responsibilities from the formal concept of R2P is necessary to secure political support for it from societies with the legitimate fear that it can be used in a colonialist or imperialist way. But it remains morally essential that these broader responsibilities be exercised under different formalities, such as protecting refugees, war victims, or victims of war crimes. The agents of such responsibility will also be multiple, including not only UNHCR, but also relevant nation-states, regional bodies, a new UN Agency for War Victims, or the International Committee of the Red Cross, to name just several. The fact that UNHCR's mandate does not cover all these forms of response does not mean there is no responsibility to carry them out. Rather, we need to explore innovative ways to accomplish the necessary tasks through diverse agents.

Part V reinforces the argument that refugees are not the only migrants in need of protection. Economic and environmental factors drive people from their homes, and the human rights of these migrants often need protection. Mary DeLorey shows how people can be placed in mortal risk by extreme poverty, by economic conditions that generate and drive conflict, and by environmental conditions. There is real obligation to protect persons fleeing from such mortal risks. Since refugee-specific rights to asylum and nonrefoulement do not cover the situations of those driven from home by economic and environmental causes, there are considerable gaps today in a human rights–based approach to protection. To remedy this, DeLorey sees a number of economic and environmental initiatives not normally associated with refugee protection as essential. These include development programs aimed at reduction of the extreme poverty and social exclusion that can drive people from their homes. Increased possibilities of legal migration to receiving countries are also called for. Such initiatives, of course, require action not only by agencies normally seen as parts of the international refugee regime. They also require action by states and intergovernmental and nongovernment organizations to support distributive justice, nondiscrimination, and environmental protection, both within and among countries.

Christopher Llanos's concluding chapter opens the way to reflection on how to keep this broad agenda of concerns from seeming so huge that it paralyzes action. It is true, of course, that protection of refugees and other forced migrants from all threats to their rights is intertwined with the full scope of global social justice. Bringing the economic and environmental causes of migration into the refugee discussion, along with internal displacement and displacement caused by war, could lead us to conclude that nothing can be done until the entire world system has been made just and peaceful. That, of course, will mean that forced migrants have to wait a very long time. Llanos, however, provides a more helpful approach by noting that moral responsibilities toward the displaced are not identical with the legal-political norms of the Refugee Convention. Responsibilities to protect forced migrants can require actions that reach beyond the Convention while leaving the requirements of the Convention fully intact. Beyond the Convention definition, an ethical framework would lead us to conceive of forced migrants as those whose basic human rights—both civil–political and social–economic—are not being protected by their home political community and who have no recourse for securing these basic rights except by turning to another community for protection.

This approach has strong parallels with Martin's argument that the international community has a duty to protect persons when their home state is unable or unwilling to do so. It has the advantage, however, of seeing that justified claims for protection can arise whenever basic human rights are being violated, whether through persecution, war, extreme poverty, or environmental dangers. If human rights provide the why of protection, this directly affects who should be protected, namely those whose basic rights are not protected by their own political communities. We can also conclude that the question of how these people are to be protected must be answered in several steps. The duty to protect falls first on one's home community. If this duty is not lived up to, it moves to the international community. Within the international framework, particular obligations arise from specific connections among peoples or states. These connections include ties of history, economic links, geographical proximity, and, in the case of asylum or its economic analogies, the physical presence of persons facing basic rights deprivation.

The protection of the rights of particular forced migrants in their distinctive social and historical circumstances thus makes particular demands for protection on particular agents, including states, intergovernmental bodies, nongovernmental agencies, churches, and citizens. Where agents or agencies capable of the necessary protective action are lacking, there is a responsibility to work to create them. In this way, more adequate protection of the universal rights of forcibly displaced people will be achieved only through particular institutions and the people who act through them.

Notes

1. Current statistics on the number of forced migrants are available in United Nations High Commissioner for Refugees, *2007 Global Trends: Refugees, Asylum-seekers, Returnees, Internally Displaced and Stateless Persons*, June 2008, 2, www.unhcr.org/statistics/STATISTICS/4852366f2.pdf (accessed April 23, 2009). The official definition of refugee is from the *1951 Convention Relating to the Status of Refugees*, art. 1, www.unhcr.org/protect/PROTECTION/3b66c2aa10.pdf (accessed May 16, 2009).

2. For the statistics, see UNHCR, *2007 Global Trends*.

3. "World Bank Updates Poverty Estimates for the Developing World," press release, http://econ.worldbank.org/WBSITE/EXTERNAL/EXTDEC/EXTRESEARCH/0,,contentMDK:21882162~pagePK:64165401~piPK:64165026~theSitePK:469382,00.html (accessed December 8, 2008).

4. UNHCR, *2007 Global Trends*, 2. See also Susan Martin's chapter in this volume.

5. See António Guterres, "People on the Move: The Challenges of Displacement in the 21st Century," International Rescue Committee-UK Annual Lecture, Royal Geographical Society, London, June 16, 2008, www.unhcr.org/admin/ADMIN/48873def4.html (accessed December 8, 2008).

6. Ibid.

7. António Guterres, "Millions Uprooted: Saving Refugees and the Displaced," *Foreign Affairs* 87, no. 5 (September–October 2008): 90–99, at 99.

8. António Guterres, United Nations High Commissioner for Refugees, Statement to the United Nations Security Council, New York, January 8, 2009, www.unhcr.org/admin/ADMIN/496625484.html (accessed April 30, 2009).

9. Executive Committee of the High Commissioner's Programme, "Note on International Protection," September 13, 2001, United Nations General Assembly document A/AC.96/951, no. 4, www.unhcr.org/excom/EXCOM/3bb1c6cc4.pdf (accessed April 20, 2009).

10. Interagency Standing Committee Principals Meeting, Palais des Nations, Geneva, December 12, 2005, Cluster Working Group on Protection Progress Report, 3, http://eos.io/pcwg/PCWG-report-dec05.pdf (accessed May 19, 2009). This definition originated with the International Committee of the Red Cross.

11. This principle has roots in both ancient Roman law and medieval canon law. See Paul E. Sigmund, "Catholicism and Liberal Democracy," in *Catholicism and Liberalism: Contributions to American Public Philosophy*, ed. R. Bruce Douglass and David Hollenbach (Cambridge: Cambridge University Press, 1994), 219. It continues to be affirmed in the 1983 Code of Canon Law of the Catholic Church, canon 119, 3.

12. Michael Walzer, *Spheres of Justice: A Defense of Pluralism and Democracy* (New York: Basic Books, 1983), 49.

13. For a very helpful discussion of how historical relationships among countries, especially colonial or other exploitative relationships, can lead to special obligations toward potential and actual migrants, see Tisha Rajendra, "For You Were a Stranger: A Christian Ethical Perspective on Immigration" (PhD diss., Boston College, 2009), chap. 5.

14. Walzer, *Spheres of Justice*, 56–61.

Part I

New Realities of Protection in a Human Rights Framework

1

Rethinking the International Refugee Regime in Light of Human Rights and the Global Common Good

Susan F. Martin

Introduction

By conservative estimates, about 45 million migrants are living outside of their home communities, forced to flee to obtain some measure of safety and security from conflict and repression.[1] The full extent of forced migration is much larger, however. Forced migration has many causes and takes many forms. People leave because of persecution, human rights violations, repression, conflict, natural and human-made disasters, and environmental hazards. Many depart on their own initiative to escape life-threatening situations, although in a growing number of cases, people are driven from their homes by governments and insurgent groups intent on depopulating or shifting the ethnic, religious, or other composition of an area. Forced migrants include persons who cross international borders in search of refuge as well as those who are internally displaced. Also of concern are stateless persons, natural disaster–affected populations, those living in areas that are or will be affected by climate change, and those involuntarily resettled as a result of development projects.

During the past decade, an increasing number of forced migrants have received assistance and/or protection from the United Nations High Commissioner for Refugees (UNHCR). Although the number of refugees, asylum seekers, and refugee returnees is lower than it was a decade ago (about 16 million in 1997), the total number of concern to UNHCR has grown. As of the end of 2007, UNHCR assumed responsibility for 37.1 million persons.[2] Refugees represented about 40 percent of this population and 43 percent was internally displaced persons (IDP). The remainder included stateless persons, asylum seekers, refugees, and internally displaced persons who were returnees. This number represents about 55 percent of UNHCR's estimated total of 67 million persons who were forcibly displaced at the end of 2007, including Palestinian refugees under the United Nations Relief and Works Administration as well as those internally displaced from conflict and natural disasters that were not under UNHCR's mandate.[3] These numbers are themselves conservative because UNHCR's estimates do not cover those displaced by environmental hazards, climate change, or development projects.

The question posed in this chapter is who among the world's forcibly displaced should be of concern to the refugee regime, and more precisely, to UNHCR. I begin with a discussion of the various categories of forced migrants, elaborating on three dimensions: where they are displaced, for what reasons, and the phase of displacement they are in. The section thereafter discusses the evolution of the refugee regime's involvement with the forcibly displaced, beginning with the League of Nations and its successes and failures, proceeding through the establishment of UNHCR and the entry into force of the 1951 United Nations (UN) Convention Relating to the Status of Refugees, and then discussing UNHCR's expanding role in using its good offices to provide assistance and protection to a widening range of forced migrants. The final section presents a framework for determining under what circumstances UNHCR should extend its good offices to the newly emerging categories of forced migrants, including those who may be displaced by the effects of climate change. I will argue that these decisions should be based on a common indicator—protection of the human rights of persons whose own governments are unwilling or unable to provide such protection.

Categorization of Forced Migrants

Policymakers within and outside of the United Nations have used a classification system that places forced migrants into specific boxes, with the assumption that standards, mandates, and programs will follow the designated classification. Of particular concern is identifying those forced migrants who need assistance and protection from the international community, generally because their own government is unwilling or unable to help them.

These categories reflect three dimensions. First, forced migrants are designated by where the displacement takes place. Those who cross international borders are designated as "refugees" or "international migrants," whereas those who remain within their national borders are "internally displaced persons" or "internal migrants." Depending on whether they have received permission to enter another country, they may also be designated "undocumented, unauthorized, or illegal" migrants.

Individuals are also designated by the causes of the forced movements. The 1951 Refugee Convention gives specific recognition to persons who flee because of a well-founded fear of persecution. If they cross an international boundary, they are refugees. Persons fleeing conflict may also be specially designated, either by Convention (e.g., the Organization of African Unity [OAU] Refugee Convention) or because the UN high commissioner for refugees uses his good offices to recognize them as refugees. By contrast, there is no international legal framework for addressing cross-border movements caused by natural disasters, development projects, environmental degradation, or climate change. The *Guiding Principles on Internal Displacement*, which were adopted by the UN in 1998, uses a broad description that encompasses all of these causes in defining who is covered by the principles. Unlike refugee law, however, the *Guiding Principles* are not legally binding international law, although based on binding human rights and humanitarian instruments. A number of governments have adopted the *Guiding Principles* into national law.

The third dimension relates to time. Forced migration is addressed through different mechanisms depending on the phase of displacement. Emergency movements often require specialized assistance and protection due to the instability of the situation. Most refugees and displaced persons are in protracted situations, however, with the average period of displacement being seventeen years or longer.[4] Although these situations are often treated as protracted crises, the needs, challenges, and opportunities differ in many ways from the emergency phase. Camps often become settlements, sometimes approaching the size of cities, with an economic life that may remain dependent on international assistance but includes employment and entrepreneurial activity. New protection issues arise over time, sometimes shifting from outside threats to internal ones as domestic and other violence erupts in response to continuing displacement. When there is a resolution to the crisis, new challenges appear, and the forced migrants may be redesignated as "returnees" or "resettled" persons. These formulations have arisen in the context of conflict-induced displacement, but they often apply in other situations. Those forced to migrate because of development projects (e.g., dams) or the effects of climate change, for example, may remain displaced for protracted periods, finding they are unable to return, perhaps permanently, to their homes and instead are treated as resettled populations.

To a large extent, categorizing the displaced by geography, cause, and time has succeeded in raising the visibility of groups of forced migrants who heretofore had been either ignored or fell between the cracks in the international system. This has particularly been the case in designating internally displaced persons as a category of concern to the international community. It also allows targeted responses to address issues arising from the specific cause or phase of an emergency. Options for those driven from their homes by conflict are different in nature and scope from those applicable to persons driven from their homes by development projects or the effects of climate change. Nor does the same approach make sense in every stage of a crisis.

There are limits, however, to the approach taken to date. The categories of forced migrants are not mutually exclusive. More often they are overlapping. The victims of humanitarian emergencies may belong to more than one group, either at the same time or in close sequence. To take the 2004 tsunami as an example, many of the survivors in Sri Lanka and Indonesia were displaced by conflict as well as natural disaster. The victims of Cyclone Nargis were harmed not only by the natural disaster but also by the persecutory policies of the Burmese government. In other situations refugees repatriate, thereby earning the designation of "returnees," only to find themselves newly designated "internally displaced persons" because they were unable to return to their home communities due to continued instability.

In many cases, drawing careful lines between categories of forced migrants hinders rather than facilitates the ability of national, intergovernmental, and nongovernmental organizations to offer appropriate assistance and protection. Agencies may too easily avoid responsibility by citing an institutional mandate to serve a specific population. Alternatively, agencies interested in intervening on behalf of a particular group may be denied the opportunity because they have no explicit mandate to do so. In the meantime the forced migrants—whether refugees or internally displaced, whether fleeing conflict, natural disasters, or other causes—may face serious deprivation of their human rights. If the government of the territory in which they seek safety is unable or unwilling to provide protection of their rights, including access to needed assistance, the cause of their displacement and their geographic location may be irrelevant to their plight. Mixed flows of people seeking asylum create dilemmas for states. As the UNHCR states in the 2008 Note on International Protection, "there are protection gaps in mixed flows, especially as regards migrants deemed 'irregular' by the authorities who fall outside established protection frameworks, but who otherwise need humanitarian assistance or other kinds of protection."[5]

Yet the complexity of this picture raises serious questions about which forced migrants should be of concern to the international community and should be accorded international protection to guarantee their rights. During the past sixty years, that question has been answered most clearly for those crossing international borders because of persecution and, to a lesser degree, conflict. Binding international law, in the form of the 1951 Refugee Convention and its 1967 Protocol, defines refugees, their rights, and the responsibility of states, and the UNHCR has a clear mandate regarding this population.

During the past decade, progress has been made in establishing a framework for international protection of internally displaced persons with the promulgation of the *Guiding Principles on Internal Displacement*, which are based on binding international law, although they are not themselves binding law. The *Guiding Principles* have been applied most often to those displaced by persecution and conflict and who thus would have been categorized as refugees had they crossed an international border The category of IDP is broader than those fleeing persecution, however, leading to some developments regarding those displaced by other causes. For example, operational guidelines based on the Principles have been developed for protecting persons affected by natural disasters, including those who are internally displaced.[6]

Trailing these developments has been a similar understanding of the rights of those who are forcibly displaced by development projects, climate change, or other environmental hazards that affect their habitat and livelihood. The World Bank and the regional development banks have established guidelines on involuntary resettlement from development projects, but these guidelines do not have the force of international law. Even less developed are international standards that define the rights of those who are internationally displaced as a result of natural disasters, environmental hazards, climate change, or other potentially life-threatening events. Decisions on admission or deportation rest fully with sovereign states, which may or may not use their discretion to permit people exposed to such risks to remain in safety.

António Guterres, the UN high commissioner for refugees, notes in a recent

Foreign Affairs article that "attempts by the international community to devise policies to preempt, govern, or direct these movements in a rational manner have been erratic."[7] He acknowledges that "new patterns of movement, including forms of forced displacement not envisaged by the Refugee Convention, have emerged."[8] Guterres calls for a global compact to tackle mass displacement, but he does not specify the nature of the international regime that might result from such a commitment on the part of states. Most specifically, he does not elaborate the role of UNHCR, or the broader refugee regime, in protecting those who have been displaced by these unenvisioned forms of displacement.

Evolution of the Refugee Regime

Understanding the evolution of the refugee regime may help identify principles that could be applied in determining who among these categories of forced migrants should be of concern to UNHCR and other agencies within the refugee regime. The refugee regime is a twentieth-century invention, initially devised as a way to address the mass displacement caused by World War I, the Bolshevik Revolution, and the collapse of the Ottoman and Hapsburg empires. While having limited success in protecting those who were displaced by these events, it failed miserably in protecting the victims of Nazi persecution. With the Allied victory in World War II, the modern regime was shaped to find solutions for the persecuted as well as those displaced by the conflict. As the next section elaborates, the refugee regime was not static in dealing with displacement. It took on new roles in dealing with displacements caused by the Cold War, decolonization, civil conflicts, and surrogate superpower conflicts.

League of Nations

In 1921 the League of Nations established the first High Commission for Refugees, charged with assisting and protecting Russian, and later, other refugees. Headed by Fridjoft Nansen, the Norwegian explorer and statesman, the high commissioner's mandate was to provide material assistance and legal and political protection.[9] Nansen was asked in 1920 to direct the repatriation of prisoners of war and then, in 1921, to direct relief efforts in response to growing famine in Russia. Then, in 1922 he arranged an exchange of about 1.25 million Greeks living in Asia Minor and about five hundred thousand Turks living in Greece. In 1925 Nansen's office succeeded in constructing villages to house upward of forty thousand Armenians in Syria and Lebanon and in resettling another ten thousand in Erivan.

After Nansen's death in 1930, the office of the high commissioner ceased to exist and instead, the Nansen International Office for Refugees, an autonomous body working under the authority of the League of Nations, was established. The office never had sufficient resources to function effectively, relying primarily on fees paid for Nansen passports, a substitute travel document issued to refugees who were unable to obtain documentation from their own governments, and on private contributions. Nevertheless, the League office provided material, legal, and financial help to about eight hundred thousand refugees.

During the 1930s, with fascism and Nazism producing massive new refugee flows, the League established a high commissioner for refugees from Germany, which also gained a mandate to assist and protect refugees from Austria and the Sudetenland region of Czechoslovakia. During the course of the 1930s, it became evident that few countries were willing to provide refuge to the German refugees, particularly those facing growing persecution because they were Jewish. In July 1938 an international conference attended by representatives from thirty-two nations convened in Evian to discuss the problem of Jewish refugees. The participants established an Intergovernmental Committee on Refugees, to be based in London, to facilitate the emigration and resettlement of German and Austrian refugees, and later, refugees from other countries. However, the Evian conference did not lead to any real pledges for the resettlement of the Jewish refugees, with many countries expressing outright bias against admission of the refugees.

At the end of 1938 the Nansen Office and the high commissioner for refugees from Germany merged and moved their offices to London. The new organization was known as the Office of the High Commissioner for All Refugees under League of Nations Protection. The new organization had little success in assisting and protecting the vast majority of Jews and others facing Nazi persecution, but it continued to provide material assistance to those refugees it could reach throughout World War II.

The tragic ramifications of the failure of the international community to come to the aid of refugees became clear with the liberation of the concentration camps. The camp survivors joined millions of people uprooted by the conflict itself. During the 1940s a number of distinct organizations were established to address the problem of refugees and displaced persons in Europe. The United Nations Relief and Rehabilitation Administration (UNRRA) was founded in 1943 to give aid to areas liberated from the Axis powers. The International Refugee Organization took over in 1946. Its main mission was to care for, repatriate, or resettle those made homeless by the war. Also, in 1948 the UN Relief and Work Administration for Palestinian Refugees was established to assist Palestinians displaced from Israel. There was another system for dealing with refugees in Hong Kong.

One of the most important but ambiguous developments in the refugee regime was adoption of the 1948 Universal Declaration of Human Rights. Article 13 establishes the individual right to move and reside freely within one's own country. That article also declares the right to leave any country, including one's own, and to return to one's own country. Having established a right to leave one's own country, the committee then turned to the problem that to be able to leave one's own country, an individual must enter another one. Member states differed considerably on how to resolve this issue. Some supported a right to asylum, but others, including the U.S. delegation, led by Eleanor Roosevelt, preferred to limit state obligations with regard to refugees. Article 14 affirms only a "right to seek and to enjoy in other countries asylum from persecution." In a very close vote, states rejected any obligation to grant asylum.

UNHCR and the UN Refugee Convention

Within just a few years, states addressed this issue again but in a very different, European-focused context.[10] The 1951 Refugee Convention and its 1967 Protocol emerged in the early days of the Cold War, largely to resolve the situation of the millions of refugees who remained displaced by the World War II and fascist/Nazi persecution. Defining refugees as persons who were unable or unwilling to avail themselves of the protection of their home countries because of a "well-founded fear of persecution based on their race, religion, nationality, political opinion, or membership in a particular social group," the 1951 Refugee Convention included geographic (Europe) and time limitations (persons displaced before 1951) that were lifted in the 1967 Protocol.[11] Since 1967 the Refugee Convention has been a universal instrument, applying to refugees worldwide.

At its core, the 1951 Refugee Convention substitutes the protection of the international community (in the form of a host government) for that of an unable or unwilling sovereign. In effect, the agency was to provide alternative protection for those who had been persecuted by their own state or who could not claim the protection of their state because of a well-founded fear of future persecution. This reasoning is based on the understanding that states produce refugees because they are unwilling or unable to protect their citizens from persecution. As Charles Keely explains, "A state is not behaving as a state when people flee or are forced out because of racial, ethnic, religious, or political reasons." He argues that the international refugee regime is "not based primarily on humanitarian feelings." Rather, the refugee regime is designed to protect the "international system of states that is threatened when states fail to fulfill their proper roles."[12]

The Convention sets out the principal obligation of states—to refrain from forcibly returning (refouling) refugees to countries in which they would face persecution. States do not have the obligation to provide asylum or admit refugees for permanent settlement, and they may relocate refugees in safe third countries that are willing to accept them. The Convention has been interpreted to require states to undertake status determinations for asylum applicants at their frontiers or inside their territories in order to determine if they have valid claims to refugee protection. While the only obligation towards refugees is nonrefoulement, in practice this has often meant admission and asylum in the host country.

The Convention drafters recognized that among refugee populations would be found individuals whose actions made them undeserving of international protection. The so-called exclusion clauses of the Convention set forth two major kinds of such individuals—human rights violators and serious criminals. Thus those who have committed a crime against peace, a war crime, a crime against humanity, or a serious nonpolitical crime are excluded from international protection.

The Convention sets out the rights of refugees who have been admitted into the territory of another country. Fundamental human rights such as freedom of religion and access to courts are guaranteed to be at least those accorded to the citizens of the state hosting the refugee. Refugees lawfully residing in a host country are guaranteed public relief in this way as well. Rights regarding employment, property, elementary public education, and housing are accorded to refugees in a manner no less favorable than those accorded to citizens of other countries. In addition, the Convention cannot be applied in a discriminatory way regarding race, religion, and country of origin.

UNHCR was charged from the beginning to find solutions for refugees, generally in the form of voluntary repatriation when conditions permitted, integration into a country of asylum, or resettlement to a third country. These solutions reflected the aim of the refugee regime to restore the refugee to a sovereign authority that would provide protection. If conditions change and the refugee is willing and able to return, that is the best solution. Otherwise, obtaining citizenship in another country would enable the refugee to enjoy state protection. Because those solutions were often not forthcoming, however, UNHCR's day-to-day activity was generally to provide assistance to those who were unable to return, integrate, or resettle.

Good Offices of UNHCR

The first big expansion of UNHCR's role in dealing with refugee issues came in 1956 with the Hungarian Revolution and the flight of Hungarian refugees into Western Europe. Although its mandate limited UNHCR's responsibility to those displaced prior to 1951, the UNHCR offered its good services to find solutions for the Hungarian refugees, generally via resettlement to the traditional immigration countries—the United States, Canada, and Australia.

In the 1960s a further expansion occurred as UNHCR was asked to assist and protect refugees in Africa and Asia who had been and were being displaced by various wars of liberation. As the numbers of refugees grew and solutions were elusive, more and more of the resources of a growing regime were spent on care and maintenance of large numbers of refugees forced out of their homes because of conflict and living in refugee camps with international assistance.

In recognition of the nature of the forced movements occurring regularly in Africa, the OAU adopted the Convention Governing the Specific Aspects of Refugee Problems in Africa in 1969. While acknowledging the 1951 Refugee Convention as the basic and universal instrument regarding the protection of refugees, the OAU Convention broadened the definition of refugees and set out other important protection provisions. The expanded definition includes those who, "owing to external aggression, occupation, foreign domination, or events seriously disturbing public order in either part or the whole of his country of origin or nationality, is compelled to leave his place of habitual residence in order to seek refuge in another place outside his country of origin or nationality."[13]

The OAU Convention explicitly forbids states from rejecting asylum seekers at the frontier. The grant of asylum is declared to be a peaceful and humanitarian act, not to be regarded as unfriendly by other states. The Convention also establishes the importance of settling refugees at a reasonable distance from the frontier of their country of origin for security reasons. This regional treaty further states that no refugee shall be repatriated against his will. Most African states are parties to the OAU Convention.

In a similar vein, the Cartagena Declaration on Refugees expands the definition of protected refugees in the Latin American region. Like the OAU definition, it supports the 1951 Convention and adds protection to those who have fled their country "because their lives, safety, or freedom have been threatened by generalized violence, foreign aggression, internal conflicts, massive violation of human rights or other circumstances which have seriously disturbed public order."[14] It emphasizes that repatriation of refugees must be voluntary and embodies principles for their protection, assistance, and reintegration. Although a nonbinding instrument, the Declaration has been endorsed by the General Assembly of the Organization of American States, and some states in the region have incorporated this definition into their own national legislation.

The OAU and Cartagena definition increasingly characterized the population of concern to UNHCR wherever in the world the population was located. UNHCR and most countries of asylum made no attempt to determine which among the large number of persons who fled conflict also had a well-founded fear of persecution, instead treating those escaping conflict as prima facie refugees. Large-scale refugee movements occurred from such places as Vietnam, Cambodia, Afghanistan, Ethiopia, Somalia, Sudan, Angola, Mozambique, Nicaragua, El Salvador, and Guatemala. In many of these cases, the military superpowers supported different sides in the conflicts, with the civil wars serving as surrogate Cold War conflicts. The international refugee regime, which was financially supported largely by the Western countries, became the protector of civilians who were forced to flee as the result of those conflicts, particularly when Communist governments took control over territory. Refugee camps often became rest and recuperation centers for fighters in the surrogate Cold War conflicts. As examples, refugee camps in Pakistan, Honduras, and Thailand were often used as staging areas for military operations in Afghanistan, Nicaragua, and Cambodia, respectively.

In 1990, with the collapse of Communism and the end to many of the surrogate Cold War conflicts, there was a major rethinking within the international humanitarian regime of how to deal with refugee issues. No longer was there a strong foreign policy rationale for a refugee regime that would support the civilian families of those fighting Communist governments. As many of the conflicts of the 1970s and 1980s ended, refugees began returning to their home countries in record numbers. The UN high commissioner for refugees adapted to the changing situation, and in 1990 the then high commissioner, Sadako Ogata, declared the 1990s to be the decade of repatriation.

At the same time, however, new refugee movements received international attention. They often occurred as the result of nationalist or ethnic conflicts, which were usually internal in nature and difficult for the Western powers to understand fully. Examples are Bosnia, Kosovo, and Rwanda. Moreover, many of the peace agreements that ended the Cold War conflicts were very fragile, and they did not necessarily take into account the fact that there were deep-seated internal problems that could lead to the resumption of fighting. Refugees who repatriated during the 1990s often returned home to high levels of insecurity. In some places, such as Afghanistan, conditions deteriorated back into full civil war and the takeover by such repressive regimes as the Taliban.

Addressing Internal Displacement

With the end of the Cold War, governments found they were able to intervene internally in countries of origin, in order to reach the displaced populations before they left, without risk of generating superpower clashes. This began in 1991, with a response in northern Iraq to the Kurdish refugees who were attempting to come into Turkey. Afraid for its own national security as a result of Kurdish insurgency, Turkey refused to allow the Iraqi Kurds to enter. The United States and its allies established a safe zone in northern Iraq so that the Kurdish refugees could return to the protected area. Humanitarian intervention has taken place in countries as diverse as the Sudan, Iraq, Bosnia, Somalia, Haiti, Kosovo, East Timor, and Afghanistan. The forms of intervention range from airlifted food drops to outright military action.

The results have been mixed. Aid reached theretofore inaccessible people in many of these cases. The deployment of peacekeepers lessened immediate reasons for flight and permitted some repatriation to take place. The root causes of displacement have not generally been addressed, however, and internally displaced populations often still remained out of reach. Moreover, safe havens established to protect civilians have too often been vulnerable to attack. Those who would have reached some level of safety as refugees in the earlier era have often been doomed to remain within their own countries, caught between the cross fires.

During the 1990s and into the present decade, troubling inequities and gaps in the international system for addressing forced migration became manifest. Francis Deng, then the UN secretary-general's representative on internally displaced persons and his colleague at the Brookings Institution, Roberta Cohen, wrote in their seminal study, *Masses in Flight*: "An array of UN agencies, humanitarian organizations, and nongovernmental organizations (NGOs) have come forward to provide protection, assistance, and development aid when governments have been unable or unwilling to meet their responsibilities. . . . None of these organizations, however, has a global mandate to protect and assist the internally displaced. Their action is ad hoc. As various agencies pick and choose the situations in which they wish to become involved, many internally displaced persons may be neglected."[15]

As the internally displaced continue to reside in their own country, of course, their rights, as those of all citizens, derive from international human rights conventions and, to the extent displacement is caused or affected by war, the Geneva Conventions. Applying these international laws to the situation of internally displaced persons, the *Guiding Principles on Internal Displacement*—developed in the late 1990s—set forth the major rights of the internally displaced and the responsibilities of sovereign authorities to such individuals prior to and during displacement. The *Guiding Principles* also look to international refugee law by analogy for guidance in certain situations. Although the principles do not have legal force themselves, they set standards that guide governments and rebel groups regarding their conduct toward civilians before, during, and following displacement. This consolidation and focusing of international law regarding the internally displaced has been adopted into domestic law by nations such as Colombia and Georgia. Important gaps in the protection framework for internally displaced persons continue to exist, however, as the human rights laws and the Geneva Conventions are laws of general applicability that were not specifically designed to address the full range of problems that the internally displaced face.

From at least the 1970s, UNHCR has aided persons still within their home countries. Often, implementing programs for returning refugees prompted UNHCR to offer its good offices to the internally displaced as well. This was the case in southern Sudan in the early 1970s when UNHCR assisted about one hundred eighty thousand returnees and about five hundred thousand internally displaced persons.[16] The UNHCR also assisted displaced people in Cyprus, in this case acting as the secretary-general's special representative and coordinator for United Nations humanitarian assistance for Cyprus.

Although UNHCR had exercised its mandate on behalf of the internally displaced, the agency had considerable discretion in determining if and when to do so unless specifically requested by the General Assembly. In March 2000, UNHCR issued a position paper clarifying its relationship to internally displaced persons. The agency made clear that its interest in this population arises from its humanitarian mandate on behalf of persons displaced by persecution and situations of general violence, conflict, or massive violations of human rights. This mandate places upon UNHCR "a responsibility to advocate on behalf of the internally displaced; mobilize support for them; strengthen its capacity to respond to their problems; and take the lead to protect and assist them in certain situations."[17] Stopping short of asserting an operational responsibility for all internally displaced persons, UNHCR set out six requirements for its involvement: "a request or authorization from the Secretary General or a competent principal organ of the UN; consent of the state concerned, and where applicable, other entities in a conflict; access to the affected population; adequate security for staff of UNHCR and implementing partners; clear lines of responsibility and accountability with the ability to intervene directly on protection matters; and adequate resources and capacity."[18]

The policy paper specified that UNHCR would be ready to take the lead where its protection and solutions expertise was particularly relevant, or where involvement with the internally displaced was closely linked to the voluntary repatriation and reintegration of refugees. Recognition was given that the linkages between refugees and the internally displaced could be complicated: "Countries of asylum may be more inclined to maintain their asylum policies if something is done to alleviate the suffering of the internally displaced, reduce their compulsion to seek asylum, and create conditions conducive to return. On the other hand, UNHCR's activities for the internally displaced may be (mis)interpreted as obviating the need for international protection and asylum."[19]

Gaps continued to persist in establishing responsibility for internally displaced persons. After trying what it called a collaborative approach that failed to fill the gaps, the United Nations shifted to what it now calls the cluster leadership approach, in which a single UN agency is responsible for coordinating activities in a particular sector. UNHCR has taken on responsibility for the protection cluster (focusing on conflict-induced displacement) as well as the emergency shelter and camp management clusters.[20] The cluster approach is being pilot tested to determine if it is effective in improving responses to IDPs. The Interagency Standing Committee (IASC) Guidance Note on Using the Cluster Approach explains that "the role of sector leads at the country level is to facilitate a process aimed at ensuring well-coordinated and effective humanitarian responses in the sector or area of activity concerned. Sector leads themselves are not expected to carry out all the necessary activities within the sector or area of activity concerned. They are required, however, to commit to being the 'provider of last resort' where this is necessary and where access, security, and availability of resources make this possible."[21] The Note also recognizes that "the 'provider of last resort' concept is critical to the cluster approach, and without it the element of predictability is lost.[22]

For agencies with technical leads (e.g., health, nutrition, water, and sanitation), the ability of the lead agency to take on responsibility is straightforward. However, the Note is more circumspect regarding the leadership for crosscutting areas such as Protection, Early Recovery and Camp Coordination: "The concept of 'provider of last resort' will need to be applied in a differentiated manner. In all cases, however, sector leads are responsible for ensuring that wherever there are significant gaps in the humanitarian response they continue advocacy efforts and explain the constraints to stakeholders."[23]

It is still too soon to know if the cluster approach will be successful in filling gaps in the institutional framework for addressing the full range of issues pertaining to forced migrants. Certainly, the willingness of UNHCR to be the "provider of last resort" in the protection of IDPs is a critical issue. It is consistent with the recommendations of the UN High-level Panel on System-wide Coherence, which recommended that "UNHCR must reposition itself to provide protection and assistance to displaced people in need, regardless of whether they have crossed an international border."[24]

UNHCR's 2007 policy on internal displacement went significantly further than its 2000 policy in specifying the circumstances under which the agency would assume responsibility: "UNHCR stands ready to contribute to the inter-agency response in situations of internal displacement in any conflict-affected country where the presence and programmes of the Office have the consent of the authorities, where the humanitarian activities of UNHCR and its partners are free from undue political or military interference, and where the security environment enables its personnel to function within acceptable levels of risk."[25] Although still constrained in terms of sovereignty and security and limited to conflict-affected countries, the 2007 policy represented a major shift from earlier policies that severely limited UNHCR's involvement with internally displaced persons. UNHCR reports in 2008 that 14 million of an estimated 25 million internally displaced from conflict fall under its mandate.[26]

During this period, UNHCR also began responding, albeit in an ad hoc way, to forced migration stemming from causes other than persecution or conflict. Although UNHCR has limited its cluster leadership to conflict-induced internal displacement, it has nevertheless been drawn into providing assistance during several notable natural disasters. In the *State of the World's Refugees*, UNHCR explained its involvement in tsunami relief: "The sheer scale of the destruction and the fact that many of affected populations were of concern to the organization prompted the move. Responding to requests from the UN secretary-general and UN Country Teams, UNHCR concentrated on providing shelter and non-food relief. In Sri Lanka, UNHCR's presence in the country prior to the tsunami allowed for a comparatively swift and sustained humanitarian intervention—including efforts focused on the protection of internally displaced persons."[27] UNHCR also assisted tsunami victims in Somalia and Aceh, Indonesia, pointing out that "the protection of displaced populations was especially urgent in areas of protracted conflict and internal displacement in Aceh, Somalia, and Sri Lanka. Furthermore, there was concern for some affected populations whose governments declined offers of international aid, such as the Dalits (formerly known as untouchables) of India and Burmese migrant workers in Thailand; it was feared they might be discriminated against and their protection needs compromised."[28] More recently, UNHCR has become involved in the international response to Cyclone Nargis in Burma and China's earthquake, providing shelter and supplies but not protection.

The potential for mass displacement from climate change is an issue that has increasingly occupied the high commissioner's attention. In several recent speeches, Guterres has given voice to his concerns: "When we consider the different models for the impact of climate change, the picture is very worrying. The need for people to move will keep on growing. One need only look at East Africa and the Sahel region. All predictions are that desertification will expand steadily. For the population, this means decreasing livelihood prospects and increased migration. All of this is happening in the absence of international capacity and political will to respond."[29] The assistant high commissioner for protection, Erika Feller, summarized the dilemma before the Executive Committee: "New terminology is entering the displacement lexicon with some speed. The talk is now of 'ecological refugees,' 'climate change refugees,' the 'natural disaster displaced.' This is all a serious context for UNHCR's efforts to fulfill its mandate for its core beneficiaries. . . . The mix of global challenges is explosive, and one with which we and our partners, government and non-government, must together strike the right balance."[30] Thus far, however, there has been no inclination on the part of the Executive Committee for UNHCR to become involved with those who cross borders because of natural disasters or climate change.

Nor is there support for UNHCR's expanded operations when it comes to helping disaster IDPs. UNHCR has made clear to the emergency relief coordinator that while it will lead the cluster on protection of conflict IDPs, it will not do the same for disaster IDPs. This cluster therefore has no leader, since the two other potential candidates—UNICEF and the Office of the High Commissioner for Human Rights—do not have the requisite capacity.

There is also debate over the expansion of UNHCR's operations when it comes to conflict IDPs. Although generally, governments on the Executive Committee of the UNHCR have been supportive of the agency's initiatives on behalf of IDPs uprooted by conflict, they have also cautioned the high commissioner that UNHCR was not the "IDP agency." A number of governments expressed concern in the 2007 Executive Committee session that "UNHCR's work with IDPs should not come at the expense of its protection of refugees."[31] The agency was also encouraged to develop exit strategies for internal displacement situations. Since then UNHCR has incorporated "When Displacement Ends: A Framework for Durable Solutions," developed by the Brookings-Bern Project on Internal Displacement and Georgetown University, into its *Handbook on Internal Displacement*.[32]

Within the academic community, the debate about the preoccupation of the refugee regime with internally displaced persons has been particularly pointed. In a keynote speech to the International Association for the Study of Forced Migration, James Hathaway, who is a law professor at the University of Michigan, raised the alarm about a shift in focus from refugees to forced migrants. He argued that refugees have a special place in international law, whereas others who migrate or are displaced do not have an explicit status. Interestingly, Hathaway argues for the special treatment of refugees because they "are seriously at risk because of who they are or what they believe." Constructing a human rights argument, he states that refugees are "doubly-deserving" of international protection, having fled "profoundly serious" risks because of unchangeable and/or fundamental characteristics.[33]

Susan McGrath and Howard Adelman, in their responses to Hathaway, point out that most refugees under UNHCR's mandate are not covered under the Refugee Convention because they have fled conflict, not persecution.[34] UNHCR's mandate had already evolved, as it used its good offices to provide assistance and protection to millions of refugees because of the humanitarian, not legal, imperative to act. To the extent that internally displaced persons meet the same criteria, there would be no reason to treat them in an essentially different manner. Cohen argues further that widespread acceptance of the *Guiding Principles on Internal Displacement*, as well as the responsibility to protect (R2P) doctrine espoused in the Millennium Summit, demonstrate a high degree of acceptance that there is an international responsibility to protect and assist internally displaced persons.[35]

Moving Forward

The debate about the scope of the refugee regime's responsibility for forced migrants has focused primarily on conflict-induced displacement, reflecting UNHCR's increasing involvement in providing assistance and protection to persons who would have been considered refugees had they crossed an international border. Despite UNHCR's occasional forays into assisting victims of natural disasters, there has been relatively little policy or academic debate on the extent to which the refugee regime should also take responsibility for those forcibly displaced for reasons other than conflict.[36] Yet as Guterres's statements indicate, the number of those so displaced could easily surpass the numbers of conflict-induced refugees and internally displaced persons in the years ahead, particularly as the impact of climate change is manifest in increased displacement. In this context, UNHCR's recent note, *Climate Change, Natural Disasters, and Human Displacement: A UNHCR Perspective*, observes that "it is legitimate to ask whether new legal protection instruments might be needed for cross-border movements that are induced by climate-related reasons. UNHCR is not seeking an extension of its mandate, but it is our duty to alert the international community to the protection gaps that are emerging."[37]

Regardless of its own concerns about mandate, UNHCR will no doubt be called upon to extend its good offices to these populations. The question is, by what criteria should UNHCR engage with those displaced by climate change, natural disasters, development projects, and other, similar causes? To answer this question, it is necessary to identify UNHCR's mandate and capabilities relative to the rest of the international community. I argue that UNHCR has evolved to protect persons whose own governments cannot or will not provide such protection. Other UN and international agencies, such as the International Organization for Migration, have a demonstrated capacity to assist persons displaced by natural disasters and environmental hazards, but only UNHCR has a history of providing protection to displaced populations.

Following this line of reason, one can divide forced migrants into four categories according to their relationship to their own governments. In the first quadrant are individuals whose governments are *willing and able* to provide protection. Those displaced by natural disasters and climate change in wealthy, democratic countries generally, though not always, fall into this category. There are examples of poorer and more authoritarian governments that also have good track records of demonstrating they are willing and able to protect their citizens affected by natural disasters and environmental hazards. Generally, displacements in these contexts are internal, not international, since the forced migrants are able to find assistance from their own governments and have few reasons to cross an international border. There is a limited role for the international community, although other governments and international organizations may offer assistance—for example, in the form of search and rescue teams, financial aid for rebuilding homes, and health professionals and other experts in disaster relief. There would be no role for UNHCR since there is no need for protection by the international community.

The second quadrant includes forced migrants in situations in which governments are *willing but unable* to provide protection to persons displaced by disaster or environmental hazards. Certainly, poor countries that do not have the financial capacity to provide assistance may fall into this category. They would like to protect their citizens from harm but do not have the capacity or resources to do so. If the affected population moves within the country of origin to find safety, a government may well attempt to fulfill its protection responsibilities by calling upon the international community to assist. There would be little reason for UNHCR to involve itself because protection is not at stake, but the international community has an important role to play in ensuring that it buttresses the willing state's ability to provide protection by offering financial and other aid. Of course, UNHCR might be called upon for material goods and expertise, as has been the case in some of the massive displacements occurring as a consequence of natural disasters, but this population would not otherwise fall within its mandate.

The third and fourth quadrants include situations in which governments are *unwilling* to provide protection to their citizens, regardless of their ability to do so. In the third quadrant, the government has the capacity to provide protection but is unwilling to offer it to some or all of its citizens. For example, the government may not spend its resources on political opponents or ethnic or religious minority groups. In the fourth quadrant, the government is both *unwilling and unable* to protect its citizens. Failed states would fit into this category because they have neither the willingness nor the ability to protect their citizens.

These are the situations in which UNHCR can play a constructive role in promoting protection for persons whose rights have been violated by states that are unwilling and/or unable to ensure their safety. In cases of internal displacement, UNHCR would need to use the same criteria the agency uses in determining whether to intervene in conflict displacement situations. The form of intervention would differ depending on the circumstances. If the agency were able to reach the affected populations, UNHCR would have an obligation to offer both assistance and protection. If state sovereignty or security conditions precluded direct access, UNHCR could still play an important role as an advocate for unprotected persons, up to and including encouraging the Security Council to intervene.

Also complicated are cases in which large numbers move across borders because of the unwillingness of their own government to provide protection. In such situations, the need for international protection will be determined by the destination country's policies and the extent to which the displaced would be harmed if returned home. If the destination country is willing and able to provide assistance and protect the cross-border population, there would be little reason for the international community to become involved. Conversely, if the destination country is unwilling or unable to assist and protect the forced migrants, or if it attempts to return the forced migrants to the home country without adequate guarantees of their protection, the international community may well have a reason to offer its assistance and protection. The complication, of course, is the absence of international law defining the rights of persons with a well-founded fear of harm from natural disasters or environmental hazards and the responsibilities of states toward them. One can nevertheless posit that if the country of origin's ability to provide protection and assistance is buttressed by the international community and the cross-border migrant could return safely, the destination country would be well within its right to return the migrants without international intervention. Conversely, if protection and assistance are unavailable in the home country, and returnees would be seriously harmed if they were to return, then the destination country has a greater responsibility to permit the forced migrants to remain, and a role for UNHCR may emerge. For example, as in conflict-induced displacement, UNHCR could offer its assistance as a way to encourage the country of destination to permit the cross-border migrants to remain until safe to return or other solutions are found for them.

Conclusions

During the past century, the international refugee regime has evolved as the international community learned from its mistakes and slowly expanded the mandate of its refugee agency to protect persons displaced by persecution and conflict. At first focused on specific nationalities and events, in the years after World War II, the refugee regime became more universal in its scope, protecting refugees throughout the world. With the end of the Cold War and the increased ability to reach persons internally displaced by conflict and persecution, the refugee regime has expanded to assume a responsibility for the protection of persons still within their home countries, particularly if the events leading to their internal displacement were similar to those affecting refugee movements. As new forms of forced migration loom on the horizon, the refugee regime may well see itself challenged to aid and protect an even larger population—those affected by climate change, environmental hazards, and natural disasters. This essay has attempted to set out criteria under which UNHCR would appropriately be the international organization to respond to these new displacements. Protection has been the hallmark of UNHCR's role in the refugee regime, and, I argue, its protection mandate should guide its responses. To the extent that states are unwilling or unable to protect their own citizens who are displaced, regardless of the cause, UNCHR would legitimately have a role to play in advocating for and, when possible, assisting and protecting, these forced migrants.

Notes

1. UNHCR reported an estimated 11.4 million refugees and persons in refugee-like situations under its care, as well as 13.7 million internally displaced persons (about half of those reported to be IDPs by the Internal Displacement Monitoring Centre) and 3 million stateless persons. In addition, there are about 4.1 million Palestinian refugees who are outside of UNHCR's mandate. See UNHCR, *2007 Statistical Yearbook* (Geneva: UNHCR, 2008) and Internal Displacement Monitoring Centre, *Internal Displacement: Global Overview of Trends and Developments in 2007* (Geneva: IDMC, 2008).

2. This number represents a modest 3 percent decline from 2006, largely because of a reduction in the number of stateless persons under UNHCR's responsibility. By contrast, in 1998 there were 22.4 million under UNHCR's responsibility, with only 4.6 million being IDPs.

3. See UNHCR, *2007 Global Trends: Refugees, Asylum-seekers, Returnees, Internally Displaced and Stateless Persons*, www.UNHCR.org/statistics/STATISTICS/4852366f2.pdf (accessed May 7, 2009).

4. See UNHCR, *The State of the World's Refugees 2006: Human Displacement in the New Millennium* (Oxford: Oxford University Press, 2006), 109.

5. UNHCR, *Note on International Protection* (Geneva: UNHCR, 2008), 5–6.

6. Brookings-Bern Project on Internal Displacement, *Human Rights and Natural Disasters: Operational Guidelines and Field Manual on Human Rights Protection in Situations of Natural Disaster* (Washington DC: Brookings Institution, 2008), www.brookings.edu/reports/2008/spring_natural_disasters.aspx (accessed May 7, 2009).

7. António Guterres, "Millions Uprooted: Saving Refugees and the Displaced," *Foreign Affairs* 87, no. 5 (September–October 2008): 90.

8. Ibid.

9. For fuller discussions of the interwar refugee regime, see Gil Loescher, *Beyond Charity: International Cooperation and the Global Refugee Crisis* (Oxford: Oxford University Press, 1993), and Michael Marrus, *The Unwanted: European Refugees from the First World War through the Cold War* (Philadelphia: Temple University Press, 2002).

10. For a fuller discussion of the early years of UNHCR, see UNHCR, *State of the World's Refugees: 50 Years of Humanitarian Action* (Oxford: Oxford University Press, 2000).

11. UN Convention Relating to the Status of Refugees, adopted on July 28, 1951 by the United Nations Conference of Plenipotentiaries on the Status of Refugees and Stateless Persons convened under General Assembly resolution 429 (V) of December 14, 1950; and Protocol to the UN Convention Relating to the Status of Refugees, entered into force on October 4, 1967.

12. Charles Keely, "How Nation-States Create and Respond to Refugee Flows," *International Migration Review* 30, no. 4. (Winter 1996): 1046–66.

13. Organization of African Unity Convention Governing the Specific Aspects of Refugee Problems in Africa Adopted by the Assembly of Heads of State and Government at Its Sixth Ordinary Session, Addis-Ababa, September 10, 1969.

14. Cartagena Declaration on Refugees Adopted by the Colloquium on the International Protection of Refugees in Central America, Mexico, and Panama, Cartagena de Indias, Colombia, November 22, 1984.

15. Roberta Cohen and Francis Deng, *Masses in Flight: The Global Crisis of Internal Displacement* (Washington, DC: Brookings Institution, 1998).

16. Louise Holborn, *Refugees: A Problem of Our Time* (Metuchen, NJ: Scarecrow Press, 1975).

17. UNHCR, *Internally Displaced Persons: The Role of the United Nations High Commissioner for Refugees* (2000), www.UNHCR.org/excom/EXCOM/3ae68d150.pdf (accessed May 3, 2009).

18. Ibid.

19. Ibid.

20. The International Organization for Migration has responsibility for camp management in the context of natural disasters.

21. Inter-Agency Standing Committee (IASC), *Guidance Note on Using the Cluster Approach to Strengthen Humanitarian Response* (November 24, 2006), www.humanitarianreform.org/humanitarianreform/Portals/1/Resources%20&%20tools/IASCGUIDANCENOTECLUSTERAPPROACH.pdf (accessed May 7, 2009).

22. IASC, *Guidance Note.*

23. Ibid.

24. UN High-level Panel on System-wide Coherence, Report of the Secretary-General's High-level Panel on System-wide Coherence: Delivering as One (2006), p. 25. http://daccess dds.un.org/doc/UNDOC/GEN/N06/621/41/PDF/N0662141.pdf?OpenElement, accessed on September 25, 2009.

25. UNHCR, *Policy Framework and Corporate Strategy: UNHCR's Role in Support of an Enhanced Inter-Agency Response to the Protection of Internally Displaced Persons* (January 2007), www.UNHCR.org/excom/EXCOM/45c1ab432.pdf (accessed May 7, 2009).

26. UNHCR, *2007 Statistical Yearbook.*

27. UNHCR, *State of the World's Refugees 2006*, 21.

28. Ibid.

29. Keynote Speech by UN High Commissioner for Refugees, Mr. António Guterres, Third Symposium on Corporate Social Responsibility and Humanitarian Assistance, Tokyo,

November 26, 2007, www.UNHCR.org/admin/ADMIN/476132d911.html (accessed May 7, 2009).

30. Statement by UNHCR Assistant High Commissioner for Protection, Ms. Erika Feller, 42nd Meeting of the Standing Committee, Agenda Item 3, June 24, 2008.

31. UNHCR, *Report of the Fifty-eighth Session of the Executive Committee of the High Commissioner's Programme*, 21, www.UNHCR.org/excom/EXCOM/471615cb2.pdf (accessed May 7, 2009).

32. Brookings Bern Project on Internal Displacement, *When Displacement Ends: A Framework for Durable Solutions* (June 2007), www.UNHCR.org/refworld/docid/469f6bed2.html (accessed May 7, 2009); and UNHCR, *Handbook for the Protection of Internally Displaced Persons*, Provisional Release (2007), www.UNHCR.org/protect/PROTECTION/4794b6e72 .pdf (accessed May 7, 2009).

33. James C. Hathaway, "Forced Migration Studies: Could We Agree Just to 'Date'?" *Journal of Refugee Studies* 20, no. 3 (2007): 349–69.

34. Howard Adelman and Susan McGrath, "To Date or to Marry: That Is the Question," *Journal of Refugee Studies* 20, no. 3 (2007): 376–80.

35. Roberta Cohen, "Response to Hathaway," *Journal of Refugee Studies* 20, no. 3 (2007): 370–76.

36. As an exception, see Roberta Cohen, "For Disaster IDPs: An Institutional Gap," The Brookings Institution, August 8, 2008. www.brookings.edu/opinions/2008/0808_natural _disasters_cohen.aspx (accessed December 21, 2009).

37. UNHCR, *Climate Change, Natural Disasters, and Human Displacement: A UNHCR Perspective* (October 2008), www.UNHCR.org/protect/PROTECTION/4901e81a4.pdf (accessed May 7, 2009).

Part II

Normative Responses

Religion, Human Rights, Gender, and Culture

2

Justice for the Displaced

The Challenge of a Christian Understanding

Agbonkhianmeghe E. Orobator

> While the disastrous war was waged, there converged on Rome almost hourly a vast mass of people, children, women, the sick, and the aged, to seek from the common father of all a place of safety and refuge. They came from the towns and villages laid waste by the invading enemies, particularly from devastated areas of Italy. This caused us to enlarge, yet further, the scope of our charity, for the cries of so many exiles and refugees touched our heart, and, moved by that same pity, we felt the need to repeat those words of Our Lord: "I have compassion on the multitude."
>
> —Pius XII, *Exsul familia* (Apostolic Constitution), August 1, 1952

As we look at the complex reality of migration, we see the various voices that compete for a hearing. One of the most neglected voices is the theological perspective.[1] The complex saga of refugees and displaced people in many parts of the world depicts the dire conditions of millions of men, women, and children.[2] Considered as a whole, and seen in its multiple forms, the crisis of forced displacement poses a challenge to governmental and nongovernmental institutions and demarcates a difficult terrain for theological and ethical analysis.

The overall perspective of this chapter is twofold. First, it examines the biblical and theological foundations of Christian approaches to the tragedy of refugees and displaced people and how these approaches provide resources for responding to the crisis of displacement as a systemic and structural problem. Second, the essay pays close attention to the combination of structural causes of displacement and the structural responses generated by a Christian understanding of this phenomenon.

We begin with a general consideration of the relationship between theology, religion, and refugees in its wider historical context. Getting the dynamics of this relationship right is critical to a correct analysis and a valid interpretation of the Christian and theological grounding of responses to the twin issues of refugees and displacement of people. The pertinence of this analysis emerges more clearly and acutely in light of the worsening conditions of forcibly displaced people. A conflagration of violence in conflict and war zones continues to drive hundreds of thousands of people from their land and home into refugee and internally displaced persons' (IDP) camps. No continent suffers the tragic consequences of this catastrophe more than Africa. Recent events in Chad, Sudan's Darfur region, Kenya, the eastern Democratic Republic of Congo, Somalia, Ethiopia, Burundi, and Zimbabwe have thrust Africa into the eye of the raging refugee storm. As Archbishop Silvano Tomasi points out elsewhere in this volume, the global profile of migration and displacement presents an alarming picture, with nearly 200 million people seeking livelihood and refuge away from the land of their birth.[3] The magnitude of this crisis underscores the necessity of a fresh and critical reappraisal of the conditions of refugees and displaced people.

Theology, Religion, and Refugees

A quick survey of situations of displacement such as refugee camps and detention centers reveals the active presence of various cadres of religious actors engaged in advocacy, protection, accompaniment, and/or the provision of humanitarian relief assistance, alongside other established governmental and nongovernment institutions.[4] Yet in the often-contested public sphere of migration and displacement, religious or faith-based organizations face the task of an ongoing clarification of the theological rationale for their roles and strategies.[5]

Tracing the contours of a Christian understanding of displacement and its theological foundations reveals two salient points. First, on the issue of migration and forced displacement, Christianity does not stand alone; nor did it invent the theology of displacement and migration. The literature of migration and displacement indicates an awareness of and sensitivity to the problems of migrants and refugees in most religious traditions.[6] Beyond some of these long-established religious traditions, there is a clear evidence of a religious and ethical concern for migrants and refugees in antiquity.[7]

The link between religion and displacement throws up an interesting irony. Religion does not function simply as a benevolent and innocuous player in the drama of displacement. One sobering fact stands out clearly, namely, that religion has been used as an instrument of displacement. Stephanie J. Nawyn notes correctly that "Religion is often a factor in the root causes of refugee migrations."[8] For example, without discounting the significance of other cofactors of displacement, the still not fully resolved crisis in southern Sudan pits the predominantly Arab Muslims of the north against the predominantly black indigenous religionist and Christian populations of southern Sudan. The religious dimension of the north–south conflict in Sudan incontrovertibly confirms Nawyn's observation that, directly or indirectly, "religion has long been implicated in why people must seek refuge elsewhere."[9] This critical awareness of the negative potential of religion invites a sober and measured consideration of the theological foundations of Christian understanding of displacement.

The volume of religious literature on various forms of migration and instances of displacement of people also serves as a pointer to the link between theology and displacement. One example of this is the plethora of ecclesiastical pronouncements on the problem of migration and displacement of people. Whether issued by the United States Conference of Catholic Bishops, the World Council of Churches, the French Episcopal Committee on Migration, the All Africa Conference of Churches, or the Zambian Episcopal Conference, each document lays claim to a theological basis. Yet, as Daniel Groody has hinted, theological claims and perspectives need to be the subject of an explicit analysis before they are made the basis of credible and effective responses to the plight of refugees and displaced people.

In the next three sections I will examine three overlapping elements of a theological framework for how Christians should respond to the human suffering facing both refugees and internally displaced people: the perspective of biblical ethics, the contribution of a theology of the Church, and the standpoint of Catholic social teaching. Thus, this chapter aims to show that migration and displacement of people define a theological and an ethical subject.

From the Memory of Displacement to a Place of Hospitality and Protection: The Perspective of Biblical Ethics

Judeo-Christian biblical ethics regulates the social construction and treatment of migrants and displaced people. Whether under the category of "alien," "sojourner," "stranger," or "exile," migrants and displaced people emerge as subjects of clearly defined and religiously sanctioned rights: "the biblical tradition puts the migrant and exile at the very center of concern."[10] Irrespective of the mythico-historical events at its origin, the biblical prescription for the ethical treatment of migrants and displaced people carries the force of divine law. Yahweh's command to the people of Israel regarding the treatment of socially deprived people, including migrants and refugees, is unambiguous:

> You shall also love the stranger, for you were strangers in the land of Egypt (Deut. 10:19, NRSV).

> You shall not oppress a resident alien; you know the heart of an alien, for you were aliens in the land of Egypt (Exod. 23:9).

> When an alien resides with you in your land, you shall not oppress the alien. The alien who resides with you shall be to you as the citizen among you; you shall love the alien as yourself, for you were aliens in the land of Egypt: I am the LORD your God (Lev. 19:33–34).

Translated into our contemporary context, these ethical injunctions of the Old Testament affirm the right to expect and the obligation to offer hospitality and protection. Associated with these are the right to settle; the right to citizenship; and, as well, the guarantee of work and economic sustenance.

The biblical traditions, attitudes, and dispositions that condition the moral category and status of migrants and refugees are derived from "a genuine historical memory" and "a bona fide recollection of the past."[11] This ethical framework harks back, first, to the nomadic experience of biblical patriarchs out of which "comes a deep appreciation for the plight of the migrant."[12] If nomadism appeared normal in the socioeconomic and geopolitical context of the pastoralist ancient Near East, other historical factors of migration and displacement were anything but congenial. Throughout the biblical saga, the twin realities of migration and displacement are provoked commonly by natural, religious, socioeconomic, and political upheavals—famine, escape from oppression, search for a better and dignified life, mass deportation, and forced exile. Deuteronomistic authors weave the experiences of migration, displacement, oppression, and deliverance of the ancestors of Israel into a "profession of faith" in the power of Yahweh:

> A wandering Aramean was my ancestor; he went down into Egypt and lived there as an alien, few in number, and there became a great nation, mighty and populous. When the Egyptians treated us harshly and afflicted us, by imposing hard labor on us, we cried to the LORD, the God of our ancestors; the LORD heard our voice and saw our affliction, our toil, and our oppression. The LORD brought us out of Egypt with a mighty hand and an outstretched arm, with a terrifying display of power, and with signs and wonders; and he brought us into this place and gave us this land, a land flowing with milk and honey. (Deut. 26:5–9)

Donald Senior notes by way of commentary that so profound was the trauma of the searing experiences of displacement that they "became embedded in the consciousness of the people of Israel and helped define their character as a people and the nature of their relationship to God."[13] Precisely, this character and this relationship also shaped Israel's attitude and treatment of migrants and displaced people. As the texts quoted earlier from the Old Testament show, having themselves been victims uprooted and forcibly displaced, the people of Israel instituted legal provisions that protected the rights and guaranteed the well-being of people in similar conditions. Yet ultimately, the timeless and universal character of the concomitant biblical ethics derives not just from the recollection of a fading, painful past but from the experience of the abiding love, justice, and compassion of Yahweh who offers deliverance to migrants, exiles, and displaced people: "For the LORD your God is God of gods and Lord of lords, the great God, mighty and awesome, who is not partial and takes no bribe, who executes justice for the orphan and the widow, and who loves the strangers, providing them food and clothing" (Deut. 10:17–18).

When we shift our attention to the New Testament, another interesting experience of displacement emerges, albeit not altogether dissimilar to the modern experience of forced migration and displacement. In the seminal document on migration, *Exsul familia*, Pius XII links the contemporary experience of migration and forced displacement to the flight into exile of the Holy Family: "The émigré Holy Family of Nazareth, fleeing into Egypt, is the archetype of every refugee family. Jesus, Mary, and Joseph, living in exile in Egypt to escape the fury of an evil king, are, for all times and all places, the models and protectors of every migrant, alien, and refugee of whatever kind who, whether compelled by fear of persecution or by want, is forced to leave his native land, his beloved parents and relatives, his close friends, and to seek a foreign soil."[14] Against the backdrop of this archetypal event, Jesus emerges as the "Proto-Refugee."[15] The divergent Lucan and Matthean accounts of Jesus's birth contain unmistakable echoes of the modern-day tragedy of displacement. In Luke it involves a perilous journey for a poor tradesman and a pregnant teenager (Luke 2:1–7). Matthew's account is more dramatic: the flight into Egypt is provoked by the murderous wrath of a despotic king and the fear of an impending large-scale infanticide (Matt. 2:13–23). Under these circumstances of "a well-founded fear of persecution," contemporary refugee protocols would have granted Mary, Joseph, and Jesus the status of prima facie refugees instantly. The two New Testament accounts lead to the poignant remark that "Jesus begins his earthly journey as a migrant and a displaced person."[16] The enduring memory of this event continues to shape the theological understanding of forced migration and displacement in the present-day context.

It needs to be said that the Gospels do not limit the refugee experience of Jesus exclusively to the circumstances of his birth and infancy. Three aspects of his life are particularly pertinent to our attempt to identify the biblical foundations of a Christian theological understanding of displacement. The first concerns the itinerant nature of his public ministry, summed up by the Lucan Jesus in a somewhat paradigmatic declamation: "Foxes have holes, and birds of the air have nests; but the Son of Man has nowhere to lay his head" (Luke 9:58). The second aspect pertains to Jesus's special concern for vulnerable women and men who have been displaced to the unstable margins of society, religion, and politics. This category included outcasts, foreigners, the terminally ill, people with disability, the poor, and the weak. Furthermore, this population of "displaced people" would become the subject of his most memorable teachings and parables, of which the Good Samaritan (Luke 10:25–37) and the Judgment of the Nations (Matthew 25:31–46) retain enduring significance in the debate about migrants, refugees, and displaced people. The third aspect relates to the wider theological notion of incarnation.

In the context of displacement, "incarnation is the principal theological hermeneutical key in this situation. God has pitched a tent with the refugees. God weeps when they weep, feels pain when they feel pain. God is with them."[17] The significance of this declaration connects with the deepest meaning of the theological reality described in the Johannine Prologue, according to which the Word of God became flesh and made a dwelling among us (John 1:14). The experience that underpins this reality is one of movement, displacement, and migration. God migrates and God moves out of a distant or remote existence of divinity toward human history, not in an abstract manner, but in a concrete, palpable experience of establishing a dwelling in time and space. The theological rapprochement suggested in this imagery of a displaced, mobile, or migrant God reinforces the ethical imperatives of hospitality, refuge, finding home and protection for the displaced and migrant peoples.

From Dispersed People to Pilgrim Community: Contribution of a Theology of the Church

The literature of the Church's theology contains numerous attempts to correlate the experience of migration and displacement with the nature and identity of the

Church. As in the case of biblical ethics, this ecclesiological approach to displacement is far from being an invention of modern-day theologians. Its roots go back to the biblical milieu. At least two historical moments can be distinguished clearly for the purposes of this chapter.

In the first instance, the early Christians lived a precarious existence. Gospel and historical anecdotes portray them as the target of religious violence and politically orchestrated persecutions leading to displacement. Even when such state-sponsored violence and persecutions did not specifically target the nascent Christian communities, they were not insulated against the predicament of the general population. Not infrequently, violent persecutions triggered displacement and migration into distant, unfamiliar territories (see Acts 8:1 ff, 11:19 ff).[18] A useful resource for the persecuted Christians flowed from the identification of their situation with the passion and death of Jesus Christ. Such a connection with the Paschal Mystery offered hope of resurrection (see Acts 5:40–41). New Testament writers characteristically imbued their accounts of forced displacement and migration with a theology of divine providence. Yet the fact remains that the events involved an involuntary movement of people across political boundaries occasioned by what refugee protocols centuries later would categorize as "a well-founded fear of persecution." As Senior has noted, "In the highly mobile and interconnected Mediterranean world of the first century A.D., the early Christians were not strangers to the experience of dislocation caused by violence and persecution. There is little doubt that they reflected on this same experience in the light of Jesus' own life and that of the history of God's people."[19]

Senior's observation is important, because it underlines how the early Christian communities set about consciously integrating their experience of displacement into a theological self-understanding. From this theological process emerged a unique definition of the meaning, nature, and identity of the community called church. For example, Acts makes a point of designating the early Christian communities as communities of "the Way" (Acts 9:2; 18:25–26; 19:9, 23; 22:4; 24:14, 22).[20] Although the early Christian communities "praised God" for the phenomenal spread of the good news "to the Gentiles" (Acts 11:18), the trajectory of their evangelical peregrinations bore marks of persecution, expulsion, and forced displacement.

From a theological perspective, today's crisis of refugees and displaced people cannot be taken simply as a historical continuation of earlier biblical occurrences unmodified except in intensity. As I will point out in the third section, the factors of displacement have become more complex and the agents more sophisticated and diverse. This analysis, however, should allow us to recognize that a theological interpretation of the historical events and circumstances of displacement belongs to the core of Catholic life.

Vatican Council II's "The Dogmatic Constitution on the Church" emphasizes the pilgrim nature and identity of the community called church in striking terms: "While on earth she [the Church] journeys in a foreign land away from the Lord . . . the Church sees herself as an exile" (no. 6). It continues: "On earth, still as a pilgrim in a strange land, following in trial and in oppression the paths he [Jesus Christ] trod, we are associated with his sufferings as the body with its head, suffering with him, that with him we may be glorified" (no. 7). This theological affirmation is linked closely with the historical experience of persecution, migration, and displacement. In reality, the ecclesiology of Vatican II adopts the chaos and trauma of forced migration and displacement as a sacramental prism through which it understands the Christian community and defines its mission in the public and social arena. "The approach of the Church to migration has increasingly emphasized its ecclesiological basis: migrants are viewed as icons of the Church, which is the people of God and the community of disciples at the service of the Kingdom."[21]

Within the ethical space circumscribed by this theology of the Church, various categories of migrants, refugees, and displaced people become the beneficiaries of special concern and compassionate care.[22] Thus, the theological concern for the plight of refugees and displaced people does not function as an accidental or convenient theological characterization. Rather, it cements the link between a radical option for people who are forced to move and the nature, identity, and mission of the community called church.[23]

Vatican II also affirms the identity of the community called church as a witness to the values of the kingdom of God.[24] The manifestation and anticipation of this kingdom make ethical demands on the church as an exile community. Bearing witness to the reality of this kingdom implies living out its values of love, inclusivity, mutuality, justice, and peace as they relate to forced displacement and migration of people.

Yet evidence from myriad situations of refugees suggests a certain "ecclesial marginalization"—besides economic and political marginalization—whereby refugees are considered passive beneficiaries of the Church's charitable services, at best, or excluded as a burden to an already impoverished ecclesial community, at worst.[25] The call that the community church see itself through the prism of refugees, however, further requires that refugees make ethical claims on the Church not as beneficiaries, but as sources of theological transformation. Peter-Hans Kolvenbach frames this point in the following words: "Despite being kept in the shadow of injustice and evil, refugees are a witness to survival in the face of adversity. This directs us towards the light of the Lord. . . . 'God is calling us through these helpless people. We should consider the chance of being able to assist them a privilege that will, in turn, bring great blessings to ourselves and our Society.'"[26]

From a Refugee to a Sacrament of Christ's Presence: The Contribution of Catholic Social Teaching

The tradition of biblical ethics, tied directly to the ecclesiology of migration and displacement, also relates closely to Catholic social teaching. When Catholic theology wades into the debate about the structural causes and possible responses to the suffering of refugees and displaced people, it grounds its argument on the resources and traditions of Catholic social teaching.

The vast body of analytical and practical resources commonly classified under the rubric of Catholic social teaching also addresses the crisis of refugees and displaced people. As Jacqueline Hagan has phrased it, "The links between theology and matters of migrant well-being are firmly carved into Catholic social theology."[27] The component documents of Catholic social teaching have a number of characteristics and foci that serve to expand our understanding of the pastoral care of migrants, refugees, and displaced people, and diverse ethical issues relating to their conditions.[28]

Broadly considered, Catholic social teaching offers some principles for discernment and priorities and indicators for action in the context of displacement, both individually and corporately, that is, as a faith community.[29] In particular, it carves out a secure ground for the treatment of refugees where human rights and justice serve as the primary conceptual markers. Within this ethical locus a refugee or a displaced person is, like every other human being, without exception, a bearer of rights. Three implications may be suggested here. First, the occurrence of displacement does not remove refugees and displaced people from the ethical ground or locus defined by human rights and the demands of justice. Second, it is incumbent on theology to question and oppose all forms of violation of the fundamental rights and dignity of the human person, no matter the agents and circumstances of such violation. Third, therefore, securing the rights of refugees and displaced people establishes the imperative of transforming unjust structures of socioeconomic and political organizations.

As a fundamental resource, Catholic social teaching seeks solutions by rethinking the problem of forced displacement within a far-reaching, global framework. Several instances can illustrate this point. For example, beyond the duty of care and protection owed to each refugee and displaced person, Catholic social teaching emphasizes the necessity of a global ethical framework that prioritizes solidarity and justice for refugees and forcibly displaced people. As the Holy See's permanent observer at the United Nations in Geneva, Archbishop Silvano Tomasi, recently affirmed, "In our interconnected world, we are linked with all displaced people by our common humanity and by the realization that the globalization of justice and solidarity is the best guarantee for peace and a common future."[30] The absence or neglect of these ethical imperatives and the lack of an effective global refugee framework to guarantee them imperil the fundamental human rights of all refugees and displaced people. Drew Christiansen further elaborates the need for a global framework as an effective response to the crisis of displacement in clear terms: "From the point of view of Catholic social teaching the paramount ethical problem in the movement of peoples today is precisely the lack of a global authority with the competence and capacity to address the needs of victimized populations in timely fashion. . . . When it comes to fundamental human rights, the basic requirement is to establish institutions which prevent their deprivation and, in the event of failure, to have in place the institutions which will undertake special efforts to protect them."[31]

On account of its global vision of the problem, Catholic social teaching has been effective in identifying and assessing some of the deeper causes of displacement. The factors include war, religious persecution, poverty, and socioeconomic and political crises, stemming from deliberate actions on the part of individuals and political institutions operating at local, state, and global levels.[32] According to Archbishop Tomasi, "displacement is not a phenomenon isolated from other social realities. It is the result of political decisions, of neglect and lack of preventive action, and also of unforeseen natural events."[33] In other words, the phenomenon of refugees and displaced people is symptomatic of systemic dislocations in society, economics, and politics. As Clement Majawa argues, "What displaced populations reveal to us all are profound shifts and stresses underlying our social economic systems. The major weakness in our system is poverty; refugee movements are like earthquakes signaling movements between the earth's tectonic plates. They are warning signs of the deep tensions within our global community."[34] Thus, as was the case even in biblical times, social, political, and economic crises generate refugees and displace people.[35] The reality of refugees and displaced people points to deeper problems of socioeconomic and political dislocations and imbalances in contemporary global dispensations.

What needs to be stressed, therefore, is that for Catholic social teaching, forced migration, whatever form it takes, represents an ethical issue. "The refugee phenomenon on the African continent, as elsewhere, is not a product of fate or stroke of misfortune but is a result of choices and decisions made individually and collectively. . . . By the very fact of having left their homes or homelands, displaced people are generally disadvantaged and are in no position to vindicate their human rights."[36] In the chaos of refugee and IDP camps, where the primary need is humanitarian relief and assistance, Catholic social teaching reminds us of the underlying variety of complex global ethical challenges.

As a consequence, Catholic social teaching affirms the complementarity of humanitarian and structural responses to the crisis of refugees and displaced people. Both are important, but neither by itself completely satisfies the need of refugees and displaced people for both charity and justice.[37] This inclusive approach enables us to characterize the task of the community called church as both a pastoral and a prophetic ministry. Not only do Christian communities and faith-based organizations offer assistance to and accompany refugees and displaced people in various locations; they also draw on a vast network of resources as "supranational religious institutions" and advocate changes at national and global levels: "The church itself is seen as an important actor in confronting the injustices that lead to forced migration, in helping to bring together warring factions and working towards peace and reconciliation."[38]

A Theological Triptych: Structural Implications of Ethical Norms

The foregoing considerations lead to a renewed affirmation of the centrality of the present-day crisis of refugees and displaced people in Christian theology and ethics. Christian responses to the needs of refugees and displaced people would appear deficient if they neglected the three theological elements just sketched and thereby risked becoming simply a form of social activism devoid of religious purpose. The following discussion summarizes the structural implications of these three theological elements.

Biblical ethics formulates a teaching that grounds a Christian understanding of displacement. In this understanding, refugees and other victims of displacement are subjects of divinely sanctioned rights, because Christianity lays claim to a total experience of life that originates from a covenantal relationship with God. "According to the Judeo-Christian Scriptures," Daniel Groody writes, "immigration is not simply a sociological fact but also a theological event."[39] The injunction to welcome and protect migrants, refugees, and internally displaced people comes as God's command. This assertion is not immune to criticism, especially because it appears gratuitous, imposing no obligation on people who do not subscribe to the underlying religious tenets. This objection notwithstanding, it bears repeating that the Christian ethical discourse on migration, refugees, and displacement appeals to a transcendent source that neither tolerates indifference nor condones injustice.

At a second level, in the midst of the refugee crisis and forced migration, a theological account of the Christian community defines the Church essentially in terms of displacement and mobility. Devoid of this understanding of the Church, our ecclesiology appears incomplete. It is true that victims of forced migration and displacement naturally turn to the Church, seeking aid and protection.[40] As an institution with a global network of centers, the Church possesses the resources to serve as a focal point for vulnerable people, particularly refugees and displaced people. Of course, one could argue with good reason that in reality not all of the Church's interventions are entirely altruistic. For example, a visit to refugee camps in eastern Africa or the Great Lakes Region would confirm that large populations of refugees and displaced people are professing members of Christian denominations on which they depend for wide-ranging religious services in addition to relief assistance.[41] This has the potential of heightening the imperative to provide humanitarian assistance and protection by churches and religious institutions. Nevertheless, in the final analysis, what grounds a Christian understanding of displacement pertains more to biblical ethics and to the theological constitution of the Church as a migrant reality endowed with an exilic vocation than to its activity as a charitable institution serving its own people:

> Welcoming the stranger, a characteristic of the early Church, thus remains a permanent feature of the Church of God. It is practically marked by the vocation to be in exile, in diaspora, dispersed among cultures and ethnic groups without ever identifying itself completely with any of these. Otherwise it would cease to be the first-fruit and sign, the leaven and prophecy of the universal Kingdom and community that welcomes every human being without preference for persons or peoples. Welcoming the stranger is thus intrinsic to the nature of the Church itself and bears witness to its fidelity to the gospel.[42]

Finally, the long history of Catholic attentiveness to and involvement in the public sphere has produced a social teaching, doctrine, and tradition that ground a theological understanding of the crisis of refugees and displaced people in the domain of fundamental rights and the dignity of the human person, as well as the imperative of justice. As Archbishop Tomasi states, "the continued effort to safeguard the human rights of all forcibly displaced people is in line with a consistent ethic of life."[43] It is important to note that, just as in the case of the ecclesiology of migration and displacement, biblical ethics serves as an important source for Catholic social teaching.[44] Rather than considering this crisis as "a nonreligious functional domain," devoid of theological warrants or rationale for action, Catholic social teaching provides alternative resources and responses within the public sphere that prioritize justice, conversion, communion, and solidarity.[45] In its clearest manifestation this teaching, tradition, or doctrine enables Christian theology to analyze the crisis of displacement, formulate an in-depth appraisal, and indicate effective responses to the structural causes of this tragedy. Stated differently, in the context of forced displacement, Catholic social teaching offers principles for reflection, criteria for judgment, and guidelines for action.[46]

The objective of establishing foundations of a Christian understanding of forced displacement and refugees will fall short if it does not attempt to distill ethical norms that generate structural responses for transforming refugee-causing factors on a global scale. It is beyond dispute that outside of natural disasters, displacements of refugees are not natural phenomena. Refugees are *caused* to flee: "Refugees are *refugeed* people."[47] Yet the question of causality is a complex one. As J. Bryan Hehir points out in this volume, although in some instances refugees can be considered "a cause of war," in most instances "refugees and IDPs . . . [are] consequences of wars." Wars and conflicts remain the most common causes, albeit not the only structural causes.[48] Thus, we bear a responsibility to seek systemic responses to the deeper causes of forced displacement. At least three such ethical prescriptions can be proposed based on the foregoing considerations.

First, in light of the central tenets of Catholic social teaching, justice and human rights, or the lack thereof, constitute vital conceptual ingredients in understanding the challenge of forced displacement. Securing justice appears paramount prior to the occurrence of displacement, which, as I have argued above, is a consequence of violations of fundamental human rights. It could be argued that concomitant structural implications exist at the political level. Ethical norms of justice and human rights necessitate international refugee protocols and conventions that are not simply reactive but essentially proactive. One way of achieving this would be to redefine more closely and strengthen the links between international agencies, instruments, and protocols that protect human rights in general and those that offer protection specifically to refugees.[49] If adequate protection is a right, it should not only be accessible as a consequence of displacement (in a refugee camp), but also as a prerequisite mechanism for safeguarding the rights of vulnerable people threatened with displacement. This argument resonates with the point made by Christiansen that "what is needed is essentially a new refugee regime, one which would include necessary revisions in international law but which also would devise the institutions that would protect and assist refugees, and *one which would, more importantly, be empowered to address effectively the political and social problems that result in refugee flows.*"[50] Thus, an effective systemic response would seek to address complex problems of poverty, conflict, human rights violations, poor governance, or lack of employment as deeper causes of forced migration.[51] With regard to the kind of ethically generated systemic response to the deeper causes of refugees and forced displacement proposed here, Tomasi makes a valid point in this volume that "the creation of a social environment where human rights are upheld and this [human] dignity is respected would be the best strategy to prevent forced displacement" (see chapter 3).

Second, hospitality represents the linchpin of a Christian approach to forced displacement. However we choose to define it, hospitality transcends a mere theoretical analysis. Practically, hospitality demands sacrifice. In various parts of the globe, concrete evidence exists of how a massive and sudden influx of refugees provokes a radical reconfiguration of the political, economic, and social landscape of host communities. There is a widespread consensus that in "many Third World countries . . . refugees represent an unacceptable strain on their limited resources."[52] Understandably, examples of lack of hospitality can be found not only in biblical and Christian traditions, but also in contemporary societies placed under enormous demographic pressures by populations of displaced people. The disproportionate burden borne by poorer nations offering hospitality to refugees translates into an ethical obligation on the part of richer nations to take more responsibility for meeting the needs of displaced people. In other words, considering the strain imposed on an already impoverished economy by unregulated refugee flows, the notion of burden-sharing assumes critical importance as a structural implication grounded on the theme of hospitality and protection of forcibly displaced people and refugees. Thus, devising an equitable mechanism of burden-sharing constitutes one of the systemic responses to the challenge of forced displacement. Arash Abizadeh makes an analogous argument for the ethical responsibility of prosperous states to keep their borders considerably more open to foreigners. The imperative of the international community to assist economically fragile and politically unstable countries—as in sub-Saharan Africa—in assuming the burden of hospitality represents an explicit structural implication of the ethical norms of a Christian understanding of forced displacement and refugees.

Third, this chapter has implicated religion as a factor of displacement. Without attempting to denigrate the commendable intervention of faith-based nongovernmental organizations, the fact remains that on several contemporary refugee issues, religion continues to play an important albeit oftentimes negative role, resulting from religious intolerance and opposing sectarian ideologies. Refugee studies tend to pay marginal attention to the connection between religion, forced migration, and displacement. In the context of defining ethical norms based on a Christian understanding, it is possible, even necessary, to identify a systemic response that draws upon the contribution of religion more positively construed. Allowing for the possibility, as Tomasi argues, that "faith insights are not a precise roadmap for normative reforms, but they do set a framework within which to move," the emphasis here is on the need to create an environment conducive to the promotion of peace, reconciliation, and dialogue among religious traditions (see chapter 3). Whether in Somalia, Sudan's Darfur region, Iraq, or Afghanistan, the breakdown in the relationship among religious traditions and allegiances counts as a deep cause of displacement and refugees. Consequently, harnessing the positive potential of religious traditions that maintain an active presence in the public sphere for a global solidarity against factors of displacement represents an important ethical, systemic response that needs to be on the agenda of refugee-serving international agencies.

Conclusion: An Enduring Challenge, an Unfinished Business

Christianity responds in diverse ways to the challenges posed by "the variegated universe of migrants—students far from home, immigrants, refugees, displaced people, evacuees—including, for example, the victims of modern forms of slavery, and of human trafficking."[53] In this chapter I have attempted to demonstrate the thesis that a Christian understanding of and responses to the phenomena of refugees and displacement are not bereft of theological resources and foundations, some of which date back to the origin of Christianity and, beyond that, to the Old Testament theology of hospitality and protection for migrants and refugees. Yet there are conceptual and practical gaps both in biblical accounts and in Christian history. This chapter has also recognized the negative role of religion as a factor in the displacement of people. The avowal of theological principles of hospitality, protection, and justice for displaced people has not always generated the required ethical behavior and practices. The legacy of lack of openness and the failure to show hospitality in Christian communities intensify the overall challenge of a theological understanding of justice for the displaced.

This investigation has identified a triptych composed of biblical ethics, the ecclesiology of migration, and Catholic social teaching. Taken together, they provide a normative Christian understanding that shapes Christian responses to the crisis of refugees and displaced people. The selection of these three items is guided by the historical affinity between religion and migratory experiences, especially those provoked by harmful socioeconomic and political factors.

I have deliberately circumscribed the scope of this chapter to explore the subject of refugees and displaced people from the perspective of Roman Catholic theology. Thus, it does not pretend to speak for all Christian traditions and denominations. Within the constitutive norms and values of this theological framework, Christian understanding recognizes, affirms, and promotes the rights of the refugee. These rights impose on church and society the obligation to welcome the stranger, protect the weak, and respect the dignity of the human person.

To be a refugee or a displaced person defines not simply a liminal sociological condition; more importantly, it embodies a theological and ethical condition. The experience of forced migration and displacement—along with their concomitant moral claims—appears to be so fundamental and constitutive of Christian discipleship that to deny or ignore it would inevitably undermine the credibility of Christian witness and weaken the identity, nature, and meaning of the community called church.

However, one reminder is important: Christianity does not enjoy a monopoly of theological responses to the crisis of refugees and displaced people. The crisis involves a multiplicity of factors. Many other religious traditions and secular organizations formulate their own partial strategies of response. This points up the necessity of cross-disciplinary approaches and dialogue among religious communities both at the level of understanding and at the level of concrete responses.

In the context of forced migration and displacement of people, the hallmark of a Christian understanding finds paradigmatic expression in the claim that at all times and in all places, the refugee or the displaced person is a bearer of inviolable rights endowed with a transcendent dignity. This claim is based neither on mere speculation nor on mere whim: it constitutes the primary tenet of Christian theological anthropology, according to which human beings embody and reflect the *imago dei*. The denial of, or resistance to, this fundamental truth underpins several refugee-causing factors. By its affirmation of the dignity and humanity of refugees and migrants as people created in the image and likeness of God, the totality of biblical and Christian understanding challenges the global conscience with regard to the evil of forced migration and displacement of people and establishes incontrovertible ethical demands of justice for the displaced.

Notes

1. Daniel G. Groody, "Fruit of the Vine and Work of Human Hands: Immigration and the Eucharist," in *A Promised Land, a Perilous Journey: Theological Perspectives on Migration,* ed. Daniel G. Groody and Gioacchino Campese (Notre Dame, IN: University of Notre Dame Press, 2008), 311–12.

2. Susan Martin's analysis of the various categories of forced migrants is helpful, but it does not obscure the fact that "human mobility today is blurring the traditional distinctions between refugees, internally displaced people, and international immigrants." António Guterres, "Millions Uprooted: Saving Refugees and the Displaced," *Foreign Affairs* 87, no. 5 (September–October 2008): 90.

3. See Global Commission for International Migration, "Migration in an Interconnected World: New Directions for Action (Report of the Global Commission for International Migration)" (Geneva: Global Commission on International Migration, 2005).

4. I have examined some faith-based organizations and their programs in refugee camps in East Africa in *From Crisis to Kairos: The Mission of the Church in the Time of HIV/AIDS, Refugees and Poverty* (Nairobi, Kenya: Paulines, 2005), 148–63. A good example of this is Jesuit Refugee Service (JRS), an arm of the religious order of the Society of Jesus, also known as Jesuits, with special focus on advocacy, service, and accompaniment of refugees and displaced people. See also Agbonkhianmeghe E. Orobator, "Key Ethical Issues in the Practices and Policies of Refugee-Serving NGOs and Churches," in *Refugee Rights: Ethics, Advocacy, and Africa,* ed. David Hollenbach (Washington, DC: Georgetown University Press, 2008), 225–44; Joint Commission for Refugees of the Burundi and Tanzania Episcopal Conferences, "The Presence of the Burundian Refugees in Western Tanzania: Ethical Responsibilities as a Framework for Advocacy," in Hollenbach, *Refugee Rights,* 53–75.

5. With regard to the issue of immigration, Tricia C. Bruce has argued that churches and church-based nongovernment organizations undertake a process of "discursive adaptation" in which religious desires and motivations are (re)formulated in more general secular terms for strategic purposes, including the need for funding. "Contested Accommodation on the Meso Level: Discursive Adaptation within Catholic Charities' Immigration and Refugee Services," *American Behavioral Scientist* 49, no. 11 (July 2006): 1489–508.

6. For example, the theme of migration and displacement is present in Judaism, Islam, and

Confucianism. See W. Gunther Plaut, "Jewish Ethics and International Migrations," *International Migration Review* 30, no. 1 (Spring 1996): 27–36; Sami A. Aldeeb Abu-Sahlieh, "The Islamic Conception of Migration," *International Migration Review* 30, no. 1 (Spring 1996): 37–57; Weiming Tu, "Beyond the Enlightenment Mentality: A Confucian Perspective on Ethics, Migration, and Global Stewardship," *International Migration Review* 30, no. 1 (Spring 1996): 58–68.

7. W. G. Plaut, *Asylum: A Moral Dilemma* (Toronto: York Lanes Press; Westport, CT: Praeger, 1995), 28.

8. Stephanie J. Nawyn, "Faith, Ethnicity, and Culture in Refugee Resettlement," *American Behavioral Scientist* 49, no. 11 (July 2006): 1510.

9. Ibid. Maryanne Loughry's chapter in this book offers further examples of how "the refashioning of many parts of Iraq along confessional lines" emerges as a key factor of displacement of refugees in Iraq and Syria.

10. Mark Franken, "The Theology of Migration" (paper presented to the board of directors of the Lutheran Immigration and Refugee Services, Baltimore, MD, October 28, 2004). For a detailed exegesis and philological analysis of the concept and meaning of various ethical categories of migrants and displaced persons, see Frank Anthony Spina, "Israelites as *gērîm*, 'Sojourners,' in Social and Historical Context," in *The Word of the Lord Shall Go Forth: Essays in Honor of David Noel Freedman in Celebration of His Sixtieth Birthday*, ed. Carol L. Meyers and M. O'Connor (Winona Lake, IN: Eisenbrauns, 1983), 321–35; Peter Muema, "Special Attention to the Tragedy of Refugees and Internally Displaced Persons within Africa in Light of the Bible," in *A Theological Response to the Tragedy of Refugees and Internally Displaced Persons in Africa*, ed. Sewe-K'Ahenda (Nairobi, Kenya: CUEA Publications, 2007), 8–12.

11. Spina, "Israelites as *gērîm*," 322.

12. Office of Migration and Refugee Services of the United States Conference of Catholic Bishops, "Welcoming the Stranger among Us: Unity in Diversity" (November 15, 2000), 8.

13. Donald Senior, "'Beloved Aliens and Exiles': New Testament Perspectives on Migration," in *A Promised Land, a Perilous Journey*, ed. Groody and Campese, 22. See also Robert Schreiter, "Theology's Contribution to (Im)migration," in *Migration, Religious Experience, and Globalization,* ed. Gioacchino Campese and Pietro Ciallella (New York: Center for Migration Studies, 2003), 170–74; Santime Matungulu, "*L'Afrique et l'immigration*," *Telema* 2–3, nos. 129–30 (April–September 2007): 66–71.

14. Pius XII, *Exsul familia.*

15. Clement Majawa, "The African Refugee-Shepherding Ecclesiology," in *A Theological Response,* ed. Sewe-K'Ahenda, 46. See also Drew Christiansen, "Movement, Asylum, Borders: Christian Perspectives," *International Migration Review* 30, no. 1 (Spring 1996): 1.

16. Senior, "Beloved Aliens and Exiles," 23; cf. Schreiter, "Theology's Contribution to (Im) migration," 174–75.

17. Orobator, *From Crisis to Kairos,* 239.

18. The theme of Pope Benedict XVI's "Message for the World Day of Migrants and Refugees" (January 18, 2009) is "*St Paul Migrant, 'Apostle of the Peoples.'*" This document refers to Paul as "a migrant by vocation" and a "missionary to migrants" whose experience serves as "an important reference point for those who find themselves involved in the migratory movement today." It can be found at the website of The Holy See, http://212.77.1.245/news_services/bulletin/news/22721.php?index=22721&po_date=08.10.2008&lang=en#TRADUZIONE%20IN%20LINGUA%20INGLESE (accessed October 9, 2008).

19. Senior, "Beloved Aliens and Exiles," 26.

20. Orobator, *From Crisis to Kairos,* 228–29; Senior, "Beloved Aliens and Exiles," 24–25.

21. Graziano Battistella, "The Human Rights of Migrants: A Pastoral Challenge," in *Migration, Religious Experience, and Globalization*, 93–94.

22. USCCB, "Welcoming the Stranger among Us," identifies the concrete manifestations of this concern as conversion, communion, and solidarity. See also Michael A. Blume, "Towards an Ecclesiology of Migration," *People on the Move*, no. 90 (December 2002), 4; Majawa, "African Refugee-Shepherding Ecclesiology," 53 ff.

23. There are interesting attempts to develop theological models of the Church based on the experiences of refugees and internally displaced people. Clement Majawa, for example, advocates a new kind of ecclesiology christened "shepherding ecclesiology," on the basis of which he argues that "the Church in Africa cannot neglect its role of speaking and acting on behalf of the oppressed, refugees, immigrants, and those in various forms of captivity." "African Refugee-Shepherding Ecclesiology," 71; see also 72–85. I also develop the idea of a "nomadic church" or "mobile church" in the context of refugees and internally displaced people. *From Crisis to Kairos*, 163 ff.

24. See Vatican Council II, *Lumen gentium (Dogmatic Constitution on the Church)*, no. 5, and *Gaudium et spes (Pastoral Constitution on the Church in the Modern World)*, no. 45.

25. Orobator, *From Crisis to Kairos*, 168 ff.

26. Letter of November 14, 2005 to the Whole Society of Jesus.

27. Jacqueline Hagan, "Making Theological Sense of the Migration Journey from Latin America: Catholic, Protestant, and Interfaith Perspectives," *American Behavioral Scientist* 49, no. 11 (July 2006): 1560.

28. Examples of Catholic social teaching documents relating to migrants, refugees, and displaced people include John XXIII, *Pacem in terris* (1963); Vatican Council II, "Pastoral Constitution on the Church in the Modern World" (1965); Paul VI, *Populorum progressio* (1967); and Pope John Paul II, *Laborem exercens* (1981) and *Sollicitudo rei socialis* (1987). To these documents we should add Zambia Episcopal Conference, "I Was a Stranger and You Welcomed Me" (Pastoral Letter of the Catholic Bishops of Zambia, June 20, 2001); Pontifical Council for the Pastoral Care of Migrant and Itinerant People, *Cor Unum, Refugees: A Challenge to Solidarity* (1992); Pontifical Council for the Pastoral Care of Migrant and Itinerant People, *Erga migrantes caritas Christi* (The love of Christ towards migrants), 2004.

29. In "Theology of Migration," 4–5; Franken summarizes five principles of Catholic social teaching of particular relevance to migrants and refugees: (1) the right not to emigrate, (2) the right to emigrate, (3) the greater obligation of powerful nations to accommodate migration, (4) the right and claim of refugees and asylum seekers to protection; and (5) the affirmation of the inalienable dignity of all migrants and refugees.

30. Archbishop Silvano Tomasi, "Globalization of Justice and Solidarity Is the Best Guarantee for Peace" (statement delivered to the UN refugee agency's annual Executive Committee meeting, Geneva, Switzerland, October 2008), Zenit News Agency, www.zenit.org/article-23906?l=english (accessed October 13, 2008).

31. Christiansen, "Movements, Asylum, Borders," 4. Cf. Kristin Heyer, "Welcoming the Stranger: What Christian Faith Can Bring to the Immigration Debate," *America*, www.america magazine.org/content/article.cfm?article_id=11117 (accessed October 5, 2008); and J. Bryan Hehir, "Catholic Social Teaching & Migration," United States Conference of Catholic Bishops Migration & Refugee Services, www.usccb.org/mrs/hehir.shtml (accessed October 9, 2008).

32. Recent church documents mention development projects, climate change, and natural disasters as factors of displacement. As Maryanne Loughry points out in her chapter in this volume, not only are there multiple causes of migration and displacement, but the various causes are also interlinked.

33. Archbishop Tomasi, "Globalization of Justice."

34. Majawa, "African Refugee-Shepherding Ecclesiology," 36.

35. Spina, "Israelites as *gērîm*," 331; Hehir, "Catholic Social Teaching & Migration." See also Donald E. Gowan, "Wealth and Poverty in the Old Testament: The Case of the Widow, the Orphan, and the Sojourner," *Interpretation* 41 (1987): 343–44, 347.

36. Peter Kanyandago, "Who Is My Neighbour? A Christian Response to Refugees and the Displaced in Africa," in *Moral and Ethical Issues in African Christianity: Exploratory Essays in Moral Theology*, ed. J. N. K. Mugambi and A. Nasimiyu-Wasike (Nairobi, Kenya: Initiatives Publishers, 1992), 173. Cf. Michael A. Blume, "Migration and the Social Doctrine of the Church," in *Migration, Religious Experience, and Globalization*, 62.

37. Orobator, "Key Ethical Issues," 240.

38. Paul Flamm, "Refugee Ministry: Towards Healing and Reconciliation," *Mission Studies* 15, no. 1 (1998): 116. On the related issue of immigration, Margarita Mooney notes: "Although bishops do not set public policy, they can influence public policy through their lobbying of political officials and by shaping the conscience of citizens. . . . The bishops can also influence the public sphere by directly providing social services." "The Catholic Bishops Conferences of the United States and France: Engaging Immigration as a Public Issue," *American Behavioral Scientist* 49, no. 11 (July 2006): 1468.

39. Daniel Groody, "A Theology of Immigration," *Notre Dame Magazine*, www.nd.edu/~ndmag/au2004/groody.html (accessed September 15, 2008).

40. Michael A. Blume, "Refugees and Mission: A Primer," *Mission Studies* 16, nos. 1–2 (2000): 164. Cf. USCCB, "Welcoming the Stranger," 4.

41. See Orobator, *From Crisis to Kairos*, 148–63; Flamm, "Refugee Ministry," 99–125; Cecilia Menjívar, "Public Religion and Immigration across National Contexts," *American Behavioral Scientist* 49, no. 11 (July 2006): 1448–49; and Jacqueline Hagan, "Faith for the Journey: Religion as a Resource for Migrants," in *Migration, Religious Experience, and Globalization*, 13–14.

42. Pontifical Council, *Erga migrantes caritas Christi*, no. 22.

43. Archbishop Tomasi, "Globalization of Justice."

44. Charles E. Curran, *Catholic Social Teaching 1891–Present: A Historical, Theological, and Ethical Analysis* (Washington, DC: Georgetown University Press, 2002), 2–3.

45. See Bruce, "Contested Accommodation," 1500.

46. Pope Paul VI, Apostolic Letter *Octogesima adveniens* (1971), no. 4; Congregation for the Doctrine of the Faith, Instruction on Christian Freedom and Liberation, *Libertatis Conscientia* (March 22, 1986), no. 72; Pope John Paul II, Encyclical Letter *Sollicitudo rei socialis* (1988), no. 41.

47. Orobator, *From Crisis to Kairos*, 56.

48. Ibid.

49. The argument here not only concerns transnational actors, like UNHCR and the UN's Office for the Coordination of Humanitarian Affairs (OCHA), as Maryanne Loughry indicates in her chapter here, but in the overall context of this chapter, it should allow space for the participation and contribution of faith-based, refugee-serving, nongovernmental organizations.

50. Christiansen, "Movements, Asylum, Borders," 4 (emphasis added).

51. Global Commission, *Migration in an Interconnected World*, 4.

52. Ebenezer Q. Blavo, *The Problems of Refugees in Africa: Boundaries and Borders* (Aldershot, UK: Ashgate, 1990), 70.

53. Pope Benedict XVI, "Message for the World Day of Migrants and Refugees" (January 18, 2009).

3

Human Rights as a Framework for Advocacy on Behalf of the Displaced

The Approach of the Catholic Church

Silvano Tomasi

Introduction

People are moving from everywhere to everywhere. More than 200 million persons live, seek and find refuge, and work in a country different from the one in which they were born. To this statistic should be added the number of people forcibly displaced within their own country due to conflicts, oppression, or natural disaster—an estimated 26–30 million people—who are a matter of growing concern worldwide. Irregular migration is ubiquitous and in the millions. The combination of adverse economic, social, and political trends places the world's poor and uprooted people increasingly at risk, and it adds to the growing scale and complexity of forced migration. Migrants of all kinds, asylum seekers, irregular economic migrants, refugees from civil wars and famine, women and children being moved about by human traffickers, and the internally displaced are all currently accorded much attention. But the scope and scale of human mobility is not a calamity, and no state is in the grips of a "pandemic" of migration that is about to overwhelm it.

Human mobility in its multifaceted aspects is not a new phenomenon; it has accompanied the unfolding of history. Prehistoric migrations peopled new territories; Phoenician and Greek trade colonies dotted the Mediterranean basin; defeated Jewish people were forcibly taken into exile to Babylon; persecution scattered the earliest Christian communities within and outside of Palestine. Examples can multiply. Today, the 3 percent of the world's population that has moved for one or another reason represents a sign of alarm that all is not well in the international community. In fact, most people would simply rather stay at home and not relocate, but they lack the option of exercising their right of not being forced to migrate. For years human mobility has been a factor resulting from, and contributing to, globalization, and that mobility has lately become a priority in the political agenda.

Economists and scholars in ethics continue to debate the implications of the movement of people. Security concerns and control of entry drive policy in most receiving countries, even if such a policy is in evident contradiction with the need to accept more people. The complexity of the debate, and the various and evolving situations in which displaced people are found, make it very difficult to translate general principles into normative legislation and clear-cut guidance for action. In an effort to advance the process, I will offer some reflections on human displacement, first as it is approached by the international community, and then by the Catholic tradition. I will attempt to note the points of convergence and the common challenges emerging from a universal perspective in a world still dominated by the decisions and legitimating function of nation-states. In conclusion, I indicate that the universal perspective must ultimately be taken as the necessary measure to ensure peaceful coexistence and sustain the enactment of norms respectful of persons and supportive of the common good.

The International Community and the Human Rights of Displaced People

The masses of people on the move could be placed along a continuum that describes the reasons for their decision to move and the form of protection they need. If we look at involuntarily uprooted people, they can be categorized roughly as refugees; groups forcibly displaced by violence, climate change, or natural disasters; and migrant workers. For each of these three categories, the international community has devised some formal instruments of protection. Refugess are covered by the 1951 United Nations (UN) Convention Relating to the Status of Refugees and by the related 1967 Protocol that removed the geographical and time limits; internally displaced persons (IDP) by the *Guiding Principles on Internal Displacement* (2001); and migrant workers by the International Labour Organization's Conventions and by the United Nations International Convention on the Protection of the Rights of All Migrant Workers and Members of Their Families, adopted by the General Assembly at its forty-fifth session on December 18, 1990. These instruments brought about pragmatic developments for implementation that further promote and defend the human rights of displaced people. Most significant are some regional instruments such as the Convention Governing the Specific Aspects of Refugee Problems in Africa (1969), the Cartagena Declaration on Refugees (1984), and the Great Lakes Pact and the Rights of Displaced People: A Guide for Civil Society (2008). There certainly is room for additional normative provisions, especially for the growing numbers of people who are in mixed flows or are escaping generalized violence, famine, and other natural disasters. The proposed draft, Convention for the Prevention of Internal Displacement and the Protection of and Assistance to Internally Displaced Persons in Africa, moves in this direction by complementing the existing norms.

Thus experience shows the dynamic evolution that has come about since the end of World War II in understanding protection as more groups, such as stateless persons and IDPs, have been included in the mandate of UN agencies. A second conclusion emerging from the conferences and resolutions of the UN deals with the shift from a total predominance of the state in provoking, regulating, and asserting objectives regarding population movements, to the felt need that the international community should assume a more effective responsibility and become involved in appropriate forms of coordination and burden-sharing at the regional and global levels. The latter development has been influenced by the desire of governments for an orderly management of population displacements and by the greater visibility assumed by the human rights of individuals.

Forced diplacement will not disappear any time soon. In 2007, fourteen noninternational conflicts, with serious humanitarian consequences, were registered in thirteen regions of the world. In addition, sixty-one international peace missions are confronted with as many complex political, military, and humanitarian crises.[1]

The two tracks on which the international community proceeds in addressing the persistent displacement of people are those of enhanced coherence in the institutional response, through tentative structures like the Geneva-based Global Migration Group, and the frequent reaffirmation of the conviction "that everyone is entitled to a social and international order in which the rights and freedoms set forth in the Universal Declaration of Human Rights can be fully realized."[2] The appeal to a democratic and equitable international order goes to the root of forced displacement, since it stresses that the responsibility for managing worldwide economic and social issues, as well as threats to international peace and security, must be shared among the nations of the world and should be exercised multilaterally. Both forced displacement and migration for survival and work are contextualized, especially now that climate change and extreme poverty and conflicts have become interrelated. They should not be seen and analyzed as isolated social phenomena, but as expressions of political and economic choices.

At the time of observance of the sixtieth anniversary of the Universal Declaration of Human Rights (UDHR), it is interesting to note that the original agreement that human rights are not necessarily tied to citizenship but to the human person has had some influence in the evolution of an international public culture. The journey from Westphalian sovereignty to supranational cooperation in handling human displacement, however, is incomplete and even contested.[3] The right to leave one's country is conditioned by the willingness of another country to accept a would-be refugee, displaced person, or hungry migrant. Thus, the freedom of movement across national boundaries is not a right, notwithstanding the tendency to recognize that a state, by itself, is unable to regulate human mobility.

The trend toward seeking transnational solutions, however, has been strengthened by the work and conclusions of the 2005 Global Commission on International Migration, established to "provide the framework for the formulation of a coherent, comprehensive, and global response to the issue of international migration." While this Commission recognized that, in the formulation of immigration policy, states exercise their sovereign right to determine who enters into and remains on their territory, it called for "greater consultation and cooperation between states at the regional level, and more effective dialogue and cooperation among governments and between international organizations at the global level. Such efforts must be based on a better appreciation of the close linkages that exist between international migration and development and other key policy issues, including trade, aid, state security, human security, and human rights."[4] One critical recommendation of the

Commission was to propose to the UN secretary-general "the immediate establishment of a high-level inter-institutional group to define the functions and modalities of, and pave the way for, an Inter-agency Global Migration Facility. This Facility should ensure a more coherent and effective institutional response to the opportunities and challenges presented by international migration."[5]

The 2006 UN High Level Dialogue on Migration and Development (HLD) supported the same line of thinking: "Participants felt that it was essential to address the root causes of international migration to ensure that people migrated out of choice rather than necessity. They observed that people often had to migrate because of poverty, conflict, human rights violations, poor governance, or lack of employment."[6] The result of the HLD was the establishment of a Global Forum on Migration and Development. This Forum is not directly part of the UN but is linked to it through a representative of the UN secretary-general. It has a mandate to discuss, in a systematic and comprehensive way, issues related to international migration and development. An assembly of state representatives, the Forum was held in Brussels in 2007, in Manila in 2008, and in Athens in 2009.

Thus the international community faces the increasing mobility of people through mechanisms that are as yet uncoordinated (the Global Migration Forum, the Global Forum on Migration and Development). There are occasional debates about the possibility of establishing a UN agency for all categories of displaced people with a role similar to that of the World Trade Organization. At the same time, global thinking on these matters remains ambivalent, with sending countries and civil society groups focusing the debate on human rights, while receiving countries emphasize security, control of borders, and national identity.

The two views could be labeled "global humanitarianism" and "national protectionism," with emphases being placed respectively on the language of universal fundamental human rights or on an understanding of displaced people as a technical, legal, political, or administrative problem. In the Human Rights Council, the traditional resolution on the human rights of migrants regularly reminds the states that the right to life, the right of a person to be free from discrimination, the right to personal freedom and security, to education and health, and to access to justice are not limited by borders and are intrinsic to all persons by virtue of their humanity.[7] The Resolution on the renewal of the mandate of the representative of the secretary-general on the human rights of internally displaced persons also directs states and civil society groups to analyse the root causes of displacement and to mainstream the "human rights of internally displaced into all relevant parts of the United Nations system."[8]

The relevance of this discussion for forcibly displaced people derives, first of all, from the fact that protection and assistance mechanisms are encouraged to converge through coherence in policy and action. Second, as the high commissioner for refugees notes, "human mobility today is blurring the traditional distinctions between refugees, internally displaced people, and international immigrants."[9] Or, as Aristide R. Zolberg put it, "Much as the international migration reflects the economic structure and concomitant processes of the international system that produces them, so the flow of refugees largely reflects the political structure of that same system."[10] Since the end of World War II, a discernible tendency appears to be that of subsuming human mobility in the total social context. What is implied is a set of interlocking variables: looking at "uprootedness" along a continuum of related causes pushing individuals and families to move, demanding a progressive recognition of the priority of human rights as inherent in any person, and finding a new balance between the state and the global community.

The Catholic Tradition vis-à-vis Displaced People

The Catholic Church has joined in the debate and, in its own way, has stimulated and effectively influenced the journey of the international community. Of historical note is the decision of the Holy See to participate in the life of the international institutions. This policy was developed at the end of World War II in response to the problem of war-displaced people, when the Church became their advocate and argued on their behalf from the perspective of the Church's experience and doctrine. The Holy See took part, as full member, in the drafting of the 1951 Refugee Convention and ratified it.[11]

Regrettably, the attempts of the international community to deal globally with population movements are somewhat erratic and have been hampered by power competition and the lack of a clear point of reference. Efforts to reform the United Nations system have come up against its agencies' fight for self-preservation. By contrast, in the social doctrine of the Church, the link between population movements, state rights, and international order is founded in the unifying, larger perspective of an integral humanism, directed to the development of every person and every people. The *Compendium of the Social Doctrine of the Church* puts it this way: "The Church aims at a 'complete form of humanism,' that is to say, at the 'liberation from everything that oppresses man' and 'the development of the whole man and of all men [and women].'" The Church's social doctrine indicates the path to follow for a society reconciled and in harmony through justice and love, a society that anticipates in history, in a preparatory and prefigurative manner, the "new heavens and a new earth in which righteousness dwells" (2 Pet. 3:13)."[12] Thus, within the framework of its social doctrine, the Catholic tradition offers an answer to human displacement that is very much in line with, and on the side of, the "global humanism" trend of the international community.

The Church's ethical approach to displacement of people has evolved in an incremental way along with the development of the broader social doctrine of the church. Leo XIII already underlined, in his encyclical *Rerum novarum*, that "men would cling to the country in which they were born, for no one would exchange his country for a foreign land if his own afforded him the means of living a decent and happy life."[13] Pius XII elaborated the right to enter another country, presented a comprehensive view of all categories related to human mobility, and legislated a systematic and specific pastoral care for uprooted persons and families.[14] John XXIII and the Second Vatican Council added the perspective of human rights and a global understanding of the common good. Paul VI highlighted the relationship of migration to the right of every person and country to development and insisted on the globalization of the social question and on the conviction that development is the new name of peace.[15]

John Paul II based his teaching on that of his predecessors and enriched it with his personal insights, both in relation to the entire social question and to specific problems. From his innumerable addresses and statements on human mobility, the complexity, urgency, and global dimension of the phenomenon were summed up when John Paul received the participants in the IV World Congress on the Pastoral Care of Migrants and Refugees. The Pope remarked,

> In this context it seems appropriate to stress that it is a basic human right to live in one's own country. However, this right becomes effective only if the factors that urge people to emigrate are constantly kept under control. These include, among others, civil conflicts, wars, the system of government, unjust distribution of economic resources, inconsistent agricultural policies, irrational industrialization, and rampant corruption. If these situations are to be corrected, it is indispensable to encourage balanced economic development, the elimination of social inequalities, scrupulous respect for the human person, and the smooth functioning of democratic structures. It is also indispensable to take timely measures to correct the current economic and financial system, dominated and manipulated by industrialized nations at the expense of developing countries. Indeed, the closing of borders is often caused not merely by a reduced or no longer existing need for an immigrant work-force, but by a productive system based on the logic of labour exploitation. . . . We must deal firmly with the causes, by seeking international co-operation to foster political stability and eliminate underdevelopment. This challenge must be met with the awareness that it is a question of building a world in which all human beings, regardless of race, religion, or nationality, can live a fully human life, free from slavery to others and from the nightmare of having to spend their life in misery.[16]

Misery, first of all, affects refugees. Arms trade, the organization of the economy, the external debt of poor countries, selfish political decisions, and similar difficulties induced Pope John Paul II to say, "The consequences of this state of affairs are to be seen in the festering of a wound which typifies and reveals the imbalances and conflicts of the modern world: the millions of refugees whom war, natural calamities, persecution, and discrimination of every kind have deprived of home, employment, family, and homeland."[17] The high number and the persistence of uprooted persons, a vulnerable group that, as such, calls for the special attention of the Christian community, prompt a clear articulation of arguments for their protection and for the motivation of concrete action on their behalf. There is a convergence between natural law and faith-inspired principles that provides a framework within which forcibly displaced persons find a response to the claims posed by their particular situation of vulnerability, and society finds the duty to assume responsibility to remedy that situation.

From the teaching of recent popes and of the bishops of the church, who recently have spoken on migration and forced displacement issues in every continent, emerging guidelines embrace the whole range of forced mobility. There is no systematic treatise in church teaching on the rights of, and the duties toward, forcibly displaced people, even though some more substantive documents as well as many occasional interventions have been officially issued by the Holy See and Episcopal conferences. From this multiplicity of documents, though conditioned by the historical circumstances within which they have been issued, it possible to see a comprehensive approach.[18]

Borders, even though clearly recognized as legitimate, are not a priority in this argumentation, and the emphasis on human rights is not defensive. These rights are seen as an instrument to enter into contact and dialogue with others. The relational understanding of the person opens the way to a widening circle of interaction that leads eventually to global solidarity. During recent decades, the framework or guideline that has evolved in the social doctrine of the church is derived from explicit references in papal encyclicals and in the documents of Vatican Council II, from the annual papal messages for Migrant and Refugee Day, and from the pastoral statements of the Holy See and of local churches. It provides a clear, consistent, and specific vision.[19] Key aspects of this ethical vision will be outlined here.

1. First of all, everyone has a right to a decent life where he or she lives, and, therefore, it is the responsibility of the state to do all that is possible to reach this goal by ensuring peaceful coexistence; economic development; access to education, health, work opportunities, and so on. Thus, Pope John Paul II said, "it is a basic human right to live in one's own country."[20] Pope Benedict XVI recently reminded the UN General Assembly that "every State has the primary duty to protect its own population from grave and sustained violations of human rights, as well as from the consequences of humanitarian crises, whether natural or man-made."[21]

2. Moving away from the dangers of violence, hunger, and oppression is a natural right of every person. Persons displaced for such reasons have the right to move with their families, to leave their countries of origin, and to enter another. Thus, we read in *Pacem in terris* that "among man's personal rights we must include his right to enter a country in which he hopes to be able to provide more fittingly for himself and his dependents. It is therefore the duty of State officials to accept."[22] *Familiaris Consortio* states that "in particular, the [1981] Synod Fathers mentioned the following rights of the family . . . the right to emigrate as a family in search of a better life."[23] In this line, the *Catechism of the Catholic Church* notes that countries with more resources have an obligation to the extent that they are able to receive needier people: "The more prosperous nations are obliged, to the extent they are able, to welcome the foreigner in search of the security and the means of livelihood which he cannot find in his country of origin."[24]

3. This general principle, however, is not absolute, since the exercise of this right needs to be regulated to take into account the common good of the receiving state: "Certainly, the exercise of such a right is to be regulated, because practicing it indiscriminately may do harm and be detrimental to the common good of the community that receives the migrant. Before the manifold interests that are

interwoven side by side with the laws of the individual countries, it is necessary to have international norms that are capable of regulating everyone's rights so as to prevent unilateral decisions that are harmful to the weakest."[25]

4. The common good in a state, on the other hand, both in the state of departure and in the state of destination, is not itself an absolute tenet. It must not be falsely understood, but considered objectively. In fact, the resources of the Earth have a universal destination to serve the needs of all persons and every person is a citizen of the universal society. "I called to mind," writes Pope John Paul II, "that although it is true that highly developed countries are not always able to assimilate all those who emigrate, nonetheless it should be pointed out that the criterion for determining the level that can be sustained cannot be based solely on protecting their own prosperity, while failing to take into consideration the needs of persons who are tragically forced to ask for hospitality."[26] While the absolute restriction of the right to leave the territory of a state is not acceptable, a limited restriction is possible, but it should be accompanied by solidarity.

5. The duty of hospitality and that of integration should be balanced in a context of the common good of society and of freedom for the individual. The biblical teaching on welcoming the stranger and Israel's memory of its liberation from slavery are points of constant reference in calling for protection, nondiscrimination, and participation. "Public authorities," teaches the Catechism of the Catholic Church, "should see to it that the natural right is respected that places a guest under the protection of those who receive him. Political authorities, for the sake of the common good for which they are responsible, may make the exercise of the right to immigrate subject to various juridical conditions, especially with regard to the immigrants' duties toward their country of adoption. Immigrants are obliged to respect with gratitude the material and spiritual heritage of the country that receives them, to obey its laws and to assist in carrying civic burdens."[27]

6. Forcibly displaced people have a just claim on the international community to be assisted in order to return to a normal existence. Charity, in addition to justice, demands a generous response, since the fundamental human rights of the displaced must be restored.

7. Displaced people searching for a more dignified life, but present in an irregular situation in a host country, are not without rights. In the words of Pope John Paul II,

> Today the phenomenon of illegal migrants has assumed considerable proportions, both because the supply of foreign labour is becoming excessive in comparison to the needs of the economy, which already has difficulty in absorbing its domestic workers, and because of the spread of forced migration. The necessary prudence required to deal with so delicate a matter cannot become one of reticence or exclusivity, because thousands would suffer the consequences as victims of situations that seem destined to deteriorate instead of being resolved. His irregular legal status cannot allow the migrant to lose his dignity, since he is endowed with inalienable rights, which can neither be violated nor ignored. Illegal immigration should be prevented, but it is also essential to combat vigorously the

criminal activities that exploit illegal immigrants. The most appropriate choice, which will yield consistent and long-lasting results, is that of international cooperation that aims to foster political stability and to eliminate underdevelopment. The present economic and social imbalance, which to a large extent encourages the migratory flow, should not be seen as something inevitable, but as a challenge to the human race's sense of responsibility.[28]

8. Cultural rights are defended. The identity of displaced people in a new environment has to be respected, especially their religion, but also their cultural traditions and expressions and always within the common good of the entire hosting society.
9. The right to return to one's home, property, and country has to be respected.
10. Finally, an international regime should be established to better manage all forced human displacement, a social phenomenon that is transnational by its nature.[29]

The foundation for the framework that I have outlined is located in the social doctrine of the church, which starts from the dignity of the human person, a dignity that is intrinsic to the person and not granted or conceded by any individual or state. Such dignity is equal in every human being and ultimately is derived from the belief that the person is made in the image and likeness of God. Therefore, the creation of a social environment where human rights are upheld and this dignity is respected would be the best strategy to prevent forced displacement. To achieve this goal, international cooperation and assistance toward development become necessary.

These strategies flow from a solidarity that is expressed in other principles of Catholic social teaching, including the oneness of the human family, the inherent duty of mutual support since we are directed to a common destiny, and the universal destination of all the goods of the earth. The three interconnected principles—human dignity, oneness in destiny of the human family, universal destiny of the goods of creation, explained also in terms of Christian theology and Revelation—establish the ideal that is the aim of the practical action of the Christian community. These principles also provide justification for a genuine global humanism.

In a world of states the social doctrine of the church may be judged as utopian. But we cannot escape the reality of our situation. As members of a state, we also are members of the universal society of all those who have the same fundamental human rights.[30] The relationship between the two forms of belonging does not entail contradiction; on the contrary, it clearly demonstrates that only states respecting and cultivating fundamental human rights on a global level can establish full freedom for their citizens and gain legitimacy in the eyes of other states.[31] This relationship is primordial and becomes critical for a correct approach to forced displacement, for the enactment of fair immigration and refugee legislation, and for any effective protection. In this regard, these basic principles of Catholic social teaching provide both inspiration and justification for the rapidly evolving concept of the responsibility to protect (R2P). The convergence of religious and humanitarian principles finds a practical application in the efforts of the international community to prevent the atrocious treatment of forcibly displaced people and ensure their protection.

Nonetheless, the tension between the ideal and the real is an existential condition that confronts the Christian. It is a dynamic tension that does not paralyze but rather stimulates the Christian to devise a rich variety of specific responses for the concrete situations that history presents. As in the case of the international community, the consequences of forced displacement have absorbed much of the energy and imagination of the Church while not forgetting that its principles are the base of prevention, an area of social concern that attracts greater attention and now prompts advocacy work and more direct involvement in any decision-making process.

The task remains unfinished even at the level of reflection. Granted that all persons have equal dignity and therefore an equal claim to protection and to the enjoyment of their fundamental human rights, whose duty would it be to provide this protection and enjoyment? Only a clear understanding of the principle of subsidiarity will help to define the operational modalities and proper management of intervention, first of all by the state, and then by transnational actors like the United Nations and regional organizations like the African Union. This remains an ongoing challenge, however, since power, national interest, compassion, and adherence to human rights may come into competition.[32] We are moving beyond legal ground into an area of higher justice and participation. Fyodor Dostoevsky (1821–1881) wrote, "beauty is the battlefield where God and the devil fight for the soul of man." Today beauty and justice overlap. Elizabeth G. Ferris states, "Any new international system will have to be based on a new consensus—a consensus that includes shared responsibility in preventing the violence that uproots people and that sees uprooted people in terms of the search for peace and justice."[33] The vision of the Church can help lay the foundations for a new international order for uprooted people.

The Affirmation of Human Rights, a Source of Action

The action of the Catholic community is clearly inspired by its global humanism derived from its faith, the ultimate measure of advocacy and service to the displaced. Faith insights are not a precise roadmap for normative reforms, but they do set a framework within which to move. Thus, the Church calls on sources from beyond the political system, including the fundamental messages of the Gospel: "I was a stranger and you welcomed me" (Matt. 25, 35), and the example of the Good Samaritan (Luke 25–37). The Church appeals to both human rights and religious arguments to make its recommendations and to undertake immediate services. The effectiveness of the human rights approach rests on its universal appeal and potential for coalition building as well as on its legitimating function vis-à-vis the state.

In translating principles into action, the Christian community is engaged in several areas that run from advocacy to immediate case assistance, but always as the implementation of human rights. Addressing the UN General Assembly, Pope Benedict XVI stated, "The promotion of human rights remains the most effective strategy for eliminating inequalities between countries and social groups, and for increasing security."[34] In this way, by pursuing the implementation of human rights on the basis of justice and charity, Christians contribute their share to the building of a just social order. As an actor in the public sphere, the Church advocates new norms to overcome unequal interdependence; calls for the protection of the most vulnerable groups, like the forcibly displaced; encourages an active role for the international community; and influences the formation of public opinion. A multiplicity of Church groups are engaged in witnessing their solidarity through their presence in refugee camps and in resettlement networks; through providing medical assistance, education, food, and job placement; through preparing laws; and even through participating in the political arena. Trafficked women and children have prompted a coalition of women religious that has compelled governments to take notice of this problem and enact legal provisions. Christian communities have shown the possibility of managing diversity, not only by living together in peace, but also by placing the gifts of everyone at the service of all. The welcome to displaced people has even made them protagonists in teaching a practical catholicity that gives evidence of the one human family to which we all belong.

Conclusion

The combination of human rights, religious belief, and theological insight helps to motivate people to pursue social justice, to rally for the rights of forcibly displaced persons and other vulnerable groups of people, and to organize. Policy recommendations are based on the understanding of the responsbilities that universal rights impose, and on the added insight and motivation brought by the light of faith. As the present Holy Father observed in his address to the United Nations,

> Discernment, then, shows that entrusting exclusively to individual States, with their laws and institutions, the final responsibility to meet the aspirations of persons, communities, and entire peoples, can sometimes have consequences that exclude the possibility of a social order respectful of the dignity and rights of the person. On the other hand, a vision of life firmly anchored in the religious dimension can help to achieve this, since recognition of the transcendent value of every man and woman favours conversion of heart, which then leads to a commitment to resist violence, terrorism, and war, and to promote justice and peace.[35]
>
> When "defending and promoting the dignity and fundamental rights of the human persons," the Church carries out her mission in the City of Man as it provides—like her Master—the intellectual vision and the practical inspiration to serve and to love by making herself the neighbhor of all the beaten, wounded, defeated, and forcibly uprooted persons she meets along her endless road.[36]

Notes

1. Stockholm International Peace Research Institute, *SIPRI Yearbook 2008* (Oxford: Oxford University Press, 2008), 72–84.

2. Human Rights Council, Resolution 8/5, "Promotion of a Democratic and Equitable International Order," 2008. The GMG consists of ten organizations that are actively involved in international migration and related issues: International Labour Organization (ILO),

International Organization for Migration (IOM), United Nations Conference on Trade and Development (UNCTAD), United Nations Development Programme (UNDP), United Nations Department of Economic and Social Affairs (UNDESA), United Nations Population Fund (UNFPA), Office of the United Nations High Commissioner for Human Rights (OH-CHR), Office of the United Nations High Commissioner for Refugees (UNHCR), United Nations Office on Drugs and Crime (UNODC), and World Bank. The GMG is an interagency group, meeting at the level of heads of agencies, that aims to promote the wider application of all relevant international and regional instruments and norms relating to migration, and the provision of more coherent and stronger leadership to improve the overall effectiveness of the United Nations and the international community's policy and operational response to the opportunities and challenges presented by international migration.

3. The discussion on humanitarian intervention to protect the fundamental human rights of individuals vis-à-vis the state is becoming clearer and more accepted. See International Commission on Intervention and State Sovereignty, *The Responsibility to Protect*, vol. 1, *The Report*, 91; vol. 2, *Research, Bibliography, Background*, 410 (Ottawa: International Development Research Centre, 2001). Pope Benedict XVI stated in his address to the UN General Assembly,

> Recognition of the unity of the human family, and attention to the innate dignity of every man and woman, today find renewed emphasis in the principle of the responsibility to protect. This has only recently been defined, but it was already present implicitly at the origins of the United Nations, and is now increasingly characteristic of its activity. Every State has the primary duty to protect its own population from grave and sustained violations of human rights, as well as from the consequences of humanitarian crises, whether natural or man-made. If States are unable to guarantee such protection, the international community must intervene with the juridical means provided in the United Nations Charter and in other international instruments. The action of the international community and its institutions, provided that it respects the principles undergirding the international order, should never be interpreted as an unwarranted imposition or a limitation of sovereignty. On the contrary, it is indifference or failure to intervene that do the real damage. What is needed is a deeper search for ways of pre-empting and managing conflicts by exploring every possible diplomatic avenue, and giving attention and encouragement to even the faintest sign of dialogue or desire for reconciliation.

Pope Benedict XVI, Address to the General Assembly of the United Nations (New York, April 18, 2008), www.vatican.va/holy_father/benedict_xvi/speeches/2008/april/documents/hf_ben-xvi_spe_20080418_un-visit_en.html (accessed March 29, 2009).

4. The Global Commission on International Migration, *Migration in an Interconnected World: New Directions for Action* (Geneva: Global Commission on International Migration, 2005), 4. Available at www.gcim.org.

5. Ibid., 82.

6. United Nations General Assembly, sixty-first session (A/61/515), Agenda item 55 (b), "Globalization and Interdependence: International Migration and Development. "Summary of the High-level Dialogue on International Migration and Development, Note by the President of the General Assembly," October 13, 2006.

7. See United Nations Human Rights Council, ninth session, "Human Rights of Migrants" (A/HRC/9/L.14), September 2008.

8. United Nations Human Rights Council, sixth session, "Mandate of the Representative of the Secretary General on Human Rights of Internally Displaced Persons" (A/HRC/6/L.46), December 11, 2007.

9. António Guterres, "Millions Uprooted, Saving Refugees and the Displaced," *Foreign Affairs* 87, no. 5 (September–October 2008): 90.

10. Aristide R. Zolberg, "International Migrations in Political Perspective," in *Global Trends in Migration: Theory and Research on International Population Movements*, ed. Ary M. Kritz, Charles B. Keely, and Silvano M. Tomasi (New York: Center for Migration Studies, 1981), 19.

11. At that time, because of its international standing and network for social assistance, the Holy See was among fifteen states invited by the UN Economic and Social Council, through Resolution 393B (XIII), to serve as members of an Advisory Committee on Refugees, a major human and political problem left over from the World War II. In 1947 a delegate of the Holy See was charged to go to Latin America to make contact with governments and Catholic organizations and thus to ensure their full acceptance of the plan for resettlement devised by the then International Refugee Organization. Due in part to these contacts and relationships, in 1951, when the UN General Assembly decided to convene a conference of plenipotentiaries with the task "to consider the Draft Convention Relating to the Status of Refugees and the Draft Protocol Relating to the Status of Stateless Persons," an invitation to participate was extended to some states that were not members of the UN, including the Holy See, which, in fact, participated with full rights. This was one of the first intergovernmental conferences in which the Holy See took part. The Conference produced one of the first conventions that the Holy See signed and subsequently ratified. This also marked the first occasion on which the United Nations Organization called upon the Holy See to take a full part in one of its organs, and such confidence has been maintained ever since. Cf. Silvano M. Tomasi, "The Diplomatic Representations of the Holy See to the United Nations and Other International Organizations," in *The Catholic Church and the International Policy of the Holy See*, ed. Fraco Imoda and Roberto Papini (Milan: Edizioni Nagard, 2008), 87–1005.

12. Pontifical Council for Justice and Peace, *Compendium of the Social Doctrine of the Church* (Rome: Libraria Editrice Vaticana, 2004), n82.

13. Pope Leo XIII, *Rerum novarum* (1891), "On Capital and Labour," n47.

14. Exsul Familia Nazarethana, Apostolic Constitution of Pius XII, August 1, 1952. Title I says, "The natural law itself, no less than devotion to humanity, urges that ways of migration be opened to these people. For the Creator of the universe made all good things primarily for the good of all. Since land everywhere offers the possibility of supporting a large number of people, the sovereignty of the state, although it must be respected, cannot be exaggerated to the point that access to this land is, for inadequate or unjustified reasons, denied to needy and decent people from other nations, provided of course, that the public wealth, considered very carefully, does not forbid this." In the introduction, the Pope writes: "Every migrant, alien, and refugee of whatever kind who, whether compelled by fear of persecution or by want, is forced to leave his native land finds models and protectors in Jesus, Mary and Joseph living in exile."

15. Paul VI, in *Populorum progressio* (1967), n3, writes, "Today it is most important for people to understand and appreciate that the social question ties all men together, in every part of the world. John XXIII stated this clearly, . . . and Vatican II confirmed it in its Pastoral Constitution on The Church in the World of Today. . . . The seriousness and urgency of these teachings must be recognized without delay. The hungry nations of the world cry out to the peoples blessed with abundance. And the Church, cut to the quick by this cry, asks each and every man to hear his brother's plea and answer it lovingly."

16. Address of The Holy Father Pope John Paul II to Congress on Pastoral Care of Migrants, October 9, 1998, nos. 2 and 3, www.vatican.va/holy_father/john_paul_ii/speeches/1998/october/documents/hf_jp-ii_spe_19981009_migranti_en.html (accessed March 29, 2009).

17. John Paul II, *Encyclical Letter Sollicitudo rei socialis*, n24. For various statements on

refugees and forcibly displaced people by Pope John Paul II, see *People on the Move*, April 14, 1984, 159–83.

18. See, for example, Pontifical Council Cor Unum-Pontifical Council for the Pastoral Care of Migrants and Itinerant People, *Refugees: A Challenge to Solidarity* (Rome: Libreria Editrice Vaticana, 1992). Pius XII, Apostolic Constitution Exsul Familia, AAS XLIV (1952) 649–704, is the first systematic official document addressing in a global way the pastoral care of displaced people and all migrants. Paul VI directed the Congregation for Bishops to issue an update of Exsul Familia, *On the Pastoral Care of Migrants* (1968), by taking into account the innovations brought about by the Second Vatican Council. A more recent review is provided in the Pontifical Council of the Pastoral Care of Migrants and Refugees's Instruction, *The Love of Christ towards Migrants* (Vatican City: Pontifical Council of the Pastoral Care of Migrants and Refugees, 2004), 80.

19. For a first attempt to identify and list the rights of displaced people, see "Jubilee Charter of Rights of Displaced People," which has been introduced in this way: "The Charter was produced by a working group that helped prepare the Jubilee for Refugees, whose members were representatives of MIGRANTES (Italian Episcopal Conference), the Jesuit Refugee Service, the Italian Council for Refugees (CIR), the United Nations High Commission for Refugees, and the Refugee Section of the Pontifical Council. As such it is not an official document of the Pontifical Council but represents a consensus of various organizations on the most important rights of refugees, which are already recognized in various instruments of international law but that need to be emphasized in our actual historical moment." Pontifical Council for the Pastoral Care of Migrants and Itinerant People, *People on the Move*, n83 (September 2000).

20. Pope John Paul II, "To the Participants in the 4th World Congress on the Pastoral Care of Migrants and Refugees" (October 9, 1998).

21. Meeting with the Members of the General Assembly of the United Nations Organization, *Address of His Holiness Benedict XVI* (New York, April 18, 2008).

22. Pope John XXIII, *Pacem in terris*, no. 106. Pope John Paul II returns often to the theme of human rights in relation to human mobility, as for example, when he writes,

> In her pastoral activity, the Church tries to take these serious problems constantly into consideration. The proclamation of the Gospel is directed towards the integral salvation of the human person, his authentic and effective liberation, through the achievement of conditions of life suitable to his dignity. The comprehension of the human being, that the Church acquired in Christ, urges her to proclaim the fundamental human rights and to speak out when they are trampled upon. Thus, she does not grow tired of affirming and defending the dignity of the human person, highlighting the inalienable rights that originate from it. Specifically, these are the right to have one's own country, to live freely in one's own country, to live together with one's family, to have access to the goods necessary for a dignified life, to preserve and develop one's ethnic, cultural, and linguistic heritage, to publicly profess one's religion, to be recognized and treated in all circumstances according to one's dignity as a human being. These rights are concretely employed in the concept of universal common good, which includes the whole family of peoples, beyond every nationalistic egoism. The right to emigrate must be considered in this context. The Church recognizes this right in every human person, in its dual aspect of the possibility to leave one's country and the possibility to enter another country to look for better conditions of life (*Message for the Day of Migrants and Refugees*, 2001, n3).

23. Pope John Paul II, Apostolic Exhortation *Familiaris Consortio*, On the Role of the Family in the Modern World (1981), n45.

24. Catechism of the Catholic Church, n2241. Family reunion is dealt with also in *De Pastorali Migratorum Cura* and in the Charter of Rights of the Family.

25. John Paul II, Message for the Day of Migrants and Refugees, 2001, n3.

26. Ibid. For the Americas in particular, the Post-synodal Apostolic Exhortation of John Paul II, *Ecclesia in America* (1999), recalls, "Church communities will not fail to see in this phenomenon a specific call to live an evangelical fraternity and at the same time a summons to strengthen their own religious spirit with a view to a more penetrating evangelization. With this in mind, the Synod Fathers recalled that 'the Church in America must be a vigilant advocate, defending against any unjust restriction the natural right of individual persons to move freely within their own nation and from one nation to another. Attention must be called to the rights of migrants and their families and to respect for their human dignity, even in cases of non-legal immigration'" (n65).

27. *Catechism of the Catholic Church*, n2241.

28. Pope John Paul II, Message for World Migration Day 1996, On Undocumented Migrants, no. 2.

29. Paul VI speaks of effective organizations to manage cooperation among states in the encyclical *Populorum progressio* when proposing an effective world authority: "Such international collaboration among the nations of the world certainly calls for institutions that will promote, coordinate, and direct it, until a new juridical order is firmly established and fully ratified. We give willing and wholehearted support to those public organizations that have already joined in promoting the development of nations, and We ardently hope that they will enjoy ever growing authority" (n78). Cf. Graziano Battistella, "Immigrazione tra libertà e controllo: Una tensione perenne," in Graziano Battistella, in his *Migrazioni: Questioni etiche*, Quaderni SIMI, 6 (Rome: Urbaniana University Press, 2008), 9–49.

30. John XXIII, *Pacem in terris*, n25, states that "the fact that he is a citizen of a particular State does not deprive him of membership in the human family, nor of citizenship in that universal society, the common, world-wide fellowship of men."

31. For an extended discussion, see Mervyn Frost, "Thinking Ethically about Refugees: A Case for the Transformation of Global Governance," in *Refugees and Forced Displacement: International Security, Human Vulnerability, and the State*, ed. Edward Newman and Joanne van Selm (Tokyo: United Nations University Press, 2003), 109–29.

32. See David Hollenbach, "Internally Displaced People, Sovereignty, and the Responsibility to Protect," in his *Refugee Rights: Ethics, Advocacy, and Africa* (Washington, DC: Georgetown University Press, 2008), 177–93.

33. Elizabeth G. Ferris, *Beyond Borders: Refugees, Migrants, and Human Rights in the Post–Cold War Era* (Geneva: WCCC Publications, 1993), 304.

34. Benedict XVI, "Meetings with the Members of the General Assembly of the United Nations Organizations," New York, April 18, 2008.

35. Pope Benedict XVI, Address to the General Assembly of the United Nations (New York, April 18, 2008).

36. "Of itself it does not belong to the Church, insofar as she is a religious and hierarchical community, to offer concrete solutions in the social, economic, and political spheres for justice in the world. Her mission involves defending and promoting the dignity and fundamental rights of the human person." World Synod of Catholic Bishops, *Justice in the World* (1971), n. 37.

4

No Easy Road to Freedom

Engendering and Enculturating Forced Migration

M. Brinton Lykes

Introduction

Institutionalized racism and ethnic strife often combine with extreme poverty and political forces as underlying causes of armed conflict forcing many to flee from home and country, as in Rwanda, the former Yugoslavia, and many other parts of the globe.[1] The official report of the United Nations (UN)-sponsored Commission for Historical Clarification in Guatemala identified a history of racism against the indigenous population and "acute socioeconomic inequalities" as direct causes of the country's thirty-six years of civil war.[2] Although cultural practices and traditional beliefs have served as resources for indigenous survival over centuries, including recent conflict and postconflict situations, many traditional beliefs and cultural practices have been deeply fractured by war or intentionally targeted by the military to limit resistance.[3]

Gender and sexual violence against women, including young girls, is also a frighteningly common dimension of armed conflict. For example, members of military and paramilitary forces frequently rape women as part of war's booty or, as human rights observers in the former Yugoslavia suggest, as part of a strategy of ethnic cleansing.[4] Although there is increasing consciousness that boys and men are also victims of sexual violence, women and girls are the more likely sufferers. These violations are extreme manifestations of the discrimination and gender violence prevalent under conditions of peace. Moreover, ethnicity, culture, language, and "race" combine with gender in complex ways, especially in war. These realities shape the particularities of women's victimization, forcing many to migrate. At the same time, gender roles can be resources for survival and resistance, both "on the move" and in contexts of refuge.

In this chapter I seek to build on the excellent work done during at least the past ten years that has filled a gap not only in our knowledge about women and girls as forced migrants, but also in national and international policies that seek to provide particular protections to women and girls on the move and in temporary shelters of refuge.[5] Recognizing the ongoing and complex dynamics of policies and practices that reflect gendered and cultured understandings, as well as ongoing debates in UN circles, this chapter seeks to trouble the waters, or complicate existing understandings and practices in forced migration.[6] Thus, I hope to contribute to the important work that refugees themselves, and the human rights activists and humanitarian aid workers who accompany them, are doing on the ground as they respond to everyday challenges facing peoples on the move. Finally, I explore possible exchanges among knowledge producers in local communities or sites of refuge and international policymakers that can provide resources for women on the move on their long road to freedom.

Despite the growing recognition that women make up nearly half of all migrants and more than half of some groups on the move, those who work with refugee women in the field, as well as those who develop gender migration policy, have stated repeatedly that a considerable gap—some might say a chasm—remains between policies and practices in this arena. As importantly, theory and its applications at the interface of gender, culture or ethnicity, and race are complex, with feminists sometimes articulating contradictory positions. At other times feminists see gender and culture as two "goods" while lacking adequate criteria to resolve difficult areas of conflict between the two. In what follows I seek to map a terrain developed by some feminists working in war zones, in economic development initiatives, and in cultural studies. I situate forced migration at the intersection of research and practice through a lens of activist scholarship. I argue that greater attention to the lived experiences and voices of refugee women and children can better inform protection and assistance in the field. It can also lead to better collective national and international responsibilities to and for refugees. Specifically, I argue that some activist scholars who accompany survivors of war and women, children, and men fleeing conflict and other disasters have generated "third voices" that offer ideas for rethinking forced migration policy and practice.[7] Thus, I draw on participatory research and action to situate the contributions of feminist activist scholarship to the theory and practice of forced migration.

Proceeding from the important debate about the complex relationships between migration and development, I draw on three distinct conceptualizations of women and gender to situate possible directions for a more fully gendered and enculturated migration praxis. Specifically, discussions of "women in development" (WID), an early stage of which focused on women working with women, conceptualized women as add-ons and largely accepted existing social structures—both those of the focal societies in which they are located and of the development programs themselves.[8] The discourse of "women and development" (WAD) emerged in the late 1970s as a corrective to the WID approach and shifted the focus to processes, including "the role of classical development [processes] in maintaining elite national and international structures of power."[9] These approaches failed, however, critically to analyze local gender relations or to problematize women's roles in everyday life and work. Thus, this work, as well as the recognition that shifting power required attention to both men and women, shifted the model to "gender and development" (GAD). More recent feminist theories and practice have emphasized further the wider social context of gender socialization and extended GAD to include attention to the environment and development. I will draw on these models to examine women on the move and argue that they contribute to better responding to the challenges of gender and migration.

Causes of Migration and Facts about Refugees

Over the past half century, the number of international migrants has more than doubled to a total of between 175 million and 190.6 million worldwide, that is, between 3 and 4 percent of the global population.[10] These numbers include those who migrate for seasonal or permanent work, for family or relational reasons, or because of sudden changes in the environment, as well as those who are stateless, those who have been trafficked or smuggled, and refugees or asylum seekers who were forced to leave due to coercion. However, if one includes the more than 4.6 million Palestinians protected by the United Nations Relief and Works Agency (UNRWA) mandate and the more than 26 million people internally displaced due to armed conflict, 13.7 million of whom are also under the care of the United Nations High Commissioner for Refugees (UNHCR) for protection or assistance, the total number of the world's displaced is closer to 235 million people, that is, nearly 4 percent of the global population.

Although there is a broad array of terms to describe those who are on the move, there are many whose migratory movements do not easily fall within traditional categories, challenging those who seek to develop new discourses and accommodate the newly identified populations. One important example is internally displaced persons (IDPs) whose reasons for displacement are similar to those of refugees but who have not crossed national borders and whose protection and care are not mandated by the UNHCR. To respond to a growing awareness of the threats facing these populations, the UNHCR developed a series of recommendations that offer some protections as well as resources to these large populations. Their rights, however, and the responsibility of states and the international community toward them, have less force than the 1951 UN Convention Relating to the Status of Refugees.

As of December 2007 it was estimated that more than 8.5 million refugees were living long-term in camps or restricted settlement situations.[11] The anatomy of refugee camps varies from place to place; in some parts of the world, camps are fenced in and gated, whereas others camps may "look no different than villages."[12] Food is usually rationed to refugees in camps, and health services are provided, but refugees do not have the same legal rights as local populations and are usually denied opportunities to work, in addition to being limited in where and how they may live.[13] Food rations may be insufficient, water scarce, and refugees may be vulnerable to attack.

There are gaps in the data on the gender and age characteristics of migrants and refugees, making it difficult to generate well-informed responses to the protection and assistance guaranteed to these peoples. According to most UN-based organs that report on the issue, data on the sex of refugees are available for only 63 percent of the populations falling under UNHCR responsibility and on age for only 42

percent of these populations. This is not surprising, given the nature of migration and the challenges it presents to enumerating refugees and migrants. What is
known is that "women represent[ed] nearly half of most populations falling under
UNHCR's responsibility" at the end of 2007.[14] According to the 2008 Global Migration Group's study on international migration and human rights, 52.2 percent of all
international migrants in the developed world were women or girls, up from 46.6
percent in 1960.

Children under eighteen represent 44 percent of the nearly 32 million people
of concern to UNHCR; 10 percent of these are under the age of five.[15] Although a
gender breakdown of these children is not available, their numbers have an important impact on the experiences and responsibilities of women on the move. As
importantly, a growing body of research suggests that girls and boys have distinctive
experiences in the conflicts and natural disasters that gave rise to their flight as well
as in subsequent experiences of migration. Among these experiences are widely
reported descriptions of gender-based and sexual violence against women and girls.
Although this is not unique to people on the move, many protections available to
women and girls living in stable environments, such as access to lawyers, police,
social service workers, and health advocates, are frequently absent in migratory processes or, when present, are often ineffective. Persistent experiences of marginalization, discrimination, and violent assault against women have been documented in
camps for refugees and displaced persons. Moreover, protections sometimes provided by traditional family structures or cultural practices are often weakened or
fractured in migration. Thus, sexual and gender-based violence interacts in complex ways with forced migration, putting women and girls at additional risk.

Many who work with migrants and on migration policy concur that there continue to be gaps in the rendering of basic protection and assistance to displaced
women and children.[16] Indeed, persecution of women is not even codified in the
Refugee Convention and women who sought protection as women have met with
resistance at national and international levels.[17] Following advocacy and lobbying in
multiple nongovernmental organizations (NGOs) and national and international
forums, some shifts in policy came in 1991, when the UNHCR issued *Guidelines on
the Protection of Refugee Women* and some individual states (e.g., Canada, Australia,
the United States, and the United Kingdom) followed with their own guidelines.[18] In
1995 the UNHCR issued additional guidelines designed to offer further protections
of refugee women in *Sexual Violence against Refugees: Guidelines on Prevention and
Response*, reacting at least in part to the UNHCR's own assessments and evaluations. These guidelines were revised in 2003 and reflect a deepening understanding
of the causes and consequences of sexual violence as well as a growing recognition
that although women are the primary targets, boys and men are also victimized.[19]

Refugee women and girls are at risk for rape, sexual abuse, exploitation, and
trafficking during and after flight.[20] The Women's Commission for Refugee Women
and Children has reported that "domestic violence is often rampant in camp settings and is the most under-reported and ignored form of gender-based violence
in refugee and IDP settings."[21] Aid workers, teachers, UN personnel, and police also

abuse refugee women and girls, despite their responsibility to protect them.[22] As the Women's Commission has reported, women and girls living in refugee camps face threats to their physical security because they "often have little choice but to risk assault by leaving the perimeters and relative 'safety' of camps" due to the need for firewood, water, and supplemental food items.[23] In addition, "the structural design of camps themselves can lead to gender-based violence when latrines and water taps are situated far from dwellings. Women and girls have been assaulted and raped when visiting latrines and fetching water. Shower areas are sometimes not secure. Communal bathrooms may not be well lit and male and female facilities may not be adequately separated."[24] Protection from abuses within refugee camps may be limited by an absence of reporting and response mechanisms, lack of punishments for abusers, and fear of breaching confidentiality.[25] In addition, women and girls who are abused by teachers or other authority figures may be particularly fearful of reporting the abuse.[26] Certain groups of women, such as elderly women, unaccompanied children, and physically or mentally disabled women and girls, also may be particularly marginalized and vulnerable.[27]

Responses to these concerns have included analysis of the design of camps to identify the multiple sites where women were exposed to increased threat. Policies have been developed requiring that the physical layout of the camps, including the placements of latrines, showers, and water sources, be designed to reduce the incidence of sexual violence against women within the camps. Health services in camps were increasingly designed to respond directly to women's and children's nutritional and health care needs, including family planning and educational and health resources related to HIV/AIDS. Sanitary resources to meet women's hygiene needs have been added to emergency medical kits distributed by first responders and in refugee camps. Psychosocial resources to address the particular needs of women who had survived sexual assault have been developed in some sites, and policies to train workers about the particular needs of women were incorporated into training.

However, the lack of consistent protections for displaced women and children may be due, in part, to a lack of resources and, as importantly, to the gap between existing policies and how they are operationalized in the field. Some have suggested that it has equally to do with how work with and for women and children has been conceptualized and incorporated into existing conventions. Put simply, the initial response to the growing recognition that the needs of many, if not most, women and children in flight were not being met was to conceptualize them as a vulnerable group in need of special protections and programs responding to their particular needs as women and children. Thus programming for—and often by—women to support reproductive health and gender-based violence counseling as well as other post-conflict initiatives reflect this women-specific programmatic response to refugee women, one that parallels the WID or, at most, the WAD focus discussed above. Providing special programming for women around a limited number of women's concerns was, at best, a partial response that did not challenge structural and systemic issues and, at least in some cases, further stigmatized women within the refugee population. In response, the UNHCR's Executive Committee has called for the "integration of considerations regarding the special needs and resources of refugee women into all aspects of UNHCR's protection and assistance activities."[28] This mainstreaming of women, reflecting a GAD perspective, sought to ensure recognition that becoming a refugee affects men and women differently and that effective responses must recognize these differences throughout policies and programs. This policy also emphasized the importance of refugee women's participation in the planning and implementation of projects, reframing them not only as a vulnerable population to be protected, but also as resources for their own and their community's development.

Despite this, Susan Martin and Maryanne Loughry, among others, report that progress in the implementation of these guidelines has been uneven, incomplete, and halting.[29] Martin attributes much of this failure to "overall financial cuts in refugee budgets, combined with inadequacies in staffing that lead to inadequate field presence of protection personnel."[30] Thus, at its most basic, continuing marginalization, discrimination, and violence against women in the camps is an indicator of the failure of UNHCR to protect and assist women. Yet reading these explanations of the UNHCR's and NGOs' failures as symptoms, rather than as the basic causes of the marginalization and oppression of women, shifts our attention from women as a special "protected population" to interrogating the fundamental conceptualization of gender underlying UN policies and practices. Moreover, it suggests the importance of questioning the two models that have characterized the UN's responses to date, that is, special programming for and the mainstreaming of women.

As suggested above, resources for developing an alternative model can be drawn from the field of feminist studies; development work in, for, and by women; and activist scholarship. The example of Guatemala will frame the discussion of this alternative, both because Guatemala is a context in which I have lived and worked over several decades and because it exemplifies the issues that are the focus here. Over nearly three generations, the conflict in Guatemala was highly racialized and gendered. At the height of the counterinsurgency, over 10 percent of the population was on the move both inside the country's borders and beyond. In the later part of the discussion I will suggest how such an alternative model might infuse current gender-based refugee policy and practices with new energies and a renewed hope for more effectively accompanying women and children on the move.

The Example of Guatemala

War destroys the fabric of social life, affecting families, communities, and institutions; threatening cultural life; and displacing large numbers of people within and beyond national borders. The material and symbolic effects of war mark individuals and communities in differing ways, distorting perception, suspending many in unresolved grief, and terrorizing and traumatizing others. Children and their parents are forced to "choose" fight or flight, joining military or guerrilla organizations or fleeing their homes, even their countries.[31] In addition, in Guatemala institutionalized racism and extreme economic inequalities ruptured the spiritual fabric of everyday life among people who had inhabited a land for centuries.[32]

Guatemalan indigenous groups have historically been discriminated against and marginalized from power, resources, and decision making within Guatemala; the gross human rights violations during thirty-six years of civil war reflect only the most recent manifestations of over five hundred years of marginalization, repression, and discrimination.[33] The economic and military elite—primarily those of Spanish descent—with international support from the United States, among others, maintained control from 1954 to 1986 through ideological campaigns, scorched earth policies, and counterinsurgent attacks that they justified in the name of preserving national identity and internal state security.[34] A repressive military regime targeted armed guerrillas as well as civilian communities where rural Mayan villagers sought to recover their historic lands to ensure their families' survival and a more equitable distribution of resources.

Analyses of military documents and testimonies gathered by peasants confirm the racism implicit in the military's beliefs about the Maya.[35] Guatemalan military officers, in interviews conducted by Michael Richards in 1983 and 1984, described the Maya in subhuman categories, as "lacking reasoning capacity" and as "lost."[36] They labeled indigenous peasants as subversives, legitimating their mass murder. This process was described by Ricardo Falla as a "partial extermination" of the rural indigenous peoples, and it was later described as genocide by the Commission for Historical Clarification (CEH).[37] The protection of the civil and political rights of an elite citizenry was invoked to legitimate the killing of others defined as threats to the security of the nation or as noncitizens or nonhuman.

In Guatemala both the archdiocesan-sponsored report on violations of human rights and the official UN-sponsored report of the CEH have documented thousands of gross violations of rights, including the murder of more than one hundred thousand people, the displacement of more than one million people at the peak of this violence, the disappearance of more than sixty thousand people, and the destruction of more than six hundred rural villages.[38] Sexual violence against women and girls was widespread, with abuses including sexual slavery; forced pregnancy, abortion, and sterilization; rape; sexual torture; mutilation; and sexual humiliation.[39] The silencing and self-silencing of many victims reflected not only their profound degradation and shame but also the destruction of cultural values, families, and wider community relations.[40] Although the violence affected rural and urban populations throughout the country, the weight of its impact was experienced by indigenous groups living within rural communities of the Guatemalan Highlands.[41] Because these acts of atrocity were embedded in the economic, linguistic, cultural, ideological, and political systems of the state, I argue that such violations of human rights constitute structural violence that underlies and informs the direct and targeted acts of violence described herein.[42]

Marcelo Suárez-Orozco described the Guatemalan situation as a "culture of terror, with its own vocabulary of sorrow (desaparecidos [disappeared], torturados [torture victims], huérfanos [orphans]) and underlying structure [that] managed consensus through violence and intimidation."[43] National leaders used everyday practices, for example, arrest, and the very rhetoric of rights to subvert their declared objectives of protecting the citizenry.[44] Analyses of systems of social control and interviews with Guatemalan military officers led Jennifer Schirmer to conclude that, under the military, Guatemalan legal structures were "appropriated and redefined as instruments for *repressively humanitarian purposes.*"[45]

Ellen Messer has argued that Guatemala "illustrate[s] most vividly the synergisms of political violence, socioeconomic marginalization, and cultural discrimination."[46] Ricardo Falla has similarly described the worst massacres of entire villages in the Ixcán of Guatemala as "collective torture" due in part to the "racial and ethnic contradiction between the *ladino* army and the indigenous communities."[47] The collective dimensions of this violence suggest that the massacres of the Maya had an impact beyond the sum total of the individuals whose rights were violated. The Maya as a people were violated in their character as a collectivity. Such brutal destruction of human life and the environment for a people whose very identity is so rooted in the land that they are known as the "people of corn," as well as the extensive sexual violence of the war, graphically illustrate extreme violations of indigenous and women's rights.[48] Despite this brutality, women were more likely than men to survive the war and to face the burdens of the psychosocial and material consequences of violence and forced displacement.

Many rural Guatemalans fled to Mexico during the conflict, and after their arrival in the refugee camps established there, Guatemalan women began to meet and to organize, seeking to address needs for health care, food, and other services.[49] International aid agencies supported the development of productive projects that were launched by women's groups, including beekeeping and chicken raising.[50] From these collectives grew Mama Maquín, a women's organization founded in 1990 that facilitated women's participation in health care and education training, women's rights workshops, and other projects. The organization focused on education, promoting literacy by training female promoters from the refugee population to teach women in the camps, and according to the UNHCR, "to link literacy education to awareness-raising on women's roles, conditions, and rights."[51]

Women's empowerment was both a goal and an outcome of these and other endeavors of the women's organizations that developed in the refugee camps in Mexico, among internally displaced women within the Guatemalan Highlands and in Guatemala City, and in Communities of Populations of Resistance.[52] Some women were able to learn Spanish, to learn to read and write, and to learn about women's health care and other concerns.[53] In the Mexican camps, many of the workshops facilitated by and for the women explicitly discussed women's rights. This rights consciousness was linked to women's participation in progressive religious organizations and guerilla movements. It was encouraged by staff of the UNCHR and supported by the women's own awareness of "asymmetrical gendered relations that existed long before [exile]."[54] Women who participated in these projects reported that they retained a sense of their rights as women after the return process had been completed.[55] As one former refugee later recounted, "what I liked about [the refugee experience] was that we learned many things, many women learned to read and to speak Spanish, we had workshops on health, women's rights, we learned to make radio programs and we communicated with the camps. . . . Above all we learned to live organized as women."[56]

Although reflective of the WAD (women and development) perspective described above—one that does not fully challenge traditional gender arrangements that are sustained by social structures—these women's activities incorporated important politicization opportunities for the women involved, which were facilitated by the wider organizations within the refugee camps. For example, the women sought involvement in negotiations over the return process, including, in particular, around women's rights to land titles. However, upon return to Guatemala, women faced resistance to their participation in political processes, economic difficulty, a highly militarized environment, and a "hardening of patriarchal values and norms" that impeded the progress begun in Mexico. All of this contributed to the splintering of women's organizations.[57] Although women's organizing and participation in decision-making structures and political processes did not continue in Guatemala at the same level as in Mexico, some long-term gains from their experiences in Mexico have been identified. Mama Maquín has continued its involvement in political activities, challenging the Central American Free Trade Agreement, educating rural communities about the dangers of globalization and Plan Panama, and "enlisting women and men collectively to analyze the local and national impacts of these new developments."[58] Many of the young women who were able to learn Spanish and to read and write, and who received other forms of education while in the camps, made finishing their education an important goal, postponing marriage and thereby "creating new opportunities . . . and a significantly different life experience than that of their mothers."[59]

Moreover, some women carried their newly developed knowledge of women's rights back into the home. As one researcher observed, in returnee communities in Los Angeles and Huehuetenango, "several couples [with whom she spoke] pointed with pride to such practices as equity between partners in household budgeting and in reproductive decisions. They also noted the reduced incidence of domestic violence against women and their greater spatial mobility. . . . The majority of the interviewees in both communities employed a human rights discourse when they described more equitable gender relations in their own homes."[60] Thus, the seeds sowed in Mexico facilitated structural changes within the home that mobilized both men and women, despite entrenched gender hierarchies within the public spheres. The stories and thick descriptions from below told by the women displaced within Guatemala and beyond its borders, as well as the women who have accompanied them, have created a "conversational space" for dialogue between local, national, and international defenders of human rights.[61] These and other examples offer an alternative perspective on the causes of forced migration that can deepen our understanding of the cultural and gendered dimensions of violence and flight, and can inform policies that might create more effective responses to, with, and for refugees and internally displaced persons.

Participatory Engagement as a Resource for Recrafting Refugee Policies

Reinstating economic, cultural, and social systems ruptured by armed conflict and from which individuals draw meaning and identity and relocating those beyond the state's borders in situations similar to their preconflict homes and communities is a fundamental part of reconstruction and healing.[62] Although people are affected in many ways, three areas in particular have been identified by those working with these communities: human capacity (i.e., skills, knowledge, and capabilities), social ecology (social connectedness and networks), and culture and values.[63] As described above in the case of Guatemala, collaborative and interdisciplinary teams responding to these factors in contexts of war, extreme poverty, and forced migration frequently speak about both empowerment of local populations and the development of human capital.

Much of the current work with forced migrants, refugees, and the internally displaced continues to see them, particularly women and children, as victims or vulnerable populations in need of protection and assistance. Yet "despite the challenges [that] women [and children] face as refugees from war, they should not be viewed as simply helpless, victimized, and unable to better their situation given the opportunity."[64] Rather, where women and children have been engaged in participatory processes and given the space to advise agencies on how to improve the conditions in refugee camps, for example, the deep wisdom of their own experiences has contributed to changing conditions in such a way as to decrease their vulnerability.[65] This contributes to ameliorating the wounds of violence and violations, as a sense of efficacy plays an important role in recovering from and responding to traumatic experiences such as those experienced by migrant women as described above.[66]

The discourse and policies surrounding forced migration increasingly note the shifts from relief, through reconstruction, toward development. According to the International Rescue Committee's Post-Conflict Development Initiative, "effort must focus on rebuilding the social welfare and economic development capacity of conflict impacted communities."[67] Such projects and programs can build skills, raise self-esteem, encourage teamwork and shared decision making, and generate local economic activity and sustainability. Such efforts may also play a key role in assuring that human rights to health, education, and well-being are not mere aspirations but material outcomes.

Participatory and action research strategies have supported community development and social change efforts over many years. Development practitioners and community-based participatory and action researchers or activist scholars, among others, have become more explicitly concerned with the role of empowerment in community development projects, including citizen engagement initiatives, participatory rural appraisal, economic development projects, health assessment, and education programs both in the United States and abroad.[68] Researchers and applied psychologists understand empowerment as encompassing four areas: perception of self-efficacy and competence; acquired knowledge, skills, and access to resources; the development of a critical consciousness; and participation in concerted action.[69]

Community development workers often describe participants' engagement in a given intervention, through participation with outside collaborators, as empowerment. Participation can facilitate greater levels of self-confidence and self-sufficiency, resources participants carry into other aspects of their lives as agents of change.[70]

Community-based participatory and action research developed in Latin America has been and continues to be strongly influenced by Paulo Freire's liberatory pedagogy and his theories of critical consciousness and empowerment. Similar approaches which assume that knowledge generates power and that people's knowledge is central to social change emerged in Asia and in Africa.[71] These efforts emphasize full and active participation of people historically marginalized from power, decision making, and knowledge construction. They stress the ideological, political, and economic dimensions of social relations in and through which all knowledge is generated.

Women have become an increasingly important focus in economic development initiatives and participatory field research. Although the feminist-infused participatory work being done in the area of development is not widely read by those in refugee contexts or by policymakers in the Northern Hemisphere, it contributes importantly to a critical analysis of activism and participatory research processes as they inform feminist analysis and vice versa. For example, Irene Guijt and Meera Kaul Shah, in *The Myth of Community: Gender Issues in Participatory Development* (1998), challenge those engaged in participatory processes who are committed to redressing power inequalities to deconstruct the local community functions of maleness and femaleness and to extend their focus on consciousness-raising to include transformation of structural or institutional systems of oppression.[72] Similarly, as Cynthia Cockburn's participatory-action informed research with a Greek and Cypriot women's organization represents, participatory processes framed from a feminist perspective can create opportunities for women to collaborate in exploring multiple lines—ethnic, sexual, national, economic—within the categories "woman" and "feminist" and what these mean "to those who have power to operationalize them, what they imply of those who are named, shaped, differentiated, and excluded by them."[73] This is particularly complex in contexts where some traditional cultural beliefs and practices relegate women to secondary positions.

Dorren Indra and other anthropologists who have engaged in participatory ethnographic collaborative research have worked alongside migrants and women on the move throughout the globe, challenging through their words and through the "third voices" reported in their studies the deeply embedded and, in the words of Barbara Harrell-Bond, "the persistent assumption on which humanitarian relief programs all over the world are based: that they, the helpers, are *rescuing helpless victims*. Their approach is based on a highly ideologized overestimation of their capacity to respond in the first place, and on the belief that without them, no one would survive."[74] Thus, through working alongside refugees and other migrants and on the ground, activist scholars seek empirical evidence to counter these long-standing and persistent ideological assumptions that are infrequently recognized by those who hold them and yet frequently seep into the interstices of our actions even if they are not manifest in our overt policies and programs.

Some of these participatory and action research and accompaniment strategies have been extended to humanitarian aid and to interventions with survivors of war and state-sponsored violence to inform collaborative approaches to rethreading social life in the context of structural economic poverty or in the wake of violence. Some engaged in such work have been particularly attentive to building it within cultural contexts of local communities and more fully incorporating women and girls.[75] As discussed above, Guatemalan Mayan refugees and forced migrants have been participants in some such research and actions. I and my colleagues have argued that work at the interface of feminism and community and cultural psychology enhances activist scholarship's contributions to centering women and culture in contexts deeply affected by war, extreme poverty, and forced migration.[76]

The use of participatory processes in addressing the challenges faced by refugees and by women on the ground, however, has its limits. While laying out the benefits of participatory processes with refugees, Lance Clark, for example, cautions that "refugee participation is no panacea that will solve all of the problems of refugee assistance programs."[77] He has identified a number of significant barriers to effective participation at work in all levels of the organizational structures of refugee assistance programs. At the highest levels, aid agencies that are reluctant to share power with refugees can marginalize those they are meant to protect due to a sense that their accountability lies with the host country and with donors, and not the refugees themselves. Similarly, Clark notes that host countries may insist that local workers be given priority over refugees in obtaining jobs or leadership roles in refugee camps and settings. Moreover, ethnic hostilities among refugee groups in a camp, or between refugees and members of the host community, can limit the collaboration necessary for effective participatory projects. Finally, Clark sees a "limited view of refugee participation" as particularly harmful to the effective implementation of participatory endeavors with refugees. He says that rather than focusing only on organizing around political issues or mobilizing labor, "one can discuss refugee participation in many ways—within phases of assistance (e.g., in emergency relief operations), in geographic terms (e.g., within programs in Pakistan), in sector areas (e.g., in providing drinking water), and many others."[78]

In working with refugee women, Andrea Cornwall cautions community-based development researchers who assume women's solidarity and identifications with other women, arguing that in local communities, women may rather see their interests as aligned with their sons or kin. Cornwall cautions that the essentialist axis of sex difference, which characterizes much of the research and activism with and among women, obscures complex and deeply contextualized constructions of power and powerlessness within local communities. In addition, many participatory projects may offer women the "tactics to grapple with" these realities but not real "strategies for change because they [these women] lack the power and agency to do so."[79] Institutional or structural barriers to women's participation in decision making and social constraints, including a lack of education, of public speaking experience, or of their critical mass in public spaces, conspire to make significant changes in power difficult to achieve. Dawn Currie challenges development theoreticians and practitioners to "develop a methodology that links social change to the experiences and needs of women as defined by women, and for social justice for women."[80] Kate Young differentiated women's practical needs as women from their strategic interests in political and social struggles for equality, and Shulamith Firestone distinguished women's reproductive and productive labor and focused on women's empowerment as involving both individual change and collective action.[81]

Moreover, drawing questions of culture into considerations of gender brings to light another layer of complexities. Valentine Moghadam and Manilee Bagheritari, who work in organizational contexts where United Nations policies are articulated and operationalized, argue—as women's rights activists and feminists—that "in order to end discrimination against women, there must be agreement that 'culture' is not a valid justification for gender inequality."[82] Thus, whereas the Convention on the Elimination of All Forms of Discrimination against Women aims to "protect women's rights in the context of cultural/traditional patterns," the Universal Declaration of Cultural Rights problematically seeks to "preserve cultural practices" without any mention of women's rights or gender.[83] Yet as anthropologist Sally Engle Merry has documented, gender and cultural practices are deeply intertwined, and violations of women's rights are actualized through local meanings of gender.[84] As she observes, "in practice, what constitutes gender violence depends on how these actions [of violence] are made meaningful. Cultural interpretation makes everyday events meaningful."[85]

Many examples exist of the use of culture and religion to justify harmful, discriminatory practices against women—practices where women's bodies are abused in the name of culture and religion—such as foot binding, forced veiling, female genital mutilation, and sex selection, among others. Feminists are not of one mind in their responses to most of these practices, with some defending the cultural rights of communities and others strongly rejecting what they argue are practices that discriminate against women. This tension between convictions about the relationships of culture and gender highlights the complexities in which these realities are engaged in local communities and international arenas. Thus, simply opening a space for local-global dialogue will not resolve complex and contentious debate where gender and culture converge. Rather, drawing heavily on the work of activist scholars to inform those conversations could open new paths toward more comprehensive policies and practices that take these conflicts seriously and recognize that particular solutions within universal aspirations may be the best—or even the only—way forward. Although a full discussion of the relationships among culture, gender, and women's rights is beyond the scope of this chapter, ongoing debates on these issues can be found in local communities, NGOs, and in international forums hosted by UN agencies, where feminists and others espouse contrasting priorities and ideological differences.

Challenges, Cautions, and Possibilities

Activist scholarship in and with local communities can engage women across significant ethnic, political, religious, racial, class, age, and sexual diversities to forge ahead in complex contexts fraught with ongoing violence and oppression that continue to characterize the lives of many forced migrants. The participatory and action research processes described in this chapter engage women at the level of their individual lives, within local communities, and through national-level public processes. I argue that such activist scholarship offers specific resources for engaging with refugees in ways that generate research and action to shift future policymaking. The fruits of this collaborative work can serve as important bridges among refugees, field workers, and policymakers in dialogue to craft a richer set of policies and practices that respond more fully with refugees and the demands of their daily lives on the move.

As noted, this work is not without challenges and risks. There is little consensus on how gendered and cultural rights should be balanced either in policy or in practice. There are also multiple challenges in seeking to converse within and across the ideological differences underlying these rights-based protections and the concrete in the field problems that emerge in work that seeks to accompany rather than to direct or supposedly help forced migrants. I enumerate a few of the risks and challenges that have emerged in my own work and in writings by human rights activist scholars.

First, although the activist scholarship informed or infused by feminist principles described in this paper offers a resource to women surviving war, wider social conditions of gendered inequalities and ongoing poverty and oppression deeply constrain what can be achieved through any single project. The conditions that breed violations of women's rights through gender oppression are some of the same that cause displacement: "racism and inequality, conquest, occupation, colonialism, warfare and civil conflict, economic disruptions and poverty."[86] Moreover, although the most recent Global Migration Group's report on *International Migration and Human Rights* delineates the critical importance of including men and masculinities within a gendered migration framework, subsequent discussions of these issues should draw more fully on the growing body of empirical research on violence and masculinities within the Northern Hemisphere, as well as some more recent work in Central America and in Africa.[87] Engendering and enculturating migration demand a critical interrogation of masculinities and power as well as careful documentation of the reproduction and ruptures of gendered power in war, migration, and peacemaking.

In addition, although participatory and activist scholarship with refugees and migrants may seek to work within a community, community has been fractured, and sometimes permanently ruptured, by armed conflict and migration. The term "community" is all too frequently—including sometimes in my own work—used to signify a geographically grounded social group with structural and associated relations and practices that seems to transcend material conditions. However, community is socially constructed, deeply ideological. Thus, as South African psychologists Alex Butchart and Mohammed Seedat have argued, its overvaluation risks ignoring or not equally valuing the "transformation of the society that perpetuates the communities' separate [and unequal] existence."[88] This overvaluation risks converting means or processes to ends in themselves and frequently ignores the historical, political, and ideological contexts in which communities are formed, thereby essentializing them in lieu of recognizing and working with them as the social constructions that they are. In a similar critique, Catherine Nolin describes Guatemalan migration patterns to Canada in which individuals, primarily urban students and labor activists, have relied primarily on their individual strengths, and their stories focus more on ruptures and separations than on the rethreading of torn communities.[89] Such critical considerations and analyses, which also include a critical analysis of Canadian immigration policies and practices, are particularly relevant as we seek to build new understanding and potential correctives to refugee policy and practice from the bottom up.

Third, the activist scholarship and participatory practices advocated here imply conflict, because, as Kate Young has observed, "empowerment is not just about women acquiring something, but about those holding power relinquishing it."[90] The examples presented here suggest processes by which women in diverse contexts facing inequality, marginalization, and social oppression struggle for survival, for the right to name who they are, and to promote change. Specifically, this work entails, in the words of Dorothy Smith, an analysis of a "'complex of organizational practices, including government, law, business and financial management, professional organization, and educational institutions, as well as discourses in texts that interpenetrate the multiple sites of power.'"[91] Yet because empowerment is both a process and an outcome, "talk of 'empowering women' [also] turns 'power' into a transferable commodity rather than a structural relation."[92] Thus some feminists and other critical scholars interrogate and renegotiate empowerment as a term or goal. For example, participants in a recent conference hosted by the University of Sussex's Pathways of Women's Empowerment project at the Institute of Development Studies (IDS) observed that the "shifting and fuzzy meanings of empowerment make it a difficult word to use" and that "some kinds of empowerment are missing from today's mainstream versions: cultural empowerment, collective empowerment, liberating empowerment, pleasurable empowerment, empowerment in the corporate sector, [and] empowerment in trade unions."[93] Yet it is only rarely that critical discussions of empowerment are included in our work with refugees and even less frequently that the contradictions described by IDS are identified and engaged through the assistance, research, and development processes.

Finally, ethical challenges inhere in the sort of activist scholarship I advocate, and they appear at various levels of the research process, beginning in negotiating with institutional ethical review boards and extending to questions of joint authorship, intellectual property rights, as well as varying—and often conflicting—interests of local, national, and international collaborators.[94] As anthropologists Ruth Krulfeld and Jeffrey MacDonald have documented, partnerships among university-based scholars, NGOs, refugees, and international policymakers may aid in the development of a gendered and enculturated forced migration policy and practice, but are also often time-consuming and frustrating, with the partnerships themselves becoming sites for the performance of power that belie our shared commitments as human rights advocates and activists to transform oppressive power relations! Moreover, these ethical considerations should not displace careful consideration of the multiple ethical challenges confronting refugees, human rights workers, and activist scholars in these collaborative processes.[95]

Despite these many challenges, experiences such as those of the Guatemalan women in refugee camps in Mexico in the 1980s and 1990s described above demonstrate how collaborations among field workers, advocates, and activist scholars who accompany refugee women can create conversational spaces for dialogue between local and international defenders of human rights. These experiences offer an alternative perspective on the causes of forced migration, one that deepens our understanding of the cultural and gender dimensions of violence and flight and could inform policies that might create more effective responses with refugees and internally displaced persons. This is the dialogic space through which local actors and international advocates can come together to create the next steps along a long road to freedom.

I conclude by extending Daphne Patai's warning: that it is challenging—if not impossible—to do truly ethical research in an unethical world.[96] The problems encountered in humanitarian aid, activist scholarship and policymaking "are political and require not only transformations in consciousness, but also, and above all, political action for their solution. Our individual research [and humanitarian aid and policymaking activities] thus returns us to the world which can be counted on to puncture any illusions that a 'correct' feminism will resolve these matters."[97] The recommended strategies in this chapter encourage those of us who respond to and work with refugees to develop relationships with them, attend to their voices and their agency, and to work with them to build on and further develop their social capacities. A focus on strengths and resilience, however, should not be read as license to ignore or deny the deep ruptures caused by migration, the traumatic experiences of violence and death, the loss and accompanying sadness, and the ongoing threats that they face. Our work must be developed within the creative spaces generated through collaborative actions that support forced migrants and refugees as we and they both attend to their social suffering and work toward transforming the systems and structures that will create more options for a better future.

Notes

I thank Erzulie Coquillon for her extensive comments on an earlier version of this chapter and for her assistance in preparing this draft for publication. In addition, I thank the conference participants for their comments on an earlier version of this chapter. Finally, and most especially, I thank the women, men, and children "on the move" for allowing me the privilege of having accompanied you in some of your war and postwar journeys. *Adelante!*

"No Easy Walk to Freedom," the title given by Nelson Mandela to his presidential address September 21, 1953, to the ANC Transvaal Conference, described how he and other ANC leaders had "been banned because we champion the freedom of the oppressed people of our country and because we have consistently fought against the policy of racial discrimination in favour of a policy which accords fundamental human rights to all, irrespective of race, colour, sex or language." He had been elected as ANC Transvaal President earlier in the year but had been served with a banning order and therefore the address was read on his behalf. The address is online at www.anc.org.za/ancdocs/history/mandela/1950s/sp530921.html (accessed

May 7, 2009). His autobiography, published in 1994, was similarly titled *Long Walk to Freedom*. I think these words capture the challenges facing forced (im)migrants/refugees and human rights activists as we face the twenty-first century. As importantly, the words capture the challenge as well as the journey we are making together.

1. Philip Gourevitch, *We Wish to Inform You That Tomorrow We Will Be Killed with Our Families: Stories from Rwanda* (New York: Picador, 1998); and Giles Wenona et al., *Feminists under Fire: Exchanges across War Zones* (Toronto: Between the Lines Books, 2003).

2. Commission for Historical Clarification (CEH), *Guatemala: Memory of Silence* (Guatemala City: Guatemalan Commission for Historical Clarification, 1999), http://shr.aaas.org/guatemala/ceh/report/english/recs1.html (accessed April 26, 2009).

3. See, e.g., Gillian T. Eagle, "Promoting Peace by Integrating Western and Indigenous Healing in Treating Trauma," *Peace and Conflict: Journal of Peace Psychology* 4 (1990): 4 (in South Africa); Noel Muchenga Chicuecue, "Reconciliation: The Role of Truth Commissions and Alternative Ways of Healing," *Development in Practice* 7 (1997): 4 (in Mozambique); Michael G. Wessells and C. Monteiro, "Healing Wounds of War in Angola," in *Addressing Childhood Adversity*, ed. D. Donald, A. Dawes, and J. Louw (Cape Town, South Africa: David Philip, 2000), 176–201 (in Angola). See Robert M. Carmack, ed., *Harvest of Violence: The Maya Indians and the Guatemalan Crisis* (Norman: University of Oklahoma Press, 1988); and Ricardo Falla, *Massacres in the Jungle: Ixcán, Guatemala, 1975–1982*, trans. Julia Howland (Boulder, CO: Westview Press, 1994).

4. Shana Swiss and Joan E. Giller, "Rape as a Crime of War: A Medical Perspective," *Journal of the American Medical Association*, 270 (1993): 612–15; Tadeusz Mazowiecki, *United Nations Commission on Human Rights: Situation of Human Rights in the Territory of the former Yugoslavia* (New York: United Nations, 1993); and Ecumenical Women's Team Visit, *Rape of Women in War* (Geneva: Ecumenical Women's Team Visit, 1992).

5. See, e.g., Doreen Indra, *Engendering Forced Migration: Theory and Practice* (New York: Berghan Books, 1999); Susan Forbes Martin, *Refugee Women* (New York: Lexington Books, 2004); Susan Forbes Martin, *2004 World Survey on the Role of Women in Development: Women and International Migration* (New York: United Nations Department of Economic and Social Affairs and Division for the Advancement of Women, 2005); Catherine Nolin, *Transnational Ruptures: Gender and Forced Migration* (Burlington, VT: Ashgate Publishing Company, 2006); Evangelia Tastsoglou and Alexandra Z. Dobrowolsky, *Women, Migration, and Citizenship: Making Local, National, and Transnational Connections* (Burlington, VT: Ashgate Publishing, 2006).

6. See, e.g., Universal Declaration on Cultural Diversity, http://unesdoc.unesco.org/images/0012/001271/127160m.pdf (accessed May 3, 2009); Convention for the Safeguarding of the Intangible Cultural Heritage, http://unesdoc.unesco.org/images/0013/001325/132540e.pdf (accessed May 3, 2009); and the Declaration on the Rights of Indigenous Peoples, www.un.org/esa/socdev/unpfii/documents/DRIPS_en.pdf (accessed May 3, 2009).

7. M. Brinton Lykes, Martin Terre Blanche, and Brandon Hamber, "Narrating Survival and Change in Guatemala and South Africa: The Politics of Representation and a Liberatory Community Psychology," *American Journal of Community Psychology* 31 (2003): 79–90.

8. Indra, *Engendering Forced Migration*.

9. Ibid., 12

10. Susie Jolly, *Gender and Migration, in Brief* (Brighton, UK: BRIDGE/ Institute of Developmental Studies, 2005); Susie Jolly, *Gender and Migration, Supporting Resources Collection* (Brighton, UK: BRIDGE/ Institute of Developmental Studies, 2005), 1; and Global Migration Group. *International Migration and Human Rights Challenges and Opportunities on the Threshold of the 60th Anniversary of the Universal Declaration of Human Rights* (New York:

United Nations, 2008), www.globalmigrationgroup.org/pdf/Int_Migration_Human_Rights .pdf (accessed April 26, 2009).

11. U.S. Committee for Refugees and Immigrants, *World Refugee Survey: Warehoused Refugee Populations* (Arlington, VA: U.S. Committee for Refugees and Immigrants, 2008), www .refugees.org/uploadedFiles/Investigate/Publications_&_Archives/WRS_Archives/2008/ warehoused%20refugee%20populations.pdf (accessed April 26, 2009).

12. Canadian Broadcasting Corporation (CBC), "Anatomy of a Refugee Camp," *Canadian Broadcasting Corporation,* June 19, 2007, www.cbc.ca/news/background/refugeecamp (accessed May 3, 2009).

13. Ibid.; U.S. Committee for Refugees and Immigrants, *World Refugee Survey.*

14. UNHCR, *2007 Global Trends: Refugees, Asylum-seekers, Returnees Internally Displaced and Stateless Persons* (New York: United Nations, 2008), 12.

15. UNHCR, *Through the Eyes of a Child: Refugee Children Speak on Violence: A Report on Participatory Assessments Carried Out with Refugee and Returnee Children in Southern Africa 2005–2007* (New York: United Nations, 2008), 12.

16. See, e.g., Martin, *Refugee Women*; Maryanne Loughry, "The Representation of Refugee Women in Our Research and Practice," in *Not Born a Refugee Woman: Contesting Identities, Rethinking Practices*, ed. Maroussia Hajdukowski-Ahmed, Nazilla Khanlou, and Helen Moussa (New York: Berghahn Books, 2008), 165–72; Indra, *Engendering Forced Migration*; and Global Migration Group, *International Migration and Human Rights Challenges.*

17. Although some aspects of gender-based violence, such as female genital mutilation (see *Matter of Kasinga*), have been found to be grounds for asylum in the United States, other forms, such as domestic violence, are not protected (see *Matter of R-A*). Both *Matter of Kasinga* and *Matter of R-A* are decisions by the Board of Immigration Appeals. *In Re Kansigna* (BIA 1996) granted asylum based upon claim of membership in a "particular social group" of women of particular tribes who have been subjected to female genital mutilation and who oppose the practice. *Matter of R-A* (BIA 2001) was once vacated by Attorney General Reno then remanded by Attorney General Mukasey to the Board of Immigration Appeals, not on remand to immigration court, the original decision rejected, for asylum purposes, claim to a "particular social group" of married domestic violence victims. Further information about the decision and its current legal status is available at http://cgrs.uchastings.edu/campaigns/ alvarado.php. U.S. lawyers and other advocates, however, are campaigning to expand the grounds of asylum related to gender-based violence. See Amnesty International, *Stop Violence against Women: Gender-Based Asylum*, www.amnestyusa.org/women/asylum, accessed November 8, 2008, (providing a brief overview of gender-based asylum claims in the United States); and Human Rights First, *Grant Rodi Alvarado Asylum & Protect Women Refugees*, http://action.humanrightsfirst.org/human_rights_first/alert-description.html?alert _id=393947, accessed November 8, 2008 (advocating for asylum of women fleeing domestic violence, where their governments are unwilling or unable to protect them, as in *Matter of R-A*).

18. UNHCR, *Guidelines on the Protection of Refugee Women* (Geneva: United Nations, online at: 1991), www.UNHCR.org/publ/PUBL/3d4f915e4.pdf (accessed May 3, 2009).

19. UNHCR, *Sexual and Gender-Based Violence against Refugees, Returnees, and Internally Displaced Persons: Guidelines for Prevention and Response* (New York: United Nations, 2003), www.UNHCRorg/protect/PROTECTION/3f696bcc4.pdf (accessed May 23, 2009).

20. Chaloka Beyani, "The Needs of Refugee Women: A Human Rights Perspective," *Gender & Development* 3 (1995): 29–35; Women's Commission for Refugee Women and Children, *Displaced Women and Girls at Risk: Risk Factors, Protection Solutions, and Resource Tools* (New York: Women's Refugee Commission, 2006); UNHCR, *Through the Eyes of a Child.*

21. Women's Commission for Refugee Women and Children, *Displaced Women and Girls at Risk*, 10.

22. Ibid.

23. Ibid.

24. Ibid., 11.

25. Ibid.

26. UNHCR, *Through the Eyes of a Child.*

27. Women's Commission for Refugee Women and Girls, *Displaced Women and Girls at Risk*, 11.

28. Martin, *Refugee Women*, 151.

29. Ibid.; Loughry, "Representation of Refugee Women in Our Research and Practice."

30. Martin, *Refugee Women*, 153.

31. Ignacio Martín-Baró, *Writings for a Liberation Psychology: Ignacio Martín-Baró*, ed. Adrienne Aron and Shawn Corne (Cambridge, MA: Harvard University Press, 1994).

32. For reviews of this literature see Graça Machel, "UN Study on the Effects of War on Children," *Peace and Conflict: Journal of Peace Psychology* 4 (1998); M. Brinton Lykes, "Terror, Silencing, and Children: International, Multidisciplinary Collaboration with Guatemalan Maya Communities," *Social Science and Medicine* 38 (1994): 543–52; and M. Brinton Lykes, "Meaning Making in a Context of Genocide and Silencing," in *Myths about the Powerless: Contesting Social Inequalities*, ed. M. Brinton Lykes, Ali Banuazizi, Ramsay Liem, and Michael Morris, 159–78 (Philadelphia: Temple University Press, 1996).

33. See, e.g., Amnesty International, *Human Rights Violations against Indigenous Peoples of the Americas* (London and New York: Amnesty International Publishers, 1992); Carmack, *Harvest of Violence.*

34. Jennifer Schirmer, cited in Ellen Messer, "Anthropology and Human Rights in Latin America," *Journal of Latin American Anthropology* 1(1995): 48–97.

35. Michael Richards, "Cosmopolitan World View and Counterinsurgency in Guatemala," *Anthropological Quarterly* 58, no. 3 (1985): 101; Falla, *Massacres in the Jungle.*

36. Richards, "Cosmopolitan World View," 101.

37. Ricardo Falla, "We Charge Genocide," in *Guatemala: Tyranny on Trial—Testimony of the Permanent People's Tribunal*, ed. Susanne Jonas, Ed McCaughan, and Elizabeth Sutherland Martinez (San Francisco, CA: Publicaciones Sinthesis, 1984), 112–19; and CEH, *Guatemala: Memory of Silence.*

38. See ODHAG/Oficina de Derechos Humanos del Arzobispado de Guatemala, *Nunca Más: Informe proyecto interdiocesano de recuperación de la memoria histórica* (Guatemala City: ODHAG, 1998); and CEH, *Guatemala: Memory of Silence.*

39. See, for example, Amnesty International, *Guatemala: No Protection, No Justice: Killings of Women in Guatemala* (London: Amnesty International, 2005); Equipo de Estudios Comunitarias y Acción Psicosocial (ECAP) and Union Nacional de Mujeres Guatemaltecas (UNAMG), *Rompiendo el silencio: Justicia para mujeres víctimas de violencia sexual durante el conflicto armado en Guatemala* (Guatemala City: F & G Editores, 2006); M. Brinton Lykes and Maria Luisa Cabrera Pérez Armiñan, *Compartir la memoria colectiva: Acompañamiento pscicosocial y justicia integral para mujeres víctimas de violencia sexual en conflictos armados* (Guatemala City: PCS-Consejeria en Proyectos, 2007); Colleen Duggan, Claudia Paz y Paz Bailey, and Julie Guillerot, "Reparations for Sexual and Reproductive Violence: Prospects for Achieving Gender Justice in Guatemala and Peru," *International Journal of Transitional Justice* 2 (2008): 192–213; and Judith N. Zur, *Violent Memories: Mayan War Widows in Guatemala* (Boulder, CO: Westview Press, 1998).

40. See ODHAG, *Nunca Más* ; CEH, *Guatemala: Memory of Silence.*

41. America's Watch Committee. *Guatemala: A Nation of Prisoners* (New York: America's Watch Committee, 1984); Amnesty International, *Guatemala: The Human Rights Record* (London and New York: Amnesty International Publishers, 1987).

42. Two examples of this structural violence are (1) the organization of more than nine hundred thousand rural men into civilian defense patrols beginning in the final days of 1981, and (2) strategies such as a "guns and beans" program wherein survivors of scorched earth extermination programs were organized into strategic villages where they were fed beans and forced to participate in reeducation programs. See America's Watch Committee, *Guatemala: A Nation of Prisoners*; Falla, *Massacres in the Jungle*; Alice Jay, *Persecution by Proxy: The Civil Patrols in Guatemala* (New York: Robert F. Kennedy Memorial Center for Human Rights, 1993).

43. Marcelo M. Suárez-Orozco, "Speaking of the Unspeakable: Toward a Psychosocial Understanding of Responses to Terror," *Ethos* 18 (1990): 353–83, at 361.

44. Frank Graziano, *Divine Violence: Spectacle, Psychosexuality, and Radical Christianity in the Argentine "Dirty War"* (Boulder, CO: Westview Press, 1992); Marguerite Feitlowitz, *A Lexicon of Terror: Argentina and the Legacies of Torture* (New York and Oxford: Oxford University Press, 1998).

45. Quoted in Messer, *Anthropology and Human Rights*, 77 (emphasis in original). See Jennifer Schirmer, *The Guatemalan Military Project: A Violence Called Democracy* (Philadelphia: University of Pennsylvania Press, 1998).

46. Messer, *Anthropology and Human Rights in Latin America*, 56.

47. Falla, *Massacres in the Jungle,* 184. The term *ladino/a* is used in Guatemala to refer to the population of mixed Spanish-Indian parentage, and often, inaccurately, to all non-Maya. See Women of Photovoice/ADMI and M. Brinton Lykes, *Voices e imágenes: Mujeres Maya Ixiles de Chajul/Voices and Images: Mayan Ixil Women of Chajul* (Guatemala City: MagnaTerra, 2000), 109.

48. Lykes, *Meaning Making in a Context of Genocide and Silencing*, 159–78. See Abigail J. Stewart, Isis H. Settles, and Nicholas J. G. Winter, "Women and the Social Movements of the 1960s: Activists, Engaged Observers, and Nonparticipants," *Political Psychology* 19 (1998): 63–94.

49. Out of the estimated one hundred thousand to two hundred thousand Guatemalans who fled to Mexico, only forty-six thousand were officially registered as refugees and given aid by the Mexican government and the UNHCR. See Carolina Cabarrús Molina, Dorotea Gómez Grijalva, and Ligia González Martínez, *Guatemalan Women Refugees: Challenges and Lessons Learned from the Refugee Camps and during Reintegration* (Washington, DC: International Center for Research on Women, n.d.).; Beatriz Manz, *Refugees of a Hidden War: The Aftermath of Counterinsurgency in Guatemala* (New York: SUNY Press, 1988); and Padre Beto Ghiglia, "Women's Organizations in Guatemalan Refugee and Returnee Populations," in *Patronage or Partnership: Local Capacity Building in Humanitarian Crises*, ed. Ian Smillie (Sterling, VA: Kumarian Press, 2001).

50. Cabarrús, Gómez, and González, *Guatemalan Women Refugees*; Patricia R. Pessar, *Women, Gender, and International Migration across and beyond the Americas: Inequalities and Limited Empowerment*, Expert Group Meeting on International Migration and Development in Latin America and the Caribbean, Population Division, Department of Economic and Social Affairs, United Nations Secretariat (Mexico City, November 28, 2005) UN/POP/EGM-MIG/2005/08.

51. Ghiglia, *Women's Organizations in Guatemalan Refugee and Returnee Populations*.

52. Amnesty International, *Guatemala: The Human Rights Record*; Beatriz Manz, "Epilogue: Exodus, Resistance, and Readjustments in the Aftermath of Massacres," in *Massacres*

in the Jungle: Ixcán, Guatemala, 1975–1982, ed. Ricardo Falla, trans. Julia Howland (Boulder, CO: Westview Press, 1994), 191–211.

53. Cabarrús, Gómez, and González, *Guatemalan Women Refugees.*

54. Pessar, *Women, Gender, and International Migration,* 9.

55. Cabarrús, Gómez, and González, *Guatemalan Women Refugees.*

56. Maria Mateo, "Una mujer Q'Anojb'al de Mama Maquin," with Manuela Camus, in *Comunidades en movimiento: La migracion internacional en el norte de Huehuetenango,* ed. Manuela Camus (Antigua, Guatemala: Junajpu, 2007): 119–50.

57. Pessar, *Women, Gender, and International Migration,* 13; Sean Loughna, *The Role of Women's Organizations during and after Conflict in Guatemala* (Arlington, VA: USAID, 1999).

58. Pessar, *Women, Gender, and International Migration,* 16.

59. Cabarrús, Gómez, and González, *Guatemalan Women Refugees,* 17.

60. Pessar, *Women, Gender, and International Migration,* 15.

61. See, e.g., AVANCSO, *Se cambió el Tiempo: Historias de vida y tradición oral de San Bartolomé Jocotenango, Quiché* (Guatemala: AVANCSO, 2002); Falla, *Massacres in the Jungle*; Maria Christina Bottinelli, Ignacio Maldonado, Estella Troya, Pablo Herrera, and Carlos Rodríguez, *Psychological Impact of Exile: Salvadoran and Guatemalan Families in Mexico* (Washington, DC: Hemispheric Migration Project, Centre for Immigration Policy and Refugee Assistance at Georgetown University, 1990); Manz, *Refugees of a Hidden War*; Beatriz Manz, *Paradise in Ashes: A Guatemalan Journey of Courage, Terror, and Hope* (Berkeley: University of California Press, 2004); James Loucky and Marilyn Moors, eds., *The Maya Diaspora: Guatemalan Roots, New American Lives* (Philadelphia: Temple University Press, 2000); Allan Burns, *Maya in Exile: Guatemalans in Florida* (Philadelphia: Temple University Press, 1993); Patricia Foxen, *In Search of Providence: Transnational Mayan Identities* (Nashville, TN: Vanderbilt University Press, 2007); Nolin, *Transnational Ruptures*; Clark Taylor, *Return of Guatemala's Refugees: Reweaving the Torn* (Philadelphia: Temple University Press, 1998); Women of Photovoice/ADMI and Lykes, *Voces e imágenes/Voices and Images.*

62. Martín-Baró, *Writings for a Liberation Psychology.*

63. Richard F. Mollica, B. Lopes Cardozo, H. J. Osofsky et al., "Mental Health in Complex Emergencies," *The Lancet* 364 (2004): 2058. See Psychosocial Working Group, *Psychosocial Intervention in Complex Emergencies: A Conceptual Framework* (Edinburgh: Psychosocial Working Group, 2005), www.forcedmigration.org/psychosocial/papers/Conceptual%20 Framework.pdf.

64. Sally Engle Merry, *Gender Violence: A Cultural Perspective* (Oxford: Wiley-Blackwell, 2009), 173.

65. See ibid., and UNHCR 2008, *Through the Eyes of a Child,* 23 (finding that "[refugee and returnee] children are very much aware of the problems they face, have devised their own protection strategies, and have creative ideas about overcoming some of the pervasive problems mentioned above. Training youth with the skills to become peer educators—for example in areas such as sexual and gender-based violence and HIV prevention—appears to be an effective way of reaching young people").

66. Judith Herman, *Trauma and Recovery* (New York: Basic Books, 1992).

67. International Rescue Committee, *The Post-Conflict Development Initiative* (International Rescue Committee, 2003), www.theirc.org/what/the_postconflict_development _initiative.html 9 (accessed May 3, 2009).

68. See, e.g., Robin McTaggart, ed., *Participatory Action Research: International Contexts and Consequences* (Albany: SUNY Press, 1997); Danielle Papineau, "Citizen Empowerment through Community Economic Development in a Multiethnic Neighborhood" (PhD diss.,

Université de Montreal, Canada, 1996); Korrie De Koning and Marion Martin, *Participatory Research in Health: Issues and Experiences* (Johannesburg: Zed Books, 1996).

69. For an overview, see Marc Zimmerman, "Empowerment Theory: Psychological, Organizational, and Community Levels of Analysis," in *Handbook of Community Psychology,* ed. Julien Rappaport and Edward Seidman, 43–64 (New York: Kluwer Academic/Plenum, 2000).

70. See Smarajit Jana, Ishika Basu, Mary Jane Rotheram-Borus, and Peter A. Newman, "The Sonagachi Project: A Sustainable Community Intervention Program," *AIDS Education & Prevention* 16 (2004): 405–14; Janet Ayres et al., *Take Charge: Economic Development in Small Communities: Empowerment for Rural Communities for the 1990s* (Ames, IA: North Central Regional Center for Rural Development, 1990).

71. Orlando Fals Borda and Muhammad A. Rahman, ed., *Action and Knowledge: Breaking the Monopoly with Participatory Action Research* (New York: Apex Press, 1991); and Anne Hope and Sally Timmel, *Training for Transformation: A Handbook for Community Workers,* vols. 1–4 (London: Intermediate Technology Publications, 1984–2000); Binaifer Nowrojee, *Shattered Lives: Sexual Violence during the Rwandan Genocide and Its Aftermath* (New York: Human Rights Watch, 1996).

72. See Andrea Cornwall, "Gender, Participation, and the Politics of Difference," in *The Myth of Community: Gender Issues in Participatory Development,* ed. Irene Guijt and Meera Khan Shah (London: Intermediate Technology Publications, 1998); Andrea Cornwall, *Making a Difference? Gender and Participatory Development,* University of Sussex Institute of Development Studies Discussion Paper 378 (Brighton, UK: Institute of Development Studies at University of Sussex, 2001); Andrea Cornwall, "Whose Voices? Whose Choices? Reflections on Gender and Participatory Development," *World Development* 31 (2003): 1325–42.

73. Cynthia Cockburn, *The Line* (London: Zed Books, 2004), 204–5.

74. Quoted in Indra, *Engendering Forced Migration,* 60. Emphasis in original.

75. See Wessells and Monteiro, *Healing Wounds of War in Angola,* among others.

76. M. Brinton Lykes, Erzulie Coquillon, and Kelly L. Rabenstein, "Theoretical and Methodological Challenges in Participatory Community-Based Research," in *Handbook of Diversity in Feminist Psychology,* ed. Hope Landrine and N. F. Russo (New York: Springer Publishing Company, 2009), chap. 2.

77. Lance Clark, *Promoting Refugee Participation in Assistance Projects,* Refugee Policy Group Working Paper (Washington, DC: Center for Policy Analysis and Research Issues, 1987), 4.

78. Ibid, 6.

79. Cornwall, *Whose Voices? Whose Choices?* 1331.

80. Dawn H. Currie, "Gender Analysis from the Standpoint of Women: The Radical Potential of Women's Studies in Development," *Asian Journal of Women's Studies* 5 (1999): 3.

81. Kate Young, *Planning with Women: Making a World of Difference* (London: Macmillan, 1993); and Shulamith Firestone, *The Dialectics of Sex: The Case for a Feminist Revolution* (New York: Bantam Books, 1970).

82. Valentine Moghadam and Manilee Bagheritari, "Cultures, Conventions, and the Human Rights of Women: Examining the Convention for Safeguarding Intangible Cultural Heritage and the Declaration of Cultural Diversity," *SHS Papers in Women's Studies/Gender Research* 1(2005): 2.

83. United Nations, *Convention on the Elimination of all Forms of Discrimination against Women,* 1979, www.un.org/womenwatch/daw/cedaw; Indra, *Engendering Forced Migration*; and Moghadam and Bagheritari, *Cultures, Conventions, and the Human Rights of Women,* 7.

84. See Merry, *Gender Violence,* 3. She defines gender violence as "violence whose meaning

depends on the gendered identities of the parties. [In other words] it is an interpretation of violence through gender."

85. Ibid., 22.

86. Ibid., 2.

87. Masculinities refers to an emergent body of social scientific research and practice that focuses on the gendered ways in which maleness is defined and performed through roles, stereotypes, and the distributions of power, resources, and decision making. See, e.g., Susan Bird, Rutilio Delgado, Larry Madrigal, John Bayron Ochoa, and Walberto Tejeda, "Constructing an Alternative Masculine Identity: The Experience of the Centro Bartolomé de las Casas and Oxfam America in El Salvador," *Gender & Development* 15 (2005): 111–21, www.informaworld.com/10.1080/13552070601179227, accessed November 8, 2008; and Simone Lindorfer, "In Whose Interests Do We Work? Critical Comments of a Practitioner at the Fringes of the Liberation Paradigm," in *Feminism & Psychology* 19, no. 3 (2009), 354–67.

88. Alex Butchart and Mohammed Seedat, "Within and Without: Images of Community and Implications for South African Psychology," *Social Science and Medicine* 31 (1990): 4.

89. Nolin, *Transnational Ruptures*. This is in comparison to descriptions of Guatemalan migratory patterns to the United States that rely heavily on community as a descriptive and analytic force, describing exile, return, and transnational communities and the agency of primarily rural Mayan peasants within these dynamics.

90. Young, *Planning with Women*, 159.

91. Quoted in Currie, *Gender Analysis from the Standpoint of Women*, 6.

92. Andrea Cornwall, *Pathways of Women's Empowerment* (openDemocracy, 2007), www.opendemocracy.net/node/34188/print (accessed May 3, 2009).

93. Rosalind Eyben, "News at IDS—Being Strategic about the Meanings of Women's Empowerment," February 27, 2008, www.ids.ac.uk/go/about-ids/news-and-commentary/february-2008-news/meanings-of-women-s-empowerment (accessed April 29, 2009). See also Pathways of Women's Empowerment, http://pathwaysofempowerment.org/ (accessed April 29, 2009).

94. See Ruth Krulfeld and Jeffrey MacDonald, *Power, Ethics, and Human Rights: Anthropological Studies on Refugee Research and Action* (New York: Rowman & Littlefield, 1998).

95. See ibid.

96. Daphne Patai, "U.S. Academics and Third World Women: Is Ethical Research Possible?" in *Women's Words: The Feminist Practice of Oral History*, ed. Sherna Berger Gluck and Daphne Patai, 137–54 (New York: Routledge, 1991).

97. Ibid., 150.

Part III

Protecting Rights at the Border

Denial of Asylum and Systemic Responses

5

Human Rights as a Challenge to National Policies That Exclude Refugees

Two Case Studies from Southeast Asia

Frank Brennan

Introduction

Recently I spoke at the Ubud Writers Festival in Indonesia. At the opening session, the organizers had to apologize for the unavoidable absence of some of the advertised speakers. I realized that there are two classes of invitees at such international events: those who can cross national borders freely and those who cannot. Many of those who cannot are not refugees. They just happen to come from countries whose nationals, when they travel, are subject to especially strict scrutiny by the host country. Some are refugees. There are often more than 10 million refugees around the globe. Even those nation-states that run large migration programs insist on their right to maintain secure borders, conduct orderly migration, and institute orderly procedures for the delivery of protection to asylum seekers and the selection of refugees for migration. Governments are keen to retain the prerogative to determine who comes into their countries, even though they are signatories to the 1951 United Nations (UN) Convention Relating to the Status of Refugees. No government admits within its jurisdiction all those who present at its border or its embassy to seek asylum. Governments argue that there is no right under the Convention for a refugee to enter their jurisdiction for the purpose of seeking asylum; there is only a right to seek asylum once one has entered the jurisdiction. Critics of government migration, refugee, and border protection policies are often able to invoke human rights arguments, agitating for more liberal policies or for particular exceptions to exclusion. While there is no doubt that national policies excluding refugees are a challenge to human rights, the extent to which human rights can be invoked as a challenge to national policies excluding refugees remains a contested issue. While such challenges may bear fruit eventually in democratic nation-states that pride themselves on the rule of law, they are unlikely to be even heard in those states yet to develop such a tradition.

In *Refugee Rights: Ethics, Advocacy, and Africa* (2008), David Hollenbach invokes what has been called the Kew Gardens Principle to expand the scope of national positive duties in sharing the burden of asylum for refugees.[1] The principle was enunciated in the academic world after an appalling murder in New York City.[2] A young woman was publicly stabbed to death while thirty-eight persons looked on, doing nothing. The principle posits that the agent has a positive ethical duty to respond to one in need, even when the agent has not caused the victim's plight, when four conditions are met:

- There is a critical need.
- The agent has proximity to the need.
- The agent has the capability to respond.
- The agent is likely the last resort from whom help can be expected.

In my dealings with governments I have found the Kew Gardens Principle not very compelling in response to government ministers who postulate that there is always a critical need when it comes to refugees seeking asylum. It is not as if the government minister is one of only thirty-eight citizens who just happen to be present when one person is in short-term critical need. The government as agent may have become the last resort from whom help can be expected only because the victim has deliberately gone to the trouble of placing herself or himself in proximity on that government's border. The agent may have the capability to respond. But it also has the capability to respond to other groups who are in equally desperate need. The Kew Gardens Principle starts to limp in these circumstances.

The human rights paradigm works when critiquing a government's treatment of an individual or discrete caseload. It does not work so well when critiquing a government's choice of one group of victims over another. If nongovernment organizations (NGOs) such as the Jesuit Refugee Service (JRS) are too stringent in their insistence on human rights and minimum standards, they may find themselves excluded by governments and even by the United Nations high commissioner for refugees (UNHCR) in the pragmatic relief of distress of some asylum seekers to the exclusion of others. But there comes a Rubicon at which such NGOs may need to say that compromise for the sake of ongoing cooperation is so unprincipled that it threatens any universal commitment to protection of the human rights of refugees. Invoking human rights for refugees is less useful when one is dealing with a government that fails to accord human rights to its own citizens and that operates in a situation of limited transparency and accountability for human rights violations against its own citizens. While NGOs, refugee advocates, and the academy invoke human rights, governments are more likely to insist on the complexity of politics and the need for compromise of rights when responding pragmatically to ongoing intractable crises. UNHCR will often be caught in the middle, having to espouse the ideals while working effectively only with the invitation and cooperation of governments.

In this chapter I illustrate the difficulties in relating human rights to refugee policies by presenting two case studies from Southeast Asia. Both governments involved, Australia and Cambodia, are signatories to the UN Convention, unlike most governments in Southeast Asia. Australia prides itself as a democracy committed to the rule of law; Cambodia is yet to take that path.

In the first case study I present an overview of the situation in Australia from 2001 to 2008. In 2001, just two weeks before the September 11 attack on the World

Trade Center, the Australian government instituted a comprehensive border protection policy that was an assault on the human rights of asylum seekers. It included a program for upstream disruption of asylum seekers traveling from Indonesia to Australia by boat; mandatory detention for those who made landfall (usually in detention facilities in the middle of the Australian desert); the Pacific Solution, which entailed removal of boat people to other countries in the Pacific Ocean (Nauru and Papua New Guinea) for processing, with no guarantee of settlement in Australia even for proven refugees; and the issuing of three-year temporary protection visas for successful asylum seekers in Australia that denied them the right of family reunion and free travel. In 2008 the Australian people elected a new government, which announced a comprehensive overhaul of the refugee system, including the abolition of the temporary protection visa and the Pacific Solution. The new government also claimed that detention would be a last resort. A year later, the Australian Human Rights Commission has published a review of immigration detention critical of the new government. In the Commission's words, "While it is true we have seen improvements in the way Australia treats immigration detainees, our report shows we are still seeing children being held in detention facilities, people being detained for prolonged and indefinite periods, and dilapidated detention centers being used for accommodation."[3]

In the second case study I describe UNHCR's failure to insist that the government of Cambodia provide basic human rights in its dealings with Montagnard asylum seekers from Vietnam and end restrictions on NGO access to such asylum seekers. In both cases, governments have insisted on border protection regardless of the impact on the human rights of asylum seekers. The incremental changes in Australia have resulted in large measure from concerted advocacy by NGOs and by parliamentarians being convinced that border protection could not be bought by overriding fundamental human rights. The lack of change in Cambodia highlights the incapacity of NGOs to influence the Cambodian political processes and the lack of interest in the human rights of foreigners by parliamentarians from a nation-state lacking a strong tradition of commitment to the rule of law.

Case Study One: The Australian Pacific Solution and Its Dismantling

All first-world countries are wrestling to achieve the correct balance between the right of sovereign border protection and the humanitarian obligations that confront any nation playing its part in the world. This case illustrates the difficulty of attaining that balance.

The 2001 Tampa *Incident*

In late August 2001 a large Norwegian container vessel MV *Tampa* was steaming from Perth to Singapore on the high seas when the captain, Arne Rinnan, received a call from the Rescue Coordination Centre of the Australian Maritime Safety Authority that a ship was in distress on the high seas.[4] Under the guidance of an

Australian Coastwatch plane, the captain sailed for about four hours to pick up 433 people from an overcrowded wooden boat, *Palapa 1*, which was within the Indonesian maritime rescue zone. Though far from the Australian mainland, the *Palapa* was only about 75 nautical miles from Christmas Island, an Australian territory in the Indian Ocean, closer to Indonesia than to the western Australian coastline. The captain intended to proceed to the Indonesian port of Merak about 250 nautical miles distant to discharge his human cargo. He then intended to complete his voyage to Singapore with a cargo of largely empty containers. His ship usually carried a crew of 27, so it was not designed or licensed to carry hundreds of people long distances; it was licensed to carry only 40 persons. Once all of the boat people were on board, 5 of the new passengers came up to the bridge to speak with the captain. According to Arne Rinnan, "They were in an aggravated mood and they said that if we did not head to Christmas Island then they would go crazy or start jumping overboard."[5] Rinnan decided that the most responsible decision he could make as a captain concerned for the safety of his ship, his crew, and his new passengers was to change course and head for Christmas Island, the nearest harbor, discharging the 433 at the closest landfall. Very soon the Australian authorities were on the radio denying him permission to enter Australian territorial waters.

By daybreak on Monday August 27, Rinnan thought that "some politics [had] got into the picture."[6] That afternoon Prime Minister John Howard told the Australian parliament, "We have indicated to the captain that permission to land in Australia will not be granted to this vessel. . . . Australia has sought on all occasions to balance against the undoubted right of this country to decide who comes here and in what circumstances, a right that any other sovereign nation has, our humanitarian obligations as a warm-hearted, decent international citizen."[7] At the diplomatic level, Australia then informed Norway that the conveying of a distress call by the Australian authorities "does not carry with it any obligation to allow the persons rescued into Australian territory."[8] Despite, or because of, the threats made to the captain by the passengers on the bridge, Australia expected the *Tampa* to take to the high seas with 460 persons aboard and forty life jackets, returning the rescued persons "either to their point of departure or to the original intended destination of the *Tampa*."[9]

On August 29, 2001, the *Tampa* entered into Australian territorial waters approaching Christmas Island. The prime minister told parliament that the captain had decided on this course of action because a spokesman for the asylum seekers "had indicated that they would begin jumping overboard if medical assistance was not provided quickly."[10] Captain Rinnan gave a different reason for his decision: "We weren't seaworthy to sail to Indonesia. There were life jackets for only forty people. The sanitary conditions were terrible."[11] Australian military personnel came aboard and took over the *Tampa*. An Australian Defence Force doctor was given forty-three minutes to make a medical assessment of the 433 asylum seekers. He reported, "Four persons required IV (2 urgent including 1 woman 8 months pregnant)." Captain Rinnan was surprised at the prompt medical assessment, because his crew had already identified ten people who were barely conscious lying in the sun on the deck of the ship. The prime minister then made a finely timed ministerial statement to parliament insisting that "nobody—and I repeat nobody—has presented as being in need of urgent medical assistance as would require their removal to the Australian mainland or to Christmas Island."[12] Some 131 fortunate asylum seekers were granted immediate asylum by the New Zealand government. The rest, having been transported to Nauru, a small mendicant island nation-state in the Pacific, awaited processing under the evolving Pacific Solution.

The Australian government set about implementing a detailed legislative response to ensure that asylum seekers boarding boats in Indonesia would be deterred from seeking landfall in Australia. The government was determined that none of the people on the *Tampa* would ever be permitted to settle in Australia. John Howard was keen to send "a message to people smugglers and others around the world that, whilst this is a humanitarian, decent country, we are not a soft touch and we are not a nation whose sovereign rights in relation to who comes here are going to be trampled on."[13] The government presumed that the message was rightly transmitted and heard, because the boats stopped coming. Others who heard the message were not convinced of the transmitter's humanitarian decency.

Having decided that most, if not all, of these prospective boat people departing Indonesia were secondary movers seeking a migration outcome, the government decided that it was time to get very tough. After all, these asylum seekers hailed from remote countries such as Afghanistan, Iraq, and Iran. It was not as if they were in direct flight from their country of persecution to the country of safe haven next door. Policymakers usually speak of "push factors" and "pull factors" in regard to refugees. Push factors are those reasons that push them out of their own country. Pull factors are those reasons that attract them to the country where they seek asylum. The government conceded that the push factors usually outweighed the pull factors when people fled their homelands with no assurance of future residence. For these boat people, the push factors included the harshness of the Saddam Hussein regime in Iraq and the oppressiveness of the Taliban in Afghanistan. It is push factors that dictate that people flee their homeland, but the pull factors may attract refugees to extend their journey to a more remote but more desirable location. As far as possible, the Australian government wanted to reduce the pull factors, and was even prepared to be punitive. It justified this approach by claiming that those arriving by boat were not seeking protection and that they could have obtained the minimal protection guaranteed by the UN Refugee Convention at other points on their journey. They were attracted to come further afield, the government said, because if they arrived in Australia, they knew they would be guaranteed resettlement there if they proved they were refugees. The government claimed that these persons were using claim to asylum to seek an optimal migration outcome—namely, permanent residence in a first-world democracy rather than protection in a poorer, more populous nation like Pakistan or Indonesia.

Australian Deterrence Theory

The government faced three problems. Or to put it another way, there were three distinct advantages that asylum seekers and people smugglers saw in making the perilous journey by boat to Australia.

- First, if asylum seekers made it to Australia, there was a good chance that the Australian authorities would find that they were refugees. Eighty-four percent of boat people were being found to be refugees, whereas only 14 percent of the contingent from the same countries of flight who presented at the UNHCR office in Indonesia were found to be refugees.
- Second, if asylum seekers were found to be refugees after they landed in Australia, they were guaranteed residence there. If they had waited in a camp in Pakistan or in a transit city such as Jakarta, awaiting a UNHCR determination, they not only had less chance of being found to be a refugee, they also had no guarantee of being resettled in a country where they would feel secure, let alone one in which they would enjoy the benefits of life in a first-world, democratic country.
- Third, if asylum seekers were granted permanent residence in Australia, they would over time be able to bring their family to join them and would be able to travel safely and legally by commercial aircraft.

From the government perspective, those coming by boat were jumping the queue in the government's annual quota of proven refugees who would be admitted from camps and transit centres throughout the world. The government was unwilling to reward those who took the initiative of coming by boat without a visa. The government strategy was

- to cooperate with the Indonesian authorities in the upstream disruption of boats;
- to positively deter boats attempting to enter Australian territorial waters;
- to keep people in remote detention centers away from lawyers and "do-gooders," reducing the access to the courts for those on shore;
- to confine the definition of refugee status;
- to process people offshore as far as possible so that they would not have any guarantee of resettlement in Australia even if they were proved to be refugees; and
- to deny refugees coming via the back door any access to family reunion.

The detention of large numbers of women and children sent shock waves around Australia as many citizens wondered how it had come to this pass. Government expressions of regret, backed by claims that there was no better way, were sufficient to appease, satisfy, and even delight many citizens. Others remained troubled that an island nation continent at the end of the earth had to resort to such measures when other first-world countries with far more pressing claims on their borders had never attempted such a strategy. The government remained convinced that if it kept its nerve and stared down those on the boats and the people smugglers, then all would be well and there could be a return to a more decent and more humane keeping of the border watch.

A Return to Decency

A new Australian government was elected in November 2007 with a commitment to improving Australia's human rights record on the treatment of boat people. The new government has now abandoned the Pacific Solution. It has abolished the temporary protection visa and is committed to restricting detention to the time needed to determine an undocumented person's identity, health, and security status. On May 13, 2008, the new government announced that "from early 2008–09, people found to be refugees will receive a permanent visa, regardless of their mode of arrival." On July 29, 2008, the new minister for immigration announced that "strong border security and humane and risk-based detention policies are not incompatible. They are both hallmarks of a mature, confident, and independent nation."[14] He went on to say that "in instituting a new processing regime for those who arrived in an excised place and claim protection, we seek to remedy those deficiencies. Henceforward, asylum seekers will receive publicly funded advice and assistance, access to independent review of unfavourable decisions and external scrutiny by the Immigration Ombudsman. These measures will build on strengthened procedural guidance for departmental decision-makers. In totality, these robust processes will deliver outcomes in which we can be confident and will reassure the world that we are meeting our international commitments."[15] The first test of the new government's border protection measures commenced with the arrival of twelve boat people in Australian waters on October 1, 2008. Minister Chris Evans said "the continuing threat of people smuggling [was] a direct result of significant long-term pressures driving the international movement of displaced people from the Middle East and Asia caused by conflict and natural disasters." He was optimistic that increased regional cooperation would stem any flow, saying that "the government has renewed efforts to work closely with regional countries including Indonesia, Malaysia, and Thailand to prevent and deter people from attempting dangerous sea journeys to Australia."[16] The opposition parties in Parliament were not so sanguine. Dr. Sharman Stone, the opposition representative responsible for the immigration portfolio, issued an alarmist statement asserting that "people smugglers are fully testing the water in response to the Rudd Government's recent weakening of border protection rules."[17]

The new Australian provisions strike a more appropriate balance between border protection and recognizing the basic human rights of unvisaed asylum seekers. If the boats started streaming towards the Australian coastline again, Australian politicians would be sure to start agitating again the politics of border protection. The Australian Human Rights Commission is still concerned about the length and uncertainty of detention for those undocumented and unvisaed asylum seekers arriving by boat. The discourse of human rights has definitely assisted in reversing the harshest aspects of Australia's recent policies aimed at excluding refugees at the border.

Case Study Two: The 2005 Tripartite Agreement concerning Montagnard Asylum Seekers in Cambodia

The government of the Socialist Republic of Vietnam, the Royal Government of Cambodia (RGC), and UNHCR signed a memorandum of understanding (MOU) agreeing "on the need to strengthen cooperation and coordination among them, to find a final solution for some 750 Central Highlands ethnic minority people currently in Cambodia's temporary sites."[18] On July 20, 2005, 94 Montagnards from the Central Highlands of Vietnam were forcibly removed from a UNHCR centre in Phnom Penh, Cambodia, and returned to Vietnam. These 94 had failed in their claims for refugee status. Then, Montagnards who were recognized by UNHCR as refugees were told to choose between resettlement in a third country or voluntary return to Vietnam within the month. Those failing to exercise a choice were threatened with forced repatriation to Vietnam. When the MOU was signed, UNHCR claimed that "the refusal of resettlement by some of the Montagnards can be seen in the context of political statements, detrimental to the asylum-space available to them in Cambodia. The MOU requires those refugees to take the protection on offer (resettlement). If they choose not to do so, they have in a way declared themselves that they do not wish to be of concern to UNHCR."[19]

The July 2005 showdown had the desired effect. There has been no need to repatriate forcibly any persons determined to be refugees. All those who were recognized as refugees, having arrived in Cambodia before January 25, 2005, decided to opt for either resettlement or voluntary repatriation.

The Cambodian government remains adamant that Montagnards will not be permitted to settle in Cambodia. Local integration is not an option on offer for any Montagnard proved to be a refugee. The Cambodian government also insists that UNHCR be kept on a short leash. The government denied UNHCR permission to open offices at or near the Vietnam border and gave it access to border crossers from Vietnam only if they present at the UNHCR office in Phnom Penh or if UNHCR receives government approval to visit the border provinces of Ratanakiri and Mondulkiri. Approval takes four to eight weeks once UNHCR lodges a request. In the meantime, Cambodian police and provincial authorities often return border crossers to Vietnam. The Vietnamese government has permitted some monitoring of returnees and their local conditions, but there is strong disagreement about these conditions between the Vietnam government and UNHCR on the one hand, and international human rights groups on the other.

Though the MOU was designed primarily to deal with a residual caseload within a six-month period, all parties have agreed to the continuation of its terms. UNHCR thinks the success of the MOU may warrant the adoption of its modalities in other refugee situations. The parties to the MOU were fortunate that there was a cohort of failed asylum seekers available for forced repatriation. The resolute conduct of the parties in relation to that cohort sent a strong message to the refugees that the parties were intent on a final solution within a strict time frame.

The History of Montagnard Influxes from Vietnam

Cambodia signed the 1951 UN Convention Relating to the Status of Refugees and the 1967 Protocol Relating to the Status of Refugees in 1992. To date Cambodia has not instituted its own refugee status determination process. UNHCR makes all determinations of refugee status in Cambodia. The Cambodian government has had a long-term policy of refusing the establishment of refugee camps on or near its borders. Though permitting UNHCR to provide its protection in Cambodia, the government no longer permits UNHCR to maintain a permanent presence outside the capital of Phnom Penh.

In 1992 the forces of the United Nations Transitional Authority in Cambodia discovered 398 Montagnard resistance fighters living in the forest in Mondolkiri province. These people were all granted permanent residence in the United States, where they established the beginnings of a large Montagnard community in North Carolina. That community has been a strong international advocate for the Montagnards in the Central Highlands of Vietnam, claiming sustained persecution and human rights abuse by the Vietnamese government.

In February 2001 Cambodia received its first large influx of Montagnards following the Vietnamese government's strong clampdown on Montagnard villagers protesting over land rights, religious persecution, and ethnic discrimination. More than nine hundred of those who crossed into Cambodia were recognized prima facie as refugees by UNHCR. Without the need for any individual refugee status determination by UNHCR, they were granted permanent residence in the United States, many of them joining the community in North Carolina. Throughout 2001, Human Rights Watch conducted extensive interviews of Montagnards and published in April 2002 its report *Repression of Montagnards.*

In July 2001 the governments of Vietnam and Cambodia attended their first tripartite meeting with UNHCR in the hope of expediting the voluntary repatriation of a further three hundred Montagnards who had crossed into Cambodia. The two governments were contemplating forced repatriation, and UNHCR was urging restraint. The Executive Committee of UNHCR had passed a resolution in 1985 declaring that "the practice of establishing tripartite commissions is well adapted to facilitate voluntary repatriation. The tripartite commission, which should consist of the countries of origin and of asylum and UNHCR, could concern itself with both the joint planning and the implementation of a repatriation programme. It is also an effective means of securing consultations between the main parties concerned on any problems that might subsequently arise."[20]

On January 21, 2002, the three parties reached agreement in Phnom Penh. It was assumed that the Montagnards would be agreeable to returning once they had received proper counseling "as an incentive for their safe and dignified return." UNHCR was to obtain and disseminate "factual, credible, and current information." The Vietnamese delegation assured "that all returnees would be well received and not subjected to punitive and/or discriminatory treatment upon return for reasons relating to their departure."[21] The Vietnamese delegation agreed to follow-up visits by UNHCR. UNHCR was to provide all transport, and UNHCR staff were to accompany the returnees to their final destinations.

But the agreement was short-lived. A month later, UNHCR signaled that the agreement was "being seriously eroded by the actions of the two governments." UNHCR announced that "an apparent agreement between the governments . . . that all the Montagnards should return by April 30, would totally undermine the idea of voluntariness."[22] UNHCR listed a number of incidents occasioning concern, including one in which "a policeman struck a number of Montagnards with an electric baton during a heated exchange with the visiting officials, prompting intervention by UNHCR staff in the camp."[23] Then, on March 23, 2002, UNHCR withdrew from the agreement when four hundred Vietnamese came across the border in buses. The convoy included Vietnamese officials who threatened and manhandled some of the one thousand Montagnards awaiting voluntary return. Ruud Lubbers, the high commissioner, wrote to both governments, "Mindful that UNHCR cannot be part of a process that no longer conforms with its mandate or principles governing voluntary repatriation, I regret to inform you that UNHCR is left with no choice but to dissociate itself from the repatriation agreement. I do not believe that the overall situation is conducive for repatriation in line with international standards and all returns should therefore be suspended."[24]

Lubbers thought that the Montagnards had been subjected to an "unprecedented and unacceptable" level of coercion to repatriate. Head of UNHCR's Asia Bureau, Jean-Marie Fakhouri, said, "The incident makes us doubt Vietnam's and Cambodia's will to resolve the Montagnard refugee issue according to the letter and spirit of the tripartite agreement."[25] And yet the agreement was posited on the presumption that one thousand Montagnards would want to return voluntarily once they were properly counseled and assured that UNHCR would be permitted to make follow-up visits.

On March 18, 2004, the Cambodian government presented UNHCR with an "Aide Memoire on Illegal Activities of the UNHCR in Cambodia," alleging that UNHCR was attracting Montagnards into Cambodia who were then undermining the sovereignty and security of the nation. The government further alleged that UNHCR was hiding its agents on the border so as to lure and attract Montagnards. The Ministry of Foreign Affairs and International Cooperation reminded UNHCR that under the Cooperation Agreement UNHCR could designate the location of its offices only "with the consent of the Government." The only authorization granted was for an office in Phnom Penh. The government insisted that UNHCR close its office in Ratanakiri. The government was considering its own refugee law, and once the law was enacted, "the Ministry would consider any request of the UNHCR on the possibility of opening its office in any area of the country." To date no law has been passed and no new office outside Phnom Penh permitted. On April 12, 2004, Cambodian Crown Prince Sihanouk begged the government and UNHCR to protect the Montagnards and not expel them from Cambodia.

On January 13, 2005, UNHCR was informed of the involuntary repatriation of four Montagnards to Vietnam. UNHCR then lodged a complaint with the Cambodian government the next day, urging the need to assess any persons before repatriating them. At this time there were about five hundred Montagnards in Cambodia. UNHCR and both governments thought it was time once again to try a tripartite agreement. It was signed in Hanoi on January 25, 2005.

The 2005 Tripartite Agreement

Both governments wanted the Montagnards returned to Vietnam, closing off the options of residence in the Cambodian forest or in Cambodian villages close to the border. The possible outcomes for the Montagnards were resettlement in a third country to be completed usually within six months, voluntary repatriation, or forced repatriation a month after the determination of their status. Such forced repatriation was to be orderly and safe "and in conformity with national and international laws." Any new arrivals would have the choice of resettlement or repatriation. No Montagnards would be permitted to remain in Cambodia more than one month after the determination of their refugee status unless they were awaiting resettlement. UNHCR had wanted a guarantee of unrestricted and unfettered access to the returnees, but the Vietnamese government would agree only to a clause providing that the government and UNHCR would consult and cooperate on visits to the returnees. To date UNHCR had no success in satisfactorily monitoring the returnees from 2001.

In its Montagnard Caseload Briefing Report of January 31, 2005, UNHCR reported that there were then 453 Montagnards in Phnom Penh who had been recognized as refugees, but that 217 (47 percent) of them were refusing offers of resettlement in a third country. UNHCR reported that "by refusing resettlement as a durable option, this group of refugees is subject to expulsion from the country of asylum for reasons of national security. Refusing the opportunity to seek legal admission to another country places the onus of responsibility on the refugees themselves. . . . Montagnard advocacy groups, including the Transnational Radical Party and Montagnard Foundation, should be strongly advised to inform this hard line group of the consequences of their political statement of remaining in Cambodia."[26]

Such statements would be expected from the Cambodian government, but they are surprising coming from UNHCR, whose staff was now more identified with the Cambodian government than with the refugees, given the staff's interest in having the tripartite agreement succeed. Human rights NGOs were dissatisfied after receiving a briefing on operationalization of the tripartite agreement on February 3, 2005.

Recognized refugees were initially given until March 25, 2005, to make a decision to be resettled in a third country. On March 21, 2005, Peter Leuprecht, the special representative of the UN secretary-general for human rights in Cambodia wrote to the acting high commissioner for refugees, urging that UNHCR suspend the operation of the MOU: "It appears that UNHCR has therefore not insisted on Cambodia abiding by its obligations under the Refugee Convention and international law, although this has not been publicly acknowledged, and no explanation or justification has been given. As I am sure you will understand, this creates great difficulties for me and others whose duty it is to ensure that Cambodia upholds international law and to give the reasons why if it fails to do so."[27]

On the next day the UNHCR staff, at a regular protection meeting with NGOs, expressed the view that "recognized refugees keep changing their mind so frequently and so many are willing to repatriate, doubts arise as to whether the refugee claims are credible."[28] The UNHCR staff said they "cannot actually support the repatriation of the recognized refugees but if RGC is insisting on the implementation of the MOU, they would not be able to actually stop them but they would not want to actively support them."[29] UNHCR interviewed all recognized refugees in the week prior to the March 25 deadline and found that 139 were still unwilling to be resettled or repatriated; "they each affirmed their desire to seek asylum in Cambodia."[30] A Technical Tripartite Meeting on the Implementation of the MOU was held on April 11, 2005. Its conclusions stated that

> UNHCR explained . . . it was encountering serious difficulties in the implementation of the MOU due to the lack of access and the possibility of independent verification of the safety of the returnees. UNHCR also pointed out that while the number of refugees refusing resettlement had gone down, there remained some 139 of them who continued to refuse repatriation or resettlement. The MOU provision that requires them to decide within one month or face return to Vietnam was proving difficult to implement due to the lack of UNHCR monitoring possibilities. The UNHCR requested the Vietnamese government for immediate access to the Central Highlands in order to obtain direct information on the safety of the returnees and as an encouragement for more Montagnards in Cambodia to opt for voluntary repatriation.[31]

UNHCR commenced a series of field trips to the Central Highlands to visit some of those who had returned voluntarily in March 2005. UNHCR's representative in Hanoi, Vu Anh Son, a Vietnamese national, was permitted access to the Highlands for a three-day monitoring trip. UNHCR Geneva reported that Son "met with local authorities and 18 returnee families" and that "there were no constraints by the authorities concerning access." Son said, "No one I met amongst the returnees claimed they were beaten or harassed during their stay in Pleiku or upon their return home. They all seemed in good shape."[32] In light of its detailed 2002 report, Human Rights Watch justifiably claimed to have better contacts in the Highlands than UNHCR. Human Rights Watch was skeptical about the UNHCR report in light of information received by Human Rights Watch about four returnees, three of whom had been beaten in Pleiku on their arrival from Cambodia. Human Rights Watch informed UNHCR that "on the morning of 18 May, all four returnees were instructed to report to local district police officials, who informed them that if people came to visit them the next day they were not to say anything about having been mistreated while in police custody in Pleiku. They were also told that if other people in the village mentioned their beatings, they would be arrested and locked up in T-20 prison and beaten worse than the other four."[33]

Human Rights Watch claimed to have reliable information that one returnee interviewed by the UNHCR representative had eight district police officers in his home when the interview occurred and that the UNHCR representative was accompanied by two government officials at all times. The UNHCR representative made further monitoring visits and was quoted by the Vietnam News Agency as having met thirty-two returnees in May and June: "I realize that they have already had a stable life, and been treated fairly. They haven't been beaten or discriminated."[34] He then gave a lengthy interview to the Vietnam News Agency that gave a glowing account of the conditions for the returnees and praised the two governments for their honoring of the tripartite agreement.[35] No UNHCR representative attempted to provide a public explanation how UNHCR was able to work so cooperatively with the Vietnamese officials, confident that returnees were not facing persecution by those same officials.

The Forced Deportation of July 20, 2005

At about 6 A.M. on July 20, 2005, Cambodian police sealed off access to the Site One Facility in Phnom Penh. They then forced 101 persons whose asylum claims had been rejected to board buses for forced repatriation to Vietnam. Of these persons, 94 were Montagnards who were subsequently delivered to their villages in the Central Highlands. The remaining 7 turned out to be Cambodians. UNHCR's associate protection officer, Inna Gladkova, told the *Cambodia Daily*, whose journalists read back the quotes to her before publication, "The Montagnards resisted passionately, many were crying and screaming as they were carried out. Some tried to jump over the compound wall but weren't successful." The press report continued, "The UNHCR 'saw someone hitting Montagnards' during the removal, Gladkova said. 'We intervened,' she said, adding that UNHCR officials physically placed themselves between police and the hill tribesmen. 'In several instances there were electric batons used to threaten Montagnards to leave the site,' though UNHCR did not directly observe anyone receiving shocks, Gladkova said."[36]

One relief worker was quoted as saying, "We heard zap-zap-zap noises and a tremendous wailing" from inside the facility. On July 26, 2005, Human Rights Watch published seven eyewitness accounts of the police behavior, including one by Sister Denise Coghlan, the longtime director of the JRS in Phnom Penh, which was UNHCR's implementing partner for assisting the asylum seekers in the closed facilities.

UNHCR went into damage control with the international media, coordinating their response from Geneva. The UNHCR spokesperson Jennifer Pagonis distanced UNHCR from the earlier comments of its assistant protection officer. Pagonis said that five UNHCR staff were present for the removal of the returnees at Site One "to ensure no excess force was applied."[37] In her Geneva press briefing, she expressed UNHCR's "firm impression" that the Cambodian authorities had "managed the return with proper restraint." She told the press that "the Cambodian authorities were receptive to our interventions and it is our firm impression that they managed the return with proper restraint. We did not observe anyone being beaten, kicked or electric batons being used to shock people."[38]

Peter Leuprecht wrote again to the high commissioner for refugees. Familiar with the ways of the Cambodian police in public with its own citizens, he had no reason to doubt the credible claims by NGO members that the Cambodian police had used excessive force on Montagnards inside a closed facility. He wrote:

> I have frequently had occasion to raise with the Government of Cambodia the use of disproportionate force in dispersing public gatherings and demonstrations. I have called for the use of electric shock batons to be banned. I am therefore very concerned about reports that the police used disproportionate force, and carried and used electric batons during the deportation. I find myself in a very difficult situation, one that is shared by the Office of the High Commissioner for Human Rights in Cambodia which tried, but was stopped by the police from monitoring the deportation. On the one hand, I am in receipt of credible reports about the deportation. On the other hand UNHCR is denying that there was anything wrong.[39]

In order to buttress the operation of the MOU, UNHCR was finding it necessary to defend the actions of the Cambodian police, implicitly discrediting human rights NGOs, one of whose most senior and respected members in Cambodia had personally witnessed the police violence that is typical of the Cambodian police and rarely defended or justified in Geneva. The demonstration deportation of the rejected asylum seekers achieved the desired result. All remaining recognized refugees in the pre-MOU caseload decided to opt for resettlement or voluntary repatriation. Those who have arrived in Cambodia since the MOU was finalized are presented with the same option. To date there has been no further forced repatriation even of failed asylum seekers. The implied threat in the MOU has worked.

NGOs like JRS and Human Rights Watch have encountered firsthand the response of UNHCR to claims that returnees have suffered abuse at the hands of Cambodian police in sight of NGO members. UNHCR Geneva has been prepared to be even more adamant in rejecting claims of abuse than its local staff in Phnom Penh, which saw some violence in the removal of July 20, 2005. These NGOs are justified in showing a high level of suspicion toward UNHCR claims that all is now well for returnees in their villages in the Central Highlands.

UNHCR is satisfied that the MOU has focused two recalcitrant governments on their responsibilities to asylum seekers. If UNHCR were not party to an agreement, it argues, there would be less prospect of third-country resettlement for this cohort of recognized refugees and there would be increased risk of forced repatriation for Montagnards, whether or not they are refugees. Regardless of the deficiencies in the monitoring process, UNHCR is confident that it enjoys more access with the MOU. UNHCR also has an assured asylum space for this cohort in Phnom Penh and it has delayed opportunities for contact with asylum seekers who have fled into the Cambodian forests. Though it would be unprincipled to threaten recognized refugees with forcible repatriation, UNHCR has satisfied itself that there has been no need to date to implement the threat. Given the low threshold for Montagnards establishing a refugee claim, some UNHCR staff also satisfy themselves that a refugee declining resettlement in a developed country may not even be a refugee despite the determination process. Anxious to maintain good relations with its MOU partners, UNHCR has been prepared to strain relations with human rights NGOs in Phnom Penh. Nevertheless, UNHCR remains confident that the NGOs will maintain their principled stance while UNHCR effects practical compromises with governments, which to date have had a poor record in their treatment of this cohort of asylum seekers. When a UN agency acts like a government, other UN agencies and NGOs will inevitably feel the strain.

States ought to have a negative duty not to refoule and a positive duty to provide refugees with the opportunity for finding a lasting solution to their plight. Guy Goodwin-Gill, however, observes that "the area continues to be governed by discretion, rather than duty, but analysis reveals that discretion to be not only confined by principle, but also structured in the light of other legally relevant considerations, including international solidarity, border sharing, and the right of functional protection enjoyed by UNHCR."[40]

On August 21, 2006, UNHCR renewed its commitment to the tripartite agreement. UNHCR thinks this compromise has produced an outcome that is better for all but ninety-four failed asylum seekers who have paid the price of maximizing what UNHCR thinks to be the best outcome for the greatest number. Cambodia has been able to delay further the development of human rights standards in accordance with international norms. UNHCR has set a precedent for other governments threatening to refoule both at the border without status determination and after status determination in country. Once UNHCR compromises on refoulement, the cornerstone of the Convention is on a slippery slope.

Conclusion

The protection of asylum seekers requires concerted cooperation between governments and other national and international actors. The invocation of human rights is a helpful way of setting, redefining, and critiquing the norms for government action, especially at the borders where governments are concerned not just with the protection of the proximate outsider but also with the ongoing security and economic well-being of the insider, as well as other policy considerations that can render foreign asylum seekers an irrelevance. The invocation of human rights helps to motivate actors, focus priorities, define mandates, and shape ethos and identity of all human agents for the better.

Governments will continue to insist on their right to assert sovereignty over their territory, and this will necessitate their control of national borders. Even democratic states respectful of the rule of law will be governed by administrations sensitive to the community's demand for security and exclusivity within those borders. Political parties that stray too far from that community sensitivity will risk electoral defeat. However, some citizens will exert influence informed by an ethic that relativizes the assertion of national sovereignty and tolerates more porous national borders. Universalizing human rights, these citizens can contribute to a popular sentiment that renders government more open and generous to those in need at the border. In less democratic states, NGOs and other actors in civil society can play a similar role.

By invoking human rights, NGOs and civil society can provide a common discourse for demanding transparency and accountability from UNHCR and governments cooperating in vexed situations such as the resettlement of Montagnards from Cambodia to Vietnam. They can also assist in moving popular sentiment in democratic nation-states. The temptation for human rights advocates is to universalize the rhetoric of human rights when there is no community consensus about the scope of such rights. Should the boats start streaming toward Australia again, I have no doubt that government will respond to community sentiment for instituting further deterrent measures again. While doing this, of course, it will reassure the community of everyone's basic decency in maintaining a border policy, migration program, and asylum processes aimed at orderly entry to Australia for those chosen by Australians for entry to the promised land of first-world wealth and human rights protection. One of the previous ministers from the government of John Howard recently reflected on that government's treatment of asylum seekers and surmised, "If there was anyone in politics who deserved a medal for political courage, it was Howard. He was the great boundary buster of Australian politics but almost never boasted about it. With Howard, even the most radical change was about restoring the kind of common sense that should always have prevailed."[41]

The rhetoric and legal entrenchment of human rights, especially for the outsider at the border of social inclusion, are key instruments in the armory of those advocates who want to challenge the common sense of the exclusivist community. Human rights can challenge the boundary busting of utilitarian or ideological governments that invoke border protection as if it were a national priority inconsistent with equitable burden sharing and decent treatment of the stranger. These instruments will be blunted and rendered useless, however, if they are wielded too often: thus, my considerable reserve about invoking the Kew Gardens Principle on the high seas or on national borders. Those of us who are free to travel across borders have an obligation to those who cannot. We must advocate their cause so that borders might be made sufficiently porous for their voices to be heard alongside ours in determining what is fair and decent treatment at those borders. Determining the extent to which human rights discourse is helpful in forcing unwilling governments to have a care for the outsider will always be a question of prudence, best judged by those at home in the local political culture.

Notes

1. David Hollenbach, "Internally Displaced People, Sovereignty, and the Responsibility to Protect," in *Refugee Rights: Ethics, Advocacy and Africa,* ed. David Hollenbach (Washington DC: Georgetown University Press, 2008), 188.

2. See John G. Simon, Charles W. Powers, and Jon P. Gunnemann, *The Ethical Investor: Universities and Corporate Responsibility* (New Haven, CT: Yale University Press, 1972), 22–25.

3. Graeme Innes, "New Report Highlights Ongoing Problems in Immigration Detention," Australian Human Rights Commission, news release, January 13, 2009, www.hreoc.gov .au/about/media/media_releases/2009/2_09.html (accessed March 23, 2009). This announced the release of the 2008 Immigration Detention Report, www.hreoc.gov.au/human_rights/ immigration/idc2008.html (accessed March 23, 2009).

4. See Frank Brennan, *Tampering with Asylum,* 2nd ed. (Brisbane, Australia: University of Queensland Press, 2007).

5. Quoted in P. Mares, *Borderline,* 2nd ed. (Sydney: University of New South Wales, 2002), 122.

6. Quoted in Brennan, *Tampering with Asylum,* 42.

7. *Commonwealth of Australia Parliamentary Debates* 30235 (House of Representatives), August 27, 2001.

8. "Note Verbale to the Royal Norwegian Embassy," Australian Government, Department of Foreign Affairs and Trade, Canberra, August 28, 2001.

9. Ibid.

10. *Commonwealth of Australia Parliamentary Debates,* 30517 (House of Representatives), August 29, 2001 (John Howard, prime minister).

11. "MS *Tampa*—Refugees at Sea," SBS Television, Australia, March 4, 2003.

12. *Commonwealth of Australia Parliamentary Debates* 30235 (House of Representatives), August 29, 2001 (John Howard, prime minister).

13. Ibid.

14. Chris Evans, *New Directions in Detention—Restoring Integrity to Australia's Immigration System*, presented at Australian National University, Canberra, July 29, 2008, www.minister .immi.gov.au/media/speeches/2008/ce080729.htm (accessed March 27, 2009).

15. Ibid.

16. Chris Evans, "Unauthorised Boat Arrivals Arrive on Christmas Island," Australian government media release, October 2, 2008, www.minister.immi.gov.au/media/media-releases/ 2008/ce08096.htm (accessed May 19, 2009).

17. Sharman Stone, "Has the Government Put People Smugglers Back in Business?" News Release, Office of the Shadow Minister for Immigration and Citizenship, Australia, September 30, 2008.

18. Memorandum of Understanding between the Government of the Socialist Republic of Vietnam, the Royal Government of Cambodia, and the United Nations High Commissioner for Refugees (UNHCR), January 20, 2005.

19. UNHCR Office (Phnom Penh), "Montagnards," Media Update, Public Information Sheet 0003, January 26, 2005.

20. UNHCR, Executive Committee Conclusion, *Voluntary Repatriation*, Resolution 40 (XXXVI), 1985, para (j), www.UNHCR.org/excom/EXCOM/3ae68c9518.html (accessed March 27, 2009).

21. "Tripartite Agreement between the Governments of Cambodia and Vietnam and UNHCR," Phnom Penh, January 21, 2002. The UNHCR Briefing Note on this agreement is "Cambodia: Agreement Signed on Vietnamese Montagnard Repatriation," January 22, 2002, UNHCR website, www.UNHCR.org/3C4d6df79.html.

22. UNHCR, Press Release, "Tripartite Agreement on Montagnards under Threat," Public Information Section, Geneva, News, February 23, 2002, www.UNHCR.org/news/NEWS/ 3c7a00e24.html (accessed April 3, 2009).

23. Ibid.

24. Letter of R. Lubbers to Governments of Cambodia and Vietnam, March 23, 2002.

25. News Report, *Agence France Press* (Geneva), March 23, 2002.

26. UNHCR (Phnom Penh) *Montagnard Caseload Briefing Report*, January 31, 2005, 3.

27. Peter Leuprecht, letter to Wendy Chamberlin, March 21, 2005.

28. Minutes of the UNHCR Protection Meeting, Phnom Penh, March 22, 2005, 1.

29. Ibid., 2.

30. UNHCR, *Briefing Note on the Progress of the Implementation of the MOU*, Tripartite Technical Meeting, Phnom Penh, April 11, 2005.

31. UNHCR Office (Phnom Penh), Conclusions of the Technical Tripartite Meeting on the Implementation of the MOU, Conclusion II, April 11, 2005.

32. "Montagnard returnees to Vietnam in good shape, says UNHCR," UNHCR Press Release, May 24, 2005; www.UNHCR.org/429322OF4.html.

33. Brad Adams, Human Rights Watch, letter to Erika Feller, UNHCR Geneva, June 22, 2005.

34. Quoted by *Xinhua News Agency* (Vietnam), June 29, 2005.

35. The full text of the interview was published by the *Vietnam News Agency* on August 7, 2005. The interview was given shortly after the UNHCR representative returned to Hanoi on June 25, 2005. He made monitoring trips to the Highlands on June 18–24, 2005.

36. *Cambodia Daily*, July 21, 2005. The journalist William Shaw confirmed on March 21, 2006, that he had read back the quotes to Gladkova, who was happy with the reportage.

37. Jennifer Pagonis, "Viet Nam: Visit to Monitor Condition of Montagnards Returning from Cambodia," UNHCR Briefing Notes, July 29, 2005, www.UNHCR.org/cgi-bin/texis/vtx/news/opendoc.htm?tbl=NEWS&id=42ea00ea25 (accessed April 5, 2009).

38. Ibid.

39. Peter Leuprecht, letter to António Gutteres, High Commissioner for Refugees, August 17, 2005.

40. Guy Goodwin Gill, *The Refugee in International Law*, 2nd ed. (Oxford: Clarendon Press, 1998), 204.

41. Tony Abbott, "The Price of Political Courage," *Weekend Australian*, January 24–25, 2009.

6

Loving Humanity while Accepting Real People

A Critique and a Cautious Affirmation of the "Political" in U.S. Asylum and Refugee Law

Daniel Kanstroom

Introduction

Certain recent trends in the refugee and asylum law of the United States have reminded me of an old *Charlie Brown* comic strip. The charmingly insecure character, Linus, stood with his security blanket tucked under his chin, staring wistfully into space. The caption, as I remember it, read: "I love mankind; it's people I can't stand."[1]

In President George W. Bush's administration, the "political" affected asylum adjudications in ways that were often subtle and sometimes pernicious. Appointments of immigration judges became improperly partisan, leading not just to legitimacy crises but to measurable disparities apparently based on ideology.[2] The Board of Immigration Appeals (BIA) faced direct attacks on its objectivity clothed in the garb of efficiency. And bars to asylum were manipulated, behind the scenes, by discretionary executive decisions. Others have effectively critiqued the ungenerous and harmful aspects of these moves. Judges have harshly criticized agency decisions and scholars have tabulated adjudication disparities. Human Rights First has poignantly described some of those barred refugees and asylum seekers: "women who were raped and enslaved by armed militias in Liberia; victims of extortion forced to pay armed terrorists in Colombia to protect their lives and their children"; democracy activists from Burma who may have innocently given minor support to groups that had not even been formally designated as "terrorist" organizations; a Christian missionary worker arrested, beaten, and jailed by the Burmese military regime, and so on.[3]

My purpose in this chapter is not to replay these critiques, but to attempt to situate them as part of the history and deep ambivalence of asylum law.[4] Dissonance between generous obligations to "mankind" or "humanity" and more restrictive concerns about certain types of people has always been present in debates over asylum seekers and refugees. In part this is because asylum law "compounds the sense of threat to immigration control."[5] Put another way, ambivalence derives from the tension between universalist laws and more particularist political practices by nation-states. The Preamble of the 1951 United Nations Convention Relating to the Status of Refugees reflects this quite clearly, as it speaks of "the principle that human beings shall enjoy *fundamental rights and freedoms without discrimination*" while recognizing that refugee and asylum law is implemented by nation-states.[6]

The tension is also apparent in the so-called exclusion clauses of the Convention, which permit states to bar from refugee status a rather wide range of criminals and other bad actors.[7] Questions abound: How much leeway do states have in defining these terms? To what extent do they or must they embody political ideas? How should states apply the general humanitarian aspirations of refugee and asylum law? Should refugee and asylum law be connected to immigration policy?

Such issues have become especially acute in the United States in recent years as national security has dominated much political and legal discourse. The proud, universalist, humanitarian achievements of refugee and asylum law have faced severe pressure. Some have even advocated changes that would subsume refugee law within rather crudely defined protectionist categories at least as strict as those of "regular" immigration laws. Indeed, a representative of the Federation for American Immigration Reform (FAIR)—a U.S.-based organization that advocates for more restrictive immigration policies—recently suggested that, due to "concern over the continuing threat from jihadist Islamic radicals," the nation's refugee admission policy should be focused not only on "whether Islamic refugees have been identified as linked to radical jihadist movements, but whether they *fit a profile of a population among whom jihadists have shown an ability to recruit.*"[8] FAIR views refugee policy as "an integral part of the nation's overall immigration policy."[9]

Much is at stake in this debate, and not only for the asylum seekers and refugees. Few politicolegal questions evoke greater passion. When a recent Canadian judicial decision concluded that the United States was not complying with its nonrefoulement obligations under the Refugee Convention, the U.S. ambassador to Canada responded immediately.[10] "The United States," he said, "welcomes more refugees than any other country in the world and remains a beacon of hope and liberty."[11] This idealistic view is widely shared. Human Rights First recites that "the principle of asylum is a deeply rooted American value, powerfully expressed since the founding of the Republic." As they note, George Washington himself once said, "The bosom of America is open to receive not only the opulent and respectable stranger, but the oppressed and persecuted of all nations and religions" as he urged the creation of "a safe and propitious asylum for the unfortunates of other countries."[12]

It is no small matter that, since 1975, the United States has resettled over 2.6 million refugees.[13] Indeed, in some years, the United States has accepted more refugees than all other countries combined, though it ranked sixth on the latest report by the World Refugee Survey in terms of the ratio between accepted refugees and national population.[14] But recent trends have not been positive.[15] Following the September 11, 2001, attacks a downward trend accelerated dramatically. In 2002 and 2003, the United States admitted 26,839 and 28,306 refugees, respectively, by far the lowest numbers in decades.[16] Though a little higher now, refugee admission numbers are still far below the averages of the 1990s.[17] A person who is in the United States may apply for asylum affirmatively to the Department of Homeland Security (DHS) or defensively in removal proceedings before the Executive Office for Immigration Review in the Department of Justice. Roughly one in five of asylum applications are granted, as discussed below.[18] In fiscal year 2007, asylum was granted to 25,230 people.[19]

Numbers, however, do not tell the whole story. Changes mandated by the USA Patriot Act of 2001 and the REAL ID Act of 2005 have led to a system of rather unfettered, but largely hidden, executive interpretive discretion.[20] Such trends should be resisted, as they surely will be by the new administration of President Barack Obama. But how? Many human rights scholars and advocates are quite wary of accepting *any* connection between political considerations and asylum law. There are perfectly understandable and defensible reasons for this, which I accept. They include

- a moral/philosophical view of asylum as inherently apolitical;
- a particular reading of the historical genesis of modern refugee and asylum law with emphasis on its religious or humanitarian aspects; and
- concerns about overtly ideological practices by governments under the guise of humanitarianism.

These concerns reflect some of the greatest achievements of the modern human rights idea. But is a purely apolitical critique of prior practice sufficiently well-focused? I will suggest, a bit polemically, that a rigid bifurcation between strong versions of ostensibly apolitical asylum and refugee law versus instrumentalist approaches to immigration law is incorrect. The reality is now—and has long been—more subtle. Put simply, asylum law has never been truly apolitical and immigration law embodies certain powerful humanitarian norms. A bright-line dichotomy may take insufficient account of the evolving relationship between refugee/asylum law and "regular" immigration laws.

The Bush administration tilted too far toward the political and to executive branch discretion, undercutting the humanitarian ideal. But the problem was not simply the penetration of policy; it was the type of policy and the way it penetrated. To maintain legitimacy and to be effectively humanitarian, we should not advocate the complete insulation of asylum from political considerations. We need a more sensitive, more comprehensive, and more pragmatic weaving together of the two strands of politicolegal discourse.[21]

This weaving might positively consider the relationship between refugee and asylum law and an array of protective measures within the "regular" U.S. immigration and deportation systems. To be sure, some dividing lines between immigration and refugee law have utility.[22] But recall that the Conference of Plenipotentiaries that completed the 1951 Convention Relating to the Status of Refugees also unanimously adopted this recommendation: "The Conference expresses the hope that the Convention . . . will have value as an example exceeding its contractual scope and that all nations will be guided by it in granting so far as possible to persons in their territory as refugees and who would not be covered by the terms of the Convention, the treatment for which it provides."[23]

U.S. immigration law now contains a variety of rather specific protective mechanisms. Consider, as a nonexhaustive list, the Violence Against Women Act, U (crime victims) and T (trafficking victims) visas, Temporary Protected Status, Cancellation of Removal, and the Convention against Torture.[24] These legal mechanisms, some with tenuous—if any—connections to traditional refugee and asylum law, may protect from removal

- victims of domestic violence;
- victims of crime or trafficking;
- those who fear harm due to ongoing armed conflict, an environmental disaster, or other extraordinary and temporary conditions;
- certain legal permanent residents; and
- certain other long-term "inadmissible or deportable" noncitizens who can demonstrate that removal "would result in exceptional and extremely unusual hardship" to legally resident or U.S. citizen relatives; and
- torture victims.

My point, emphatically, is not that U.S. immigration law is especially generous in general.[25] Indeed, it is often quite restrictive and harsh. But this patchwork quilt of specific protective measures evidences certain deep underlying humanitarian urges that have garnered specific political support. The fact that they are listed completely separately in the immigration statutes reflects history and politics, not rational planning or anything close to coherent philosophical thought.[26] Still, a basic underlying concept is protection from certain specific types of serious harm. One could certainly imagine a more unified approach to that basic concern, as a matter of legislation, executive discretion, and judicial review.[27]

There are, of course, great potential risks to such thought experiments. One wonders if anything remotely comparable to the Refugee Convention could be achieved today. But the brutal fact is that, for many millions, the current regime is simply inadequate. As Thomas Nagel once wrote, "It is important to try to imagine the next step, even before we have come close to implementing the best conceptions already available."[28] Perhaps consideration of such alternative pathways might help us to strike a better balance between political and legal factors in refugee and asylum cases as well as to sketch the outlines of a more just, comprehensive, and durable system. My hope is to inspire a creative synthesis between the best principles of the political and the universally humanitarian; or, if you will, between Linus's love of humanity and his concerns about real people. But first we must refine our critique of current practices.

Adjudication Disparities and the Rise of the Political in Asylum Law

The infiltration of the political in asylum adjudications has recently arisen in at least three ways. First, concerns have been raised about appointments within the Department of Justice. Second, the reorganization of the BIA has raised questions of

political bias.[29] And, finally, low quality decision making and adjudication disparities have rankled appeals courts and others.[30]

A brief outline of how the U.S. refugee and asylum systems work is useful here.
Persons who fear persecution or who have suffered it in their country of nationality
may seek refugee status from outside the United States. To qualify, an applicant must
be a refugee as defined by the immigration statute and be of "special humanitarian
concern" to the United States.[31] Eligibility is determined on a case-by-case basis,
and thus a large measure of executive branch discretion is always involved. Certain
special cases, such as opponents of Chinese population control laws, are also recognized.[32] And broad determinations of need are made by the president in consultation with Congress each year, which inevitably injects policy considerations into the
otherwise largely humanitarian enterprise.[33]

Asylum is different.[34] Generally, any noncitizen who is present in the United
States or at a port of entry may apply for asylum if she or he meets the refugee
definition.[35] Cases proceed on two tracks: affirmatively, which means filing with an
asylum officer, or defensively, in removal proceedings before an immigration judge,
within the Executive Office of Immigration Review (EOIR) of the Department of
Justice.[36]

Department of Justice Appointments

The U.S. immigration administrative court system exists within the Department
of Justice comprising immigration judges and the Board of Immigration Appeals
(BIA), appointed by the attorney general.[37] In July 2008 the Justice Department's
Office of Professional Responsibility (OPR) and its inspector general (IG) published
a report which concluded that the Department had used an illegal, highly partisan,
politicized process to appoint immigration judges with conservative political credentials.[38] Though noting that "both Department policy and federal law prohibit
discrimination in hiring for career positions on the basis of political affiliations," the
investigation found "that [Monica] Goodling improperly subjected candidates for
certain career positions to the same politically based evaluation she used on candidates for political positions."[39]

The report found that many of these appointees had little or no immigration law
expertise and that the process had left a large number of needed immigration judge
positions unfilled. OPR and IG recommended that the Department "clarify its policies regarding the use of political or ideological affiliations to select career attorney
candidates" because "the Department's guidance on this issue is inconsistent."[40]

BIA Streamlining and Reorganization

The BIA was plagued by problems of massive delays through the 1990s.[41] In 2002
Attorney General (AG) John Ashcroft sought to address this by a process of "streamlining."[42] Instead of hearing cases in three-member panels and issuing written
opinions, as it had for years, the BIA was ordered to decide most appeals through

summary orders by individual Board members. In a move that many observers found counterintuitive at the very least, the AG also eliminated twelve of the twenty-three Board seats. Among the advantages cited for such a move was that "the continued expansion of the Board has . . . had significant institutional costs including effects on the cohesiveness and collegiality of the Board's decision making process, and the Department's perception of the uniformity of its decisions."[43]

The reality was that the most liberal members of the BIA, as measured by the percentages of their rulings in favor of noncitizens, were eliminated.[44] The effects were dramatic. In less than a year, summary affirmances increased twentyfold.[45] The nature of BIA decisions also changed: decisions in favor of noncitizens fell from 25 percent to 10 percent.[46] Many thousands of administrative appeals were also simply rejected without any written explanation.

One prominent scholar, Stephen Legomsky, has referred to the entire episode as a "war on independence."[47] As he wrote, "the Attorney General . . . sent unmistakable signals to both the immigration judges who preside over deportation hearings and the appellate adjudicators who review them. The message was simple: 'You rule against the government at your personal peril.'"[48]

The American Bar Association Commission on Immigration Policy, Practice & Pro Bono put it this way: "The Department of Justice's announcement . . . created an incentive to 'play it safe.' . . . This change in composition of the Board detracts from a public perception of fair and impartial decision making and also deprives the Board of a variety of viewpoints that is valuable in the appellate process."[49]

Adjudication Disparities and Judicial Criticism

We will never know how many asylum cases were denied due to improper political biases. But there was an apparent decline in the quality of adjudications, perceived by reviewing courts. There was also a surge in immigration appeals caused by the so-called streamlining.[50]

The Seventh Circuit Court of Appeals, in particular, became scathingly critical of various aspects of immigration decisions.[51] In a 2003 case the court concluded that "the elementary principles of administrative law, the rules of logic, and common sense seem to have eluded the Board in this *as in other cases*."[52] In 2005 it wrote that "the immigration judge's unexplained conclusion is hard to take seriously."[53] In another case, the court concluded that "the procedure that the [immigration judge] employed in this case is an affront to [petitioner's] right to be heard."[54] Other circuits have been similarly critical. The Second Circuit wrote that "the immigration judge's finding is grounded solely on speculation and conjecture."[55] The Third Circuit noted that "the tone, the tenor, the disparagement, and the sarcasm of the [immigration judge] seem more appropriate to a court television show than a federal court proceeding."[56] The Ninth Circuit held that "the [immigration judge's] assessment of Petitioner's credibility was skewed by prejudgment, personal speculation, bias, and conjecture."[57]

Academic studies have corroborated that such concerns were well founded in asylum cases. A 2006 study that examined asylum cases from 1994 through early

2005 found denial rates for 208 immigration judges ranged from a low of 10 percent to a high of 98 percent. Eight judges denied asylum to nine out of ten of the applicants, while two judges granted asylum to nine out of ten.[58]

A 2007 study of asylum adjudication patterns concluded that "one judge is 1820 percent more likely to grant an application . . . than another judge in the same courthouse" and "one U.S. Court of Appeals is 1148 percent more likely to rule in favor of a petitioner than another U.S. Court of Appeals considering similar cases."[59] More generally, the study concluded that "in the world of asylum adjudication, there is remarkable variation in decision making from one official to the next, from one office to the next, from one region to the next, from one Court of Appeals to the next, and from one year to the next, even during periods when there has been no intervening change in the law."[60]

Do these discrepancies reflect ideological bias? Perhaps. A preliminary analysis of the asylum decisions by the sixteen judges who were appointed after consideration of their political credentials found that "on average, they were more likely to rule against asylum seekers than their colleagues on the same court who had been appointed according to the department's politically neutral rules."[61] In 2006 former attorney general Alberto Gonzales promised an "improvement plan."[62] Researchers, however, concluded in 2008 that "the Justice Department has failed to implement measures that would increase oversight of immigration judges, [or] to make the immigration appeals process more rigorous."[63] One hopes and expects that the new administration will do better.

Exclusions from Protection

Matthew Gibney wrote in 2004 that "U.S. resettlement policy has been generous but not humanitarian, while asylum policy has been humanitarian but not generous."[64] Certain recent interpretations of exclusions from protection, however, were neither humanitarian nor generous. The Refugee Convention, in Article 1(F), excludes persons who have committed "a crime against peace, a war crime, or a crime against humanity"; "a serious non-political crime"; or "acts contrary to the purposes and principles of the United Nations."[65] An extensive interpretive gloss has developed regarding these provisions, which straddle the lines between the universal and particular, the political and the legal. As one group of experts has noted, "Exclusion poses a serious moral dilemma to host states, which may explain the long avoidance in confronting its true dimensions."[66]

U.S. statutory law contains similar exceptions and preclusions. They were undoubtedly originally intended to be construed in conformity with international law. But interpretations—and the list of exceptions itself—have diverged from such norms. As a result, both the generosity and the humanitarian openness of the U.S. asylum system have been significantly limited.

Material Support

Much of the recent problem of the "political" in asylum derives from concerns about national security.[67] The U.S. government has strictly applied the provisions of the Patriot Act and the REAL ID Act against refugees and asylum seekers. As Donald Kerwin has observed, however, many such restrictions "adopted in the name of 'national security' violate the rights of refugees and asylum seekers, and do little to enhance public safety."[68] Perhaps the clearest example of this phenomenon is the so-called material support bar to refugee admission and asylum.[69]

There is a baroque interplay between certain inadmissibility and removal grounds, which apply generally to "regular" immigration cases, and asylum cases.[70] For the purposes of his chapter, I will not retrace that complicated pas de deux other than to cite it as a clear example of a blurring of the lines between refugee and asylum law and immigration law.[71]

In short, any noncitizen who has provided "material support" to an individual "terrorist" or to a "terrorist organization" is barred from asylum. The asylum seeker may be barred if he "knows, or reasonably should know" that the object of his support "has committed or plans to commit a terrorist activity."[72] The term "terrorist activity" includes such actions as airplane hijacking, sabotage, assassination, and kidnapping. However, it also includes the use of a "dangerous device (other than for mere personal monetary gain), with intent to endanger, directly or indirectly, the safety of one or more individuals or to cause substantial damage to property."[73] Obviously, this could cover a very wide range of conduct that most people would probably not describe as terrorism.

The specific term "material support" is buried deep within the inadmissibility statute as part of the definition of "engage in terrorist activity." It is largely undefined, though it includes, among other things, "to commit an act that the actor knows or reasonably should know, affords material support, including a safe house, transportation, communications, funds, transfer of funds or other material financial benefit, false documentation." Such support may be either directly for the commission of a terrorist activity or to any individual "who the actor knows or reasonably should know," has committed or plans to commit a terrorist activity; to "a terrorist organization" specifically designated; or even to "a group of two or more individuals, whether organized or not, which engages in, or has a subgroup which engages in," a very wide range of "terrorist activities."[74] The executive branch, in its "sole unreviewable discretion" may decide not to apply the material support bar. Given the breadth of the definitions, the opposite is also true: the bar may be applied to a very wide range of seemingly innocent activities.

The standard of proof for the government in such cases has been held to be remarkably low. As the BIA put it in 2005, the bar applies "where, under the circumstances, information about an alien supports a reasonable belief that the alien poses a danger—that is, *any nontrivial degree of risk*—to the national security."[75]

Similarly, the *mens rea* requirements regarding the intent to contribute are virtually nonexistent. The BIA has rejected the idea that there must be a link between the provision of material support to a terrorist organization and the intended use by that recipient organization of the assistance to further a terrorist activity.[76]

Thus, the statute, already complex to the point of virtual incomprehensibility, embodies numerous loose *mens rea* standards such as "reasonably should know" and very broad definitions.[77] As interpreted by the BIA, it is a paean to executive discretion.[78] This discretion has been quite harshly exercised. Consider the word "material." It can mean virtually any level or type of support (even *de minimis* amounts of funds and support provided by children).[79] DHS has argued that the list of examples in the statute was intended to have "an expanded reach and cover virtually all forms of assistance, even small monetary contributions."[80]

In the end, such questions get funneled down to the discretion provided in the statute to "waive" the bars.[81] In 2007 the executive began to mitigate some of its prior harshness. DHS secretary Michael Chertoff announced that the bar would no longer apply to certain individuals who provided support under duress to certain "terrorist" groups "if warranted by the totality of the circumstances."[82] In April 2007 the exceptions were expanded.[83] Still, the model remains one of unfettered executive discretion. Consider the range of factors that DHS will now balance in its sole and presumably unreviewable discretion:

> whether the individual could have avoided, or took steps to avoid, providing material support;
> the severity and type of harm inflicted or threatened;
> to whom the harm was directed; and
> in cases of threats alone, the perceived imminence of the harm threatened and the perceived likelihood that the harm would be inflicted.

The government will also consider

> the amount, type, and frequency of the support provided;
> the nature of the activities committed by the terrorist organization;
> the individual's awareness of those activities;
> the length of time since the support was provided;
> the individual's conduct since that time; and
> "other factors."[84]

DHS has authorized the application of the exemption to specific groups and has expanded group waiver designations.[85] These are positive developments. But the main point is that the legal asylum regime has largely moved from a politicolegal standard to one that is purely policy based and virtually immune from judicial scrutiny.

The number of cases affected by the bars is not trivial. According to the State Department, some 13,000 refugees who would otherwise have been admitted to the United States in fiscal year 2006 remained in refugee camps and urban detention centers. Many of those deemed likely to be excluded from the United States because of the material support bar are simply no longer considered for admission.

The cases of some 650 asylum seekers as well as an estimated 6,500 adjustment of status cases were placed on hold because of the material support bar.[86] Particularist statutory models have also emerged. In 2008 President Bush signed a law that authorizes DHS and the Department of State to exempt members of the African National Congress from the material-support bar with respect to anti-apartheid activities.[87]

Persecutors

Is there a less discretionary, less policy-based way to proceed with such highly charged terms? I believe so. Consider the U.S. legal approach to persecutors. The U.S. refugee definition excludes "any person who ordered, incited, assisted, or otherwise participated in the persecution of any person on account of race, religion, nationality, membership in a particular social group, or political opinion."[88]

The word "persecution" is not defined in the 1951 Convention, the 1967 Protocol, or the Immigration and Nationality Act.[89] But its interpretive history has been one of executive and judicial dialogue, quite unlike the designation model for material support. Though formulations have varied considerably over the years, persecution may now generally be defined under U.S. law as "the infliction of suffering or harm upon those who differ . . . in a way regarded as offensive."[90]

The preclusion harkens back to exclusion grounds relating to those who aided the Nazis in Germany during the 1930s and 1940s.[91] In the context of Nazi denaturalization cases and the 1948 Displaced Persons Act, the U.S. Supreme Court recognized that the definition has potentially ambiguous boundaries.[92] As the Court recognized, certain "cases may present more difficult line-drawing problems."[93] But it remains a *legal* question. Lower U.S. courts have used a wide variety of methods to achieve a workable definition. Indeed, in one recent case, the Third Circuit Court of Appeals, simply turned to dictionaries.[94] The court was satisfied with this definition of "persecute": "to harass in a manner to injure, grieve, or afflict [usually] because of some difference of outlook or opinion[;] set upon with cruelty or malignity . . . to cause to suffer or put to death because of belief (as in a religion)."[95]

To be sure, the word "persecution" has been interpreted quite rigidly by administrative authorities, barring even those who assisted persecutors involuntarily or under duress.[96] The Supreme Court, however, recently held that this interpretation "rested on a mistaken legal premise" and needed to be reevaluated against the backdrop of the history and purposes of the Refugee Act of 1980.[97] The Court noted that it had twice previously recognized that "'one of Congress's primary purposes' in passing the Refugee Act was to implement the principles" agreed to in the 1967 Protocol and the 1951 Convention Relating to the Status of Refugees.[98] Unsurprisingly, when applied to former Nazis, strict preclusions have generally elicited little outrage from the human rights community.[99] In other contexts, however, the BIA, despite its general rigidity on the preclusion, has recognized the potential danger. In a Salvadoran asylum case, the BIA noted that "as the concept of what constitutes persecution expands, the group which is barred from seeking haven in this country also expands, so that eventually all resistance fighters would be excluded from relief."[100]

Serious Nonpolitical Crimes

Under international law, a person with a well-founded fear of very severe persecution "should only be excluded for the most serious reasons."[101] The United Nations High Commissioner for Refugees (UNHCR) Handbook requires that "a 'serious' crime must be a capital crime or a very grave punishable act."[102] Further, all the relevant factors—including any mitigating circumstances—must be taken into account. Many argue that an act must be grossly disproportionate to the political objective sought in order to constitute a serious nonpolitical crime.[103] Of course, states are not required to extend the protection of the refugee regime to those who have committed crimes such as bombings, murders, and torture. However, "the explicit exclusion of persons who have committed nonpolitical crimes implies that individuals who have been accused of or even committed serious political crimes may qualify as refugees."[104] Thus, the lynchpins are "seriousness" and the "political." As the UNHCR Handbook puts it, "The political element of the offence should also outweigh its common-law character. This would not be the case if the acts committed are grossly out of proportion to the alleged objective. The political nature of the offence is also more difficult to accept if it involves acts of an atrocious nature."[105]

Finally, some argue that a balance should be struck between the offense and the harm the applicant would face. The president of the 1951 Conference stated that "when a person with a criminal record sought asylum as a refugee, it was for the country of refuge to strike a balance between the offenses committed by that person and the extent to which his fear of persecution was well-founded."[106]

The U.S. Supreme Court, however, has been quite deferential in its consideration of what constitutes a "serious non-political crime."[107] In *INS v. Aguirre-Aguirre* an asylum seeker from Guatemala was alleged to have "burned buses, assaulted passengers, and vandalized and destroyed private property" as part of a political protest.[108] The Supreme Court highlighted the deference to be owed to the executive branch in the immigration context, "where officials exercise especially sensitive political functions that implicate questions of foreign relations."[109] Asserting that such decisions "may affect our relations" with other countries, the Court viewed the issue as more one of policy than of law.[110] As to humanitarian balancing, the Court held that the lower court's error was "clearest" in that context.[111] The Court made clear that the "U.N. Handbook may be a useful interpretative aid, but it is not binding on the Attorney General, the BIA, or United States courts." In the end, the asylum decision "is incumbent upon the Contracting State in whose territory the refugee finds himself."[112] In effect, this reading prioritizes the political approach to asylum and withholding both procedurally (as deference) and substantively.[113]

Should/Can Asylum Law Be Separated from Political Considerations?

The law of asylum has always been connected to implicit political substrata.[114] How are the "oppressed and persecuted" cited by Washington distinguished from their oppressors and persecutors? I sometimes pose the question to my students this way: had George Washington lost the Revolutionary War and fled to another country with a modern-type asylum system, would he have been eligible for asylum? Perhaps; but this surely would have been more likely in France than in an ally of England.

Political and Adjudication

How should a freedom fighter be distinguished from a terrorist? Lists are superficially tempting. I am sure that few would fight passionately for the right of each actively engaged Nazi to an individualized asylum hearing. But lists are inevitably both over- and underinclusive. One of the signal achievements of the modern regime of asylum law was the rejection of group designations in favor of case-by-case adjudication against general standards.[115] Asylum, to use Ronald Dworkin's metaphor about rights, is a trump card played by an individual against state sovereignty.[116] And so it should remain. To be sure, individualized adjudication is "at best a crude and incomplete way to respond to the complex realities that the world presents."[117] It can be chaotic and arbitrary if unmoored from any centralized consistency. Thus, what is needed is a meaningful dialogue between executive discretion and judicial review as both sides seek the proper balance. U.S. asylum law allows highly discretionary calculations, some interpretive, some ultimate.[118] As the Supreme Court put it in 1987, "A finding that an alien is a refugee does no more than establish that 'the alien may be granted asylum in the discretion of the Attorney General.'"[119]

This idea, too, has deep roots. Consider the full statement from which Washington's famous "oppressed and persecuted" quotation is taken: "The bosom of America is open to receive not only the Opulent and respectable Stranger, but the oppressed and persecuted of all Nations and Religions; whom we shall welcome to a participation of all our rights and privileges *if, by decency and propriety of conduct, they appear to merit the enjoyment.*"[120] The U.S. idea of asylum is thus considerably more complex than it might at first appear. Grounded in generous humanitarianism, it is also discretionary, and in some sense always political. Who decides "propriety of conduct"? In most cases it is the executive. Still, executive decisions become illegitimate if they are too political in a partisan sense.[121]

Scholars have struggled to distinguish the legitimately political from the illegitimate as they have traced the evolution of asylum from ancient origins, to an exception to extradition norms for certain "political" criminals, to a right of states to give protection to a newly conceptualized special class: exiles and refugees.[122] Its humanitarian nature has long been evident, connected to the practice of sanctuary in holy places.[123] The Old Testament tells of God instructing Moses to designate cities of refuge "for the children of Israel, and for the stranger, and for the sojourner among them" (Num. 35:9–15). But asylum rights, such as they are, have never been completely divorced from political considerations. Christian von Wolff noted in the mid-eighteenth century that "[by] nature the right belongs to [exiles] to dwell in any place in the world which is subject to some other nation."[124] But this right was always "tempered with recognition of the fact of sovereignty."[125] The very word "right" in this context often confuses. It can indicate a right of states to grant asylum as well as the right of an individual to be considered for asylum.[126] Indeed, under the Universal Declaration of Human Rights, a person has a right to "seek and to enjoy in other countries asylum from persecution," but not a right "to be granted" asylum.[127]

The Political in U.S. Asylum Law

In the United States, the political aspect of asylum has loomed especially large for many years. The terminology often used for asylum law in the United States embodies the tension between the moral/legal and the political, between individual rights and state sovereign power. Consider the subtitle of a recent, excellent book by Phillip Schrag that dealt with U.S. legislative battles over asylum in the 1990s. The primary title, *A Well-Founded Fear*, was taken from the statutory definition of a refugee, but the subtitle is *The Congressional Battle to Save Political Asylum in America*. The statute that governs U.S. asylum law does not precede "asylum" with the adjective "political."[128] And yet a recent search I conducted in the LEXIS Law Reviews and Journals database for the term "political asylum" returned 1,421 hits. The same search in the Federal Immigration Cases and Agency Decisions database returned 1,772 hits, including this one from the U.S. Supreme Court: "Respondents in this case are a Florida lawyer who represents undocumented Haitian nationals seeking *political* asylum in the United States and three of his clients."[129] What, if anything, does the widespread acceptance of this modifier by U.S. legal academics, lawyers, and judges imply?

One concern is its impact on the legal nature of asylum adjudications. Law aspires, often vainly, to neutral principles of adjudication. In asylum law, the aspiration is buttressed by the ostensibly apolitical nature of the definition of "refugee."[130] The line between the humanitarian and the political in the United States has been sharply drawn by human rights advocates. In a highly influential article written nearly a quarter century ago, the late Arthur Helton wrote: "Three years after the passage of the Refugee Act of 1980, its mandate that uniform and neutral standards be utilized in the asylum adjudication process remains unfulfilled. Rather, the Act's mandate is subservient to foreign and domestic policy considerations which continue to dominate asylum decision making. Indeed, the standards and practices used in the asylum process, including alien interdiction and detention programs, have served to jeopardize the very right of asylum."[131] Note the connection in this passage between two distinct issues: the betrayal of "uniform and neutral standards" and the use of harsh practices that impede access to the process itself. Interdiction, detention, and other such practices clearly remain compelling problems. But note, too, that Helton titled his article "Political Asylum . . . An Unfulfilled Promise."

We must first decide what the phrase "policy considerations" and the adjective "political" signify. Is the latter an accurate modifier, surplus, or epithet? The adjective works to differentiate so-called economic refugees from the term of art, "refugee," as it is understood in both international and U.S. law.[132] This, I suspect, is at the strongest root of recent colloquial usage of "political asylum."[133] As one commentator wrote in 1938, the "essential quality" of a refugee was "one who has sought refuge . . . as a result of *political* events which rendered his continued residence in his former territory impossible or intolerable."[134]

Political offenses have long been an exception to U.S. criminal exclusion laws. The earliest federal laws excluding convicts from immigrating provided an exemption for "political offenses."[135] The line between political refugees and economic migrants also has a long pedigree, the full history of which is beyond the scope of this chapter. We can, however, trace its most immediate U.S. roots in the asylum context back to the 1948 Displaced Persons Act, which distinguished refugees from other "regular" immigrants and embodied a "new, seemingly cogent, rationale for linking humanitarian concerns for certain groups of refugees with the interests of the U.S. state."[136] Soon thereafter, the 1950 Internal Security Act forbade deportation to a country where the "alien" would face "physical persecution" (a phrase interpreted to have more political than economic connotations).[137]

The word "asylum" did not appear in U.S. immigration statutes until 1980. One of Congress's primary purposes was to bring U.S. refugee law into conformance with the 1967 Protocol. There were many statements indicating that the new statutory definition of "refugee" should be interpreted in conformance with the Protocol.[138] But the developing asylum concept was, in the United States, already deeply linked to political considerations.

The political modifier thus differentiates cognizable from noncognizable asylum claims.[139] It may also differentiate prosecution from persecution. In a case involving coup plotters from Ghana, for example, the court recognized the need for "an accurate assessment of the political conditions existing in the particular country."[140]

But here a more complex problem emerges: this inquiry requires a normative political distinction to be made between legitimate "freedom fighters against totalitarian regimes [versus] those who act against democratic governments that respect basic rights."[141] Adjudicators are often understandably uncomfortable with this endeavor. As two members of the BIA once noted, "The majority wades in dangerous waters when it presumes to make judgments as to the legitimacy of sovereign nations by scrutinizing their political systems."[142] But there seems no easy way around these "dangerous waters." Indeed, this normative aspect of politics seems inherent in the asylum enterprise.

Of course, the word "political" may have a quite different meaning. It may connote a partisan or an ideological application of the law. This is a much more controversial proposition for asylum law—linked as it is to the etymology of "political" in the sense of policy. Indeed, this usage may test the outer bounds of the legitimacy of refugee and asylum "law" as law. So it seems that our task is not so much to separate the political from asylum, but to differentiate the legitimate from the illegitimate versions of the political.

The difficulty of this task is exacerbated by separation of powers concerns and uncertainly about the line between the rule of law and discretion. The roots of political entry practices for refugees in the United States are connected more to executive action than to statutory law.[143] In the 1950s, 1960s, and 1970s, the discretionary executive power known as parole accounted for hundreds of thousands of entrants, ranging from participants in the 1956 Hungarian uprising to large numbers of Cubans and Vietnamese. Critiques of excessively partisan determinations were often made by proponents of a more forceful legislative role, as well as by those who questioned the legitimacy of their ideological aspects.

Before the United States acceded to the 1967 Protocol, the use of parole power was highly—indeed unabashedly and ideologically—political. As Arthur Helton reported, of 232,711 pre-1968 parolees, the total number from "non-Communist Europe" was 925, as compared with 32,000 from Hungary, 185,487 from Cuba, and so on.[144] In the 1960s the spillover of ideology into refugee and proto-asylum laws was unsurprising.[145] Indeed, the first codification of a U.S. refugee admissions law was the so-called seventh preference category.[146] One could hardly imagine a more partisan refugee law—it limited admissions to those who had fled persecution from a "Communist or Communist-dominated country."[147]

Following its accession to the Protocol in 1968, the United States was bound to apply the nonideological definition of a "refugee." Nevertheless, parole continued to be utilized in a highly political way. Of 608,000 parolees admitted from 1968 to 1980, only 7,000 came from non-Communist countries.[148] Arthur Helton contended that immigration authorities were still "frustrating implementation of the Protocol and acting inconsistently with its *generous underlying humanitarian philosophy*."[149]

All of this implicated real separation of powers concerns. One of the great goals of the Refugee Act of 1980 was to end (or at least to limit) ideological refugee and asylum decisions. There were two aspects to this goal. The first was whether the standard ought to be nonideological. On this point, there was a general consensus. But the second, more subtle, issue was who should make such decisions as whether a fear was well founded or whether a person had persecuted others? The executive branch, through the Department of Justice, argued strongly from the very start that the "well-founded fear of persecution" test should be the "well-founded fear of persecution in the *opinion of the Attorney General*."[150]

As enacted, the Refugee Act's standard for refugees and asylum seekers was designed to be "compatible with the humanitarian traditions and international obligations of the United States." The Act was an attempt to accommodate the executive desire for policy-based flexibility with the goals of stability, predictability, and control.[151] It was designed "to excise ideological bias from immigration law and to facilitate bringing refugees into this country by requiring that only a well-founded fear of persecution be established."[152] This was a great and important achievement, no doubt. But in practice, the second question, that of who decides a claim, was never definitively resolved: the executive made the first decision, often with an eye toward policy concerns and particular conceptions of security. But judicial review—based on the nonideological statute—was fully available.

The tensions became acute again due to the persistence of ideologically biased decisions. Immigration and Naturalization Service (INS) statistics from 1983 showed that "seventy-eight percent of the Russian, sixty-four percent of the Ethiopian, fifty-three percent of the Afghan, and forty-four percent of the Romanian cases decided received political asylum, all involving persons fleeing Communist-dominated regimes. On the other hand, asylum was granted in less than eleven percent of the Philippine, twelve percent of the Pakistani, two percent of the Haitian, two percent of the Guatemalan, and three percent of the Salvadoran cases."[153]

In 1984 the government granted 328 Salvadoran asylum cases and denied 13,045. It granted 3 Guatemalan claims while denying 753.[154] Further, the executive practice of admitting special categories of parolees also continued with so-called Cuban/Haitian entrants and the like.[155] In short, the 1980s, which began with strong humanitarian, apolitical promise, ended with the tension between the universalist and particularist visions clarified but unresolved.

During the Clinton administration, focus turned to questions of bias, but also to basic competence. An Asylum Corps was created and new professional asylum officers received special training in "international human rights law, conditions in countries of origin, and other relevant national and international refugee law."[156] But in fiscal year 1992, asylum seekers filed some 103,000 applications, climbing to around 150,000 in the next years, double the expectation. A huge backlog of unadjudicated applications developed.[157]

Concern mounted that the system was too loose, open to too many applicants, too subject to abuse and that it had, in fact, been abused by nondeserving applicants. This critique was invigorated by two terrorist acts on U.S. soil by two noncitizens who had reportedly sought asylum.[158] INS implemented major changes to the asylum system, expanding its staff, improving training, streamlining procedures, and restricting work permits. The impact was profound: new asylum applications dropped from some 124,000 in fiscal year 1994 to under 47,000 in fiscal year 1996.[159] Nevertheless, pressure continued for a stronger legislative fix. The 1996 Illegal Immigration Reform and Immigrant Responsibility Act (IIRIRA) had powerful effects on the U.S. asylum system.[160] IIRIRA imposed a one-year deadline on applying for asylum, delayed work authorization, created a new system known as "expedited removal," and provided for the detention of asylum seekers. The question that many human rights advocates have asked ever since is, "What has been the human cost of these restrictions?"[161]

Conclusion

It has been suggested that human rights discourse "is increasingly acquiring the status of a universally understood and accepted mode of moral communication."[162] If this was ever true regarding refugees and asylum seekers, it has certainly been a highly dubious recent proposition in the United States. As Lavinia Limón recently noted, "Wealthy industrial nations utilize policies designed to limit the number of refugees that enter their territory . . . [they] claim national security reasons, ethnic and/or religious conflict, or a lack of tolerance from their own citizens. . . . No matter the rationale the result is the same—refugees are denied their rights under international law."[163] Because nonrefoulement and asylum rightly remain the ideal of apolitical humanitarian remedies, the struggle to purge the system of bias and improper political criteria is crucially important.

However, this does not necessarily counsel human rights advocates to argue in purely humanitarian or universalist terms. A more unified legal approach to forced migration is a timely and worthy goal. Until U.S. immigration law embodies a more comprehensive approach to extreme hardship cases, though, we must at least struggle to maintain balance and fairness in asylum adjudications. This does not—and cannot—mean jettisoning the inevitable legitimate political components of asylum. It means sifting through the more and less legitimate meanings of the "political" and then prioritizing the best moral and legal component as far—and as clearly—as possible.

Notes

1. Thanks to David Hollenbach for directing me to a somewhat more literary source for the same sentiment: "The more I love humanity in general, the less I love man in particular" (Fyodor Dostoyevsky, *The Brothers Karamazov*, chap. 4). See also Thomas Nagel, *Equality and Partiality* (New York: Oxford University Press 1991), 4. ("The impersonal standpoint in each of us produces, I shall claim, a powerful demand for universal impartiality and equality, while the personal standpoint gives rise to individualistic motives and requirements which present obstacles to the pursuit and realization of such ideals.")

2. These are administrative law judges, employed by the Department of Justice, though they have much adjudicative independence. Their decisions are subject to review by the Board of Immigration Appeals, also part of the Department of Justice, and then may be reviewed by federal courts.

3. Human Rights First, *Abandoning the Persecuted*, 2006, www.humanrightsfirst.info/pdf/06925-asy-abandon-persecuted.pdf (accessed May 5, 2009). The Burmese government had accused the missionary of trying to convert children to Christianity and ordered that the mission's orphanage be closed. He was warned that he would be arrested because of his work at the mission orphanage because he attempted to convert children and because he allegedly gave a pair of binoculars to the Chin National Front.

4. This tension has recently led to many blunt, overt mechanisms such as interdiction. See Matthew J. Gibney, *The Ethics and Politics of Asylum: Liberal Democracy and the Response to Refugees* (Cambridge: Cambridge University Press 2004).

5. David A. Martin, "The Refugee Concept: On Definitions, Politics, and the Careful Use of a Scarce Resource," in *Refugee Policy: Canada and the United States*, ed. Howard Adelman (Toronto: York Lanes Press, 1991), 39. Put another way, asylum "holds a unique immunity to the measures for deliberate decisions concerning intake that are available, at least in theory, in other subfields of immigration law." Ibid.

6. 189 U.N.T.S. 137, signed July 28, 1951. Emphasis added. Also from the 1951 Convention: "States . . . will do everything within their power to prevent this problem from becoming a cause of tension between States."

7. These clauses exclude "any person with respect to whom there are serious reasons for considering that

1. he has committed a crime against peace, a war crime, or a crime against
    humanity . . . [or]
2. he has committed a serious non-political crime outside the country of refuge
    prior to his admission to that country as a refugee; [or]
3. he has been guilty of acts contrary to the purposes and principles of the
    United Nations."

8. Jack Martin, "Reforming Refugee Admissions, Comment from the Federation for American Immigration Reform (Fair) to the FY-2008 Refugee Admissions Program Stakeholders' Meeting Chaired By Asst. Secretary of State Ellen Sauerbrey," June 6, 2007, www.fairus.org/site/PageServer?pagename=ReformingRefugeeAdmissions (accessed May 5, 2009). Emphasis added.

9. This view leads FAIR to conclude that refugee policy should be shaped by such characteristics as "ability to learn English and find well paying jobs [because] increasing evidence of assimilation problems and cultural clashes can jeopardize [the U.S.] generous spirit." Ibid.

10. On December 29, 2005, the Canadian Council for Refugees, Amnesty International, and the Canadian Council of Churches, along with a Colombian asylum seeker in the United States, challenged the designation of the U.S. as a safe third country for refugees. On November 29, 2007, Justice Michael Phelan of the Canadian federal court upheld the challenge, finding, inter alia, that it was "unreasonable to conclude that the US complies with its non-refoulement obligations under the Refugee Convention and the Convention against Torture." On June 27, 2008, a federal Court of Appeal allowed an appeal brought by the government. The court overturned Justice Phelan's ruling, though it did not find the U.S. a safe country for all refugees. In September 2008 an application was filed with the Supreme Court of Canada for leave to appeal the decision.

11. David H. Wilkins, quoted in Adam Liptak, "U.S. Is No Haven, Canadian Judge Finds," *New York Times*, December 10, 2007, sidebar.

12. Human Rights First, "Asylum and Expedited Removal," www.humanrightsfirst.org/refugees/reports/due_process/due_pro_I.htm (accessed May 5, 2009).

13. Testimony on "Oversight Hearing: U.S. Refugee Admissions and Policy," by Kenneth Gavin on behalf of Refugee Council USA before the Senate Committee on the Judiciary Subcommittee on Immigration, Border Security, and Citizenship, www.jrs.net/reports/index.php?lang=en&sid=1340.html (accessed May 5, 2009).

14. Statistics available at www.refugees.org/uploadedFiles/Investigate/Publications_&_Archives/WRS_Archives/2008/resettlement%20by%20country.pdf (accessed May 5, 2009).

15. In the 1990s refugee admissions averaged around 100,000 per year. In 1999 the United States resettled 85,076 refugees; in 2000, more than 72,000; and in 2001, some 69,000. DHS, *2003 Yearbook of Immigration Statistics*, Office of Immigration Statistics, September 2004, 53, www.dhs.gov/xlibrary/assets/statistics/yearbook/2003/2003Yearbook.pdf. See Donald Kerwin, "The Use and Misuse of 'National Security' Rationale in Crafting U.S. Refugee and Immigration Policies," *International Journal of Refugee Law* 17, no. 4 (2005): 749–63.

16. The Refugee Council USA, U.S. Refugee Admissions Program for Fiscal Year 2004 (May 2003), 4.

17. See Kelly J. Jefferys and Daniel C. Martin, "Refugees and Asylees: 2007," in DHS, *Annual Flow Report 2007*, July 2008. The annual average number of refugee arrivals has been about fifty thousand during the 2000 to 2007 period. Some forty-eight thousand persons were admitted to the United States as refugees during 2007. The leading countries of nationality for refugees were Burma, Somalia, and Iran.

18. See TRAC, "The Asylum Process," http://trac.syr.edu/immigration/reports/159/index.html (accessed May 5, 2009).

19. DHS, FY 2007, Table 16, U.S. Department of Homeland Security; U.S. Citizenship and Immigration Service (USCIS); Refugee, Asylum, and Parole System (RAPS); and the U.S. Department of Justice (DOJ), Executive Office for Immigration Review (EOIR).

20. The Uniting and Strengthening America by Providing Appropriate Tools Required to Intercept and Obstruct Terrorism Act of 2001, Pub. L. No. 107-56, 115 Stat. 272 (2001). The REAL ID Act was a rider to the Emergency Supplemental Appropriations Act for Defense, the Global War on Terror, and Tsunami Relief, Pub. L. No. 109-13, Div. B, Title I, 119 Stat. 231, 302-23 (2005). The Act changed certain evidentiary standards in asylum cases and redefined certain terrorism exclusions, as discussed more fully below. The Act makes a person deportable unless he or she can show "by clear and convincing evidence" that he or she did *not* know that a group he or she supported was involved in broadly defined terrorist activities. It also expanded the concept of "material support" to include soliciting to *any* member of a terrorist organization. See Marisa Silenzi Cianciarulo, "Terrorism and Asylum Seekers: Why the REAL ID Act Is a False Promise," *Harvard Journal on Legislation* 43, no. 1 (2006): 101–43.

21. See *Murray v. The Schooner Charming Betsy*, 6 US (2 Cranch) 64, 117–18 (1804) (an act of Congress ought never to be construed to violate the law of nations if any other possible construction remains).

22. "Governments and the publics to which they respond insist on a general framework whereby international migration is controlled and normally subject to deliberate decisions by the polity as to who should be admitted and on what terms." David A. Martin, T. Alexander Aleinikoff, Hiroshi Motormura, and Maryellen Fullerton, *Forced Migration Law and Policy*, Thomson West American Casebook Series (Eagan, MN: Thomson West, 2007), 3.

23. UN Conference of Plenipotentiaries on the Status of Refugees and Stateless Persons, *Final Act of the United Nations Conference of Plenipotentiaries on the Status of Refugees and Stateless Persons*, July 25, 1951, A/CONF.2/108/Rev.1, www.UNHCR.org/refworld/docid/40a8a7394.html (accessed 13 May 2009).

24. The original Violence against Women Act of 1994 (VAWA) (P.L. 103-322, 108 Stat. 1902) was introduced in Congress in 1990 and enacted as part of the Violent Crime Control and Law Enforcement Act of 1994 to address the problems of domestic violence, sexual assault, and other forms of violence against women. VAWA included measures to reduce the frequency of violence against women, provide services to victims of gender-based violence, and hold perpetrators accountable. Its immigration provisions empowered battered immigrant women to obtain lawful immigration status without relying on the assistance of an abusive citizen husband. A variety of such protective measures are now part of U.S. immigration law. VAWA 1994 also allowed abused spouses placed in removal proceedings to seek cancellation of removal, a form of discretionary relief from removal available to individuals in unlawful immigration status with strong equities, after three years rather than the seven ordinarily required. The statute also granted similar rights to minor children abused by their citizen or lawful permanent resident parent, whose immigration status, like that of the abused spouse, would otherwise be dependent on the abusive parent. Further protections were contained in VAWA 2000, Division B of the Victims of Trafficking and Violence Protection Act of 2000 (H.R. 3244), P.L. 106-939. U and T visas were also created by VAWA 2000. They are now codified at 8 U.S.C. § 1101(a)(15)(T) and (U). TPS is a temporary immigration status granted to eligible nationals of designated countries (or parts thereof). Congress established a procedure by which the attorney general may provide TPS to aliens in the United States who are temporarily unable to return safely to their home country because of ongoing armed conflict, an environmental

disaster, or other extraordinary and temporary conditions. 8 U.S.C. §1254a; and 8 C.F.R. § 244. On March 1, 2003, pursuant to the Homeland Security Act of 2002, Public Law 107-296, this authority was transferred from the attorney general to the secretary of homeland security. TPS beneficiaries may remain in the United States and may obtain work authorization. But TPS does not lead to permanent resident status. Cancellation of Removal, 8 U.S.C. §1229b. Convention against Torture and Other Cruel, Inhuman, or Degrading Treatment or Punishment (CAT), 1468 U.N.T.S., done Dec. 10, 1984. Nonrefoulement-type protections under CAT were implemented by the Foreign Affairs Reform and Restructuring Act of 1998 (FARRA), Div. G., Pub. L. 105-277, 112 Stat. 2681. See 8 CFR 208.16-.18 and 8 CFR 208.30-.31 (defining the scope of protection that may be ordered by immigration judges pursuant to CAT).

25. See Daniel Kanstroom, *Deportation Nation: Outsiders in American History* (Cambridge, MA: Harvard University Press, 2007).

26. Ironically, though, the net result may well have been a rather more generous regime than might have been achieved had the problem of forced migration been considered more comprehensively.

27. For example, some have suggested that "the central ranking principle must be the immediacy and degree of life-threatening violence." A. Zolberg, A. Suhrke, and S. Aguayo, *Escape from Violence: Conflict and the Refugee Crisis in the Developing World* (New York: Oxford University Press, 1989), 272. Alex Aleinikoff once suggested that a more unified model could be grounded on the idea of "loss of community as the fundamental harm." T. Alexander Aleinikoff, "From 'Refugee Law' to the 'Law of Coerced Migration,'" *American University Journal of International Law and Policy* 25, no. 9 (1993–1994): 25–27. In his view this would allow "combinations of protection . . . return (when conditions permit) or the creation of community elsewhere" (ibid., 27).

28. Nagel, *Equality and Partiality*, 7.

29. See Evelyn H. Cruz, "Double the Injustice, Twice the Harm: The Impact of the Board of Immigration Appeals's Summary Affirmance Procedures," *Stanford Law and Policy Review* 481, no. 16 (2005): 507.

30. See, e.g., Jaya Ramji-Nogales et al., "Refugee Roulette: Disparities in Asylum Adjudication," *Stanford Law Review* 60 (2007): 295; and Eliot Walker, "Asylees in Wonderland: A New Procedural Perspective on America's Asylum System," *Northwestern Journal of Law and Social Policy* 1, no. 1 (2007): 2. ("That the American asylum system has fallen into disrepute is no longer a significantly contested point of debate.") See also, e.g., Adam Liptak, "Courts Criticize Judges' Handling of Asylum Cases," *New York Times,* December 26, 2005; Sydenham B. Alexander III, "A Political Response to Crisis in the Immigration Courts," *Georgetown Immigration Law Journal* 21, no. 1 (2006): 9–10; *Benslimane v. Gonzales,* 430 F.3d 828, 830 (7th Cir. 2005); and Memorandum to Immigration Judges from Attorney General Alberto Gonzales, January 9, 2006, www.humanrightsfirst.info/pdf/06202-asy-ag-memo-ijs.pdf (accessed May 6, 2009). See also Memorandum from Alberto Gonzalez, August 6, 2006, www.usdoj.gov/opa/pr/2006/August/06_ag_520.html (outlining twenty-two proposed changes in asylum adjudication, including performance evaluations for immigration judges and testing on immigration law).

31. This definition of refugee was incorporated into the Immigration and Nationality Act by the Refugee Act of 1980, conforming to that contained in the 1951 United Nations Convention relating to the Status of Refugees and the 1967 Protocol. A refugee must also not be firmly resettled in any foreign country, and be otherwise admissible under the Immigration and Nationality Act. Spouses and minor children of qualifying refugees may derive status and also enter the United States as refugees, either accompanying or following to join the principal refugee.

32. Prior to 2005 there was an annual ceiling of one thousand persons who could be granted refugee or asylee status under this provision. Applicants beyond the one thousand cap who were otherwise approved were given conditional grants of asylum. The REAL ID Act of 2005 eliminated this annual cap on asylum approvals based solely on Chinese population control.

33. In 2007, for example, nationals of Cuba, Vietnam, and the countries of the former Soviet Union were designated, as were extraordinary individual protection cases for whom resettlement is requested by a U.S. ambassador anywhere. Before the beginning of each fiscal year, the president consults with Congress to establish a worldwide refugee admissions ceiling for that year and to set allocations for five geographic regions and an "unallocated reserve." In 2007, the total ceiling for refugee admissions was seventy thousand.

34. The United States uniquely differentiates between the standards for asylum and withholding (nonrefoulement). See *INS v. Stevic*, 467 US 407 (1984); *Matter of Acosta*, 19 I&N Dec. 211 (BIA 1985); and *INS v. Cardoza-Fonseca*, 480 US 421 (1987). The Court has held that the standard of "more likely than not" for withholding is much higher than the standard of a "well-founded fear" of persecution. *Cardoza-Fonseca*, 480 US 421, 431 (1987). Even a 10 percent probability of harm may constitute a "well-founded fear." But the elaboration of the standard has inspired continuing executive/legislative and judicial conversation. As the Supreme Court observed in a footnote, "How 'meaningful' the differences between the two standards may be is a question that cannot be fully decided in the abstract. . . ." Ibid., n31; see also *Matter of Mogharrabi*, 19 I&N Dec. 439 (BIA 1987).

35. Applicants are required to apply for asylum within one year from the date of last arrival or to establish that an exception applies based on changed or extraordinary circumstances. When a claim for asylum is barred because of the one-year filing deadline, a noncitizen may still apply for withholding of removal or Convention against Torture protection. The burden of proof, however, is higher: asylum claimants must show that they have a "well-founded fear of persecution," while withholding requires proof that persecution is "more likely than not."

36. For recent asylum statistics, see Jefferys and Martin, *Refugees and Asylees: 2007.*

37. Indeed, decisions of the BIA may be reviewed and overturned by the attorney general personally. Noncitizens may appeal certain BIA decisions to the U.S. Courts of Appeals.

38. *An Investigation of Allegations of Politicized Hiring by Monica Goodling and Other Staff in the Office of the Attorney General* (July 28, 2008). In addition, a report on the Department's Honors Program and Summer Law Intern Program made other recommendations to address allegations of politicized hiring in the Department. See *An Investigation of Allegations of Politicized Hiring in the Department of Justice Honors Program and Summer Law Intern Program* (June 24, 2008). The recommendations included revising the Department of Justice Human Resource Order to emphasize that the process for hiring career attorneys must be merit based and to specify that ideological considerations cannot be used as proxies to discriminate on the basis of political affiliations. Attorney General Michael Mukasey announced that the Department intended to implement all of its recommendations.

39. *An Investigation of Allegations of Politicized Hiring by Monica Goodling*, 135.

40. Ibid., 140.

41. See United States Department of Justice, Executive Office of Immigration Review, Board of Immigration Appeals, www.usdoj.gov/eoir/biainfo.htm (accessed February 18, 2009).

42. For a thorough analysis of the recent problems at the Board of Immigration Appeals, see Dorsey & Whitney LLP, study conducted for the American Bar Association Commission on Immigration Policy, Practice, and Pro Bono, Re: Board of Immigrations Appeals: Procedural Reforms to Improve Case Management (2003), www.dorsey.com/files/upload/Dorsey

StudyABA 8mgPDF.pdf. See also ABA Commission on Immigration Policy, Practice & Pro Bono, Seeking Meaningful Review: Findings and Recommendations in Response to Dorsey & Whitney Study of Board of Immigration Appeals Procedural Reforms (2003), www.abanet .org/publicserv/immigration/bia.pdf. In addition, see, Evelyn H. Cruz, "Double the Injustice, Twice the Harm: The Impact of the Board of Immigration Appeals' Summary Affirmance Procedures," *Stanford Law and Policy Review* 6, no. 16 (2005): 481–512; Lory Diana Rosenberg, "Lacking Appeal: Mandatory Affirmance by the BIA," *Bender's Immigration Bulletin* 9, no. 3 (2004): 91; Bradley J. Wyatt, "Even Aliens Are Entitled to Due Process: Extending Mathews v. Eldridge Balancing to Board of Immigration Appeals Procedural Reforms," *William & Mary Bill of Rights Journal* 12, no. 2 (2004): 605–35; Sydenham B. Alexander III, "A Political Response to Crisis in the Immigration Courts," *Georgetown Immigration Law Journal* 21, no. 1 (2006): 2–59.

43. *Board of Immigration Appeals: Procedural Reforms to Improve Case Management*, 67 FR 54878 (August 26, 2002).

44. See Peter J. Levinson, "The Facade of Quasi-Judicial Independence in Immigration Appellate Adjudications," *Bender's Immigration Bulletin* 9 (2004): 1154–64.

45. The increase was from 3 to 60 percent of the Board's decisions. See Dorsey and Whitney report cited in note 42, Appendix 3; see also "The Surge of Immigration Appeals and Its Impact on the Second Circuit Court of Appeals," www.abcny.org/pdf/report/AppealSurge Report.pdf (accessed May 5, 2009).

46. "Surge of Immigration Appeals."

47. Stephen H. Legomsky, "Deportation and the War on Independence," *Cornell Law Review* 91, no. 2 (2006): 369–81.

48. Ibid.

49. ABA Commission Report, cited in note 42. The author was a member of the Commission and currently serves as an advisory member.

50. See Stanley Mailman and Stephen Yale-Loehr, "Immigration Appeals Overwhelm Federal Courts," *New York Law Journal*, December 27, 2004, p. 3, reprinted in *Bender's Immigration Bulletin* 10 (2005): 45; John R. B. Palmer, Stephen Yale-Loehr, and Elizabeth Cronin, "Why Are So Many People Challenging Board of Immigration Appeals Decisions in Federal Court? An Empirical Analysis of the Recent Surge in Petitions for Review," *Georgetown Law Review* 20, no. 1 (Fall 2005): 1–94.

51. See also *Benslimane v. Gonzales*, 430 F.3d 828 (7th Cir. 2005), in which Judge Richard Posner wrote, "Our criticisms of the Board and of the immigration judges have frequently been severe." He cites *Dawoud v. Gonzales*, 424 F.3d 608, 610 (7th Cir. 2005) ("the [immigration judge's] opinion is riddled with inappropriate and extraneous comments"); *Ssali v. Gonzales*, 424 F.3d 556, 563 (7th Cir. 2005) ("this very significant mistake suggests that the Board was not aware of the most basic facts of [the petitioner's] case"); *Soumahoro v. Gonzales*, 415 F.3d 732, 738 (7th Cir. 2005) (*per curiam*) (the immigration judge's factual conclusion is "totally unsupported by the record"); and *Kourski v. Ashcroft*, 355 F.3d 1038, 1039 (7th Cir. 2004) ("there is a gaping hole in the reasoning of the Board and the immigration judge").

52. *Niam v. Ashcroft*, 354 F.3d 652, 654 (7th Cir. 2003) (emphasis added).

53. *Grupee v. Gonzales*, 400 F.3d 1026, 1028 (7th Cir. 2005).

54. *Sosnovskaia v. Gonzales*, 421 F.3d 589, 594 (7th Cir. 2005).

55. *Chen v. U.S. Dep't of Justice*, 426 F.3d 104, 115 (2d Cir. 2005).

56. *Wang v. Attorney General*, 423 F.3d 260, 269 (3d Cir. 2005); see also, *Fiadjoe v. Attorney General*, 411 F.3d 135, 154-55 (3d Cir. 2005) (the immigration judge's "hostile" and "extraordinarily abusive" conduct toward petitioner "by itself would require a rejection of his credibility

finding"); *Korytnyuk v. Ashcroft*, 396 F.3d 272, 292 (3d Cir. 2005) ("it is the [immigration judge's] conclusion, not [the petitioner's] testimony, that 'strains credulity'").

57. *Lopez-Umanzor v. Gonzales*, 405 F.3d 1049, 1054 (9th Cir. 2005).

58. See Transactional Records Access Clearinghouse (TRAC), "Immigration Judges," http://trac.syr.edu/immigration/reports/160/ (accessed December 20, 2009).

59. Jaya Ramji-Nogales, Andrew I. Schoenholtz, and Philip G. Schrag, "Refugee Roulette: Disparities in Asylum Adjudication," *Stanford Law Review* 60, no. 2 (2007): 295.

60. Ibid., 302.

61. See TRAC, "Bush Administration Plan to Improve Immigration Courts Lags," http://trac.syr.edu/immigration/reports/194/ (accessed May 6, 2009).

62. The plan promised some twenty-two new measures, including performance evaluations; an immigration law exam for new immigration judges and Board members; budgets increases for new immigration judges, law clerks, and staff attorneys for the BIA; technological and support improvements; improvements to the BIA's "streamlining" practices; a new code of conduct for immigration judges and the BIA; improved mechanisms to detect poor conduct and quality by immigration judges; and a pilot program to assign assistant chief immigration judges to serve closer to the immigration courts that they oversee. www.lexis .com/research/retrieve?_m=1b88ff5c3f090e3cfffda5958f02f31f&csvc=bl&cform=search Form&_fmtstr=FULL&docnum=1&_startdoc=1&wchp=dGLzVlz-zSkAA&_md5=1f666fcea cbb0f00a8c385641d62154a-n133. Press Release, U.S. Department of Justice, "Attorney General Alberto R. Gonzales Outlines Reforms for Immigration Courts and Board of Immigration Appeals" (August 9, 2006), www.usdoj.gov/opa/pr/2006/August/06_ag_520.html; Memorandum from Attorney Gen. Alberto Gonzales to Immigration Judges (January 9, 2006), www .humanrightsfirst.info/pdf/06202-asy-ag- memo-ijs.pdf; Memorandum from Attorney Gen. Alberto Gonzales to Members of the Board of Immigration Appeals (January 9, 2006), www .humanrightsfirst.info/pdf/06202-asy-ag-memo-bia.pdf.

63. Memorandum from Attorney Gen. Alberto Gonzales (January 9, 2006). On the positive side, however, TRAC has concluded that "the agency has substantially completed improvements in other areas, publishing standardized court procedures, assigning supervisory judges to all courts, and providing new resources to support the work of immigration judges."

64. Gibney, *Ethics and Politics of Asylum*, 159.

65. Article 33(2), which deals with nonrefoulement, also provides that "the benefit of the present provision may not, however, be claimed by a refugee whom there are reasonable grounds for regarding as a danger to the security of the country in which he is, or who, having been convicted by a final judgment of a particularly serious crime, constitutes a danger to the community of that country."

66. See Chaloka Beyani, Joan Fitzpatrick, Walter Kälin, and Monette Zard, "Exclusion from Protection," *International Journal of Refugee Law*, Special Supplementary Issue (2000): 2.

67. See Daniel Kanstroom, "Reaping the Harvest: The Long Rhetorical Struggle over Deportation in the 'Nation of Immigrants,'" *University of Connecticut Law Journal* 39 (Spring 2007): 1911.

68. Donald Kerwin, "The Use and Misuse of 'National Security' Rationale in Crafting US Refugee and Immigration Policies," *International Journal of Refugee* Law 17 (2005): 749, 756 (arguing "for a more nuanced and rigorous sense of 'national security' in crafting refugee and immigration policy"). See also David Cole and Jules Lobel, *Less Safe, Less Free: Why America Is Losing the War on Terror* (New York: The New Press, 2007).

69. See Susan Benesch and Devon Chafee, "The Ever-Expanding Material Support Bar: An Unjust Obstacle for Refugees and Asylum Seekers," *Interpreter Releases* 83, no. 11 (2006): 466.

70. 8 USC 1182(a)(3)(B). Although, as noted above, U.S. immigration law has long banned a wide range of dissidents, anarchists, and others from entry, the immediate history of the relevant "material support" and "engaging in terrorist activities" bar may be traced to 1990.

71. Similar exclusions apply to withholding of removal. See 241(b)(3)(B)(iv), which applies to being a "danger to the security of the United States." Following the general inadmissibility provision, there is also a statement that an alien who is described in INA 237(a)(4)(B) shall be considered an alien whom there are reasonable grounds for regarding as a danger to the security of the United States. But the bar does not apply to "deferral of removal" under the Convention against Torture. See 8 CFR 208.16(b)(4)(2) and 208.17(a) (any person falling within INA 241[b][3][B] [which covers security exclusion and exclusion for having committed a particularly serious crime] may be granted deferral of removal to the country where he or she is "more likely than not" to be tortured).

72. INA § 212(a)(3)(B)(iv)(VI), 8 U.S.C. § 1182(a)(3)(B)(iv)(VI).

73. INA § 212(a)(3)(B)(iii)(V), 8 U.S.C. § 1182(a)(3)(B)(iii)(V). There are three "tiers" of terrorist organizations. Tier I and Tier II are for terrorist groups designated by the secretary of state in consultation with or upon the request of the attorney general or the secretary of homeland security.

74. (Tier III). INA § 212(a)(3)(B)(vi)(III), 8 U.S.C. § 1182(a)(3)(B)(vi)(III).

75. In *re A.H.*, 23 I & N Dec. 774 (A.G. 2005) (emphasis added). This means simply that "there is information that would permit a reasonable person to believe that the alien may pose a danger to the national security." Ibid.

76. *Matter of S-K-*, 23 I&N Dec. 936 (BIA 2006).

77. Note that this arises in two distinct places. First, the person contributing must know, or reasonably should know, that the transfer of funds involves material support. Second, the material support may be to someone who the provider reasonably should know has committed or plans to commit a terrorist act.

78. 212(d)(3)(B)(i) The secretary of state, after consultation with the attorney general and the secretary of homeland security, or the secretary of homeland security, after consultation with the secretary of state and the attorney general, may conclude in such secretary's sole unreviewable discretion that subsection (a)(3)(B)(i)(IV)(bb) or (a)(3)(B)(i)(VII) shall not apply to an alien, that subsection (a)(3)(B)(iv)(VI) shall not apply with respect to any material support an alien afforded to an organization or individual that has engaged in a terrorist activity, or that subsection (a)(3)(B)(vi)(III) shall not apply to a group solely by virtue of having a subgroup within the scope of that subsection. The secretary of state may not, however, exercise discretion under this clause with respect to an alien once removal proceedings against the alien are instituted under section 240.

79. See Margaret D. Stock, "Providing Material Support to a Foreign Terrorist Organization: The Pentagon, the Department of State, the People's Mujahedin of Iran, & the Global War on Terrorism," *Bender's Immigration Bulletin* 11 (June 1, 2006): 521, 531; see also *Matter of S-K-* (1,100 Singaporean dollars over eleven months was material).

80. *Matter of S-K-*.

81. As noted, the statute provides that the secretary of state or the secretary of homeland security, after consultation with each other and the attorney general, may conclude as a matter of "unreviewable discretion" that the material support ground of inadmissibility "shall not apply." *Matter of S-K-*. See Melanie Nezer, "The Broad Scope of the 'Material Support' and Other Terrorism-Related Grounds of Inadmissibility," *LEXIS Expert Commentaries,* December 2007.

82. This applied to Tier III. On February 20, 2007, Secretary Chertoff exercised his discretion to apply these provisions for individuals who provided such support to the Karen National Union/Karen National Liberation Army (KNU/KNLA); Chin National Front/Chin

National Army (CNF/CAN); Chin National League for Democracy (CNLD); Kayan New Land Party (KNLP); Arakan Liberation Party (ALP); Tibetan Mustangs; Cuban Alzados; and Karenni National Progessive Party (KNPP). Six days later he applied the exemption to nondesignated organizations (Tier III) if a totality of the circumstances justifies the exemption. See Exercise of Authority under Sec. 212(d)(3)(B)(i) of the Immigration and Nationality Act, Michael Chertoff, secretary of homeland security (Feb. 26, 2007), 72 Fed. Reg. 9954-58 (March 6, 2007) (series of notices).

83. Exercise of Authority under Sec. 212(d)(3)(B)(i) of the Immigration and Nationality Act, Michael Chertoff, secretary of homeland security (April 27, 2007), 72 Fed. Reg. 26,138 (May 8, 2007).

84. Ibid. This includes individuals who have provided material support to the Revolutionary Armed Forces of Colombia (FARC), the United Self-Defense Forces of Colombia (AUC), and the National Liberation Army of Colombia (ELN).

85. Material support—including voluntary support—may now be excused for individuals who supported the following groups (see www.rcusa.org/index.php?page=refugee-waivers):

- certain Hmong Refugees from Laos (who provided support to "certain Hmong individuals or groups" prior to December 31, 2004);
- certain Montagnards from Vietnam (who provided support to the Front Unifié de Lutte des Races Opprimées (FULRO) before December 31, 1992);
- the Arakan Liberation Party (Burma);
- the Chin National League for Democracy (Burma);
- the Chin National Front (Burma) and the Kayan New Land Party (Burma);
- the Karenni National Progressive Party (Burma);
- the Karen National Union (Burma);
- the Cuban Alzados (Cubans who supported armed groups opposing Fidel Castro in the 1960s); and
- the Tibetan Mustangs (Tibetans engaged in resistance against the Chinese).

However, any person who has actually taken up arms in support of any Tier III organization remains ineligible for admission. The person's spouse and children are inadmissible to the United States if the person has engaged in armed conduct within the past five years. See 8 U.S.C. § 1182(a)(3)(B)(iii)(IX).

86. Nezer, The Broad Scope, 5. There are now special procedures for adjudicating such cases. See Joseph E. Langlois, Chief, Asylum Division, Office of Refugee, Asylum, and International Operations, USCIS, HQASM 120/16.1, "Processing of Asylum Division Cases Involving Material Support" (June 1, 2007), reprinted in *Bender's Immigration Bulletin* 12 (App. E) (July 15, 2007): 924, 974.

87. See www.whitehouse.gov/news/releases/2008/07/20080701-1.html (accessed May 6, 2009). The politics of this bill might be gleaned from two pieces of legislation signed contemporaneously by the president: the "Fannie Lou Hamer, Rosa Parks, and Coretta Scott King Voting Rights Act Reauthorization and Amendments Act of 2006" and a law that authorizes the award of a Congressional Gold Medal to Edward William Brooke III.

88. See 8 U.S.C. §1158(b)(2)(A)(i) and 8 U.S.C. §1231(b)(3)(B)(i).

89. The Protocol relating to the Status of Refugees was opened for signature on January 31, 1967. *19 U.S.T. 6223*, T.I.A.S. No. 6577, 606 U.N.T.S. 267. It was ratified by the United States on October 4, 1968. 114 CONG. REC. 29,607 (1968). The Protocol expressly incorporates the terms of the Convention relating to the Status of Refugees, opened for signature on July 28, 1951, 189 U.N.T.S. 137. The preclusion is reiterated in the sections governing grants of asylum and withholding of removal. See 8 U.S.C. §§ 1101(a)(42) (refugee definition), 1158(b)(2)(a)(1)

(asylum bar for persecutors), and 1231(b)(3)(B)(i) (withholding of removal bar). It is, however, recognized as a crime against humanity. It is defined in the ICC statute as "the intentional and severe deprivation of fundamental rights contrary to international law by reason of the identity of the group or collectivity." Article 7(2)(g). See Pejic, "Article 1F(a): The Notion of International Crimes, in Exclusion from Protection," *International Journal of Refugee Law,* Special Supplementary Issue (2000): 41. See also M. Boot, R. Dixon, and C. K. Hall, "Crimes against Humanity," in *Commentary on the Rome Statute of the International Criminal Court, Observer's Notes Article by Article,* ed. Otto Triffterer (Oxford: Beck/Hart, 2008), 51–56.

90. *Ghaly v. INS,* 58 F.3d 1425, 1431 (9th Cir. 1995).

91. See former INA 241(a)(19); now at 8 U.S.C. §1227(a)(4). See Martin et al., *Forced Migration Law and Policy,* 382.

92. Displaced Persons Act of 1948 (DPA), 62 Stat. 1009; *Fedorenko v. United States,* 449 U.S. 490, 514 n34. The Court found that "an individual who did no more than cut the hair of female inmates before they were executed cannot be found to have assisted in the persecution of civilians." However, "persecution" was not ambiguous when applied to an armed camp guard "who was issued a uniform and armed with a rifle and a pistol, who was paid a stipend and was regularly allowed to leave the concentration camp to visit a nearby village, and who admitted to shooting at escaping inmates on orders from the commandant of the camp." Ibid.

93. *Fedorenko v. United States.*

94. "We refer to standard reference works such as legal and general dictionaries in order to ascertain the ordinary meaning of words." *United States v. Geiser,* 527 F.3d 288, 294–95 (3d Cir. Pa. 2008).

95. *Webster's Third New International Dictionary* (Springfield, MA: Merriam-Webster, 1981), 1685. The court noted that Black's Law Dictionary defines "persecution" as "violent, cruel, and oppressive treatment directed toward a person or group of persons because of their race, religion, sexual orientation, politics, or other beliefs," *Black's Law Dictionary,* 8th ed. (St. Paul, MN: Thomson West, 2004), 1178.

96. *Matter of Fedorenko,* 19 I&N Dec. 57 (BIA 1984); *Matter of Laipenieks,* 18 I&N Dec. 433 (BIA 1983).

97. *Negusie v. Holder,* 129 S. Ct. 1159 (March 3, 2009).

98. *Negusie v. Holder,* 1166.

99. But even there, some reviewing courts have differed, requiring at least proof of "active personal involvement." *Laipenieks v. INS,* 750 F.2d 1427 (9th Cir, 1985); see Michael J. Creppy, "Nazi War Criminals in Immigration Law," *Georgetown Immigration Law Journal* 12 (1998): 443.

100. *Matter of Rodriguez-Majano,* 19 I&N Dec. 811 (1988).

101. Guy Goodwin-Gill and McAdam, *The Refugee in International Law* (New York: Oxford University Press, 1996), 178.

102. UNHCR, *Handbook on Procedures and Criteria for Determining Refugee Status,* par. 155 (Geneva: UNHCR, 1979).

103. *McMullen v. INS,* 788 F.2d 591 (9th Cir. 1986).

104. *Dwomoh v. Sava,* 696 F. Supp. 970, 978 (D.N.Y. 1988).

105. "UNHCR Handbook on Procedures and Criteria for Determining Refugee Status under the 1951 Convention and the 1967 Protocol Relating to the Status of Refugees" (Geneva: UNHCR), 152. Two decades ago, the Ninth Circuit similarly developed a "balancing approach including consideration of the offense's 'proportionality' to its objective and its degree of atrocity." *McMullen v. INS,* 596, referring to Goodwin-Gill and McAdam, *Refugee in International Law,* 61.

106. Statement of the President of the Conference, Conference on Territorial Asylum, UN Doc. A/CONF.2SR.29, at 23, July 19, 1951, as cited in James C. Hathaway, *The Rights of Refugees under International Law* (Cambridge: Cambridge University Press, 2005), 224n226. See also Statement of Mr. Larsen of Denmark, Conference on Territorial Asylum, UN Doc. A/CONF.2/SR.24, at 13, July 17, 1951, in ibid., at 225n227. As the UNHCR Handbook states: "In applying this exclusion clause, it is also necessary to strike a balance between the nature of the offence presumed to have been committed by the applicant and the degree of persecution feared" (156).

107. U.S. statutory law, like Article 1(F) of the Geneva Refugee Convention, bars those for whom "there are serious reasons for believing that the alien has committed a serious non-political crime outside the United States." It applies both to asylum and withholding claims. Note that U.S. law also bars "those who have been convicted of a particularly serious crime in the United States" and those against whom there are "reasonable grounds for regarding the alien as a danger to the security of the United States." See 8 U.S.C. §1158(a)(2)(A)(ii); 1231(b) (3)(B)(ii).

108. 526 U.S. 415 (1999). The Ninth Circuit had held that a balance was required between the seriousness of the offense and the gravity of the persecution faced by the applicant. Further, the court held that a standard of whether the acts were "atrocious" was required, as was some consideration of "political necessity" and "success."

109. *Aguirre-Aguirre*, citing *INS v. Abudu*, 485 U.S. 94 (1988).

110. "The judiciary is not well positioned to shoulder primary responsibility for assessing the likelihood and importance of such diplomatic repercussions." *Aguirre-Aguirre*.

111. The BIA had rejected this approach and the Court held that "the BIA's reading of the statute . . . is the more appropriate one." See *In Matter of Rodriguez-Coto*, 19 I.&N. Dec. 208, 209-210 (1985).

112. *INS v. Cardoza-Fonseca*, 480 U.S. at 439n22 (quoting UN Handbook, at 1, P[ii]).

113. *Aguirre-Aguirre*, 526 U.S. 415, 428 (U.S. 1999); see also *T. v. Secretary of State for the Home Dept.*, 2 All E. R. 865, 882 (H. L. 1996) (Lord Mustill). ("The crime either is or is not political when committed, and its character cannot depend on the consequences which the offender may afterwards suffer if he is returned.")

114. See Deborah E. Anker and Michael J. Posner, "The Forty Year Crisis: A Legislative History of the Refugee Act of 1980," *San Diego Law Review* 19, no. 9 (1981): 13–14.

115. See David Martin, "Reforming Asylum Adjudication: On Navigating the Coast of Bohemia," *University of Pennsylvania Law Review* 138 (1990): 1247. Perhaps a better phrasing of this would be that it is a "supplementation" of broad categories of refugees to be admitted by governments according to various policy criteria.

116. Of course, an "asylum seeker" is simply a person with a claim to be a refugee. See Gibney, *Ethics and Politics of Asylum*, 10.

117. Martin, "Reforming Asylum Adjudication," 1278.

118. See, e.g., *Kalubi v. Ashcroft*, 364 F.3d 1134, 1137 (9th Cir. 2004). ("Asylum is a two-step process, requiring the applicant first to establish his eligibility for asylum by demonstrating that he meets the statutory definition of a 'refugee,' and second to show that he is entitled to asylum as a matter of discretion.") For a discussion of the various aspects of discretion in immigration law, see Daniel Kanstroom, "The Better Part of Valor: The REAL ID Act, Discretion, and the 'Rule' of Immigration Law," *New York Law School Law Review* 51 (2006–2007): 161, 167–80; Daniel Kanstroom, "Surrounding the Hole in the Doughnut: Discretion and Deference in U.S. Immigration Law," *Tulane Law Review* 71 (1997): 703, 731–51.

119. *INS v. Cardoza-Fonseca*, 480 U.S. 421, 428 n5 (1987); see also 8 U.S.C. § 1158(b).

120. "Address to the Members of the Volunteer Association and Other Inhabitants of the Kingdom of Ireland Who Have Lately Arrived in the City of New York, December 2, 1783." John C. Fitzpatrick, ed., *The Writings of George Washington* (Washington, DC: U.S. Government Printing Office, 1938), vol. 27, 254. Emphasis added.

121. The problem also appears, however, in the more concrete obligations that states have accepted to respect the right of a refugee against nonrefoulement (i.e., to be returned to any country where he or she is likely to face persecution, serious harm, or torture). See Article 33 of the Convention relating to the Status of Refugees, July 28, 1951 (entry into force, April 22, 1954); 189 U.N.T.S. 137; see also UNGA res. 8(1), February 12, 1946, para.(c)(ii) (accepting that refugees or other displaced person who express "valid objections" to returning to their countries of origin should not be compelled to do so). Although the assessment of whether a refugee is a "danger to the security of a country" is a task largely left to state authorities, the threshold for such a vague criterion must be very high if the nonrefoulement principle is to be respected. It should be recalled that some of the early drafters of what was to become Article 33 took a quite absolutist position on such issues. Louis Henkin, for example, stated that "no consideration of public order should be allowed to overrule that guarantee" (quoted in Goodwin-Gill and McAdam, *Refugee in International Law*, 204n14). See also Goodwin-Gill, 235–37.

122. Reportedly, a Hittite king of the second millennium B.C. proposed a treaty to another ruler that said, "I affirm on oath . . . when a refugee comes from your land to mine he will not be returned to you. To return a refugee from the land of the Hittites is not right." UNHCR, *The State of the World's Refugees: The Challenge of Protection*, 1993, 33, www.UNHCR.org/4a4 cbda96.html (quoted in Martin et. al., *Forced Migration Law and Policy*, 29). The Belgian Extradition Treaty of 1833 and the Franco-Swiss Treaty of 1831 are said to have been the first to embody the principle that political offenders should not be extradited. Paul Weis, "Recent Developments in the Law of Territorial Asylum," *Human Rights Journal* 1 (1968): 378. However, the practice is much older than that. See E. Reale, "Le droit d'asile," *Hague Recueil* 63 (1938-I): 473; A. Grahl-Madsen, "The European Tradition of Asylum and the Development of Refugee Law" in *The Land Beyond: Collected Essays on Refugee Law and Policy by Atle Grahl-Madsen*, ed. P. Macalister-Smith and G. Alfredsson (The Hague: Martinus Nijhoff, 2001); and Guy S. Goodwin-Gill and Jane McAdam, *The Refugee in International Law,* 3rd ed. (Oxford: Oxford University Press, 2007), 355.

123. UNCR, *The State of the World's Refugees*, 33. The Greek word *asylou* means a place that may not be violated, a sanctuary. Paul Weis, "Recent Developments," 378.

124. Wolff, *Jus Gentium Methodo Scientifica Pertreatatum* (1764), 147 (quoted in Goodwin-Gill and McAdam, *Refugee in International Law*, 355)

125. Goodwin-Gill and McAdam, *Refugee in International Law*, 355.

126. Paul Weis, "Recent Developments."

127. Article 14, para. 1. The conventional current formulation is that there is no individual right to asylum under international law, as contrasted, perhaps, with a right to nonrefoulement. See also Martin, "Refugee Concept."

128. See 8 U.S.C. §1158 ("Asylum procedures").

129. *U.S. Dep't of State v. Ray*, 502 U.S. 164 (1991). Emphasis added.

130. In the 1951 Geneva Convention relating to the Status of Refugees and the 1967 Protocol as transplanted to the U.S. Refugee Act of 1980. Refugee Act, Pub. L. No. 96-212, 94 Stat. 102 (1980) (defining a refugee as "any person who is outside any country of such person's nationality or, in the case of a person having no nationality, is outside any country in which such person last habitually resided, and who is unable or unwilling to return to, and who is unable or unwilling to avail himself or herself of the protection of, that country because of

persecution or a well-founded fear of persecution on account of race, religion, nationality, membership in a particular social group, or political opinion"). The Refugee Act also repealed geographical and political limitations on the asylum process, created a statutory right to seek asylum in the United States, eliminated numerical caps on yearly grants of asylum, and required that the attorney general establish procedures for asylum cases.

131. Arthur C. Helton, "Political Asylum under the 1980 Refugee Act: An Unfulfilled Promise," *University of Michigan Journal of Law Reform* 17 (Winter 1984): 243.

132. It is not my purpose in this chapter to critique fully the political-economic dichotomy or to grapple with its deep moral and legal problems. Among scholars, it has precious few defenders on the merits. But see Martin, "Refugee Concept" (arguing that the exclusion of protection under asylum law of disaster victims, socioeconomic migrants, and civil war victims may be justified because as an "entitlement system," asylum is not necessarily "indispensable for affording such shelter in these circumstances, particularly because the need for such haven is more reliably temporary.") The economic refugee is, of course, not the only gap in legal protection regimes. In recent years, hundreds of millions of people have been forcibly displaced as a result of conflicts, natural disasters, severe environmental changes, smuggling, human trafficking, and "development projects." Millions of others are "internally displaced persons," that is, persons who have been forced to flee their homes suddenly or unexpectedly in large numbers, as a result of armed conflict, internal strife, systematic violations of human rights or natural or man-made disasters, and who are within the territory of their own country. Sadly, the scope of human suffering around the world and the need for relief is incalculable, even as its victims remain largely unrecognized as refugees or as possessing any sort of a right to safe haven or protection. See Forced Migration Online, "What Is Forced Migration?" www.forcedmigration.org/whatisfm.htm (accessed May 13, 2009). As Andrew Shacknove wrote more than two decades ago, "neither persecution nor alieneage captures what is essential about refugeehood. . . . Persecution is but one manifestation of a broader phenomenon: the absence of state protection of the citizen's basic needs. It is this absence of state protection which constitutes the full and complete negation of society and . . . which justifies the persecutee's claim to refugeehood [and] the claims of person deprived of basic needs as well." Andrew Shacknove, "Who Is a Refugee?" *Ethics* 95 (1985): 274–84.

133. See, e.g., Goodwin-Gill and McAdam, *Refugee in International Law*, 16, noting how states have long limited the rights of "economic refugees" though the term "has long been disfavoured."

134. J. H. Simpson, *Refugees—A Preliminary Report of a Survey* (1938), 1 (quoted in ibid., 19; emphasis added).

135. See Act of March 3, 1875, ch. 141 §5, 18 Stat. 477. See Martin, Aleinikoff, Motormura, and Fullerton, *Forced Migration Law and Policy*, 74.

136. See Gibney, *Ethics and Politics of Asylum*, 143

137. Internal Security Act of 1950, Ch. 1024, §23, 64 Stat. 987, 1010. The 1952 Immigration and Nationality Act—the foundation of modern U.S. immigration law—adopted this phrase in its early development of nonrefoulement-type protections (also called "withholding of deportation" or "withholding of removal"). The current standard forbids removal to a country where the "alien's life or freedom would be threatened" because of the alien's race, religion, nationality, membership in a particular social group, or political opinion. 8 U.S.C. §1231(b)(3).

138. *INS v. Cardoza-Fonseca*, 480 U.S. 421, 436–7 (1987).

139. For a normative analysis of this divide that favors the political, see Gibney, *Ethics and Politics of Asylum*, 12 ("the needs of refugees . . . are more urgent than those of migrants escaping poverty . . . refugees have the strongest claim to our attention").

140. *Dwomoh v. Sava*, 696 F. Supp. 970 (SDNY 1988).

141. For an insightful treatment of this subject, see Walter Kälin and Jörg Künzli, "Article 1F(b): Freedom Fighters, Terrorists, and the Notion of Serious Non-Political Crimes," in "Exclusion from Protection," ed. Chaloka Beyani, Joan Fitzpatrick, Walter Kälin, and Monette Zard, special supplementary issue, *International Journal of Refugee Law* 2 (2000): 46; see also UNHCR, "Background Note on the Application of the Exclusion Clauses," *International Journal of Refugee Law* 15 (2003): 502.

142. *Matter of Izatula*, 20 I&N Dec. 149, 155 (BIA 1999). Carolyn Patty Blum, "License to Kill: Asylum Law and the Principle of Legitimate Government Authority to 'Investigate Its Enemies,'" *Williamette Law Review* 28 (1992): 719.

143. It should be noted in this regard that the entire enterprise of U.S. immigration law has long been a somewhat confused mix of legislative and executive power to which the judiciary pays great—sometimes virtually complete—deference. To be sure, this idea of plenary power has always been a very uneasy and rather unstable doctrine, especially when powerful human rights or separation of powers claims are involved. But it endures. See Kanstroom, *Deportation Nation*.

144. About 15,000 for Chinese processed in Hong Kong and 224 from the USSR. Helton, "Political Asylum under the 1980 Refugee Act," 245 (compiled from Schmidt, "Development of United States Refugee Policy," *INS REPORTER* [Fall 1979], 1–3); World Refugee Crisis: The International Community's Response, Report to the Committee on the Judiciary, 96th Cong., 1st Sess. 213 (1979).

145. The Cold War, for many, clearly legitimized ideological immigration laws. In fact, laws of exclusion and deportation had long been quite specifically ideological, barring anarchists and Communists. See Kanstroom, *Deportation Nation*, chap. 3.

146. It was embodied within the 1965 revisions to U.S. immigration law.

147. Also included were countries "within the general area of the Middle East." Immigration and Nationality Act Amendments of 1965, Pub. L. No. 89-236, §3, 79 Stat. 911, 913. See also the 1953 "Refugee Relief Act" (which had used a similar formulation for a limited number of escapees. See Philip G. Schrag, *A Well-Founded Fear: The Congressional Battle to Save Political Asylum in America* (New York: Rutledge, 2000), 24. Throughout this period, the statutes contained no special provisions for asylum seekers, who were handled under less formal administrative procedures that reflected similar biases.

148. Helton, "Political Asylum under the 1980 Refugee Act," 248.

149. Ibid., 249 (emphasis added).

150. Ibid. (emphasis added). The Department argued that "[otherwise] it would be entirely subjective with the alien claiming refugee status whether his fear of being persecuted was well-founded [or not]." See Western Hemisphere Immigration: Hearings on H.R. 367, H.R. 981, and H.R. 10323, before the House Subcommittee on Immigration, Citizenship, and International Law of the Committee on the Judiciary, 94th Cong., 1st and 2d Sess. 18 (1976) (quoted in Helton, "Political Asylum under the 1980 Refugee Act," 250).

151. See David Martin, "The Refugee Act of 1980: Its Past and Future," *Michigan Yearbook of International Legal Studies* (1982): 91–96; and Gibney, *Ethics and Politics of Asylum*, 151.

152. Helton, "Political Asylum under the 1980 Refugee Act," 251–52.

153. Ibid., 254.

154. Elizabeth G. Ferris, *The Central American Refugees* (New York: Praeger, 1987), 126.

155. See Gibney, *Ethics and Politics of Asylum*, 155.

156. See 55 *Federal Register* 30674–88 (1990), codified at 8 CFR § 208.1–208.31.

157. See Gregg Beyer, "Affirmative Asylum Adjudication in the United States," *Georgetown Immigration Law Journal* 6 (1992): 253; Gregg Beyer, "Establishing the United States Asylum Corps: A First Report," *International Journal of Refugee Law* 4 (1992): 455; Gregg Beyer,

"Reforming Affirmative Asylum Processing in the United States: Challenges and Opportunity," *American University Journal of Refugee Law and Policy* 9 (1993–1994): 43–78.

158. In January 1993 a Pakistani gunman killed two CIA employees in Langley, Virginia. A month later a car bomb exploded beneath the World Trade Center in Manhattan.

159. Approval rates also climbed and applications were adjudicated much faster.

160. Omnibus Consolidated Appropriations Act of 1997, Pub. L. No. 104-208, Div. C, 110 Stat. 3009-546 to 3009-724 (1996).

161. See United States Commission on International Religious Freedom, *Report on Asylum Seekers in Expedited Removal*, February 8, 2005, www.uscirf.gov/index.php?option=com_content&task=view&id=1892 (accessed May 13, 2009).

162. Bhikhu Parekh, "Finding a Proper Place for Human Rights," in *Displacement, Asylum, Migration*, ed. K. Tunstall (Oxford: Oxford University Press, 2006), 17–43.

163. Lavinia Limón, "A Race To the Bottom," World Refugee Survey 2008.

7

Closed Borders, Human Rights, and Democratic Legitimation

Arash Abizadeh

The world as we know it is divided into territorially bounded states, each of which has traditionally asserted the sovereign right coercively to regulate its own internal affairs, its relationships with outsiders, and the territorial and civic boundaries between the internal and external. According to the ideology of state sovereignty, internally, the state is the final and absolute political authority over its particular territory and its inhabitants; externally, the state is not subject to any other authority outside its own territory; and, concerning the boundaries between these two realms, the state has the sovereign right unilaterally to determine who may cross and under what conditions. The state is the final arbiter of internal, external, and boundary questions.[1]

To say that the state is the final arbiter of these political questions may imply that it has the authority to decide them according to its own will, independent of any moral criteria—that is, how it decides these questions is morally arbitrary. One of the most powerful challenges to this potentially decisionist feature of the ideology of state sovereignty has come from the liberal egalitarian tradition. Internally, liberal egalitarians have argued that respect for the moral freedom and equality of persons places moral limits on how the state may legitimately treat its own population. Liberal egalitarians initially formulated these limits in terms of individual natural rights, which later evolved into doctrines of human rights. Externally, these human rights were also thought to place moral limits on how the state could legitimately treat outsiders—for example, in war. And, finally, these rights came to be seen as placing moral limits on how the state could regulate its own boundaries—for example, in its treatment of refugees.

My focus here is on the third aspect of sovereignty, namely, boundary sovereignty. Liberal egalitarian critics have more recently gone well beyond the question of refugees to argue that respect for the freedom and equality of persons requires an interstate regime of borders open to almost everyone, either because of a basic human right to free movement or because of considerations of global distributive justice. I shall argue that these moral considerations do indeed speak powerfully in favor of borders considerably more open than the norm today. However, my thesis is that the liberal egalitarian discourse of human rights, no matter how radical in its critique of the ideology of state sovereignty, fails to address a crucial feature of this ideology. This is not to say that the discourse of human rights should be abandoned. Far from it: it is an invaluable component of an adequate critique of absolute sovereignty. The point is, rather, that it is not enough to engage in a substantive moral argument about what the state's moral duties are—for example, to foreigners. One must also address the procedural political question of who has the legitimate authority to decide what rights and duties to act on in cases of disagreement. One must address the jurisdictional question of who legitimately has the authority to determine the laws through which political power is exercised, whether internally, externally, or over boundaries.

Indeed, the claim that the state is the final arbiter need not imply the absence of external moral criteria concerning rights and duties. The ideology of state sovereignty may instead rest on a procedural-political claim about who has the legitimate authority to make the final judgment, in cases of disagreement, about what these moral rights and duties are and what they mean in legal and political practice.[2] This political dimension of the state sovereignty view is left intact by the liberal egalitarian doctrine of human rights. To challenge it, we must turn instead to a second, equally powerful critique of the state sovereignty view, namely, the democratic theory of popular sovereignty. While the liberal egalitarian discourse of human rights does indeed provide a moral vocabulary to critique today's relatively closed state borders, activists concerned with the injustices of the current Westphalian regime of border control must also address the legitimacy of the political processes within which foreigners' claims to free movement are adjudicated. It is true that challenging state control over boundaries by appealing to democratic theory may initially seem counterintuitive: The democratic principle of self-determination is often taken to imply the right of the democratic polity unilaterally to determine its own border policies, free from interference by outsiders and the moral demands they make. But this view rests on a mistaken reading of democratic theory. The democratic theory of popular sovereignty, I shall argue, denies that the state has the right unilaterally to control its own boundaries. Whether or not the right to free movement urged by some liberal egalitarians merits legal recognition, its legitimate recognition or denial must be the result of democratic processes giving participatory standing to the foreigners who assert such a right. The moral discourse of human rights cannot be pursued in isolation from a political discourse about democratic participation.

Citizenship: A Contrast with the Subject or the Foreigner?

The ideology of state sovereignty emerged in early modernity along with the absolutist state.[3] The point of legal and political institutions, according to the state sovereignty model, is to keep the peace; therefore, legitimate authority simply arises from the capacity to impose social order and protect from attack. Whoever has de facto power rules legitimately and ought to be obeyed.[4] It was very much against this ideology, which focused exclusively on the political obligations of the individual, portrayed as a mere subject of political power, that liberal egalitarian political ideology first emerged. Beginning with the assumption of the moral freedom and equality of the individual, liberal egalitarians have argued that the legitimate scope of political authority and obligation must be limited by terms reflecting the purposes for which free and equal persons would be motivated to join with others to cooperate in society. Those subject to political power do not merely have obligations, but also enjoy rights as members of political society.[5] They must also be recognized as rights-bearing citizens.

Two sets of rights were traditionally emphasized in the liberal tradition. Classical liberals, primarily concerned with the threat of coercion to individuals' freedom, emphasized civil rights enabling citizens freely to undertake contracts and protecting them from unwarranted interference by the state or others. Later, social liberals, primarily concerned with the threat of inequality to social justice, emphasized social (or socioeconomic) rights guaranteeing some minimum level of economic welfare and security, equalizing socioeconomic opportunities, and/or minimizing socioeconomic inequalities. Such rights, whether civil or social, imply significant moral constraints on state sovereignty, constraints that liberals sought to institutionalize via constitutional arrangements such as separation of powers and federalism, as well as constitutionalized rights protecting persons' status as citizens rather than as mere subjects. Moreover, although the liberal egalitarian challenge to state sovereignty initially emerged within the internal state context, and thus focused on the rights of the citizen within political society, in principle the recognition of the freedom and equality of persons committed liberal egalitarianism to the rights of man, or human rights—operative both within and across political societies.

As both the state sovereignty model and the discourse of human rights make clear, there is no conceptual link between the status of political membership and the enjoyment of equal rights as such. Indeed, one of the political achievements of the modern national state, reflecting the demand that subjects of political power be recognized as equal citizens, was to fuse the status of political membership and equal rights together in the single category of national citizenship. Prior to the Revolution of 1789 in France, for example, rights and privileges were attached primarily to class membership rather than political membership: French subjects did not enjoy equal rights, nor were foreigners necessarily denied privileges. The Revolution fused together political membership and equal rights. However, while this fusion in the status of citizenship ostensibly created a new internal realm of inclusion and equality, it also ironically simultaneously created an external realm of exclusion and inequality. For the citizen was constituted not only in contrast to the mere subject, but also in contrast to the foreigner, whose nonmembership ostensibly justified unequal treatment by the state.[6]

Liberal Egalitarian Arguments for Open Borders

The question is whether the coercive regulation of this distinction between citizen and foreigner—used to justify unequal treatment by the state, including regulation of entry into the state's territory—is fully compatible with the liberal egalitarian doctrine of human rights. According to this doctrine, there exist obligations owed to human beings either simply by virtue of their humanity or by virtue of relations that they share apart from membership in a common political society.[7] It is widely recognized, of course, that one function of human rights is to restrict the state's internal sovereignty. But the liberal egalitarian doctrine of human rights also clearly has implications for the state's boundary sovereignty, that is, its sovereign discretion over its own boundary laws. Under the overwhelming influence of the state sovereignty model, for example, customary international law traditionally held that emigration is a privilege at the absolute discretion of the sovereign state.[8] But for the liberal tradition, the right of exit has always been absolutely crucial for legitimating the state's exercise of power; the right of any person freely to leave a state's territory (and the right of a citizen freely to return to it) is today widely recognized and, indeed, enshrined in the 1948 Universal Declaration of Human Rights.[9] A more far-reaching moral constraint on the state's boundary sovereignty concerns the rights of refugees, namely, persons who flee their home and fear returning because of a threat to their life or some basic liberty. Many liberal egalitarians have argued that duties of humanitarian assistance morally require states to permit such persons entry to their territory. While this demand goes considerably further than the rights and obligations recognized by current international law and state practice, it is nonetheless still quite limited: it concerns only one specific class of foreigners.[10]

Yet the basis for such obligations and rights is, according to liberal egalitarians, the moral freedom and equality of *all* persons. Recently some have accordingly argued that the freedom and equality of each human being create a strong presumption in favor of opening borders to everyone. They argue, in other words, for a universal right of immigration, not just emigration. Two major arguments for open borders have been advanced, one appealing to the value of freedom, the other to equality. Both arguments begin with a simple empirical observation: that when the state closes its borders, it uses coercion, which inherently restricts persons' freedom. The second argument draws on a further observation: that in a world with extreme levels of material poverty and inequality, when a prosperous state closes its borders, it effectively uses coercion to protect the prosperity of its own citizens by depriving the worst off from opportunities to share in it. These observations are important because to say, as liberal egalitarians do, that all human beings are free and equal, is implicitly to question all coercively enforced boundaries that restrict freedom and entrench inequality.

Classical liberals focus on the first observation. Liberals typically argue that there are some basic liberties so fundamental to a free life that they can only be legitimately restricted for the sake of the basic liberties themselves.[11] These are the liberties that civil rights are designed to protect above all, such as freedom of expression. Freedom of movement is often thought to be one of these basic liberties, because without it individuals would not be able to pursue their own choices and projects about how to live; it is not only an important liberty in its own right, but a prerequisite to guaranteeing other basic liberties.[12] This is in part why, for example, liberal democracies typically recognize a civil right to free movement within their own territory. Hence, the first major liberal argument for a strong presumption in favor of open borders is that the same considerations justify a basic human right to free movement across state boundaries. Joseph Carens has argued that, because a basic liberty is at stake, states have a prima facie duty to keep their borders open to everyone; the only way border coercion could be justified is if it were for the sake of enhancing basic liberties themselves.[13]

If freedom of movement is indeed a basic liberty, and states have a corresponding prima facie duty to keep their borders open to all, then to resist the conclusion that states have an all-things-considered duty one must show that closing borders to some persons is in fact necessary for protecting some other basic liberties. So, for example, even domestically the civil right to free movement does not mean that a person can go just anywhere on the state's territory. For the sake of public order and security, which are necessary to protect basic liberties and civil rights as a whole, movement may be legitimately restricted (e.g., by traffic regulations). For the sake of protecting the right to free association, or property rights, or persons' capacity to engage in private contracts, free movement may also legitimately be restricted (e.g., a person cannot enter a home without the owner's permission). And so on. Similarly, it may be permissible (or even required) for some states to close their borders to some for the sake of protecting basic liberties themselves.

The question is whether any such basic liberties would be threatened by (more) open borders. Some have argued that given current levels of global economic inequality, if prosperous states were to open their borders to everyone, they might experience a massive, speedy rise in population levels, which in turn might lead to chaos and a general breakdown in public order. First, the sheer numbers may overwhelm the state's capacity to maintain security and protect the civil rights of those in its territory; second, the great number of poor immigrants could instigate a collapse of the domestic economy, which in turn would lead to more general chaos; and, third, the sheer numbers, and cultural diversity, of the new arrivals could overwhelm the society's capacity to integrate them, leading to social collapse.[14] The debate, therefore, turns on the empirical question of what levels of immigration the state could handle before nearing this threshold of collapse. I take it that today's prosperous states can afford vastly more open borders than is their current practice. (A similar argument points not to the numbers, but to potentially illiberal or subversive immigrants, who might effectively destroy the state's liberal institutions; the most extreme example is an immigrant intent on terrorism. The problem with this argument is that liberal egalitarian ideals normally forbid the state to curtail basic liberties on the basis of its evaluation of a person's character or intentions. As Philip Cole has pointed out, for example, a liberal state is not justified in expelling its citizens simply because it believes they are a threat.[15])

Critics of open borders, however, often go further, and simply deny that free movement across state boundaries is a basic liberty at all. Michael Blake, for example, has argued that the right to free movement only arises within a particular institutional context. The state must recognize free movement domestically as a basic liberty in order to justify its imposition of a coercive legal system on free and equal persons within its territory. Since the state does not coercively impose its legal system on outsiders, however, it has no duty to recognize their freedom of movement (into its own territory).[16] The difficulty with this account lies in explaining why, if what triggers the requirement of justification is state coercion, border coercion should be any different.[17] Other critics pursue a different strategy. A powerful justification for recognizing free movement as a basic liberty, after all, is that it is necessary for protecting individuals' freedom to choose and pursue their own projects from among an adequate range of valuable options. David Miller has argued, however, that except for cases where one's state of origin fails to provide these options (such as in the case of refugees and failed or tyrannical states), free movement within one's own state is sufficient to protect such options.[18] The difficulty with this argument arises from the fact that much of the world's population lives in states that do systematically fail to provide these options, an observation that points to the second major argument for open borders.

The second argument is made by social liberals who appeal to the values of equality and justice. Granting that interstate movement may not be a basic liberty, they nonetheless insist that, given the massive levels of poverty and inequality in the world and the failure of many states to provide their populations with an adequate range of valuable life options, prosperous liberal states in particular have a duty to keep their borders open to the global poor. Considerations of justice impose either a duty of humanitarian assistance in the face of great (and desperate) need or a duty to redress global inequalities. The duty arises because, according to liberal egalitarians, the state must recognize the equal moral worth of each person: The coercive restriction of individuals' freedom by the state requires a justification recognizing the inherent freedom and equality of all. Therefore, insofar as border coercion protects and entrenches global poverty and inequality, it is illegitimate.[19] Here, entry and/or membership are viewed not as something to which persons have a basic right, but as a valuable socioeconomic good that must be distributed according to global principles of distributive justice that concern either absolute levels of poverty or relative levels of inequality.[20]

One way to challenge this argument is empirically: It might be asked whether immigration is an effective means for combating global poverty. While Stephen Perry has argued that immigration may in some respects be more effective than direct foreign aid because it avoids the potential for bureaucratic inefficiencies or corruption associated with aid, James Woodward argues that open borders would fail to help those most in need because immigration is an option only for those with the financial means of leaving.[21] Indeed, it is possible that—because of the brain drain phenomenon—open borders would be positively detrimental to those left behind in impoverished countries. Others have argued, however, that the brain drain phenomenon, along with the possibility of emigration abroad thanks to education, simply increases incentives for education in the country of origin, and that any losses are offset by the phenomenon of family remittances. The World Bank estimates that officially recorded remittance flows to developing countries totaled $265 billion, or 2 percent, of Gross Domestic Product in 2007.[22]

Perhaps the more promising, or at least broader, challenge to the equality and justice argument is normative: a rejection of the assumption that states and/or their citizens are obliged (to foreigners) to reduce global poverty or inequality. According to Rawlsian social liberals, the point of principles of distributive justice, after all, is to regulate shared social or political institutions. Many Rawlsians have therefore concluded that unless persons share such institutions, they cannot have duties of justice to each other. Critics of global justice simply deny that the world's population shares the relevant institutions. Michael Blake, for example, has argued that the point of principles of justice is to legitimate coercive political institutions; that duties of justice consequently arise only between persons whose lives are regulated by shared coercive institutions; and that, since there is no global state, there are no global duties of justice.[23] Again, the challenge here is to show why the interstate system of border coercion does not qualify as the relevant kind of coercive institution, especially since a key function of such coercion is effectively to defend global inequalities. Alternatively, Samuel Freeman has argued that the point of principles of distributive justice is to regulate the distribution of goods jointly produced by social cooperation; that social cooperation only truly exists when there are shared sociopolitical institutions regulating the fundamental terms of cooperation; and that such institutions are confined to within states (or, at most, to within the European Union).[24] But the term "social cooperation" either refers to mere social interaction or, more strongly, it exists only when people interact on the basis of fair principles of reciprocity or justice. On the one hand, if social cooperation means mere social interaction, then today's levels of globalization seem enough to give rise to demands of justice.[25] On the other hand, if social cooperation means that people already are fulfilling their duties to each other, then it seems that the argument perversely implies that duties of justice arise only between people who are already fulfilling their duties to each other![26]

In any case, as even most critics of global justice are willing to concede, a liberal egalitarian doctrine of human rights does suggest that all human beings have a social right to minimum levels of material subsistence, so that citizens of affluent states have a duty to reduce extreme poverty abroad. More often than not, liberal critics of global justice simply wish to deny that citizens of affluent states have a duty to reduce inequality beyond such levels.[27] Yet given the appalling levels of global destitution, even this concession would seem enough to carry the second argument for open borders: states would have a prima facie humanitarian duty to open their borders not just to political or religious refugees, but to all economic (and even environmental) refugee candidates, that is, to all those who have fled their homes because their basic or fundamental human rights are at stake—a rather enormous number.[28] Critics of open borders would then need to show that such prima facie duties to foreigners, whether to reduce poverty or inequality, are overridden by other considerations in favor of closing borders.

Liberal Egalitarian Arguments for Closed Borders

For social liberals, the most important such consideration is the welfare state and the social rights it is meant to protect. At least three potential arguments for closed borders, grounded in welfare considerations, have been suggested. First, given the enormous levels of global inequality in our world, open borders would permit such massive levels of immigration to prosperous industrialized states that, as a result, their economies would collapse, destroying the welfare state's capacity to function. Second, even if prosperous states' economies survived, their capacity to sustain a welfare state would still collapse, or at least come under so much strain as to compromise the state's capacity to fulfill putative special responsibilities to its own current citizens (and perhaps residents).[29] Third, even in a world much more equal than our own, as long as there were no global state, open borders would unfairly disadvantage citizens of any state in which citizens pay into lifelong welfare schemes more generous than the global norm.

No state has a duty to adopt policies leading to the collapse of its economy. If open borders would lead to economic collapse, even the coercive exclusion of impoverished foreigners could be justified, consistently with the equal moral worth of all, because otherwise not only would native citizens suffer, but impoverished immigrants would find no relief either. Moreover, if opening borders would lead to the welfare state's collapse, then even if the duties of distributive justice were global in scope, closing borders could be justified to foreigners on the grounds that the long-term prospects for global justice depend on the consolidation (not destruction) and gradual expansion of existing social welfare institutions and social rights. Yet as Veit Bader has suggested, these justifications for closing borders would be consistent with respecting the freedom and equality of foreigners only if the states invoking them also discharge their obligations of global justice by other means (such as foreign aid).[30] Moreover, it is an open question whether opening borders would indeed lead to massive, stability-threatening levels of migration: Domestic fears over the rise of immigration triggered by more open borders are typically vastly exaggerated.[31] Furthermore, as Howard Chang has argued, as a matter of empirical fact, prosperous liberal states can afford to open their borders to vastly greater numbers of immigrants than they currently do, without the collapse of their economies or welfare state.[32] Indeed, given their ageing populations, it is arguable that the continuing prosperity of the industrialized economies in the North, and their capacity to sustain the welfare state, actually depend on permitting greater numbers of immigrant workers.[33]

Rather than arguing that open borders would lead to the complete collapse of the economy or welfare state, a weaker claim is that open borders would harm prosperous countries' impoverished native citizens. Poor immigrants would strain the welfare state's social services, or wage competition between migrants and poor native citizens would push the latter's wages down, or a large immigrant presence would decrease the political pressure for programs of distributive justice. Stephen Macedo has recently argued that these putative harms to the domestic poor justify closing borders because the state has special obligations for the welfare of its current citizens.[34] Yet even if it were true that greater immigration would weaken the political motivation for redistribution programs, Macedo's argument would still face several problems. One is that if immigration weakens such motivation because of some contingent fact about native citizens, such as their unjustifiable mistrust or dislike of immigrants, then the mere fact fails to provide a moral justification for closing borders.[35] (It provides, rather, a justification for policies designed to minimize anti-immigrant sentiment.)

But the main problem with Macedo's argument lies in his appeal to special obligations. Special relationships give rise to special obligations to favor the interests of insiders, in a manner compatible with the impartial recognition of the freedom and equality of all, only if they do not serve to reinforce—especially via coercion—preexisting inequalities in the distribution of resources between insiders and outsiders.[36] Yet this is precisely the condition that today's borders violate.[37] As Scheffler points out, the only way in which putative special obligations could rightly arise and persist, despite reinforcing inequalities, is if "those who are not members of the putatively duty-generating groups and relationships are given the opportunity to join and voluntarily decline to do so."[38] In other words, special obligations between citizens could only arise if they did not serve to reinforce preexisting inequalities or if the boundaries demarcating them were open.

Joseph Heath has advanced a third social liberal argument for closed borders. The welfare state is usually only able to recognize social rights and provide benefits, such as free universal health care or old age pensions, thanks to mandatory taxes paid by citizens (and residents). This is why welfare states directly tie the social rights of citizenship to the obligations of citizenship: Citizens who wish to live under an extensive welfare state must necessarily accept the collective burden of financing it. These obligations, moreover, are usually spread throughout the entire life cycle of a citizen: Young adults, for example, usually pay taxes at a rate much higher than the health care benefits they presently receive would warrant, but later in life, as senior citizens, they will receive health services much greater than the taxes they will pay. Annual contributions, in other words, do not directly pay for the services enjoyed that year.

The fusion of social rights and obligations in the status of citizenship, and the fact that the rights/obligations ratio varies greatly from one life stage to another, present a fundamental problem for open borders. If different polities adopted different tax and welfare regimes, open borders would create incentives for people to live their healthy and productive working years in polities with low taxes and minimal welfare services, and emigrate to a high-tax state with generous welfare programs in their hospital-prone and nonworking years. In other words, without a global federal state to enforce a global taxation regime, productive citizens living in states with generous welfare regimes risk becoming suckers open to interstate exploitation—even if we lived in a world without today's global poverty and inequalities. Therefore, Heath concludes, without a global state, open borders would be unfair to productive native citizens, because their lifetime contributions would be susceptible to exploitation by immigrants who benefit from the welfare state without having contributed their fair share.[39] The problem with Heath's argument, however, is that it wrongly assumes that justice requires social benefits be distributed only to those who have contributed to making them possible. Whatever the plausibility of this assumption for the issue of socioeconomic inequality, it has none at all for cases of poverty, destitution, and absolute need: Justice requires extending benefits to persons in dire need, even if they have not been able to make any earlier contributions (and even if other third parties have failed to do their fair share).[40] Given the levels of absolute global poverty, Heath's argument has minimal applicability to today's world.

Beyond protecting the economy or welfare state, some liberals have also argued that the state has a right (if not a duty) to close its borders to foreigners to protect the integrity of its citizens' culture. Will Kymlicka has argued, for example, that meaningful freedom or autonomy requires an adequate range of valuable options, and that a person's culture is the "context of choice" providing it: A culture is the source of beliefs about what is valuable and offers options corresponding to those beliefs. Therefore, closing borders is justified as the necessary means for protecting citizens' cultural "context of choice" from being submerged or destroyed by immigration.[41] But this argument has very limited application. Cultural change is a risk to individuals' autonomy only if the culture that provided them with valuable options is eroded *and* they are unable to assimilate to the new cultural forms replacing it, in the sense that they are unable to see the new cultural options as having value.[42] This disorienting, anomie-inducing form of assimilation generally occurs only in cases of very rapid assimilation or of assimilation through oppression. The argument therefore does not justify protecting citizens' culture from immigration-induced change per se, but only from rapid and disorienting, or oppressively imposed, change.[43] Michael Dummett has even argued that the only circumstance in which high levels of immigration might submerge a native culture in this way is when a political society is colonized or subjected to the rule of oppressive invaders, and never simply because of open borders.[44]

Democratic Arguments against Open Borders

In light of these empirical and substantive-moral considerations, I conclude that the liberal egalitarian doctrine of human rights demands boundaries vastly more open than the ones legally enforced by today's states. This conclusion will, of course, be merely one among many interpretations of the balance of moral reasons. Others, whether appealing to liberal egalitarian or other premises, will draw different conclusions. The crucial procedural-political question is who, in the face of disagreement about which laws should guide the coercive exercise of political power, has the legitimate authority to determine those laws. While the ideology of state sovereignty may claim that there are no substantive moral considerations that must guide the state's border policies, it also claims that, whatever the balance of moral reasons, the state has the legitimate, unilateral right (without the participation of outsiders) to rule on what these reasons are and determine its own border policies. The liberal egalitarian discourse of human rights challenges the first, substantive-moral, dimension of the ideology of state sovereignty, but it leaves intact the second, procedural-political dimension.

It is the democratic theory of popular sovereignty that challenges the state sovereignty view on this second, political dimension. Not the state, but the people is sovereign, according to democratic theory.[45] Like liberal egalitarians, democrats thus demand that those subject to state power be also recognized as citizens. But while liberal egalitarians have emphasized the civil and social rights of citizenship, the rights emphasized by the democratic model of citizenship are political rights of participation: According to this model, the citizen must not only be protected by the law, but actively engaged in formulating it.[46] The people subjected to political power must also be, in some sense, the author of the laws through which power is exercised. In the face of substantive-moral disagreements, laws are democratically legitimate insofar as they are the outcome of political procedures giving voice to those all who will be subject to them.

Despite their critique of the ideology of state sovereignty, however, partisans of the democratic model of citizenship have typically sided against liberal egalitarians who argue, on moral grounds, for open borders. These theorists typically advance two arguments: first, that closed borders are *instrumentally* necessary for ensuring the empirical preconditions of viable democratic practice; and second, that democratic self-determination *intrinsically* entails the unilateral right to control one's own borders, including the moral permission to close it to foreigners.

The instrumental argument, advanced by a number of authors, is that viable democratic practice requires a "community of character" with a shared national public culture, which would be undermined by open borders.[47] A shared national public culture is necessary either to effect social integration democratically, to ensure the levels of social trust necessary for democratic deliberation, or to ground a shared national identity necessary for democratic projects.[48] In my view, these points speak in favor of regulated immigration but are compatible with levels of immigration vastly higher than current practice. First, as I have argued elsewhere, democratic social integration, social trust, and shared identity are not dependent on a single national public culture in any thick sense of the term.[49] Second, even if democratic politics depended on a minimal level of cultural homogeneity, and even if this required state-sponsored policies of integration, such policies are not dependent on closed borders, as demonstrated by open borders within regionally diverse federal states or within a union of states. Third, even if democratic politics required policies fostering high levels of social trust, such policies are compatible with open borders, since well-designed sociopolitical institutions are perfectly capable of fostering such trust in contexts of diversity.[50]

The more fundamental argument is the intrinsic one that a democratic polity has the legitimate moral discretion unilaterally to determine its own border policies. This is not an argument for closed borders per se, but against the putative duty to open borders. The argument appeals to the democratic principle of self-determination, which follows from the doctrine of popular sovereignty. The doctrine that the people subject to the exercise of political power be able to see itself as the author of the laws through which power is exercised requires, as Frederick Whelan has put it, that "the operation of democratic institutions should amount to 'self-determination,' or control by the people over all matters that affect their common interests." Since the "admission of new members into the democratic group" counts as "such a matter" affecting "the quality of their public life and the character of their community," then self-determination grounds a polity's unilateral right to control its own boundaries.[51] This is why Michael Walzer has argued that "admission and exclusion . . . suggest the deepest meaning of self-determination."[52]

The question, however, is whether the distinction between citizen and foreigner, once it is coercively regulated by the state, is compatible with the democratic demand that those subject to state power be recognized as equal citizens. Implicit to the demand that subjects also be citizens is not only a claim about what goes along with being a citizen, namely a set of equal rights, but also about who *ought* to be recognized as a citizen, namely all those subject to the state's exercise of political power. Of course, even within so-called democracies, in practice there have been many historical examples (such as women and colonized persons) of subjects of political power deprived of full citizenship and the attending participatory rights. But future demands for further inclusion, as equal members of the people, could always be made by asking whether the currently constituted boundaries of citizenship were legitimate according to the normative aspirations internal to democratic theory itself, that is, whether the equation of subject and citizen had been fully realized in practice.[53]

The problem with the self-determination argument arises from the fact that, in one crucial respect, the state's enforcement of boundaries is different from any other instance of its exercise of political power. If the state exercises power over, and enforces its laws against, only those persons within its own territory, then at least in principle it can confine the scope of its power to its own citizens by recognizing the entire subject population as equal citizens. However, this is not possible, even in principle, if the state seeks coercively to enforce its territorial and civic boundaries against foreigners, that is, to regulate if and how foreigners can immigrate to its territory and/or naturalize as citizens. This is a unique conceptual feature of boundaries: Constituting and enforcing them always necessarily subjects both insiders and outsiders to the exercise of political power.[54] Call this the unboundedness of subjection. The question is how democratically to legitimate such an exercise of power, which subjects individuals to state power in the very act of constituting them as noncitizens who are deprived of the associated civil, social, or political rights.

In other words, when what is at issue are boundary laws, the appeal to self-determination begs the question of who the relevant collective self rightly is. Civic boundary laws are what provide the answer to who the collective self is; one cannot point to an already-existing collective self when the boundary laws themselves are in question.[55] Since the constitution and enforcement of boundaries is one of the most significant ways that political power is exercised over human beings, the boundaries of a democratic polity cannot be the taken-for-granted starting point of democratic theory, simply imported as is from history and exempted from the demands of legitimation. Insofar as boundaries are politically and coercively enforced on an ongoing basis, they are not prepolitical, historically given facts beyond the scope of democratic legitimation.[56] Insofar as boundaries are politically and coercively enforced, the democratic principle of legitimation requires that the laws by which they are enforced be the outcome of political processes in which those subject to the boundary laws enjoy a right of democratic say. Since boundary laws governing immigration and naturalization subject both citizens and noncitizens to the state's exercise of political power, from a democratic point of view both citizens and non-citizens ought to have a right of democratic participation in determining those laws. Insofar as a set of political rights are attached to the status of citizenship, of course, noncitizens will not enjoy the same political rights in the determination of a polity's laws; but in the case of its boundary laws in particular, given the unboundedness of subjection, political rights of participation cannot be tied exclusively to the bounded status of citizenship without violating the basic principle of democratic legitimation. To be democratically legitimate, regimes of border control must be democratically justified to all those subjected to them.[57]

Conclusion

The liberal egalitarian discourse of human rights provides a powerful critical tool for activists to address the injustices of the Westphalian regime of border control. According to the ideology of state sovereignty, which underwrites that regime, the state has full discretion to determine its own boundary laws—it is the final arbiter. The liberal egalitarian doctrine of human rights, I have argued, challenges this supposed discretion: Respect for the moral freedom and equality of persons, and the fundamental human rights that protect them, implies that today's states, particularly prosperous liberal states, have a moral duty to keep their borders considerably more open to foreigners than is the norm today. From a liberal egalitarian perspective, the coercive restriction of people's freedom to cross state boundaries faces a heavy burden of justification, a burden met only under restrictive empirical conditions. This is especially true given today's appalling levels of global poverty and inequality and the desperate threats to people's life, liberty, and security. Just how much more open borders must be, in light of human rights considerations, will depend on empirical circumstances. Since I have suggested that current circumstances justify at least some degree of closure, the question is *who* should be permitted entry; my argument suggests that those whose basic human rights are most urgently at stake have the strongest moral claims against prosperous liberal states.

I have also argued, however, that while the tools provided by the discourse of human rights (and state duties) are necessary, they are by themselves insufficient fully to address the shortcomings of the current interstate regime of border control. There are at least two major reasons—one instrumental, the other intrinsic—for why it is insufficient to make a substantive-moral case about what the state's moral duties to foreigners are. First, in order for moral rights and obligations to shape real-world state actions, they must find institutional articulation in legal and political structures. This, in turn, requires that those who defend such rights have political standing to be able to shape these legal and political structures. If those whom such human rights are designed to protect have no voice in the political process, it is that much less likely that these rights will find legal and political expression. Even if they did find political expression, such rights could easily be ignored by institutions democratically unaccountable to those who bear them. Moreover, the specific articulation of rights and obligations would in any case fail to reflect the particular needs, views, and experiences of those excluded from participation. As Brinton Lykes has emphasized in this volume, it is important for those who advocate on behalf of migrants to recognize them not merely as victims in need of rights protections, but as agents whose own participation is required to articulate, institutionalize, and implement those rights.[58]

Second, without the participation of those subject to political power in the determination of the laws by which power is exercised, such exercise will lack one of the most important grounds for political legitimacy in today's world: democratic legitimacy. Indeed, unless human rights find legal articulation via political processes in which those protected by them are able to participate, they may easily be dismissed by some as a foreign, culturally imperialist imposition. Regarding borders in particular, the democratic principle of legitimation, according to which all those subject to the exercise of political power ought to have a right of democratic say over how that power is exercised, requires that the laws governing borders be determined in political processes in which foreigners can participate.

This is not a call, however, for boundary laws to be determined by a simple majority vote of citizens and foreigners. Simple majoritarianism as a model of democratic politics is just as inadequate for boundary questions as it is for domestic politics: Democratic legitimation requires not just the participation of those subject to the exercise of political power, but participation on terms consistent with the freedom and equality of those subjects. The threat of majoritarian tyranny therefore rules out simple majoritarianism. The most plausible models of democratic legitimation take seriously the dual commitment to the democratic principle of popular sovereignty, on the one hand, and the rule of law, human rights, and group-differentiated rights on the other.[59] This means that political boundaries—namely, differentiated political jurisdictions—are crucial to democratic practice, and that citizens of different jurisdictions are not necessarily owed the same participatory rights in determining the laws that govern any given, particular boundary.[60]

Which particular cosmopolitan or transnational political institutions should be adopted depends heavily on the details of particular circumstances, but it goes without saying that today's state institutions would resist their development in any case. The question then is how an appeal to the discourse of democratic legitimacy could serve practical political purposes. The answer, at least in the short term, is that applying the principles of democratic legitimation to border questions may help to shape public opinion and the terms of public debate in liberal democratic societies. Migrant activists do not simply seek to influence state actors; they also seek to shape public opinion. Without mobilizing public opinion, it may be impossible to adequately defend migrants' rights in any case. Moreover, anti-immigrant populations in prosperous liberal countries are themselves often motivated by a sense of their own voicelessness and impotence in the face of larger social forces; they often fail to empathize with foreign migrants and migrants' human rights because they see themselves as the victims of migration. In part, this sense of helplessness and lack of empathy may arise precisely from the lack of common, democratically accountable political institutions in which each group's needs and fears could be articulated and negotiated. The discourse of democratic participation and empowerment might serve to address the needs and anxieties of both migrants and native citizens.

In short, border activists can ill afford to ignore the democratic supplement to human rights discourse. In the face of potential moral disagreement, one must go beyond substantive-moral questions and also address the procedural-political question of who has the legitimate authority actually to decide upon the laws that govern state boundaries. Not only must activists seek to ensure that states live up to their moral duties to foreigners in their border laws, they must also seek to reform the political processes by which those laws are determined. Foreigners, especially those most in need, have a right to help formulate the coercive laws that govern their lives. To treat foreigners according to terms over which they have no say should be seen for what it is: a profound compromise of a polity's democratic credentials.

Notes

For valuable comments, I am grateful to David Hollenbach, David Rasmussen, and participants at the Conference on Forced Migration, Center for Human Rights and International Justice, Boston College, November 20–22, 2008. I am also grateful to Oxford University Press for permission to draw on material from my "Citizenship, Immigration, and Boundaries," in *Ethics and World Politics*, ed. D. S. A. Bell (Oxford: Oxford University Press, forthcoming).

1. Hedley Bull, *The Anarchical Society: A Study of Order in World Politics* (New York: Macmillan, 1977), 8; F. H. Hinsley, *Sovereignty*, 2nd ed. (Cambridge: Cambridge University Press, 1986), 26; and Stephen D. Krasner, *Sovereignty: Organized Hypocrisy* (Princeton, NJ: Princeton University Press, 1999).

2. This was arguably Thomas Hobbes's view: The sovereign has "duties" but nonetheless, in practice, must be free from any earthly judge about what his duties are and whether he has lived up to them.

3. Quentin Skinner, *The Foundations of Modern Political Thought*, Vol. 2, *The Age of Reformation* (Cambridge: Cambridge University Press, 1978); Quentin Skinner, *Visions of Politics*, Vol. 2, *Renaissance Virtues* (Cambridge: Cambridge University Press, 2002), chap. 14.

4. A classic example of a model emphasizing de facto control is that of Thomas Hobbes, *Leviathan*, ed. by Richard Tuck (1651, Cambridge: Harvard University Press, 1996). On Hobbes's de factoism, see Kinch Hoekstra, "The *de facto* Turn in Hobbes's Political Philosophy," in *Leviathan after 350 Years*, ed. Tom Sorell and Luc Foisneau (Oxford: Clarendon Press, 2004).

5. A classic example is John Locke, *Two Treatises of Government*, ed. Peter Laslett (1690, Cambridge: Cambridge University Press, 1988).

6. Rogers Brubaker, *Citizenship and Nationhood in France and Germany* (Cambridge, MA: Harvard University Press, 1992).

7. On the contrast between these two alternative accounts of human rights, see Charles R. Beitz, "Human Rights and the Law of Peoples," in *The Ethics of Assistance: Morality and the Distant Needy*, ed. Deen K. Chatterjee (Cambridge: Cambridge University Press, 2004).

8. David C. Hendrickson, "Political Realism and Migration in Law and Ethics," in *Free Movement: Ethical Issues in the Transnational Migration of People and of Money*, ed. Brian Barry and Robert E. Goodin (University Park: Pennsylvania State University Press, 1992), 223–25.

9. Article 13 proclaims that every person "has the right to leave any country, including his own, and to return to his country."

10. The Convention and the Protocol Relating to the Status of Refugees (1951, 1967) only recognize as refugees those fleeing social and political persecution (not those fleeing famine, economic destitution, war, environmental disaster, or gender-based persecution) and who have already crossed a state boundary. (Under current international law, persons who have fled their homes but have remained within the territory of the state are labeled "internally displaced persons" rather than refugees.) Furthermore, rather than obliging states to take refugees in, the Convention and Protocol simply oblige them not to expel and return refugees who have already entered, back to the territory where their lives or freedoms are threatened. For criticism of the current interstate refugee-rights regime, see Michael Dummett, *On Immigration and Refugees* (London: Routledge, 2001); Robert McCorquodale, "International Law, Boundaries, and Imagination," in *Boundaries and Justice: Diverse Ethical Perspectives*, ed. David Miller and Sohail H. Hashmi (Princeton, NJ: Princeton University Press, 2001), 150–51. Drawing on Catholic social teaching, Christopher Llanos argues that a refugee should be defined as "any person who is the victim of ongoing basic human rights failures in her/his home political community for reasons other than involvement in criminal behaviour, for whom there is no reasonable recourse to that political community for redress of these failures, and who now wants to participate temporarily (e.g. until reasonable possibilities for redress in the home political community open up) or permanently in another political community." Christopher Llanos, "The Distinction between Refugees and Economic Migrants," in *Conference on Forced Migration*, Center for Human Rights and International Justice (Boston: Boston College, 2008). See also chap. 12 of this volume.

11. John Rawls, *A Theory of Justice* (Cambridge, MA: Harvard University Press, 1971); and John Rawls, *Political Liberalism* (Cambridge, MA: Harvard University Press, 1996), lecture 8.

12. Rawls, *Political Liberalism*, 335.

13. Joseph H. Carens, "Aliens and Citizens: The Case for Open Borders," *Review of Politics* 49, no. 2 (1987): 251–73; Joseph H. Carens, "Immigration and the Welfare State," in *Democracy and the Welfare State*, ed. Amy Gutmann (Princeton, NJ: Princeton University Press, 1988), 215; John H. Carens, "Migration and Morality: A Liberal Egalitarian Perspective," in *Free Movement: Ethical Issues in the Transnational Migration of People and of Money*, ed. Brian Barry and Robert E. Goodin (University Park: Pennsylvania State University Press, 1992).

14. For public order and civil rights, see Carens, "Aliens and Citizens"; and Carens, "Migration and Morality," 30; on economic collapse, see John Isbister, "A Liberal Argument for Border Controls: Reply to Carens," *International Migration Review* 34, no. 2 (2000): 630; for the emphasis on social integration, see Will Kymlicka, "Territorial Boundaries: A Liberal Egalitarian Perspective," in *Boundaries and Justice: Diverse Ethical Perspectives*, ed. David Miller and Sohail H. Hashmi (Princeton, NJ: Princeton University Press, 2001); Christian Nadeau, "Républicanisme, immigration, et design institutionnel," *Raisons politiques* 26 (May 2007): 83–100; and David Miller, "Immigrants, Nations, and Citizenship," *Journal of Political Philosophy* 16, no. 4 (2008): 371–90.

15. Philip Cole, *Philosophies of Exclusion: Liberal Political Theory and Immigration* (Edinburgh: Edinburgh University Press, 2000), 142–43.

16. Michael Blake, "Immigration," in *A Companion to Applied Ethics*, ed. Raymond Gillespie Frey and Christopher Heath Wellman (Oxford: Blackwell, 2003), 228–29; and Michael Blake, "Universal and Qualified Rights to Immigration," *Ethics and Economics* 4, no. 1 (2006): 4–5.

17. Arash Abizadeh, "Cooperation, Pervasive Impact, and Coercion: On the Scope (not Site) of Distributive Justice," *Philosophy & Public Affairs* 35, no. 4 (2007): 318–58.

18. David Miller, "Immigration: The Case for Limits," in *Contemporary Debates in Applied*

Ethics, ed. Andrew I. Cohen and Christopher Heath Wellman (Oxford: Blackwell, 2005), 196. See also Stephen R. Perry, "Immigration, Justice, and Culture," in *Justice in Immigration*, ed. Warren F. Schwartz (Cambridge: Cambridge University Press, 1995), 106–8.

19. Carens, "Aliens and Citizens"; Carens, "Migration and Morality."

20. James Woodward, "Commentary: Liberalism and Migration," in *Free Movement: Ethical Issues in the Transnational Migration of People and of Money*, ed. Brian Barry and Robert E. Goodin (University Park: Pennsylvania State University Press, 1992), 62.

21. Perry, "Immigration, Justice, and Culture," 103; Woodward, "Commentary," 64–65.

22. Dilip Ratha, Sanket Mohapatra, and Zhimei Xu, "Outlook for Remittance Flows 2008–2010," *Migration and Development Brief* 8, (November 11, 2008), http://siteresources .worldbank.org/INTPROSPECTS/Resources/334934-1110315015165/MD_Brief8.pdf (accessed January 15, 2009). For a survey of the literature and analysis of the impact of the brain drain and family remittances, see Riccardo Faini, "Remittances and the Brain Drain: Do More Skilled Migrants Remit More?" *World Bank Economic Review* 21, no. 2 (2007): 177–91.

23. Michael Blake, "Distributive Justice, State Coercion, and Autonomy," *Philosophy and Public Affairs* 30, no. 3 (2002): 257–96; and Thomas Nagel, "The Problem of Global Justice," *Philosophy & Public Affairs* 33, no. 2 (2005): 113–47.

24. Samuel Freeman, "Distributive Justice and *The Law of Peoples*," in *Rawls's Law of Peoples: A Realistic Utopia?* ed. Rex Martin and David A. Reidy (Oxford: Blackwell, 2006); and Samuel Freeman, "The Law of Peoples, Social Cooperation, Human Rights, and Distributive Justice," *Social Philosophy & Policy* 23, no. 1 (2006): 29–68.

25. Charles R. Beitz, *Political Theory and International Relations*, 2nd ed. (Princeton, NJ: Princeton University Press, 1999); and Allen Buchanan, "Rawls's Law of Peoples: Rules for a Vanished Westphalian World," *Ethics* 110 (July 2000): 697–721.

26. Abizadeh, "Cooperation, Pervasive Impact, and Coercion."

27. See David Miller, "The Limits of Cosmopolitan Justice," in *International Society: Diverse Ethical Perspectives*, ed. David R. Mapel and Terry Nardin (Princeton, NJ: Princeton University Press, 1998).

28. For the significance of basic human rights violations, including of social rights, see Henry Shue, *Basic Rights: Subsistence, Affluence, and U.S. Foreign Policy*, 2nd ed. (Princeton, NJ: Princeton University Press, 1996).

29. Robert E. Goodin, "If People Were Money . . . ," in *Free Movement: Ethical Issues in the Transnational Migration of People and of Money*, ed. Bryan Barry and Robert E. Goodin (University Park: Pennsylvania State University Press, 1992), 11.

30. Veit Bader, "The Ethics of Immigration," *Constellations* 12, no. 3 (2005): 331–61.

31. A good illustration of this was the consternation in the fifteen pre-2004 member states of the European Union over expansion plans in 2004 and 2007. Many feared that, because of lower wages and higher unemployment in the new Central and Eastern European member states, lifting migration controls would trigger massive labor migration to the more prosperous Western European states. As such, the treaties of accession permitted temporarily maintaining some restrictions against workers from states acceding in 2004 and 2007. Although most EU-15 states initially opted for transitional restrictions, some, facing labor shortages, did not, and by 2009 only four maintained them against the 2004 acceding states. The empirical evidence suggests that the ensuing labor migration had largely positive effects for EU-15 economies, and that in any case, there was considerably less migration than anticipated. Indeed, several reports concluded that there was little evidence of an expansion-induced surge in workers or welfare expenditures in pre-2004 states. Ray Barrell, John FitzGerald, and Rebecca Riley, "EU Enlargement and Migration: Assessing the Macroeconomic Impacts," *NIESR Discussion Paper*

No. 29 (March 2007), www.niesr.ac.uk/pubs/DPS/dp292.pdf (accessed January 20, 2009); European Commission, *COM(2008) 765: The Impact of Free Movement of Workers in the Context of EU Enlargement* (Brussels: Commission of the European Communities, 2008), http://ec.europa.eu/social/main.jsp?catId=508&langId=en (accessed January 19, 2009).

32. Howard F. Chang, "Liberalized Immigration as Free Trade: Economic Welfare and the Optimal Immigration Policy," *University of Pennsylvania Law Review* 145, no. 5 (1997): 1147–1244.

33. UN DESA, *Replacement Migration: Is It a Solution to Declining and Ageing Populations?* (New York: United Nations Department of Economic and Social Affairs, Population Division, 2001), www.un.org/esa/population/publications/migration/migration.htm (accessed May 1, 2009).

34. Stephen Macedo, "The Moral Dilemma of U.S. Immigration Policy: Open Borders versus Social Justice?" in *Debating Immigration*, ed. Carol M. Swain (New York: Cambridge University Press, 2007). See also Woodward, "Commentary," 69; and Isbister, "Liberal Argument for Border Controls."

35. Ryan Pevnick, "Social Trust and the Ethics of Immigration Policy," *Journal of Political Philosophy* 17, no. 2 (2009): 146–67.

36. This is because of what Scheffler calls the "distributive objection." Samuel Scheffler, *Boundaries and Allegiances: Problems of Justice and Responsibility in Liberal Thought* (Oxford: Oxford University Press, 2001), 74. See also Arash Abizadeh and Pablo Gilabert, "Is There a Genuine Tension between Cosmopolitan Egalitarianism and Special Responsibilities?" *Philosophical Studies* 138, no. 3 (2008): 348–65.

37. See Carens, "Immigration and the Welfare State," 219, 222, 227; and Bader, "Ethics of Immigration," 346.

38. Scheffler, *Boundaries and Allegiances*, 74.

39. Joseph Heath, "Immigration, Multiculturalism, and the Social Contract," *Canadian Journal of Law and Jurisprudence* 10, no. 2 (1997): 343–61. Heath also gives what I think is an additional but distinct argument: Even if in principle there are duties of global justice, these duties are conditional on some assurance that others are fairly living up to their global duties as well (such as opening their borders, providing foreign aid, etc.). Absent a global state, our duties are void, because otherwise we would be interstate "suckers." See also Joseph Heath, "Rawls on Global Distributive Justice: A Defence," in *Global Justice, Global Institutions: Canadian Journal of Philosophy Supplementary*, vol. 31, ed. Daniel Weinstock (Calgary, Canada: University of Calgary Press, 2005).

40. See Pablo Gilabert, "Contractualism and Poverty Relief," *Social Theory and Practice* 33, no. 2 (2007): 277–310.

41. For the "context of choice" argument, see Will Kymlicka, *Multicultural Citizenship: A Liberal Theory of Minority Rights* (Oxford: Clarendon Press, 1995), 83; Joseph Raz, *Ethics in the Public Domain: Essays in the Morality of Law and Politics*, rev. ed. (Oxford: Clarendon Press, 1995), 83–84; and David Miller, *On Nationality* (Oxford: Clarendon Press, 1995), 84, 146. For critical discussion, see Alan Patten, "The Autonomy Argument for Liberal Nationalism," *Nations and Nationalism* 5, no. 1 (1999): 1–17. For its application to borders, see Heath, "Immigration, Multiculturalism, and the Social Contract," 349; Kymlicka, "Territorial Boundaries."

42. Patten, "Autonomy Argument for Liberal Nationalism," 8–11. Furthermore, to warrant protection on grounds of autonomy, the culture in question must itself be a culture that values autonomy; otherwise, while the culture might provide valuable options to its members, it would nonetheless undermine the first and third conditions of autonomy. In other words, cultures that do not value autonomy would fail to foster "the range of capacities, self-understandings, and attitudes that they require to be in a position to shape and direct their

own lives" and would fail to protect individuals from coercion and manipulation should these individuals seek unorthodox life options (7).

43. Perry, "Immigration, Justice, and Culture," 95, 115; Bader, "Ethics of Immigration," 352.

44. Dummett, *On Immigration and Refugees*, 20–21.

45. For the contrast between state sovereignty and popular sovereignty, see Skinner, *Visions of Politics*, vol. 2, chap. 14.

46. For the three kinds of rights, see T. H. Marshall, "Citizenship and Social Class," in *Citizenship and Social Class and Other Essays* (Cambridge: Cambridge University Press, 1950). For the contrast between the liberal and democratic-republican models of citizenship, see Michael Walzer, "Citizenship," in *Political Innovation and Conceptual Change*, ed. Terence Ball, James Farr, and Russell L. Hanson (Cambridge: Cambridge University Press, 1989); Dominique Leydet, "Citizenship," *Stanford Encyclopedia of Philosophy* (2006), http://plato .stanford.edu/entries/citizenship/ (accessed August 5, 2008).

47. For variations of this argument, see Michael Walzer, *Spheres of Justice: A Defence of Pluralism and Equality* (Oxford: Blackwell, 1983); Frederick G. Whelan, "Citizenship and Freedom of Movement: An Open Admission Policy?" in *Open Borders? Closed Societies? The Ethical and Political Issues*, ed. Mark Gibney (New York: Greenwood Press, 1988), 29; Kay Hailbronner, "Citizenship and Nationhood in Germany," in *Immigration and the Politics of Citizenship in Europe and North America*, ed. W. R. Brubaker (Lanham, MD: University Press of America, 1989), 72; Kymlicka, "Territorial Boundaries"; and Miller, "Immigration," 199–200.

48. For these arguments, see Dominique Schnapper, *La communauté des citoyens: Sur l'idée moderne de nation* (Paris: Gallimard, 1994); Miller, *On Nationality*; and Miller, "Immigrants, Nations, and Citizenship." A similar argument is made by those who appeal to a civic republican conception of democratic citizenship. Civic republicans typically argue that, in addition to political rights, democratic-republican political participation requires civic virtues and a willingness to sacrifice for the common good; this public spiritedness, in turn, must be motivated thanks to high levels of social trust and a strong sense of patriotic identification with one's polity and fellow citizens. See Walzer, "Citizenship"; David Miller, "Bounded Citizenship," in *Cosmopolitan Citizenship*, ed. Kimberly Hutchings and Roland Dannreuther (New York: St. Martin's Press, Inc., 1999); Leydet, "Citizenship"; and Linda Bosniak, *The Citizen and the Alien: Dilemmas of Contemporary Membership* (Princeton, NJ: Princeton University Press, 2006).

49. Arash Abizadeh, "Does Liberal Democracy Presuppose a Cultural Nation? Four Arguments," *American Political Science Review* 96, no, 3 (2002): 495–509; and Arash Abizadeh, "Liberal Nationalist versus Postnational Social Integration: On the Nation's Ethno-Cultural Particularity and 'Concreteness,'" *Nations and Nationalism* 10, no. 3 (2004): 231–50. See also Andrew Mason, *Community, Solidarity, and Belonging* (Cambridge: Cambridge University Press, 2000).

50. On social trust, see Pevnick, "Social Trust." Furthermore, if high levels of immigration were a threat to integration, then one would expect the country, among prosperous democracies, with the highest rates of per capita immigration—Canada—to fare worst in measures of integration. To the contrary, on all relevant indicators, Canada fares extremely well and, indeed, better than other comparable countries in this regard. Ironically, it is Kymlicka who presents the evidence. Will Kymlicka, *Finding our Way: Rethinking Ethnocultural Relations in Canada* (Toronto: Oxford University Press, 1998), chap. 1. This evidence, however, must be weighed against Macedo's observation that immigration to Canada is tightly controlled, and that Canada picks its immigrants with an eye to social integration. Macedo, "Moral Dilemma of U.S. Immigration Policy."

51. Whelan, "Citizenship and Freedom of Movement," 28.

52. Walzer, *Spheres of Justice*, 62.

53. See Robert A. Dahl, *Democracy and Its Critics* (New Haven, CT: Yale University Press, 1989), chap. 9.

54. Arash Abizadeh, "Democratic Theory and Border Coercion: No Right to Unilaterally Control Your Own Borders," *Political Theory* 35, no. 1 (2008): 37–65.

55. This point is, of course, a variation of the boundary problem in democratic theory. See Frederick G. Whelan, "Prologue: Democratic Theory and the Boundary Problem," in *Nomos 25: Liberal Democracy*, ed. J. Roland Pennock and John W. Chapman (New York: New York University Press, 1983).

56. Sofia Näsström, "The Legitimacy of the People," *Political Theory* 35, no. 5 (2007): 624–58.

57. I have made this argument at length in Abizadeh, "Democratic Theory and Border Coercion."

58. For the argument that human rights must be articulated through democratic processes, see also Jürgen Habermas, *The Inclusion of the Other: Studies in Political Theory*, ed. Ciaran Cronin and Pablo De Greiff (Cambridge, MA: MIT Press, 1998).

59. As Jürgen Habermas has suggested, the principles of human rights and popular sovereignty are grounded in the same considerations and so in some sense are co-original. The realization of both principles is necessary for the exercise of political power to be consistent with respect for freedom and equality of all. Habermas, *Inclusion of the Other*, chap. 10.

60. This principle of differentiated participatory rights is already familiar to democratic practice from federalist arrangements, which grant differentiated participatory say to citizens of different regions or provinces, and from parliaments, in which rural electoral units are typically less populous than urban ones.

Part IV

Protection in the Face of Conflict and War

8

The Experience of Displacement by Conflict

The Plight of Iraqi Refugees

Maryanne Loughry

An anticipated consequence of the U.S. invasion of Iraq in 2003 was the displacement of a proportion of the Iraqi population. Population displacement and refugee movements as a result of conflicts have been known phenomena for much of the ancient and modern eras. In the last century the international community has put processes, legal instruments, and agencies in place to deal with such displacement. Today's question is, how adequate are these responses?

This chapter argues that the protection and assistance received by the vast majority of the forcibly displaced no longer meet minimum standards. It will examine the present-day international response to those displaced by the Iraqi war in an attempt to ascertain the characteristics of a contemporary displaced population, the needs of this population, and the responses available to them.

In recent times, even though the number of refugees (those people who cross borders because of a well-founded fear of persecution) is lower than in the 1980s, the United Nations High Commissioner for Refugees (UNHCR) has been called upon to provide assistance and protection to an increasing number of forced migrants, many of whom are outside the agency's original mandate.[1] Now more than ever, the world recognizes that there are mixed populations of forced migrants and complex explanations for the reasons these people have felt compelled to leave their homes. Current attempts to adapt existing responses to these newer displaced populations, as well as more familiar displaced groups, are stretched thin. Adequate responses are not in place when new crises erupt.

António Guterres, the United Nations high commissioner for refugees, has declared the twenty-first century the century of migration. It has begun with multiple patterns of movement and forced displacement, where the number of internally displaced people outstrips the number of refugees by more than two to one, and where an estimated 200 million people work in countries where they do not have citizenship.[2] The challenges of this reality are enormous, and existing institutions struggle to respond adequately to these people's needs. Arguably, it is the people on the move who can give us the best insight into the response required for those who are displaced and the yawning gaps that are opening up in these responses.

Forced Migration Today

More than a half century has passed since nations responded to events following World War II and established the office of the United Nations (UN) High Commissioner for Refugees as well as signing into effect the 1951 United Nations Convention Relating to the Status of Refugees to protect those who had left their country, fleeing persecution and war. Those who were not identified as refugees were seen to be migrants. While the definition has never been completely straightforward, there is now considerable complexity surrounding issues of who is a refugee, who lives in refugee-like settings but has not crossed a border, who is a forced migrant, and who is a migrant. Linked to the complexity of defining these groups of people on the move is the concern of who and which international agencies are responsible for assisting and protecting them. Many now argue that the concept of "refugee" is too limited and that the traditional distinctions between refugees, internally displaced people, and international immigrants have become blurred, given the realities of modern-day population movement.[3]

The roots of migration are multifaceted, with ever-increasing numbers of people being forced to move because of the growing links between a number of causes, including extreme economic deprivation, climate change and the resulting environmental degradation, and conflict. The majority of those who are forced to move today do so because of more than one of these causes, and in their various displacement settings they are frequently in dire need of protection and assistance; yet they are not, according to the 1951 Refugee Convention, considered to be refugees.[4]

The face of forced migration today is significantly different from the reality that was being addressed in 1951, when the Refugee Convention was drafted, and in 1969, when the international community last adopted a protocol that modified the way the Convention was to be interpreted in the light of the refugee reality at the time. In today's reality, four key factors shape contemporary experiences of forced displacement: the majority of those displaced are in refugee-like settings within the borders of their own country (internally displaced persons); those who do cross borders are rarely resettled in third countries; those in refugee settings are there for protracted periods of time; and in 2009 the forcibly displaced are more likely to be residing in urban settings than refugee camps.

Internally Displaced Persons (IDPs)

The nature of modern-day conflict has meant that millions of people are intimately caught up in, and experience firsthand, local and regional disputes. When forced to flee their homes because of the threats, violence, and loss of livelihood resulting from the conflict, the vast majority of the displaced population does not cross borders into neighboring countries but rather is forced to move to safety within its own country, frequently living with extended families and in refugee-like settings with few resources and limited protection and assistance. On its website, the Internal

Displacement Monitoring Centre estimates that there are presently 26 million internally displaced worldwide.[5] In the last two decades awareness has grown that there are greater numbers of internally displaced people than those who cross borders for protection and that there is a need to formulate a new response for this group of forced migrants. Such a response will require sensitivity to the fact that they are still within their own country but that their government is no longer able or willing to provide them with the necessary assistance and protection. In 1998 the protection needs of populations internally displaced were given recognition through the formulation of the *Guiding Principles on Internal Displacement*.[6] These *Principles* identify the rights and guarantees relevant to the protection of persons from forced displacement and to their protection and assistance during displacement as well as during return or resettlement and reintegration.

Convention Refugees

Those forced migrants who cross borders in search of protection nowadays find themselves in settings where the durable solution of resettlement is a very limited option and where return to their own country is not yet possible. Unlike previous decades, when countries such as the United States, Canada, and Australia resettled large numbers of refugees who had fled Communism and repressive regimes, resettlement quotas in these countries are now much smaller and targeted. In 1980 the United States, which has historically been the world's largest resettlement country, had a refugee resettlement ceiling of 231,700; by 2004 this had dropped to 70,000, while just over 40,000 were actually allowed entry.[7]

The 1990s was seen as the decade of repatriation rather than resettlement, with millions of refugees returning to their country of origin, frequently before all the conditions for a safe return had been met. This is still the reality in many countries throughout the world. One of the many examples is the plight of Afghan refugees repatriated to Afghanistan from Pakistan. Many have returned to very unstable situations that are exacerbated by severe drought and food shortages. In November 2008, during a visit to one of the camps in eastern Afghanistan where returnee refugees live, Guterres commented: "These are the poorest of the poor, the most vulnerable of the vulnerable."[8]

Protracted Refugee Settings

Without resettlement options and with home countries too unsafe to return to, many of today's forced migrants remain in protracted refugee settings. In August 2008 the website of the U.S. Committee for Refugees and Migrants (USCRI), a leading U.S. refugee advocacy agency, estimated that nearly seven million refugees have lived in refugee camps and segregated communities for over ten years. In these settings the refugees are frequently denied basic human rights, such as the right to earn a livelihood and freedom of movement and residence.[9] In recent years USCRI has referred to those who have been in such protracted refugee settings for more than ten years as "warehoused" refugees.[10]

In the twenty-first century, United Nations agencies and nongovernment organizations (NGOs) have been forced to undertake shifts in mandates in an effort to respond to present-day reality, especially with regard to the assistance and protection needs of the forcibly displaced. Notably, the office of the United Nations High Commissioner for Refugees (UNHCR) now works with refugees and with internally displaced persons as well. While internally displaced persons were not in UNHCR's original mandate, the international community has come to ask more of the agency because of its experience and on-the-ground presence. In recent years, UNHCR has actively assisted up to 13.7 million internally displaced, out of an estimated total of 26 million.[11] Additionally, again because of its expertise, especially in providing temporary shelter, UNHCR has also been called upon to provide assistance to populations displaced because of natural disasters, such as the tsunami that devastated Asia in December 2004. All of these requests and responses have not only reshaped UNHCR and its original mandate, but have also stretched the expertise and the response that the agency can now provide to different displaced populations.

At a more strategic level, the international community—as a result of all the changes that have occurred in forced migration settings—has developed what has become known as the "cluster approach" for responding to displaced populations that require immediate assistance. In the situation of internally displaced persons, this has meant that while mindful of the sovereignty of nation-states and the human rights of citizens, many conflict situations today frequently require a response by actors other than the state.[12] Usually under the coordination of the UN Emergency Relief Coordinator, UN agencies and NGOs are attempting to work together to develop a more comprehensive and coordinated response to emergencies, often regardless of the agency's primary mandate. Such a response has been seen to be necessary to address the complexity of today's population flows.[13]

Urban Refugee Settings

In recent decades, population growth, migration, and failing rural economies have resulted in the rapid growth of urban populations in the developing world.[14] Within these urban populations are more and more refugees, who in previous times would have resided in refugee camps. Many have come to urban settings, trading the assistance they receive in camps to escape the lack of opportunity in protracted refugee settings and to access resources that are available within the cities.[15] Frequently without work rights, these refugees reside in urban slum settings, eking out an existence in the informal economy. Within these urban settings the refugees frequently lack adequate protection. In places where they exist, the refugees seek help from NGOs that are mandated to provide legal and medical assistance and occasional material assistance in the form of clothes and food. There are many protection concerns for urban refugees who are vulnerable to labor and sexual exploitation; trafficking; and, in some settings, violent attacks due to xenophobia as well as a general shortage of resources available to the urban poor among whom they reside. In December 1997 UNHCR formulated an urban refugee policy. This policy is presently being revised by UNHCR. It is well recognized that UNHCR has neither the means nor the methods to respond to the protection needs of urban refugees. This is of increasing concern to UNHCR and other partner organizations, because it is now known that there are more refugees residing in urban settings than in dedicated refugee settings such as refugee camps. At the end of 2007, UNHCR estimated that 8.8 million, or 77 percent, of the world's 11.4 million refugees were residing in urban settings.[16]

Iraqi Refugees and Their Experience of Conflict and Displacement

Today there is no more powerful an example of the modern-day experience of displacement by conflict than that of the Iraqi people. Their situation very clearly illustrates the needs of those forcibly displaced and the challenges facing those attempting to address these needs.

The displacement that has resulted from the present war in Iraq is complex, the human costs high, and the humanitarian response inadequate. The Iraqi response is presently UNHCR's largest operation. Some 2 million of the 11.4 million refugees under UNHCR's mandate are Iraqi. These Iraqi refugees primarily reside in countries that border Iraq: Syria, Jordan, and Lebanon, although there are a number of Iraqis seeking asylum in industrial countries as well. Large in number and resulting from a highly publicized war, the Iraqi refugees' situation is seen to be dire and the response to their plight underresourced. One only has to look at the titles of recent reports by human rights groups reflecting on the Iraqi situation in 2008 to glean what significant human rights observers think of the failure by states and humanitarian actors to address the needs of those who have been forced to flee the Iraqi conflict: International Crisis Group's *Failed Responsibility: Iraqi Refugees in Syria, Jordan, and Lebanon*; Amnesty International's *Iraq Rhetoric and Reality: The Iraqi Refugee Crisis*, and Human Rights Watch's *From Exile to Peril at Home*.[17] All three human rights groups, as well as other experts in forced migration and human rights, have critically examined the plight of the Iraqi refugees and found it to be a crisis that is deepening and without an end in sight.[18]

Like many other displacement settings, Iraq has a history of displacement. Under the former regime of Saddam Hussein, one million people are estimated to have been displaced as a result of abuses.[19] Clearly the Iraqi people are no strangers to war, persecution, and displacement. As we all know, in March 2003 a multinational coalition force, primarily consisting of U.S. and United Kingdom forces, invaded Iraq ostensibly with the belief that Iraq had manufactured weapons of mass destruction that could be used against Western nations. At the time of the invasion, it was anticipated that there would be large flows of Iraqi refugees into neighboring countries. This was an expected cost of the war.

Humanitarian agencies waited on Iraq's borders, but the anticipated numbers of refugees did not arrive. Instead, tens of thousands were displaced internally through military activities and increasing sectarian violence. The displaced remained within Iraq, and it was not until the sectarian violence culminated in the bombing of the Shi'ite mosque in Samarra in February 2006 that neighboring countries came to receive the anticipated large numbers of refugees.

Some movement, however, happened earlier. In 2005, on account of the deteriorating security within parts of Iraq, significant numbers of Iraqis crossed into Jordan, and during 2006 and 2007 large numbers of Iraqis are reported to have continued to enter Jordan. In 2007 official estimates suggested that there were between 750,000 and 1 million Iraqis residing in Jordan. In the same year, the government of Syria reported that approximately 2,000 Iraqis were arriving each day.[20] The Syrian Arab Republic and UNHCR currently estimate that more than 1 million Iraqis are now living in Syria.[21] In 2006 the Iraqis became the leading nationality seeking asylum in industrial countries, with 22,200 Iraqis seeking asylum in Europe and other industrialized countries in 2006 and a further 19,800 in the first six months of 2007.[22] An additional 100,000 Iraqi refugees are in Egypt; 54,000 in Iran; 40,000 in Lebanon; and 10,000 in Turkey.[23] Within Iraq it was estimated that more than 700,000 people were internally displaced between February 2006 and March 2007. Overall, UNHCR estimated that in September 2007, over 60,000 Iraqis were being displaced from their homes each month.[24] The Internal Displacement Monitoring Centre estimates that in mid-2008 there were over 2.8 million internally displaced persons in Iraq.[25]

To put these numbers into historical context, the displacement of the Iraqi population in the last few years has been the largest population movement in the Middle East since the creation of Israel in 1948. More than 15 percent of Iraqis have left their homes.[26]

Responding to Large-Scale Displacement

Faced with such large-scale displacement of the Iraqi people and a sense that the emerging consequences of this displacement had not been appreciated, UNHCR convened an international conference in April 2007 to focus attention on the emerging humanitarian crisis in the Middle East. The conference had three aims: to sensitize the international community to the humanitarian impact, to seek commitments from the international community to address immediate and foreseeable needs, and to identify targeted responses to specific problems.[27] In his opening statement at the conference, the UN high commissioner for refugees spoke of how the massive displacement of the Iraqis had gone largely unnoticed because those displaced were not in visible camps but rather were housed in host communities in Iraq and in neighboring states, making for the largest urban caseload ever dealt with by UNHCR.[28] At the conference, the burden placed on the neighboring countries was emphasized, and members of the international community were asked to support countries that were shouldering the burden. UNHCR asked countries with resettlement programs to increase existing targets and to be more flexible in their selection criteria. Financial support and other forms of support from humanitarian programs were also sought from the international community. The countries hosting the refugees were asked to continue to provide an essential "protection space for the Iraqi refugees."[29]

When Nations Are Invited to Share the Burden

With 95 percent of those fleeing Iraq remaining in the Middle East, the emerging humanitarian crisis was located in countries that UNHCR perceived to have limited capacity to respond adequately for a sustained period of time. Both Syria and Jordan had initially opened their borders to the Iraqis, treating them as guests and not refugees. It is argued that both countries experienced positive impacts on their economy as a result.[30] The growing number of Iraqis began, however, to place considerable burden on services such as the health and education systems of the host countries. In Syria and Jordan, Iraqi children were given free access to public schooling, and while not all Iraqi families took this opportunity because of other costs such as uniform and school supplies, many classrooms were overwhelmed. Many Iraqis had already become familiar with the Syrian health system during the time of the sanctions on Iraq, but now more than ever they challenged the system by presenting special medical needs. Other pressures were placed on the host communities: Jordan reported water shortages, and Jordan, Lebanon, and Syria all experienced steep hikes in accommodation, fuel, and food costs. Some of these trends were consistent with international trends but were frequently attributed to the large numbers of Iraqis. All of these effects are thought to have contributed to growing animosity between the host communities and the refugees. Eventually the pressure became too much, and in 2007 Jordan closed its border to further Iraqis. Late in October 2007 Syria responded by placing visa restrictions on the Iraqi population, with the majority of refugees securing visas as a result of either serious medical conditions, their children being registered in Syrian schools, or themselves being registered with the Iraqi Chamber of Commerce.

As of 2009 the financial support requested from the international community has not materialized in the amounts required and pledged at the 2007 international conference. Considerable pressure has been placed on the United States to meet the shortfall and to fund the required humanitarian assistance because of the prominent role the country played in invading Iraq. Estimates of costs borne by the United States on the war per day have been compared to funds pledged to assist the Iraqi refugees, and many potential donors have waited for the United States to take a more significant lead in donating to asylum countries. There has also been mounting criticism that the Iraqi government has not done enough with its own oil revenues to alleviate the suffering of its people.

In the asylum countries, UNHCR and other humanitarian agencies have also struggled to respond adequately to the influx. The registration of refugees for assistance and protection has been extremely slow. In the UNHCR Global Appeal update 2009, UNHCR in Jordan estimated that in January 2009 it would be assisting 65,000 Iraqi refugees out of an estimated population of 450,000.[31] In February 2009, UNHCR in Syria reported the registration of 224,000 refugees from a population estimated to exceed 1 million.[32]

The total number of Iraqi refugees in the Middle East is contested. Some sources consider the governments' estimates to be inflated and others contend that given the size of the flows and the lack of computerized immigration systems, it is not possible to have a more accurate number. Regardless, in February 2008 António Guterres visited Syria, Jordan, and Iraq to see firsthand the plight of the Iraqis displaced by the war; he is reported to have stated at a meeting in Damascus with senior foreign diplomats that the actual numbers of refugees were of little relevance because UNHCR did not have adequate funds and resources to manage the caseload it had identified.[33]

In receiving states, the sheer volume of arrivals has placed enormous burdens on limited resources, and UNHCR has focused much of its attention on supporting government structures so that Iraqis could have access to public services including education, health, and other community services.

Protection in Urban Refugee Settings

The Iraqi refugees in the Middle East live in urban settings where they are dependent on their own savings or remittances from relatives in Iraq to survive. Of the 8.8 million refugees now residing in urban settings, 2.2 million are Iraqi.[34]

It is well known that assistance and protection for refugees in urban settings is a particular challenge, and one that UNHCR and most humanitarian agencies have struggled with. Recent surveys reaffirm that many persons of concern in urban areas do not have permission to work and do not receive basic assistance from the state where they have asylum, UNHCR, or other humanitarian agencies. Such situations result in cases of destitution, compounded by the political, economic, and social environment of the particular location.[35] The latest survey of Iraqi refugees in Syria found that 20 percent were living on less than one hundred dollars per month.

Most Iraqi refugees are living in rental accommodation in the suburbs of Amman and Damascus. They frequently share rooms with other Iraqi families and have increasingly limited capacity to pay the high rents that are demanded of them. They are prey to landlords who evict them with very short notice should another tenant with more money seek the same accommodation. Much of the accommodation is overcrowded, poorly heated or ventilated, and inadequately furnished. As the Iraqis run out of their own money, they are forced to move to smaller accommodation or accommodation that is on the edge of these cities. For registration and any other assistance, the onus is on the refugee families to travel to UNHCR and other humanitarian agency offices for assistance. This can be expensive and in some instances burdensome if there are elderly, children, people with disabilities, and female-headed households. Many Iraqi refugee families are afraid when moving around the city for fear of meeting former enemies or even former abductors. Communication with the refugees is through mobile phones, and many have inadequate information about the assistance they are entitled to and the role of agencies such as UNHCR. Information about resettlement options and return and visa requirements are peppered with misinformation and gossip. Many of the registered refugees are considered eligible for assistance, but limited funds have restricted what assistance can be given.[36]

In urban settings such as Amman and Damascus, the Iraqi refugees are less visible than in refugee camp settings, as they are dispersed throughout the suburbs. They blend with other Iraqis who have been in these cities since before the current war, and as their finances dwindle they are identified less as refugees and more as urban poor. The problems associated with registration and providing adequate assistance can result in increased poverty and isolation. Some Iraqi women and girls are reported to have resorted to commercial sex work in order to provide funds for their families, and there are reports of child trafficking. Since January 2008, UNHCR in Syria has identified more than 450 survivors of sexual, gender-based violence, the majority of whom have been identified at registration.[37] Women have reported rape, forced prostitution, trafficking, forced marriage, economic and sexual exploitation, and domestic violence. It is important to bear in mind that given the fact that only an estimated 20 percent of the Iraqi refugee population have been registered, these numbers are inevitably much higher. While a very sensitive topic in most countries, it is documented that Syria is a destination country for men from neighboring Middle East countries who are looking for the services of prostitutes. The involvement of Iraqi women and girls in prostitution in Syria is a concern for UNHCR and other international agencies. UNHCR is supporting safe houses in Damascus that are accommodating women and children who have experienced gender-based violence. Most of these safe houses are managed by local church organizations. International agencies are also accessing Iraqi women and girls who are in prison and juvenile detention centers on charges of prostitution. The Iraqi refugees are not formally allowed to work, although some do derive income from the informal work sector. Children are also reported to be involved in child labor. Many families have become more dependent on welfare from mosques and churches.

In recent years, refugee studies have made a significant shift from considering refugees to be vulnerable individuals to seeing them as a resilient group of people possessing agency. The challenge for the Iraqi refugees in the Middle East is whether the resilience they display can be sustained over time in such adverse settings.

In a January 2008 briefing in Geneva, UNHCR reported survey findings of Iraqi refugees interviewed while registering in Damascus between October 31 and November 25, 2007.[38] Everyone interviewed reported experiencing at least one traumatic event, and in 2007 one in five, or more than nineteen thousand refugees, have been registered as victims of torture and/or violence in Iraq. These statistics highlight the nature of the conflict that the refugees have fled and, more significantly, the pressing needs that they bring with them to the countries of asylum.

When registering in the Middle East with UNHCR, Iraqis are interviewed by national registration staff, many with limited training in identifying protection cases. The refugees themselves are not given advice on how best to present their situation. The waiting time for an interview for registration has varied from three months to one year, depending on the numbers of staff deployed by UNHCR. In recognition that some of the refugees may have urgent needs, a protection telephone hotline has been established in Syria, but it is staffed only during working hours and is frequently unavailable. This is a source of concern, given the vulnerability of the population and the recent nature of the events from which they have fled.

What Durable Solutions Are Available Today?

The Iraqi statistics only highlight the manifest needs of the Iraqi people in asylum countries. These statistics, however, only give us some of the picture because of the relatively few refugees who have registered; in August 2008 only three hundred thousand out of a possible 2 million were registered with UNHCR in the countries surrounding Iraq.[39] What is not known is the experience and needs of the Iraqi refugees who are fending for themselves without assistance.

Overall, while the situation in Iraq appears to have improved in recent months, UNHCR still considers the country to be too unsafe for return. In September 2008 UNHCR urged the European Union ministers of justice and home affairs, at their meeting in Brussels, to reaffirm their commitment to the protection of Iraqi refugees and to agree on the establishment of an EU resettlement program.[40] UNHCR had earlier reported that Iraqi asylum seekers had a very different recognition rate, depending on where they claimed asylum in countries other than the Middle East.

Between April 2007 and September 2008 only 14,600 Iraqi refugees were resettled from the Middle East. Some 60 percent of those resettled went to the United States. Clearly, resettlement is not going to be an option for most of the Iraqi refugees. While UNHCR has made valiant efforts to put forward Iraqi refugees for resettlement, quotas have been missed and refugees have experienced enormous delays due, in no small part, to the religion of most of them and concerns in the resettlement countries about the sectarian violence in Iraq spilling over into their own borders.[41]

It has also become clear that many Iraqi refugees will never be able to return to their homes. Displacement continues in Iraq. In September 2008 nine thousand Christians fled Mosul from what appears to be a concerted act of intimidation to remove Christian Iraqis from districts to which they had previously fled to for safety. In Syria large numbers of the Iraqi refugees are Christian and many believe they will be forced to remain in Syria because of the refashioning of many parts of Iraq along confessional lines.

The Face of Displacement Today

The landscape of refugees in the world has changed dramatically in recent decades, and states. UN and humanitarian agencies have struggled to keep up with these changes and to provide the responses that are demanded today.

As evidenced by the displacement following the war in Iraq, the level and cost of displacement is immense but not always immediately obvious, because the displaced people are more likely to move within their own country, reliant on their own resources, with very limited access to international protection and assistance.

The internally displaced are frequently displaced multiple times and only flee to neighboring states when they have exhausted the options available to them in their own country. It is now ten years since the establishment of the *Guiding Principles on Internal Displacement*. Walter Kalin, the UN secretary-general's special representative for the human rights of internally displaced persons, recently argued that before these guidelines were drawn up, internally displaced persons were neglected and not included in humanitarian programs.[42] The Iraqi cases show that the majority of those displaced by conflict today still do not have the assistance they require because of ongoing political instability and the limited access for international agencies in the countries of conflict. When the displaced do reach countries of asylum, they are now more likely to be in urban settings, where they struggle to make ends meet and frequently find themselves vulnerable to labor exploitation and poverty. While refugees have increasingly fled to urban settings in recent years, agencies such as UNHCR are still not adequately equipped to deal with such settings and are more accustomed to providing assistance programs in refugee camps. These urban settings of asylum are predominantly in developing and Middle Eastern countries with limited capacity to meet the needs of their own population.

While Jordan and Syria are not yet considered protracted refugee settings, UNHCR has identified an asylum fatigue in those nations.[43] Both countries are experiencing burdens on both economic and social structures. The Iraqi refugees are increasingly considering return to Iraq, not because it is now thought safe to do so, but because they have depleted their finances and can no longer afford to stay away from Iraq. Frequently, voluntary repatriation is the only option. Moreover, those who do return find themselves returning to cities that have been "carved into sectarian enclaves."[44] The displaced are often not returning to their previous homes, as these have been taken over or destroyed. In January 2008, Human Rights Watch interviewed Iraqis who had returned to Baghdad in late 2007 and found that they were now displaced again in Iraq, most living in rented accommodation in neighborhoods where they felt safe. When asked why they had returned, they cited the visa restrictions placed on them by the country of asylum and the legal ban on employment.

Regarding all refugees, few are resettled today, although in 2007 there was an increase in UNHCR resettlement submissions in response to refugees in protracted refugee settings.[45] In total, UNHCR made 99,000 resettlement submissions, and the actual number of departures to resettlement countries was just under 50,000. A quick examination of trends in refugee statistics shows that of the 11.4 million refugees, a small number will be resettled, a significant number will remain warehoused or in protracted refugee settings, and others will return to their own countries, often before conditions are safe. For the Iraqi population there is immense political pressure to declare the war over and the country stable. Presently, Iraqi refugees can remain in countries of asylum with limited funds and diminishing resources, or they can take their chances back in Iraq and either join the other Iraqis internally displaced or, in the rare exception, return to their own home.

Today's response to those displaced is clearly located within a political setting in which where a person comes from matters, and where a person goes counts.

Nations pledge to join with other nations to share the burden of the displacement. Frequently, however, these pledges do not materialize. UNHCR and other humanitarian organizations are stretched to assist and protect those under their mandate. In recent times, the number of people requiring protection and assistance under these mandates has increased, but the resources have not.

Overall, it is the displaced themselves who most heavily bear this reality. They actively engage with their setting and seek to find assistance in places that are best suited to them and their families. In settings of internal displacement and urban asylum, the displaced live in isolation, with limited dependence on each other and less reliance on humanitarian agencies. Much of the burden is placed on the economy and services of the state within which they are displaced. Over time they can be described as refugee, asylum seeker, urban poor, slum dweller, or economic migrant. It depends on the snapshot of time in which the displacement is examined and the political climate in which the displaced reside.

Notes

1. Susan Martin, "Rethinking the International Refugee Regime in the Light of Human Rights and the Global Common Good," in this volume.

2. António Guterres, "People on the Move: The Challenges of Displacement in the 21st Century" (lecture, Royal Geographical Society, London, June 16, 2008), www.theirc.org/uk/uklibrary/irc-uk-annual-lecture-2008.pdf (accessed November 19, 2008).

3. Ibid.

4. See the 1951 United Nations Refugee Convention: "Refugee: Any person who is outside any country of such person's nationality or, in the case of a person having no nationality, is outside any country in which such person last habitually resided, and which is unable or unwilling to return to, and is unable or unwilling to avail himself or herself of the protection of that country because of persecution, or a well-founded fear of persecution on account of race, religion, nationality, membership in a particular social group or political opinion," www.UNHCR.org/protect/PROTECTION/3b66c2aa10.pdf (accessed May 19, 2009).

5. Internally displaced persons are defined in the *Guiding Principles on Internal Displacement* as "persons or groups of persons who have been forced or obliged to flee or to leave their homes or places of habitual residence, in particular as a result of or in order to avoid the effects of armed conflict, situations of generalized violence, violations of human rights or natural or human-made disasters, and who have not crossed an internationally recognized State border." www.reliefweb.int/ocha_ol/pub/idp_gp/idp.html (accessed May 7, 2009). The Internal Displacement Monitoring Centre, www.internal-displacement.org (accessed March 3, 2009). UNHCR reported to the 2008 Executive Committee that there are presently 11.4 million refugees or persons in a refugee-like situation. The number of refugees rises to 14 million if Palestinian refugees are included. Palestinian refugees are assisted under the mandate of the United Nations Works and Relief Agency (UNWRA). UNHCR, "Note on International Protection," June 30, 2008, www.UNHCR.org/excom/EXCOM/488dd0e12.pdf (accessed November 19, 2008).

6. Office of the High Commissioner for Human Rights, "Guiding Principles on Internal Displacement" (February 11, 1998), www.unhchr.ch/html/menu2/7/b/principles.htm (accessed December 5, 2008).

7. Erin Patrick, "The U.S. Refugee Resettlement Program," *Migration Policy Institute*, June 2004, www.migrationinformation.org/USfocus/display.cfm?ID=229#3 (accessed December 5, 2008).

8. Adam Ellick, "Afghan Refugees Return Home to a Life of Desperation," *International Herald Tribune*, December 3, 2008, www.iht.com/articles/2008/12/03/asia/03refugees.php (accessed December 5, 2008).

9. U.S. Committee for Refugees and Immigrants, "Statement Calling for Solutions to End the Warehousing of Refugees," August 2008, www.refugees.org/uploadedFiles/Investigate/Anti_Warehousing/statement.pdf (accessed October 15, 2008).

10. Ibid.

11. UN High Commissioner for Refugees, "Note on International Protection," June 30, 2008. A/AC.96/1053, www.UNHCR.org/refworld/docid/486902122.html (accessed November 19, 2008).

12. UNHCR, "Internally Displaced Persons: Questions & Answers," www.hsc.usf.edu/nocms/publichealth/cdmha/toolkit_dm/Documents/PDF/UNHCR—Internally%20Displaced%20Persons.pdf (accessed November 19, 2008).

13. Ibid.

14. Loren B. Landau, "Urban Refugees," Forced Migration Online, February 2004, www.forcedmigration.org/guides/fmo024/ (accessed February 10, 2009).

15. UNHCR, "State of the World's Refugees 2006—Safeguarding Asylum," www.UNHCR.org/publ/PUBL/4444d3c32f.html (accessed February 10, 2009).

16. UNHCR, "2007 Global Trends," June 2008, www.UNHCR.org/statistics/STATISTICS/4852366f2.pdf (accessed February 10, 2009).

17. International Crisis Group, "Failed Responsibility: Iraqi Refugees in Syria, Jordan, and Lebanon," July 10, 2008, www.reliefweb.int/rw/RWFiles2008.nsf/FilesByRWDocUnid Filename/ONIN-7GELXM-full_report.pdf/$File/full_report.pdf (accessed November 20, 2008); and Amnesty International, "Iraq: Rhetoric and Reality: The Iraqi Refugee Crisis," June 15, 2008, www.amnesty.org/en/library/info/MDE14/011/2008/en (accessed November 20, 2008); and Human Rights Watch, "From Exile to Peril at Home," September 22, 2008, www.hrw.org/legacy/english/docs/2008/09/22/iraq19868_txt.htm (accessed November 19, 2008).

18. Expert research organizations such as the Brookings Institute and the Institute for the Study of Forced Migration, Georgetown University, have also researched the Iraqi refugee response.

19. International Displacement Monitoring Centre, "Challenges of Forced Displacement within Iraq," December 29, 2008, www.internal-displacement.org/8025708F004BE3B1/(http InfoFiles)/07A9E0C588CD5FECC12575240047DB82/$file/Iraq_Overview_Dec08.pdf (accessed February 9, 2009).

20. UN News Centre, "Spiralling Iraqi Refugee Problem Forces UN Agency to Double Aid Target," July 12, 2007, www.un.org/apps/news/story.asp?NewsID=23221&Cr=iraq&Cr1= (accessed February 12, 2009).

21. UNHCR, "2006 Country Operations Plan for Syrian Arab Republic," www.UNHCR.org/home/PROTECTION/43327caa2.pdf (accessed November 19, 2008).

22. UNHCR, "Statistics on Displaced Iraqis around the World," September 2007, www.UNHCR.org/cgi-bin/texis/vtx/home/opendoc.pdf?tbl=SUBSITES&id=470387fc2 (accessed November 20, 2008).

23. Nir Rosen, "The Flight from Iraq," *New York Times Magazine*, May 13, 2007, www.nytimes.com/2007/05/13/magazine/13refugees-t.html (accessed November 20, 2008).

24. Internal Displacement Monitoring Centre, "Challenges of Forced Displacement within Iraq," December 29, 2008, www.internal-displacement.org/8025708F004BE3B1/(http InfoFiles)/07A9E0C588CD5FECC12575240047DB82/$file/Iraq_Overview_Dec08.pdf (accessed May 14, 2009).

25. Ibid.

26. Nir Rosen, "The Flight from Iraq."

27. UNHCR, Proceedings of International Conference on Addressing the Humanitarian Needs of Refugees and Internally Displaced Persons inside Iraq and in Neighbouring Countries, April 17–18, 2007, Palais des Nations, Geneva, www.UNHCR.org/cgi-bin/texis/vtx/events?id=45e44a562 (accessed December 17, 2008).

28. "Opening Statement by António Guterres," in UNHCR, Proceedings of International Conference on Addressing the Humanitarian Needs of Refugees and Internally Displaced Persons inside Iraq and in Neighboring Countries, April 17, 2007, Palais des Nations, Geneva, www.UNHCR.org/cgi-bin/texis/vtx/events?id=45e44a562 (accessed November 20, 2008).

29. UNHCR, "Humanitarian Needs of Persons Displaced within Iraq and across the Country's Borders: An International Response," April 17, 2007, www.UNHCR.org/events/EVENTS/4627757e2.pdf (accessed December 15, 2008).

30. Patricia Weiss Fagen, "Iraqi Refugees: Seeking Stability in Syria and Jordan" (Washington, DC: Institute for the Study of International Migration, Georgetown University, 2007).

31. UNHCR *Global Appeal 2009 Update*, Iraqi situation, 247, www.UNHCR.org/publ/PUBL/4922d4230.pdf (accessed February, 10 2009).

32. UNHCR, "Syria Update," February 2009, www.un.org.sy/forms/publications/files/UNHCR_Syria_Update_February_2009.pdf (accessed March 3, 2009).

33. R. Comeau, personal letter to author, February 18, 2008.

34. UNHCR, Global Trends 2007, www.UNHCR.org/statistics/STATISTICS/4852366f2.pdf (accessed February 10, 2009).

35. See the recent study, "The Local Integration of Refugees in Belarus, Moldova, and Ukraine: A Strategy for Action," European Union 2008, http://soderkoping.org.ua/page17181.html (accessed November 19, 2008).

36. In May 2008 UNHCR was forced to admit that it was struggling to meet the needs of Iraqi refugees in Jordan and Damascus because of rising fuel and energy costs. UNHCR has only received half of the funds it requested for 2008. Rising food costs have meant that UNHCR has already had to reduce the size of food packages in 2008.

37. UNHCR, "Syria Update," August 2008, www.un.org.sy/forms/publications/files/UNHCR%20Syria%20Update_August%202008%20-%20FINAL.pdf (accessed October 18, 2008).

38. UNHCR, "The Iraqi Situation, 2007," www.UNHCR.org/cgi-bin/texis/vtx/iraq?page=briefing&id=4795e6222 (accessed October 18, 2008).

39. UNHCR, *Global Appeal Update 2009*, Iraqi Situation.

40. William Spindler, UNHCR spokesperson, "UNHCR Urges Reinforced EU Commitment to Protection of Iraqi Refuges," Briefing Note, September 23, 2008, www.UNHCR.org/cgi-bin/texis/vtx/iraq?page=briefing&id=48d8be5c6 (accessed October 18, 2008).

41. UNHCR International Protection note 2008 reports that UNHCR exceeded its target of twenty thousand submissions for 2007, although departures were significantly less, www.UNHCR.org/excom/EXCOM/488dd0e12.pdf (accessed March 3, 2009).

42. Walter Kalin, "Strengthening the Rights of Internally Displaced Persons" (speech, Brookings-Bern Project on Internal Displacement, October 16, 2008, Brookings Institute, Washington, DC), www.brookings.edu/opinions/2008/1016_internal_displacement_kalin.aspx (accessed November 19, 2008).

43. UNHCR, "Update on UNHCR's Operations in the Middle East and North Africa," Executive Committee 2008, www.UNHCR.org/excom/EXCOM/48dcfcd42.pdf (accessed September 22, 2008).

44. Human Rights Watch, "From Exile to Peril at Home: Returned Refugees and Iraq's Displacement," September 22, 2008, www.hrw.org/legacy/english/docs/2008/09/22/iraq 19868_txt.htm (accessed November 19, 2008).

45. UNHCR, "Note on International Protection," June 30, 2008, www.UNHCR.org/excom/ EXCOM/488dd0e12.pdf (accessed March 3, 2009). Protracted populations include 3 million Afghans in Iran and Pakistan, 336,000 Burundians in Tanzania, 192,000 Somali in Kenya, 162,000 Sudanese in Uganda, 160,000 Eritrean in Sudan, 125,000 Myanmarese in Thailand, 113,000 Angolans in the Democratic Republic of Congo, and 108,000 Bhutanese in Nepal (total of 4,196,000).

9

The Ethics and Policy of War in Light of Displacement

J. Bryan Hehir

The question addressed in this chapter is what are the challenges and implications for the just war ethic (JWE) arising from the human, moral, and political situations of refugees and internally displaced persons (IDP) produced by modern wars? To respond to this question, I will examine four themes: (a) the historical model of the JWE; (b) the development of doctrine in the JWE; (c) the reality of refugees and displaced persons; and (d) the rethinking (again) of the JWE.

The Historical Model: A Synthetic Statement

The JWE today appears, explicitly or implicitly, in a wide range of publications, policy debates, official documents, and military manuals of discipline and instruction. Often these contemporary uses of the JWE are made without attention to or awareness of the historical narrative that has brought the tradition to its present form. Intellectual and/or moral traditions are inevitably open to use in this fashion; their arguments have achieved the status of public property, and the understanding of them is often divorced from earlier formulations.

Since the specific purpose of this chapter is to ask if change, expansion, or reconstruction of the moral categories of the JWE is necessitated or warranted by the persistence of thousands of refugees and displaced persons issuing from wars across the globe, it is useful to survey the ways in which the ancient ethic (now spanning sixteen centuries) has developed in the distant and recent past. Such an approach requires a style that rightfully makes professional historians apprehensive, but it may provide resources for addressing a contemporary situation that is unlikely to be solved soon.

LeRoy B. Walters concluded his detailed textual study of the JWE with the guidance that it is best understood as a tradition of moral argument rather than a single theory.[1] The tradition admits of diverse theoretical statements best distinguished from one another rather than understood as a tight, parsimonious product. At the root of the multiple theories, however, lies a basic conviction that war fits within the moral universe, that in spite of its tragic character and consequences, war can be justified within stringently drawn conditions. The fundamental condition is that war be used in defense of multiple moral values. The shorthand formulation, war on behalf of justice, points to a broader range of values that legitimates the uniquely challenging action of the systematic, organized killing always inherent in the act of war.

From this basic assertion that some killings are not murder arises the corollary that many killings and many wars do not meet the standard of moral justification. Attending to this dual assertion of moral principle, the tradition of the JWE then builds a complex fabric of principles, rules, distinctions, and conclusions that shapes the contemporary statement of the ethic.

The development of the fabric of the ethic is commonly identified with (but not fully explained by) its association with key individuals. The position of Augustine (d. 430), a moderate realist reading of human nature and human history, joined with his moral understanding of war as a public, political act, established the early formulation of key categories in the ethic. War must have a just cause (a significant public harm that must be opposed for the good of the community) and a proper authority (those with the responsibility for the community). Augustine acutely joined these public arguments about war to an awareness of the powerful psychological forces at work that are catalyzed by warfare. The moral argument of right intention addressed both issues of motivation (war should not be fought out of hatred) and purpose (not revenge but the establishment of a just peace).

Aquinas (d. 1274) perpetuated Augustinian insights about the public character of justifiable violence, but he also opened consideration of the means of warfare in more detail than the Augustinian legacy provided. The most significant example of the means question is Aquinas's treatment of self-defense, which yielded the insight into the subsequently named principle of double effect, a modern staple for analyzing all uses of power. John Finnis's detailed treatment of Aquinas focuses extensively on his prohibition of the directly intended killing of civilians. James T. Johnson locates the defense of civilian life in a broader set of authors (including canonists and professional soldiers).[2]

By the end of the medieval period, the fundamental distinction in the JWE between just cause (*jus ad bellum*) and just means (*jus in bello*) is established. The priority lies with the *jus ad bellum* arguments, but changes in both politics and war by the seventeenth century made it increasingly difficult for either religious or moral authorities to enforce the complex just cause criteria. The new phenomenon of sovereignty, understood as the refusal by political leaders to acknowledge any superior authority or judgment over their decisions, made the task of moral restraint more complex and more difficult.

The transition from the medieval world to the modern world of sovereign states required one of the several developments in the just war tradition that has kept it relevant to the worlds of war and politics. The architects of the modern theory of JWE (Vitoria, Suarez, and Grotius) were not prepared to cede moral judgment to the claims of sovereign states, but they did focus new and detailed emphasis on the means of warfare, seeking to limit and humanize policies that sovereign rulers now believed were their right to employ solely in the interests of their state (*raison d'état*). The modern period (the seventeenth to twentieth centuries) filled out the basic structure of the JWE. Categories previously held but not elaborated (e.g., proportionality) and questions made more explicit by sovereignty (could war be just on both sides?) were examined in detail by modern moralists as well as legal scholars and secular philosophers.

By the mid-twentieth century, two characteristics were evident concerning the JWE. First, analytical developments had produced a more expansive and finely honed set of criteria; second, in the major wars of the first half of the century, the moral tradition was ignored and violated. The paradox was that a highly developed moral structure had been marginalized; it existed but exerted little impact on events.

The expanded criteria were summarized in diverse ways. The jus ad bellum contained just cause, right intention, last resort, possibility of success, and proportionality. The *jus in bello* consisted of the principle of noncombatant immunity and the rule of proportionality, along with the interpretive guide of the double effect.

The fact of two brutal world wars in Europe in fifty years and the stunning opening of the nuclear age at Hiroshima and Nagasaki catalyzed reflection about the absence of just war thinking in the first half of history's most violent century. One theologian in the United States emerged as a significant voice, but Reinhold Niebuhr did not use the JWE in his influential commentary on World War II and the Cold War era. Niebuhr was at best ambivalent about the value of the just war categories.[3] His abiding doubts about Natural Law ethics (the source of the JWE) and Catholic rationalism made acceptance of the just war ethic's clear lines and multiple distinctions (e.g., the double effect) very difficult for Niebuhr. Others saw in the tradition a way for serious moral reflection to reenter the debate about politics and strategy.

The two leading catalysts for renewal of the JWE were theologians: John Courtney Murray. and Paul Ramsey.[4] Beginning in the late 1950s, they sparked interest in the JWE inside and outside the Christian church. In turn they served as mentors for the next generation of scholars. James Turner Johnson brought the historian's eye for complexity, continuity, and discontinuity to the long just war tradition; James Childress found unused potential for renewing the tradition by invoking modern categories of ethical reflection; an ecumenical community loosely connected but whose members drew on each other's work created a new wave of scholarship from the 1960s onward. (Charles West, Max Stackhouse, Ralph Potter, David Hollenbach, John Langan, and Kenneth Himes all represented this second generation of modern research and writing.)

A unique contribution to the renewal of the JWE was the work of Michael Walzer.[5] Steeped in Western political philosophy, Walzer's style of analysis was to draw together principles of the tradition and illustrative cases that exemplified the tradition at work. His impact on the American academic community was unique. By the 1970s Walzer was joined by other scholars, principally international relations experts, who joined just war analysis with their empirically oriented work. (Joseph Nye, Stanley Hoffmann, Michael Howard, Lawrence Freedman, Robert Tucker, and Bruce Russett exemplified this contribution.) This diverse body (and many others) resorted to the JWE, but also interpreted it in different ways. In spite of differences in the historical, political, and strategic judgments they made, during the second half of the past century just war ideas were pervasively present in policy debates about war and peace. The capacity of the tradition for development was also evident. To that we turn.

Development of Doctrine: Within and Beyond the Classical Model

Since the ultimate objective of this chapter is to assess the capability of the classical model to respond to the refugee crisis, I wish first to summarize how the JWE has developed in the recent past. The nuclear age and cases of intervention called for development within the traditional ethic. More recently, developments have been proposed to expand the categories of the JWE beyond the tradition.

Development Within

The eruption of the nuclear age initiated by the atomic bombing of Hiroshima and Nagasaki in 1945 posed a quantitative challenge with qualitative consequences for the traditional ethic of war. The bombings of 1945 demonstrated an entirely new capacity of destructive power, sufficiently different from the past to challenge directly the central affirmation of the JWE, that the only morally legitimate war is a limited war.[6] The first group to grasp the empirical difference of atomic weapons was the community of scientists who produced them; Robert Oppenheimer, Hans Bethe, and Victor Weisskopf were among those who became early advocates for control of the new age and its weapons. Political analysts such as Bernard Brodie and Hans Morgenthau followed the scientists. The moral analysis of the significance of the new era came more slowly, taking substantial shape in the 1950s. Again, Niebuhr, Murray, and Ramsey led the way, each representing a distinctive style of analysis.

As the nuclear age moved beyond the bombings of World War II, its issues deepened in complexity. The capacity for destruction embodied in new weapons moved ahead in geometric progression. But the challenge was no longer simply the size or number of the weapons. New questions, with a paradoxical logic, were put to strategists and moralists alike. Historically, the JWE did its work when war was being actively considered or had begun. In the nuclear age the questions of moral legitimacy shifted from use to the complexities of deterrence theory. Now the JWE had to answer questions of both use and the highly structured threat to use. Among just war moralists three positions emerged. The first was held by those who had supported the JWE through World War II but became convinced on either proportionality or discrimination grounds that the only moral response to the use of nuclear weapons was to rule them out absolutely.[7] A second position focused on the intentionality embodied in deterrence theory, arguing that a murderous intent made deterrence effective and therefore made it impossible to defend.[8] A third position either ruled out or barely acknowledged justifiable use but sought to legitimate some forms of deterrence.[9] Consequentialist analysts using the JWE made a straightforward defense of deterrence as effective and necessary to forestall the ultimate evil of a nuclear exchange. Nonconsequentialists sought to draw a barrier against use as tightly as possible and then concentrate on targeting doctrines and war planning to rule out direct targeting of civilians.

In all of these statements of the JWE, the categories of the traditional doctrine were stretched to the limit. Clearly, the classical authors up through the 1940s had not encountered a problem of these new dimensions.[10] The three uses of just war previously outlined were not compatible; hence various authors were designated as giving up on the tradition or disfiguring it by accommodating the new realities of the age. Purely philosophical versions of the JWE could move toward a consequentialist reading more easily than Catholic theologians could; the consequentialist conclusions about deterrence reflected fairly closely the mainline position in the strategic community, namely that deterrence was a dangerous necessity yet the only viable stabilizing strategy for a world with thousands of nuclear weapons. The position that sought to prevent use and yet hold to a version of deterrence while maintaining the principle of discrimination as an exceptionless rule maintained continuity with earlier tradition but also embodied deep tensions in the categories of the ethic.

A more clear-cut example of development within the tradition arose in the post–Cold War period of the 1990s. The problem that evoked it was humanitarian military intervention. The cases extended from the Horn of Africa to Central Africa to the Balkans in Europe. The classical version of the JWE focused primarily on interstate warfare, particularly after the rise of modern sovereignty in the seventeenth century. The moral doctrine was reinforced by the United Nations Charter, which protected sovereignty, condemned interstate aggression, and prohibited military intervention among states except for the narrowly defined case of genocide.[11]

The post–Cold War decade saw multiple states erupt into political, ethnic, and religious violence. The casualties approached or even surpassed what cases of aggression had produced. But the very foundation of international order was grounded in sovereignty and nonintervention. A substantial division arose between the moral doctrine and the political-legal doctrine grounded in the charter and often reinforced by international law. From Somalia to Rwanda to Bosnia to Kosovo, moral arguments were made to employ force as a last resort.[12] But careful moralists recognized this legitimation of intervention as a high-risk strategy. The nonintervention principle fulfilled a valuable normative and political role in a world of almost two hundred sovereign states. To invoke intervention as a conclusion required moralists to provide a justification with a double purpose: first, to illustrate continuity with the moral tradition, and second, to provide a response the political-legal community was entitled to expect.

The development that occurred in the 1990s was essentially the reworking of the JWE to produce a theory of just intervention. Following the logic of just war, moralists began by affirming the value of the nonintervention principle but then relativizing it to the status of a presumption. Next, using the category of just cause, they specified which reasons could override the nonintervention norm. There was not a single consensual list of exceptions, but three seemed broadly supported: genocide (applied to Rwanda), ethnic cleansing (applied to Bosnia), and failed states (applied to Somalia). There were also differences. The first concerned the scope or scale of human rights violations that rose to the level of a casus belli. Beyond cause, there were debates about "proper authority": Did intervening states need UN authorization? What constituted "last resort" in intervention cases where delay could make success impossible? The question of *Jus in Bello*, which dominated the nuclear debate, was a secondary issue when intervention was the question. By the end of the 1990s, just intervention was a recognized category in the just war tradition.[13] Perhaps the best recognition of its standing as a moral theory was the way in which several of the basic just war categories were incorporated into the pathbreaking document of the International Commission on State Sovereignty and Intervention, *The Responsibility to Protect* (2001). This document redefined the meaning of sovereignty and recast the intervention debate from a right to intervene to a responsibility to protect (R2P). Its status is still fragile in the world of law and politics, but it has moved the debate on intervention to a new level of discourse. In many ways the development of the moral theory paved the way.[14]

Development beyond the Tradition: Pre- and Postbellum

The examples of adapting the JWE to the nuclear age and to issues of humanitarian intervention are what I call development *within* the tradition. In both cases, the classical model of just war categories was employed; the work of development involved refining the categories (to address deterrence theory) and restructuring the categories (to address intrastate war). I call the subject of this section development *beyond* the tradition because it raises the two areas now being examined widely that seldom were addressed in the classical model. Both of these areas, pre- and postbellum issues, are works in progress. My purpose is to use them as illustrative efforts that hold potential to engage issues touching upon refugees/IDPs in conflict situations.

First, I deal with prebellum issues. The phrasing here is my own and it is awkward. I use it to point to a body of work now being developed under the rubric of "peace building." Scott Appleby of Notre Dame University's Kroc Center has been deeply involved in this work. He describes peace building as "a broad range of activities, including conflict prevention and management. The transformation of conflict through mediation, the implementation of negotiated settlements and the longerterm building of civil society and democratic institutions; and, not least, 'second order' efforts, such as the building of human rights regimes and the promulgation of secular and religious laws and ethical traditions conducive to peaceful relations."[15] Appleby has a broad and deep understanding of the peace building scholarly community. His very description cuts across a vast and differential range of activities.

What does this add to or replace in the traditional JWE? The motivation behind this work is to prevent conflicts, particularly within nations, from rising to the level of war. In that sense it is prebellum, because it seeks to intervene before the *Jus ad Bellum* judgment would be made that war is legitimate, necessary, and the only means left to address conflicts in a society. This work, theoretical and practical, gained prominence in the 1990s when intrastate warfare was the source of much of the violence in the world, from Central Africa to southern Europe. Peace building seeks to join the resources of religious traditions with secular disciplines of conflict resolution, negotiation skills, and basic work of social transformation through socioeconomic and legal reforms in divided societies. Some of its theorists and practitioners are committed pacifists who find the JWE unsatisfactory as a normative guide. But others are not principally critical of the JWE; they simply want to restrict the full-scale resort to war as stringently as possible.

Peace building has similar characteristics to the work of preventive diplomacy, seeking methods of intervention and negotiation before the tipping point of violence. It would not be useful, nor do its advocates want, to fold peace building into the JWE. They in fact draw upon different sources in the Catholic tradition. Peace building is closer to Catholic social teaching as found in the papal tradition than it is to the moral categories used in the JWE. It is perhaps best to conceive of peace building and the JWE as correlative resources rooted in the Catholic tradition (but not only there) that can be used independently in situations of potential or actual conflict.

Second are postbellum issues. Discussion of a *jus postbellum* also has been catalyzed by the patterns of warfare in the 1990s. Internal conflicts, often involving strong ethnic, religious, and nationality factors, evoked debates about humanitarian intervention and produced ideas about *jus postbellum*. Michael Walzer, in a review of the JWE in 2004, wrote of "the need for an expansion of just war theory." He described it as a response to the wars of the 1990s and noted that "more work is necessary here, in both the theory and practice of peacemaking, military occupation, and political reconstruction."[16] Brian Orend responded to this call by devoting two chapters to *Jus postbellum* in his book *The Morality of War* (2006). In his chapter, "Justice after War," Orend focuses on war termination and the moral duties incumbent on those who have fought a just war.[17] He focuses his examples on interstate war and develops useful categories for framing the postbellum arguments. His range of considerations runs from proportionality to punishment of those guilty of war crimes to compensation and rehabilitation. As useful as his chapter is, I think it will take added reflection to deal with the duties that follow upon a just intervention in an internal conflict. Often the suffering and rehabilitation in these settings will require more extensive engagement by the wider international community than interstate war required in the past. Obviously, the gold standard of such international assistance was the Marshall Plan. This is unlikely to become the norm today, but something approaching it will be needed lest the original intervention be simply a destructive, wasted effort.

Refugees, Displacement, and War

The ethics of war must remain in constant contact with the facts of war. James Gustafson once wrote about the need to understand the empirical fabric of a problem before moving to moral analysis.[18] John Courtney Murray distinguished the *questio facti* and the *questio juris*; his meaning was that a clear understanding of the intricacies of a problem preceded moral judgment about it.[19] A basic theme of this volume is the search for systemic causes of and solutions to the problem of forced migration. War, in various forms, is a systemic problem of world politics, and war is a principal source of refugees in the world today. Both of these statements require elaboration.

The systemic character of war is rooted in the very nature of world politics. The international system since the seventeenth-century has been comprised of independent sovereign states. The system of states today is truly global in scope for the first time in world history. Sovereignty means the refusal to accept any superior authority—secular or sacred—over the status of the state. Precisely because all states possess the characteristic of sovereignty, the modern state system is described as "anarchic" in nature. The term does not mean constant chaos, but it does mean there is no legitimate, universally recognized center of authority in world politics. The corollary to this anarchic structure is that each state possesses the right of self-help. Since no higher authority exists that can guarantee the security of a state or its population, each sovereign state has the political-legal right to recourse to war under certain conditions. Those conditions, specified morally in the just cause criteria of the JWE, are set forth legally and politically in the UN Charter. The Charter and the organization of the United Nations itself have modified the anarchic character of the system of states up to a point. Conversely, the criteria of the charter are designed to restrict without denying the right of states to resort to force. On the other hand, the United Nations itself is not an authority over states but among states.

War, therefore, is a systemic problem because it responds to the very decentralized structure of world politics. In that sense it must be counted as one of the deep, systemic causes of forced migration. In addition, the evidence is clear that various forms of warfare in the twentieth century produced waves of refugees. Niall Ferguson, in his mammoth volume, *The War of the World* (2006) has described the last century as "the most violent in history."[20] The statement complements the title of a much earlier book by Raymond Aron, *The Century of Total War* (1954). These descriptions are readily employed and repeated in various forms because the past century and this decade have been permeated by various forms of warfare. Classifications abound, but a simple chart might identify two great wars (1914–18, 1939–45); the Cold War (1945–90), with its multiple subconflicts from Korea to Vietnam to Afghanistan; the four Middle East Wars; the Great Lakes War of Central Africa in the 1990s; the first and second Gulf wars; and the multiple intrastate wars that followed upon the collapse of the Cold War. The systemic reality of war has produced a worldwide pattern of forced migration.

Myron Weiner was one of the leading scholars of migration and refugee issues during his long career. In 1996 he published an illuminating article in the journal *International Security*, the foremost journal of political-strategic thought in the United States. Weiner distinguished five types of war and charted the refugees produced by them from 1969 to 1992. His five types included interstate wars, anticolonial wars, ethnic conflicts, nonethnic civil conflicts, and flight from repressive regimes. His aggregate statistics for these wars show that 1969 produced 9,756,000 refugees; 1982 produced 7,721,000 refugees; and 1992 produced 16,551,000 refugees.[21] Weiner cautions that such statistics are open to significant margins of error, and he specifies how each kind of war yielded different refugee flows. I have not found a comparable article tracking refugees and war in the period 1993–2008. But a broader generalization can be safely made. Weiner's study ended in 1992, just as the succession of intrastate wars of the 1990s was beginning. Save for the first Gulf War (1990–91), the dominant form of warfare in the 1990s was not war between states but within states. The fact that these explosions of violence occurred just after the end of the Cold War tempts one to a *post hoc, propter hoc* conclusion. One of the earliest of these wars, the Balkan conflicts of the 1990s, may well be traced to the collapse of the superpower pressures to keep Yugoslavia a single state throughout the Cold War, but there is no systematic evidence that the mix of ethnic, religious, and civil conflicts that erupted within states in the 1990s was caused by the collapse of the Cold War. Safe generalizations would be that (a) each had its own unique character; (b) the roots of each were distinct from the Cold War; (c) the Cold War may have intensified their character; and (d) the world paid more attention to these areas of conflict in Africa, the Balkans, and South Asia after the superpower nuclear rivalry was no longer on center stage in world politics.

However complex the causes of these conflicts were, the results in terms of refugees produced are clear and compelling. Two examples, continents apart and dramatically different in their demographics, their socioeconomic structure, and their cultural and religious composition exemplify the scale of the refugee crisis produced by warfare in the 1990s.

For Yugoslavia, Myron Weiner again is the source, this time in his 1995 book, *The Global Migration Crisis*: "The largest contemporary flow from successor states is from former Yugoslavia. . . . The disintegration of Yugoslavia led to a war in which the principal actors regarded the forced exodus of minorities as part of the process by which they created homogeneous ethnic states. The result was a massive exodus among the successor states. Croatia bears the burden of 425,000 refugees in a population of 4.5 million, but an estimated 425,000 refugees had also fled to other countries by mid-1992."[22]

For the Great Lakes area of Africa (Democratic Republic of Congo), the report of the United Nations high commissioner for refugees, *The State of the World's Refugees* (2006), summarizes the human cost of The Great War in Africa: "It is estimated that 3.5 million people have perished in Eastern Congo since 1998. . . . Furthermore according to UN estimates some 29,000–40,000 children soldiers have been recruited into the ranks of warring groups and more than 40,000 women have been victims of sexual assault. . . . Between 1999 and 2003 more than 50,000 people were killed and some 600,000 displaced in Ituri alone, with 10,000 refugees entering Uganda. The population displacement peaked in mid-2003, by which time a total of 3.4 million Congolese had been forced to flee their homes."[23]

These examples (in terms of numbers) in the Balkans and Africa, although extreme in numbers, were similar to multiple conflicts of the 1990s. The names are well known: Somalia, Rwanda, Sierra Leone, Liberia, and Kosovo. All of these intrastate conflicts produced refugee flows, IDPs, or both. To complete the general sketch of war and refugees/IDPs, however, we need to enter the first decade of the twenty-first century, when the September 11, 2001, attacks on the United States then led to war in Afghanistan and Iraq. These wars are perhaps best classified as interstate wars, but they also each have dimensions of internal ethnic and sectarian conflicts. Both have produced thousands of refugees and comparable numbers of IDPs within their borders.

A chapter with a different purpose could expand upon both the quantitative scope of the war–refugee relationship and illustrate aspects of similarity and difference in these multiple conflicts from 1990 to 2008. Having tried to highlight both the systemic roots of the problem in warfare and the connection between war and displacement, my more limited purpose is to connect key aspects of this survey with the systemic character of world politics today.

First, refugee flows are not unique to modern warfare; they have tragically accompanied war for centuries. But today the forced migration of people is one of the transnational characteristics of world politics. The large-scale movement of refugees is one dimension of an increasingly globalized market and globalized communication system. None of the wars of 1990–2008 had refugees as a primary object of concern, but unlike past ages, the world had multiple ways of knowing about this community of refugees, migrants, and IDPs. One could well say that given their suffering and their moral significance they did not get sufficient attention, but their fate has been made known and the cause of their suffering is identified. In principle this should make response to their needs more effective. In fact this often was not the case.

Second, the internal conflicts, either ethnic or civil (to use Myron Weiner's categories), that have produced refugees and IDPs forced to the surface of world politics the most substantial challenge to the classical concept of sovereignty in the modern era. The very factor that made concerted international action inadequate—respect for sovereignty—finally produced a systematic critique of this basic notion in the debates about humanitarian intervention.

Third, the wars of 2001–8 arising from transnational terrorist attacks were associated with a new challenge to security and order: nonstate actors with the capacity to produce violence akin to that generated by a sovereign state. This new threat on the world stage impacted the refugee question not only in the conflicts of the Middle East, but in the unwillingness of states to admit refugees seeking asylum into their countries.

The war–refugee nexus, therefore, encompasses transnationality, interstate and intrastate warfare, terrorist threats, and increased security measures within states. All of which render refugees more vulnerable.

Rethinking the JWE: Obligations to Refugees and IDPs

The ultimate objective of this chapter is to review, assess, and (if needed) reshape the JWE from the perspective of its potential impact on the status and welfare of refugees and IDPs. It is clear from the earlier parts of the chapter that change and development have been a characteristic of the just war narrative. Change has been the product of external forces along with internal review and restructuring of the

JWE. From Augustine through Aquinas, the normative focus of the ethic was on cause, authority, and intention. This reflected, in part, the ability of the Catholic Church to use the JWE effectively on the decisions of political leaders in a basically unified Christian empire and commonwealth. The focus of the ethic shifts in a post-Reformation world decisively shaped by consolidation of political power in the sovereign state. While the custodians of the JWE (both Catholic and Protestant authors) refused to simply endorse the sovereign's conception of the *droit de guère*, they were sufficiently acute politically to recognize that their primary leverage now rested with limiting the way war was fought. The rise of attention to the *jus in bello* criteria in the sixteenth and seventeenth centuries was later (as noted above) greatly intensified in the twentieth century in the face of wholly new forms of military power and technology.

Change is possible and has been effective in the just war history. How then shall the tradition evaluate the challenges posed for it by the evident moral urgency posed by the way war today can devastate the lives of refugees and IDPs? A synthetic snapshot of this problem is evident in the cases of war noted earlier in this essay. My purpose is not to provide a "thick" description of the plight of refugees and IDPs, but to move to normative reflection in light of their morally compelling situation.

The first question to ask, the question that arose in light of new political and military challenges in earlier stages of history, is whether the very architecture and structure of the JWE is appropriate to the challenge now faced. Since the very nature of the JWE is a *grenzmoral*, a "limit case" in the moral universe—barely moral, but moral—each new moral challenge to the doctrine will likely raise questions about the very premises of the doctrine itself. To be sure, the plight of refugees and IDPs will not be seen in the world of high politics as a challenge equal to the nuclear age, but in the normative order, built upon the unique dignity of every person, the suffering of refugees and IDPs must be given serious reflection. To test the ethic at its very foundation, one must begin with its essential premise. That premise locates war within the moral universe; it then states two corollaries. First, some uses of force are morally legitimate but not all. Second, the nature of the political order requires the possibility of using coercion to meet challenges to order and justice that no other political methods can address. These basic assertions are the core justifications supporting specified uses of force. They are grounded in three intellectual conclusions: a Christian realist anthropology, a consensual view of world politics, and a reading of history.

Christian realism is not simply an endorsement of the broader realist tradition; it is certainly not to be equated with Hobbesian realism. Augustine captured the realist conviction that sustained his ethic of war in the formula stating that war is the result of sin and the remedy for sin.[24] Even in the context of a world of grace, Augustine recognized the potential liabilities of a fallen nature and a fallen world: at the personal and societal level aggression was always possible. Hence restraint of aggression was necessary.

The consensual view of world politics is a secular contribution. It reduces to the assertion that the international arena is anarchic, devoid of a center of political authority. In that setting each sovereign state reserves the right to resort to self-help, the use of force when necessary to protect basic interests and values. In a world of self-help, an ethic of war that limits the use of force, but does not rule it wholly out of order, provides a strong but flexible framework for moral analysis.

The historical argument simply highlights the ever-present possibilities of both aggression and war. The record, sobering and sorry as it is, should not be taken as the best humanity is capable of, but it does reinforce the conviction that force in the name of justice is a justifiable conclusion.

The fundamental question is whether the JWE can still be an appropriate framework to evaluate war, given the plight of refugees and IDPs. The answer here is offered in the affirmative.

Having moved in this direction, the burden of proof of this conclusion devolves to an analysis of the constituent categories of the JWE, asking critically whether they take the basic realities of how war affects refugees and IDPs into consideration. The relevant categories to be examined are cause, last resort, and proportionality as well as means.

The relationship of the just cause category to refugees and IDPs can be examined in two ways: first, refugees as a cause of war, and second, refugees and IDPs as consequences of wars fought for other reasons. In the first instance the plight of refugees can serve as a compelling reason to justify the use of force by states as authorized by the UN Charter. The clearest case of this would be when refugees fleeing from a conflict within a state are identified as a threat to international peace and security. In such an instance, chapter VII of the UN Charter can be invoked to authorize collective action by states. Prior to the year 2000, such authorization by the Security Council was regarded as the sole justification for the international community to override the "domestic jurisdiction" of sovereign states. The latter phrase, found in Article 2(4) of the UN Charter, served as a partial barrier against measures used to pressure states on human rights grounds. These pressures—moral, legal, political, or economic—were regarded as having only limited legitimacy against the claims of a sovereign state to control events within its own borders. Until the 1990s the arguments about sovereign claims of domestic jurisdiction versus moral-legal claims made in the name of human rights against repressive regimes were overwhelmingly focused on nonmilitary measures. The outside pressures were the identification and documentation of human rights abuses, the shaming of states through publicity, the application of transnational pressure by human rights organizations, and various forms of economic sanctions.[25]

The explosion and implosion of states in the 1990s brought a qualitatively different urgency to the issue of human suffering and claims of sovereign autonomy. The conditions of open warfare within states, the cases of the collapse of civil authority, highly visible policies of ethnic cleansing and/or religious oppression, and the rising salience of thousands of refugees and IDPs created by these conditions pushed the international argument beyond shaming and sanctions to the question of military intervention.

There were two possible ways of approaching the legitimacy of military action. The first, already noted, was a UN Security Council finding that refugee flows were endangering international peace and security so that collective action under chapter VII of the UN Charter was justified and authorized. The point to be noted about the logic of this policy is that while refugees (not IDPs) were the "cause" of military action, they were not the primary political or legal consideration. The primary justifying factor was not the welfare of refugees themselves but the impact of refugee flows on other countries. True to the original logic of the UN Charter, the overriding of state sovereignty (in the country to be invaded) could be undertaken only in terms of international order and security. While the status and condition of refugees was morally recognized, their plight did not catalyze action.

The chapter VII argument was embedded in the UN system from the beginning, but it was not often invoked because of the challenge it posed to state sovereignty and the difficulty of gaining consensus in the Security Council. The 1990s brought new attention to the role of chapter VII but not a new argument about its content. Refugees were a factor in invoking chapter VII, but they were a *secondary* consideration to order and security.

A different way of understanding the plight of refugees and IDPs as a cause to justify the use of force was to consider them as the primary reason for action. The logic of this case was not dependent on refugee flows reaching such a proportion that international order was at stake. Moreover, this case allowed IDPs standing as a cause, something the chapter VII argument did not recognize, since IDPs remained within the state causing the refugee flows. The second case of cause was rooted not in the logic of the UN Charter but in the UN Declaration of Human Rights. It is the pre-2000 argument raised to a new level: the argument that force should be used against a state or a country because of the internal conditions existing therein. The chapter VII justification did not explicitly cover this case. But this is precisely the case that the responsibility to protect declaration is designed to address. It overrides domestic jurisdiction claims in the name of human rights. This constitutes development of doctrine within the political-legal order but is grounded in prior moral reasoning. The R2P argues that sovereignty itself is not simply to be understood as protection against outside interference by other states and/or international institutions. Rather, sovereignty involves the responsibility of states to guarantee basic human rights of citizens.[26] If such a fundamental responsibility is not being fulfilled, then other actors in the international system (states, international institutions, or both) become responsible agents to protect the basic rights of the citizens in question. The logic of the R2P position is to place primary weight on why refugees and IDPs are being created by the situation within a sovereign state. In this case the condition of the refugees and IDPs is the central finding to justify possible forms of intervention, not the threat to international order. The refugees/IDPs become the just cause for diplomatic, then military, action. It is important to stress that the R2P logic does not posit force as the immediate response to mass atrocities or less severe human rights abuses.[27] But it does include the possibility of such action, which is the point to make when considering refugees/IDPs as a legitimating cause of military intervention.

Refugees/IDPs understood as a consequence of war moves the just war analysis in a different direction. Refugees as a cause—those in need of defense or protection or protection or rescue—highlights the basic position of the JWE: some events or situations can justify war. But every war or intervention has drastic human consequences, intended and unintended. Indeed, one of the ways to understand the multiple criteria of the JWE beyond just cause is to see them as placing additional constraints on the right to war precisely because war is both a violent and unpredictable instrument of justice. Just cause by itself does not legitimate the use of force. Among the unintended but likely consequences of war is the creation of refugees/IDPs. Focusing on both the likelihood of this fact and the surge of refugees and IDPs produced by intrastate and interstate violence in the last half of the twentieth century moves the argument from why force should be used (refugees as cause) to why force should not be used (refugees as consequence). Refugees/IDPs who result from wars waged not on behalf of them but on other grounds are casualties of war. Since the historical record yields few instances of wars fought because of refugees/IDPs, it is likely that their fate, their status, and vulnerability would have little weight in why and how states would decide to undertake war.

The principal moral leverage of refugees/IDPs as casualties is rooted in the fact that the vast majority of them are civilians. Even if one presumes that these civilians were not the intended targets of attack, the sheer numbers of refugees/IDPs caught up in interstate and intrastate conflicts today requires specific, focused attention in weighing the moral calculus of war. Could the prospect of refugees/IDPs as civilian casualties of war be sufficient to override an otherwise just cause? In other words, would the prospective harm to refugees/IDPs be sufficient to forestall states from (a) resisting aggression across an international boundary (e.g., the First Gulf War) or (b) intervening to prevent severe human rights violations (e.g., ethnic cleansing)? In either case, the prospective damage to refugees/IDPs alone would seldom forestall an otherwise just cause argument. In a given case, combined with other factors, the status of refugees/IDPs could tip the balance on whether war should be undertaken. To conceive of how an argument could be made for the status of refugees as key to beginning a war, we should join a last resort and proportionality defense of refugees and IDPs.

The argument here is that an otherwise just cause exists to use force, but the prospect of refugees/IDPs as prospective casualties of war weighs against resort to force. Two preliminary conditions need to be addressed. First, both refugees and IDPs, as noted above, are part of the civilian population; the argument presumes that the state pursuing a just cause will not directly target *any* sector of the civilian population. Second, it must be recognized that beginning with World War II, where half of the casualties were civilians, the trend of an increasing percentage of civilian casualties has continued, particularly in intrastate conflicts characterized by religious, ethnic, and nationality conflicts. Any resort to force must address these two realities. Targeting civilians is always wrong; but civilians die in large numbers even if not directly targeted. These two propositions have been a part of the moral debate about war for over three decades. By themselves they have not led most supporters of the JWE to forestall a just cause argument for using force. The examples that illustrate these conclusions include the first Gulf War, Somalia, and Kosovo, among others.

The question asked in this essay is whether the plight of refugees/IDPs adds a unique dimension to the broader issue of civilian suffering in modern warfare. Using Myron Weiner's categories, it is clear that refugees are a constant factor in all forms of warfare (interstate wars, ethnic conflicts, civil wars, and persecution by authoritarian or revolutionary regimes). While the broader category of civilian casualties encompasses refugees, it is reasonable and useful to specify their status as a distinct cost of warfare. How might that influence a moral assessment of the use of force? The answer lies in using last resort and proportionality in tandem.

Both of these criteria yield important but usually less than definitive conclusions about the exercise of *jus ad bellum*. Both presume a just cause exists, and they provide guidance regarding how/whether the just cause should be pursued militarily. The "last resort" category is inherently imperfect in its guidance; Michael Walzer has expressed doubts about its normative value.[28] But if one begins the JWE with the understanding that the burden of proof rests on authorities beginning a war, then last resort functions as a test of the bona fides of the authority's claim that war is now truly the only means of redress. Walzer's critique of the category is that it can be used to make any resort to force impossible. If so, it is being badly used; when rightly used, last resort imposes both restraint and reflection about possible alternatives to force. By highlighting *how* war impacts refugees, one can provide a resource in determining whether reasonable means short of war have been exhausted and whether some uses of force will be more protective of civilians and refugees than others.

The consideration of last resort should feed into the judgment about Proportionality, another component element of *jus ad bellum*. This category can function in two ways prior to the decision to go to war. First, it asks what kind of force is appropriate for the threat posed by just cause. Second, what calculus of costs and benefits is being used in deciding upon war in a given case. This second judgment, a consequential calculus, is—like last resort—inherently less than definitive. But being forced to think through the proportionality test is part of what moral judgment adds to political-strategic calculation when deciding upon war. Proportionality is a richer moral category than last resort; it takes one more deeply into the specifics of what war will entail. It also can draw upon the lessons of similar uses of force in the past. Here is where the understanding of war and refugees as casualties of war can be included in the broader calculus of the moral decision to use force. The experience of the 1990s is particularly valuable; the combined categories of ethnic conflicts and civil conflicts throughout the decade provide concrete evidence of how these intrastate wars create refugees and IDPs; how these two groups remain unprotected and often uprooted after the conflict ends; and what the multiple costs—moral, human, financial, political—are when refugees and IDPs remain displaced in camps and without a stable future. A different essay focused on case studies of the aftermath of the 1990s would provide the raw material for proportionality judgments about war and refugees.

What impact might be expected of the combined resources of last resort and proportionality? First, while refugees/IDPs are surely among the most visible casualties of the kinds of war most likely in the world today (i.e., ethnic and civil conflicts), I am not sanguine that they will be treated as an independent variable in assessing the prospective costs of war. By this I mean that it is unlikely their prospective status could act as a veto over a broader decision that war is necessary in political-strategic terms. Second, I do believe that an argument made with solid and specific historical references and a detailed catalogue of the multiple ways war contributes to the plight of refugees/IDPs during war and in postconflict situations can be used to shape a broader political-moral argument about whether war is a wise choice in a given instance. In summary, refugees/IDPs can be made to count more heavily than in the past; they will count most effectively, I believe, as part of a broader fabric of argument joining Last Resort, Proportionality, and the fate of civilians in warfare. Given the way decisions about war are made, even when moral arguments are seriously considered, I do not believe refugees/IDPs will, by themselves, be the sole criterion of decision making.

Precisely because the urgent moral claims of refugees/IDPs are unlikely to provide the political-moral weight to prevent war in cases when a justified cause exists, it is important to focus on two moral questions: *jus in bello* and *jus postbellum*.

The *jus in bello*, the just means principles, can be invoked whether the protection of refugees is the cause of war or whether refugees will be threatened in wars fought for other reasons. In either case, scrutiny of the means of warfare can be heightened by paying attention to the threats posed to refugees. The basic imperatives can be stated simply. First, refugees/IDPs cannot be directly targeted in a conflict; second, refugees/IDPs must be part of the calculation of proportionality—even if the war is being fought on their behalf. Beyond these conclusions, more specific scrutiny should be given to how to protect refugees/IDPs caught in a conflict. Professor Barry Posen has pursued this question from the perspective of politics and strategy. Posen does not draw moral conclusions, but he seeks to balance the calls to use military force to address internal conflicts producing refugees/IDPs against the human costs of doing this.[29] One can feel in his article the burden of someone who knows the specific costs of war in detail. At best he is hesitant to conclude that war is an instrument suited to relief of refugees/IDPs. To be sure, he does not doubt that on both political and moral grounds they command the conscience of others to act. But he has doubts whether those who urge military action fully understand the risks entailed.

Two cases not discussed by Posen illustrate his well-founded restraint about simply endorsing the use of force: Kosovo and Darfur. In both instances, just cause for action by states and international institutions undoubtedly has been clear. In Kosovo, major military action was undertaken, and in the end, it contributed to a political outcome widely (if not universally) supported. Indeed, I advocated military action at the time, aimed at the Serbian state. But advocates of such action must at best acknowledge on proportionality grounds that bombing may well have increased the refugee/IDP numbers in the short term. As yet, I do not see reasons to reverse my initial judgment, but the mixed results of military action gives one pause. Therefore, the case of Darfur becomes a problem of both great clarity and some complexity. The clarity is the human suffering of a people that cries out for relief. There is no ambiguity about just cause for some action beyond what has been done thus far. The principal aggressor has been the Sudanese state, although conflicts among the groups in Darfur add to both the misery of the situation and the definition of who should be restrained. Multiple diplomatic, economic, and even peacekeeping measures have been tried, but the fundamental plight of the people of Darfur remains unaddressed.[30] The military option, beyond the methods of peacekeeping, has been urged. This exemplifies Posen's dilemma. It has been observed that there are three wars within Sudan: the North–South conflict, a challenge from militants in Darfur against Khartoum, and conflicts among the Darfuri militants. Military action has been most often urged against Khartoum for failure to protect its citizens, indeed, for orchestrating attacks upon them. Air power is usually suggested, to be used against the state.

Two questions remain: Will it be effective and will it intensify the North–South conflict? To the first, it seems unlikely that air power without a much expanded peacekeeping force would be sufficient. Expanding the latter before any decision on air power is taken is necessary. It might be that expanded peacekeeping forces might be sufficient in themselves. To the second, it is legitimate, given the costs of the North–South struggle, to weigh how actions in Darfur might reopen the worst of the prior conflict in the south of Sudan. Based on my limited reading of the case, I would not rule out military action against the Sudanese government, but the Kosovo case (plus the Iraq case) has enhanced my sense of restraint regarding the costs and benefits of major military action in a divided nation. Posen himself usefully outlines a series of measures that the military can undertake in defense of refugees/IDPs. They include safe zones (the geographical protection given the Iraqi Kurds after the first Gulf War), safe havens (a protected area, "a sheltered refuge" where "victims can flee their homes without fleeing their country"), and an enforced truce (the invading military create an area in a failed state where they are in control of law and order).

Posen identifies the tactical complexity of executing any of these options. His objective is clearly not to discourage rescue of refugees/IDPs, but to press advocates of military power to assess what will be needed, what capabilities are available, and what human costs will inevitably accompany the use of military power. I find this sobering analysis helpful and wise; I would not rule out the possibility and/or necessity of military action in specific cases, but Posen gives us excellent guidelines to assess Last Resort and Proportionality in cases of internal conflict.

Finally, a crucial resource in defense of refugees/IDPs is the newly initiated analysis of *jus postbellum*, identified earlier as one of the lines of development for the JWE. Any planning for intervention in an ethnic or civil conflict should include explicit plans for refugees/IDPs. The *jus postbellum* should include plans for which institutions are responsible for the living conditions, welfare, and future status of refugees. It should include measures to prevent the emergence in refugee camps of an insurgent military presence. And it should include some sense of a reasonable time frame for permanent settlement of refugees and resettlement of IDPs within the affected state. This is not an exhaustive list, but the concept of *jus postbellum* places on the agenda of a just war the opportunity to focus on the needs of refugees/ IDPs before they are lost on the world's radar screen.

Conclusions: Questions, Objections, and Recommendations

Faced with the compelling fact of refugees and IDPs as one of the major consequences of war in the world today, this chapter has focused on the role the JWE might play in simultaneously using and limiting military power in political conflicts, whether they are intrastate, transnational, or interstate wars. The chapter has confronted the paradoxical role the JWE has played and continues to play in political conflicts. Paradoxical because it asserts the possibility that the use of force can be an instrument of justice, but that it also can be the cause of unjustified death and destruction. The chapter as originally conceived focused primarily on how states and international institutions should attend to the often-ignored plight of refugees/IDPs in conflicts, and how a paradoxical ethic might both oblige the use of force (the role of rescue) and also set limits on whether or how force should be used at all.

The chapter has attempted to answer both questions. But it clearly has left open issues arising out of the specific nature of the conflicts that are most prone to produce the suffering of refugees/IDPs. The authors of other chapters in this volume and the commentary of Jesuits and other practitioners working directly with refugees/IDPs deepen the tension between war as an instrument of justice and a method of destruction. To some degree their specific questions are part of the broader debate of the last two decades on humanitarian military intervention. The phrase itself is contested: as noted above, humanitarian relief organizations often object to using the adjective humanitarian in any connection with military methods or means. Several of my colleagues in this project reflected that objection or at least skepticism about the linkage. Absolute opposition to all use of military force was not the position taken by my colleagues; the memory of Rwanda illustrated cases when nothing short of coercion would have prevented genocide. In a sense, the two cases of Rwanda and Kosovo define the debate about humanitarian and military realities. Rwanda demonstrates what can occur when all coercive power resides with those committed to use it without restraint. Kosovo demonstrates that coercion intended to prevent harm can also be a contributing factor to violence and chaos. Humanitarian intentions, methods, and objectives will never reside easily alongside force and coercion. The moral question, however, remains whether excluding coercion—as last resort—from policy will make some humanitarian work impossible.

Beyond skepticism about invoking the JWE, African participants in the Boston College conference particularly focused on aspects of conflicts that the traditional JWE needs to address. Most of the questions raised were about the means and methods of war. While the traditional ethic is accustomed to addressing the role of states, the potential of UN peacekeeping, or (lately) terrorist organizations, the internal conflicts of Africa are often fueled by private armies, employing child soldiers and operating in conflicts either independently or with the collusion of political states. Such private actions violate simultaneously just cause (they do not have one), proper authority (they are not one), and just means (they do not recognize them). Understanding when these highly destructive players fit in a conflict requires a wider lens than JWE may usually employ. Supplementing their role—indeed making it possible—is the international/transnational arms trade that both states and private interests fuel in a globalized market.

From Cambodia to Afghanistan come stories of another just means problem: the methods used by the United States, primarily, when it commits troops to combat, humanitarian or otherwise. Particular methods are the issue: first, the reliance on airpower and the capacity to control and direct it; second, the use of cluster bombs, which inflict indiscriminate damage and remain after conflicts subside as a continuing danger; and third, the use of landmines, which do exactly the same. The first issue attracts much attention, even if results are mixed. The second and third issues are best addressed by seeking international prohibition of them as methods of war in any situation.

Using the lens of the lives of refugees and IDPs is not the conventional method of analyzing world politics and modern warfare. Such a perspective will never likely be the primary focus of such analysis. But the record of the past twenty years, the arguments about the responsibility to protect, and the testimony of those who know the suffering of refugees/IDPs coalesce to say this reality deserves a seat at the analytical and policy table.

Notes

1. LeRoy B. Walters, "Five Classic Just-War Theories: A Study in the Thought of Thomas Aquinas, Vitoria, Suarez, Gentili, and Grotius" (PhD diss., Yale University, 1971), 420.

2. James T. Johnson, *Just War Tradition and the Restraint of War* (Princeton, NJ: Princeton University Press, 1981), 122 ff.

3. For examples of Niebuhr's analysis and his differences with Natural Law categories, see D. B. Robertson, ed., *Love and Justice: Selections from the Shorter Writings of Reinhold Niebuhr* (Cleveland, OH: Meridian Books, 1967), 46–54, 232–37.

4. John Courtney Murray, "Remarks on the Moral Problem of War," *Theological Studies* 20 (1959): 40–60; and Paul Ramsey, *The Just War: Force and Political Responsibility* (New York: Charles Scribner's, 1968).

5. Michael Walzer, *Just and Unjust Wars: A Moral Argument with Historical Illustrations* (New York: Basic Books, 1977).

6. Ramsey, *Just War*, is the most expansive text analyzing the moral challenges of the nuclear age; Murray and Niebuhr offer similar but not identical analyses. For an assessment of the political-strategic nature of the nuclear age, see McGeorge Bundy, *Danger and Survival: Choices about the Bomb in the First Fifty Years* (New York: Random House, 1988); see also Lawrence Freedman, *The Evolution of Nuclear Strategy* (New York: St. Martin's Press, 1981).

7. For examples, see Walter Stein, ed., *Nuclear Weapons and Christian Conscience* (London: Merlin Press, 1961).

8. For an argument reflecting this position, see John Finnis, Joseph Boyle, and Germain Grisez, *Nuclear Deterrence, Morality, and Realism* (Oxford: Clarendon Press, 1987).

9. Two examples are David Hollenbach, *Nuclear Ethics: A Christian Moral Argument* (New York: Paulist Press, 1983); and National Conference of Catholic Bishops, *The Challenge of Peace: God's Promise and Our Response* (Washington, DC: U.S. Catholic Conference, 1983).

10. A uniquely rigorous and insightful argument that pre-dated the nuclear age but focused on the key moral issues that nuclear weapons would raise was John C. Ford, "The Morality of Obliteration Bombing," *Theological Studies* 5 (1944): 261–309.

11. For a survey of the issues raised by Humanitarian Military Intervention, see J. L. Holzgrete, "The Humanitarian Intervention Debate" in *Humanitarian Intervention: Ethical, Legal, and Political Dilemmas*, ed. J. L. Holzgrete and Robert O. Keohane (Cambridge: Cambridge University Press, 2003), 15–52; and Michael Byers and Simon Chesterman, "Changing the Rules about Rules? Unilateral Humanitarian Intervention and the Future of International Law," in Holzgrete and Keohane, 177–203.

12. James T. Johnson, *Morality and Contemporary Warfare* (New Haven, CT: Yale University Press, 1999), 71–118; and Stanley Hoffmann, "The Politics and Ethics of Military Interventions," *Survival* 37 (Winter 1995–1996): 29–51.

13. Kenneth Himes, "The Morality of Humanitarian Intervention (Notes on Moral Theology)," *Theological Studies* 55, no. 1 (March 1994): 82–105.

14. Report of the International Commission on Intervention and State Sovereignty, *The Responsibility to Protect* (Ottawa: International Development Research Centre, 2001), 1–8.

15. Scott Appleby, "Religion as an Agent of Conflict Transformation and Peacebuilding," in *Turbulent Peace*, ed. Chester A. Crocker, Fen Osler Hampson, and Pamela Hall (Washington, DC: United States Institute of Peace, 2001), 822.

16. Michael Walzer, *Arguing about War* (New Haven, CT: Yale University Press, 2004), xiii.

17. Brian Orend, *The Morality of War* (Peterborough, Ontario, Canada: Broadview Press, 2006), 160–89.

18. James Gustafson, "Christian Ethics and Social Policy," in *Faith and Ethics: The Theology of H. Richard Niebuhr*, ed. Paul Ramsey (New York: Harper Torchbooks, 1957), 121, 126–27.

19. John Courtney Murray, *We Hold These Truths: Catholic Reflections on the American Proposition* (New York: Sheed and Ward, 1960), 271–72 (an edited version of Murray, "Remarks on the Moral Problem").

20. Niall Ferguson, *The War of the World: Twentieth Century Conflict and the Descent of the West* (New York: Penguin Press, 2006), xxxiv.

21. Myron Weiner, "Bad Neighbors, Bad Neighborhoods: An Inquiry into the Causes of Refugee Flows," *International Security* 21 (1996): 12–13.

22. Myron Weiner, *The Global Migration Crisis Challenge to States and to Human Rights* (New York: HarperCollins, 1995), 30.

23. UNHCR, *The State of the World's Refugees: Human Displacement in the New Millennium* (Oxford: Oxford University Press, 2006), 68.

24. Frederick H. Russell, *The Just War in the Middle Ages* (Cambridge: Cambridge University Press, 1975), 16.

25. For examples of how the rise of human rights arguments affected work policies, see R. J. Vincent, *Human Rights and International Relations* (Cambridge: Cambridge University Press, 1986).

26. Report of the International Commission, *Responsibility to Protect*, 8. Note on p. 9 the discussion of terminology; the Commission rightly points out the critique offered by humanitarian organizations to the joining of the adjective humanitarian with any military actions. The reframing of the intervention question to the responsibility to protect moves the discussion forward, even though the earlier phrase of humanitarian intervention is widely used.

27. See Gareth Evans, *The Responsibility to Protect: Ending Mass Atrocity Crimes once and for All* (Washington DC: Brookings Institution Press, 2008), 43, 59.

28. Michael Walzer, "A Just War?" in *The Gulf War Reader: History, Documents, Opinions,* ed. Micah L. Sifry and Christopher Cerf (New York: Random House, 1991), 304–5.

29. Barry Posen, "Military Responses to Refugee Disasters," *International Security* 21 (1996): 72–111.

30. Richard Just, "The Truth Will Not Set You Free," *The New Republic,* August 27, 2008, 36–47; and Scott Straus, "Darfur and the Genocide Debate," *Foreign Affairs* 84 (2005): 123–33.

10

Reinserting "Never" into "Never Again"

Political Innovations and the Responsibility to Protect

Thomas G. Weiss

With the possible exception of the prevention of genocide after World War II, no idea has moved faster or further in the international normative arena than the "responsibility to protect," commonly called R2P, the title of the 2001 report from the International Commission on Intervention and State Sovereignty (ICISS).[1] This chapter, like others in the volume, contains a strong dose of ethics, but its main purpose is to explore political innovations that could make "never again" an actuality instead of an aspiration. As Princeton University's Gary Bass puts it in his history of early efforts to halt mass atrocities, "We are all atrocitarians now—but so far only in words, and not yet in deeds."[2] Or as David Rieff writes, "there is considerable evidence of changing norms, though not, of course, changing facts on the ground."[3] More specifically still, the title of a 2008 Stanley Foundation report put it another way: "actualizing the responsibility to protect."[4] In other words, we require additional measures and the mobilization of political will to ensure the provision of the global public good of protecting and assisting forced migrants.

The UN Security Council's inability to address the woes of the Democratic Republic of Congo (DRC), and especially its painful dithering since early 2003 over massive murder and displacement in Darfur, demonstrate the dramatic disconnect between multilateral rhetoric and the reality of protecting and aiding the displaced.[5] As Roméo Dallaire, the Canadian general in charge of the feeble United Nations (UN) force during the 1994 slaughter in Rwanda, lamented, "Having called what is happening in Darfur genocide and having vowed to stop it, it is time for the West to keep its word."[6] Normative change often is a necessary but insufficient condition for mobilizing the political will to act.

The "responsibility to protect" is a more politically acceptable reformulation of the more familiar "humanitarian intervention."[7] At the outset, it suffices to say that R2P redefines sovereignty as contingent rather than absolute, and R2P locates responsibility for human rights in the first instance with the state. But it also argues that if a state is unwilling or unable to honor its responsibility, or itself becomes the perpetrator of atrocities, then the residual responsibility to protect the victims of mass atrocity crimes shifts upward to the international community of states, ideally acting through the Security Council.

The most reliable indicator of suffering in war zones traditionally has been the number of refugees, who are, in the vernacular or according to the text of the 1951 UN Convention Relating to the Status of Refugees, exiles who flee across the borders of their country of origin. Physical displacement is prima facie evidence of vulnerability, because people who are deprived of their homes and communities and means of livelihood are unable to resort to traditional coping capacities. When such people are forced migrants within their own countries, especially as a result of war, however, they may be even more vulnerable.

Whatever one's views about legal niceties or political necessities, the ratio of refugees to internally displaced persons (IDPs) has reversed dramatically over the past two decades. The number of refugees at the beginning of the twenty-first century is fewer than 10 million while the number of IDPs is considerably higher—depending on who is counting, certainly as many as 26 million people have been internally displaced by wars in some fifty countries (13 million in Africa, 3 million in Asia, 2.5 million in Europe, 3.5 million in the Middle East, and 4 million in the Americas), and similar or even greater numbers were displaced by natural disasters and development projects.[8] When IDP data were first gathered in 1982, there was one IDP for every 10 refugees; at present the ratio is approximately 2.5:1.

Whereas international law entitles refugees to physical security and human rights protection in addition to assistance to offset their other vulnerabilities, no such legal guarantees exist for those who participate in an "exodus within borders."[9] Agencies seeking to come to the rescue of persons who have not crossed a border often require permission from the very political authorities responsible for the displacement and abuse.

While the origins of the responsibility to protect emerged from work by Francis Deng and Roberta Cohen, who pursued the cause of IDPs, analytical and practical distinctions between refugees and internally displaced persons increasingly seem insignificant.[10] At the same time, David Hollenbach correctly points out that "humanitarian concern with the protection of internally displaced people has been one of the stimuli for a serious reconsideration of the meaning and implications of the sovereignty of the nation-state."[11] The slavish respect for the sovereign prerogatives of states was undermined by efforts on behalf of IDPs, whose assistance and protection were viewed as especially subversive because outsiders were seeking ways to succor and protect victims of human rights abuse within a state. So the concept of "sovereignty as responsibility" was one way to square the circle, maintaining the fiction of state sovereignty and its corollary of nonintervention but in fact making room for international action in the face of mass atrocities. Although not so attributed, the opening lines of the ICISS report sound as if they had come from the word processor of Deng and his Brookings colleagues: "State sovereignty implies responsibility."[12]

A dramatic illustration of the potential mass appeal of R2P appeared in Pope Benedict XVI's April 2008 address to the General Assembly. In his words, "The principle of 'responsibility to protect' was considered by the ancient *ius gentium* as the foundation of every action taken by those in government with regard to the governed." While R2P "has only recently been defined, . . . it was always present implicitly at the origins of the United Nations, and is now increasingly characteristic of its activity."[13] Normally, the Vatican takes far more time to weigh in so clearly in favor of an emerging norm, but this declaration came only a few years after the 2005 World Summit session of the UN General Assembly endorsed R2P. The impact of the pope's support on the foreign policies of Latin American countries, for example, may be substantial. It reinforces the earlier judgment about R2P by former *New York Times* columnist Anthony Lewis, who sees R2P as "the international state of mind," and by one of its harshest opponents, Mohammed Ayoob, who admits its "considerable moral force."[14]

Occasionally, my generic optimism is rewarded, for instance by the results of the November 2008 U.S. presidential elections and, before that, the civic engagement during the primaries. But such domestic progress is rarely matched for the global challenges of war and peace or human rights. It is certainly difficult for anyone exploring the history of genocide and mass atrocities to remain optimistic. We can easily recall crimes committed by governments against their own citizens and evils allowed by other governments unwilling or unable to stop them. The "never again" moments since the Holocaust include Cambodia, Rwanda, and Srebrenica. Every time, collectively we ask in horror and shame how we could have let it happen once again.

However, I firmly believe that we have had an ethical breakthrough of sorts: R2P qualifies as emerging customary law after centuries of more or less passive and mindless acceptance of the proposition that state sovereignty was a license to kill. In the interest of full disclosure, I was the ICISS research director and the Ralph Bunche Institute at The CUNY Graduate Center, which I direct, houses the Global Centre for the Responsibility to Protect.

This chapter has three parts. The first provides the historical backdrop of human rights. The second examines more specifically the evolution of the R2P norm and actual efforts to protect civilians in the 1990s. The third part proposes five political innovations that could reduce the disparities between rhetoric and reality.

The Human Rights "Grapevine"

The history of diplomacy and international law shows that states accept limits on their conduct.[15] In a speech at the United Nations in 1948, Eleanor Roosevelt presciently predicted that "a curious grapevine" would spread human rights ideas.[16] More specifically for our purposes, the Universal Declaration of Human Rights requires that states protect individual and social rights; the Geneva Conventions and various treaties and covenants prohibiting torture, trafficking in persons, or nuclear proliferation similarly restrict the behavior of states. Moreover, there has been a shift in the understanding of sovereignty, spurred not only by globalization and technological advances but also by a growing sensitivity to human rights and by a reaction to atrocities perpetrated upon citizens by their own leaders. Sovereignty is increasingly defined not only as a license to control those within one's borders but also as a set of obligations toward citizens. Kofi Annan spoke of the sovereignty of the individual as well as of the state.[17] Francis Deng, now the special representative on the prevention of genocide and the former representative of the UN secretary-general on internally displaced persons, developed the concept of "sovereignty as responsibility."[18] Chief among those responsibilities, he and others argued, is the responsibility to protect citizens from the most atrocious forms of abuse. In terms of values, and simply put, people should come before sovereigns.

Our collective lack of historical perspective and institutional memory can make it hard to recall the extent to which human rights were so much more marginal to geopolitics and everyday politics not only at the UN's founding in 1945 but also, for instance, when Amnesty International took form in the 1960s and Human Rights Watch in the 1970s. If we fast forward to the September 2005 World Summit in New York on the occasion of the UN's sixtieth anniversary, human rights were the third pillar of the world organization's architecture, along with security and development.[19] More specifically, the largest-ever gathering of heads of state and government agreed unanimously to protect people from four extreme forms of abuse: genocide, war crimes, ethnic cleansing, and crimes against humanity.

During the first half of the 1990s, twice as many resolutions were passed as during the UN's first forty-five years. Many of these contained repeated references, in the context of Chapter VII enforcement actions, to humanitarian and human rights crises amounting to threats to international peace and security, and they repeated demands for parties to respect the principles of international humanitarian law. The unanimous 1992 decision in Security Council resolution 794 to authorize the U.S.-led intervention in Somalia, for example, set a modern multilateral record for redundancy by mentioning "humanitarian" eighteen times. In short, today's normative and political landscape for humanitarian intervention is substantially different from that dominating international relations during the Cold War.

Is there a downside? The International Council on Human Rights Policy answers, "As their standing and influence have increased, human rights have also been more actively contested."[20] The transformation of the Soviet Union, the differences in North–South perspectives on universality of rights, and the importance of economic and social versus political rights, and more recently the global war on terror have caused many governments to revisit, restrict, or reverse the application of human rights.

This is the ambiguous and sometimes contradictory context within which to situate the highly volatile topic of outside intrusions, including military intervention, on human rights and humanitarian grounds. On the one hand, the responsibility to protect is not new; on the other hand, it reframes and reaffirms the primary and continuing responsibilities of states to protect their populations within the contemporary, contested climate. With the advent of R2P, the larger international community of states accepted for the first time the collective responsibility to act should states fail to protect citizens from genocide, ethnic cleansing, war crimes, and crimes against humanity. R2P thus imposes two obligations—the first upon

each state individually, the second on the international community of states collectively. Skeptics and foes remain, to be sure, but the long debate over whether to act
has become, instead, a discussion about how and when to act. The new activism also
explains why the humanitarian field is asking many questions about its orientation
and operations.[21]

Evolution of the R2P Norm

The historical trajectory captured by the snapshot found in paragraphs 138–39 of
the 2005 *World Summit Outcome Document* is breathtaking—moving from the early
1990s with Frances Deng and Roberta Cohen's sovereignty as responsibility to help
internally displaced persons, to Secretary-General Kofi Annan's "two sovereignties,"
to the ICISS. At a minimum, state sovereignty seems less sacrosanct today than in
1945. Richard Haass even proposes a bumper sticker, "abuse it and lose it."[22]

The ICISS identified two threshold cases or unequivocal just causes for taking
action across borders: large-scale loss of life and ethnic cleansing, under way or anticipated. Humanitarian intervention also should be subject to four precautionary
conditions: right intention, last resort, proportional means, and reasonable prospects of success. Finally, the Security Council is the preferred decision maker, or just
authority. That many would rightly see R2P as an adaptation of just war doctrine
is easy to understand, even if the effort was purposefully not so labeled in order to
avoid the political complications arising from its western provenance.

The differences between the World Summit paragraphs and the original ICISS
formulation are not trivial, but caricatures of the former's being R2P lite or providing a license for imperial intervention are exaggerations. The text agreed to by more
than 150 princes, presidents, and prime ministers is woollier, wordier, and wafflier
than one would like, but the World Summit's language nonetheless reflects a unanimous and historic agreement to protect citizens from mass atrocities. The core of
R2P remains: state sovereignty does not include the license to commit murder and
other conscience-shocking crimes.

The so-called new wars of the 1990s witnessed precedent-setting military interventions to come to the rescue of civilians in northern Iraq in 1991, Somalia in 1992,
and Haiti in 1994; later in the decade, Kosovo and East Timor also were important
victories for civilians.[23] Others disagree with my positive evaluation of the overall
beneficial impact of many of these efforts.[24] However, the more important thought
here is that the ICISS moved beyond the largely sterile political confrontations of the
1990s that accompanied the horrors of Rwanda and the Balkans when the Security
Council was unable to act. The pitched battles about whether there was or was not
a right to intervene were fought between partisans of humanitarian intervention
like me and the defenders of unrestricted and sacrosanct state sovereignty, who saw
humanitarian intervention as a Trojan Horse for imperial intervention or as a desta-
bilizing factor for international society.[25]

The Responsibility to Protect report found a way to square the circle, to put forward a more politically acceptable way to halt mass atrocity crimes. Kofi Annan was the first head of the world organization to systematically use the secretary-general's bully pulpit almost continually to champion human rights. As a result, he was obliged to wear the equivalent of a diplomatic flak jacket at the end of the 1990s after he dared suggest that people were more important than sovereignty. Annan met with a predictable salvo of vituperative attacks in the General Assembly and elsewhere. When he received the first copy of the ICISS report, he quipped, "I wish I had thought of that."

R2P is a new normative tool to help protect the most basic human right, life itself. It makes a dent in the age-old practice of what Hugo Slim has documented as "killing civilians."[26] Robert J. Rummel's scholarly career has been spent counting how many people have been killed through wars, pogroms, genocides, and mass murder. His estimate for the twentieth-century alone is 217 million.[27] And of course this figure does not include the many more uncounted who have lived diminished lives as refugees, IDPs, detainees, widows or widowers, orphans, and paupers.

As a result of the R2P norm, the notion of outside military intervention for human protection purposes is more feasible than it has ever been in the modern era, even if it remains far from palatable and certainly should not be the first policy option. Such intervention is not really a North-versus-South issue, but that is how it is often parsed in UN circles. The ICISS tried to overcome this dysfunctional fiction not only by having cochairs from the North and the South, but also by having a geographical balance among the other ten commissioners. ICISS also held ten consultations in both the Northern and Southern Hemispheres to expose the views of governments, scholars, NGOs, and journalists. The cacophony cannot be summarized except to say that what was notable, in historical perspective, is that nowhere did a substantial number of people argue that intervention to sustain humanitarian objectives was never justifiable. Rwanda's horror had a clear impact: few policymakers, pundits, or practitioners dared to exclude humanitarian intervention in principle. This change, for those of us who follow such developments, was momentous.

The R2P norm broke conceptual ground in three ways. First, the primary responsibility to protect rights resides in a sovereign state and its government. So in addition to the usual attributes of sovereignty that students encounter in undergraduate and graduate international relations and law courses and in the 1934 Montevideo Convention—people, authority, territory, and independence—there is another, namely a modicum of respect for basic human rights. In other words, the traditional emphasis on the privileges of a sovereign has made room for modest responsibilities. Moreover, when a state is unable or manifestly unwilling to protect the rights of its population—indeed, especially when it is the central perpetrator of abuse—that state temporarily loses its sovereignty, along with the accompanying right of nonintervention, and an international responsibility results to assist and protect that population.

Second, ICISS turned the language of humanitarian intervention on its head and moved away from the language of intervention, detested at least in much of the global South, which had become visible and widespread after debates in France starting in the mid-1980s. The movement away from the "right to intervene" and toward the "responsibility to protect" was accompanied by the removal of the "H" word.[28] Taking away the adjective "humanitarian" was crucial because it meant that particular situations should be analyzed and evaluated rather than simply blessed as "humanitarian." For anyone familiar with the number of sins justified by the use of that adjective during the colonial period, this change involves more than mere semantics. In particular, the language marked a dramatic shift in the focus away from the rights of outsiders to intervene and toward the rights of populations at risk to assistance and protection and the responsibility of outsiders to come to the rescue.

Third, ICISS developed a three-part framework that included the responsibility to prevent and the responsibility to rebuild before and after the responsibility to react in the eye of a storm. In conceptualizing international responsibilities, deploying international armed forces is thus neither the first nor the last step. The full spectrum of activities is integral to R2P and essential to dispel the impression that only military intervention matters.

Thus, in what Gareth Evans aptly calculates to be "a blink of the eye in the history of ideas," R2P evolved from the prose and passion of an international commission to a broadly accepted international norm.[29] It is a norm with a substantial potential to evolve further in customary international law and to contribute to the evolution of the ongoing conversations about the responsibilities of states that are expected as characteristics of legitimate sovereigns.

Normative developments and political reality are rarely in synch, however. Sometimes norm entrepreneurs scramble to keep up with events, and sometimes they are ahead of them.[30] In this case the humanitarian interventions in northern Iraq in 1991 and Somalia in 1992 were actually endorsed by the United Nations before there was any significant discussion of conditioning state sovereignty on human rights. Plotting the growing normative consensus about R2P on a graph would reflect a steady growth since the early 1990s, whereas the actual operational capacity and political will to engage in humanitarian intervention during the same period—like the transformed humanitarian system—has witnessed peaks and troughs.[31] Hence, the 2005 World Summit marked the zenith of international normative consensus about R2P. But the blowback from September 11, 2001, and the war in Iraq, along with the absence of substantial military capacity in the West besides the American one, which is tied down in Afghanistan and Iraq, explains the current decline in actual humanitarian intervention in spite of the horrors in Darfur, the DRC, Somalia, Burma—and the list goes on. This is another manifestation of what I called "collective spinelessness" in the Balkans.[32]

It is worth spending a moment on the war in Iraq, which sometimes is a bit of a conversation stopper for R2P.[33] The blowback from Iraq means that military intervention for human protection purposes is no longer on the side of the angels. Many fear Washington will manipulate it and strengthen the rationale for preemptive strikes against so-called rogue states and terrorists. The emerging norm of the responsibility to protect has been contaminated by association with the Bush administration's spurious humanitarian justifications for invading Iraq after the supposed links to al-Qaeda and the possession of weapons of mass destruction were exposed as vacuous. The position of the United Kingdom may have been even more damaging. In March 2004 Tony Blair offered a most worrisome example of abusing R2P when he applied it retroactively to Iraq. "We surely have a duty and a right to prevent this threat materializing," Blair announced, "and we surely have a responsibility to act when a nation's people are subjected to a regime such as Saddam's."[34]

In spite of incantations by numerous actors—including the ICISS, the secretary-general's High-level Panel on Threats, Challenges, and Change; secretaries-general Kofi Annan and Ban Ki-moon; and the World Summit—the responsibility to protect is oftentimes a harder sell these days than earlier because a Bush-like administration might manipulate any imprimatur. A rigorous application of R2P would not lend itself to becoming a veiled pretext to intervene for preemptive purposes, especially if the Security Council's authorization were a sine qua non for an authorization.[35] But this is scarce consolation for those who see Washington's and London's loose application of humanitarian rhetoric to Iraq ex post facto. In brief, it is hard to dismiss out of hand the fiercest claims that R2P conceals an imperial agenda.

The notion that the rights of human beings trump state sovereignty, while radiating briefly across the international political horizon, is now overshadowed as the U.S. military is tied down in Afghanistan and Iraq, with the latter morphing into a vague humanitarian intervention. Because the United States cannot commit significant political and military resources to human protection, political will and the operational capacity for humanitarian intervention have evaporated. Yet the cosmopolitan logic underpinning R2P is uniquely compelling for international relations, "given the fact that sovereignty is one of the few principles that has universal appeal among national elites and mass publics."[36]

The current moment's diplomatic atmosphere could be described as toxic in UN diplomatic circles, which may not bode well for advancing the responsibility to protect norm in the immediate term. Beginning with the fall 2007 General Assembly debates concerning the appointment of the special representative on the prevention of genocide and the special adviser with a focus on R2P, the most backward-looking states have again been sharpening their swords and are attempting to skewer proponents of R2P by arguing in public forums everything ranging from "the summit rejected R2P" to "R2P exists only in the minds of Western imperialists." In essence, the responsibility to protect flies in the face of strongly held views by states, especially younger ones in the global South, about the sacrosanct nature of state sovereignty. The 1965 General Assembly resolution 20/2131 on the "Inadmissibility of Intervention" asserted: "No state has the right to intervene, directly, or indirectly, for any reason whatsoever, in the internal or external affairs of any other state." The animus in North–South relations today, in my view, is akin to that of the mid-1970s in the heyday of confrontation over the establishment of the New International Economic Order (NIEO).

That does not make political innovation for R2P easy. Innovation never is. "The crisis in Iraq has revived more traditional interpretations of state sovereignty," United Nations High Commissioner for Refugees (UNHCR) António Guterres notes. "But a reinvigorated global consensus on the R2P has to be forged nonetheless."[37]

Five Political Innovations

It is tempting to compose a short paragraph recommending a radical international political innovation, namely, that states actually implement the international agreements that they have signed and even ratified. While awaiting that unlikely development, however, my road map for innovations that would help R2P has something for everyone: for analysts, conceptual clarity; for civil society, a long-term strategy; for UN reformers, a consolidated relief agency; for the military, more robust and numerous forces in Europe; and for weak, fragile countries, enhanced state capacities. Progress here would help move us along what Ramesh Thakur and I call the "unfinished journey" toward better global governance.[38]

Conceptual Clarity

The lengthy 2005 *World Summit Outcome Document* was agreed by consensus; but like most diplomatic compromises, the agreement on the responsibility to protect meant that differences were papered over and that the usual suspects were not really on board. As a UK House of Commons document put it, "It also is somewhat ironic that in trying to use language to take heat out of the policy debate, R2P has become an amorphous concept meaning vastly different things to different people."[39]

My first political innovation may be dismissed because it reflects the scholar's penchant for more research, but it nonetheless is essential to push forward the conceptual understanding of R2P. To be sure, practical actors must seek new structures and processes, both national and international, to ensure that timely and adequate preventive and reactive responses are forthcoming. We also need to build political bases so that when a new atrocity takes place (e.g., Darfur) or a potential one is looming (e.g., DRC, Iraq, or Kenya), the actual response is predictable. But if ridding the world of mass atrocities is to become more feasible, we also must get the concepts right, which is a comparative advantage of people like the contributors to this volume. We need to frame the issues correctly and to embed moral instincts so that there are fewer stumbling blocks to a global effort to protect civilian populations at risk.

There are two kinds of challenges to the Goldilocks problem of getting the R2P porridge just right. To date, we have not been clear enough about describing exactly what the responsibility to protect is about, to what kinds of situations it applies, and what kinds of policies are essential at different stages in the evolution of crises that threaten to degenerate into mass atrocities. This has permitted second-guessing among governments that are genuinely confused or skeptical. While engaging the spoilers is not a priority, having more precise concepts for honest skeptics is.

The first conceptual challenge is to ensure that R2P not be seen too narrowly. It is not, and this cannot be said too frequently, only about the use of military force. R2P is not a synonym for humanitarian intervention. As mentioned above, this task is especially pertinent after the rhetoric in Washington and London morphed into a humanitarian justification for the war in Iraq when weapons of mass destruction (WMDs) and links to al-Qaeda proved to be nonexistent.

Also as specified earlier, R2P is above all about taking effective preventive action. It is about identifying situations that are capable of deteriorating into mass atrocities and bringing to bear all appropriate preventive political, diplomatic, legal, or economic responses. Paragraphs 138–139 of the World Summit Outcome Document stress that the responsibility to prevent is very much of the state itself, and part of the outside or international prevention responsibility is to help countries to help themselves. And if prevention fails, reaction becomes necessary. But here too we need to develop an entire tool kit of nonmilitary measures that go from persuasive to intrusive, from less to more coercive, which is true of military measures as well. We require action long before the only option remaining is the U.S. Army's 82nd Airborne Division, and we also require a commitment after deploying outside military forces. R2P prevention and R2P peace building have to be distinct from the normal panoply of preventive and postconflict measures, or there is no value added for the responsibility to protect label.

This feeds into, ironically, the second conceptual challenge at the opposite end of the spectrum: R2P is not about the protection of everyone from everything. While broadening the perspective from reaction to include prevention and peace building was a conceptual step forward, the downside has been opening the floodgates to appeals to address too many problems under this rubric. For example, part of the support at the World Summit reflected a desire to mobilize more support for root-cause prevention, or investments in economic and social development. As bureaucrats invariably seek justifications for what they are doing or new pet projects, we run the risk that there is nothing that may not figure on the R2P agenda. It is emotionally and perhaps politically tempting to say that we have a responsibility to protect people from HIV/AIDS and small arms, or the Inuit from global warming.

But such pleas are counterproductive; it is not sensible to make the responsibility to protect overlap with the full scope of human security. The uncomfortable truth is that R2P is irrelevant for many types of forced migration—both the push and the pull of armed conflict and economic opportunity—unless they involve mass atrocities. Displacement, actual or anticipated, has to be truly horrific before R2P comes into play. In brief, if it means everything, it means nothing. The responsibility to protect has to be focused because we do not wish to lose the sharp agenda that can energize political will and action at least in the worst cases. The value of R2P is as a rallying cry for visceral international reactions in the face of such conscience-shocking crises as mass murder and ethnic cleansing.

Longer-term Strategy

It is important to develop a longer-term strategy, one that takes the best from the original ICISS report and the *World Summit Outcome Document* but is not constrained by either.[40] There are a number of challenges if we are to consolidate and advance the R2P norm. Among them is the confusion about R2P that persists even among its most ardent proponents, so that the norm is being characterized inappropriately. In the aftermath of the World Summit, diplomatic opponents of R2P have become more adept than proponents in making their case, with the result that the claims of hard-line opponents sometimes go unchallenged. The overall debate on the responsibility to protect within the United Nations often is skewed because of the diplomatic skills and power of a few key third world states and because the secretary-general's job description and the current incumbent's disposition mean that addressing and satisfying the concerns of the most determined opponents assumes pride of place. The strength of the opposition has often been compounded because proponents do not have sufficiently coherent strategies to get R2P to a point where it will galvanize timely action to save lives.

Civil society's norm entrepreneurs can make a difference. R2P supporters need to advocate for an alternative vision that is intellectually and doctrinally coherent and clearly expressed. The long-term goal is protecting the essence of the R2P norm such that it triggers effective action to save lives from mass atrocities. The more immediate goal is ensuring that R2P supporters influence the purpose and tenor of any debate on R2P in the General Assembly so that the 2005 agreement is not weakened. The secretary-general's promising July 2008 speech in Berlin was followed by a disappointing laundry list instead of a strategy in a document to the General Assembly early in 2009.[41] A debate followed within the Assembly in July 2009, the first time since the adoption by the World Summit. As one independent assessment summarized, "What emerged was a clear commitment from the vast majority of member states to the prevention and halting of atrocity crimes. Indeed, only four countries sought to roll back what heads of state had embraced."[42]

The R2P notion is a complex and multifaceted. Earlier, in discussing the need for conceptual clarity, we saw that some observers hope that the responsibility to protect can be a springboard for all international responses to prevent and resolve armed conflicts, while others see it as a framework for international efforts to protect civilians. Still others see it as a basis for military intervention. Whatever else it may be, R2P is fundamentally about overriding sovereignty when mass atrocities occur; and so the concept will always be fraught. Diplomacy to keep all of the countries happy all of the time is a fool's errand.

Civil society should mobilize around a narrow notion of R2P for those situations that require highly intrusive and rapid outside military and civilian responses. The strategy should not take seriously the disingenuous and convoluted arguments from those, such as the 2008 Non-Aligned Movement leadership of Cuba, Malaysia, and Egypt, who will never be mollified by conceptual arguments. At the same time, the strategy should avoid the all-embracing approaches (something for everyone) usually favored by coalition builders in civil society as well as in the UN secretariat. Anything other than a narrow focus on the responsibility to protect civilians from mass atrocities will needlessly politicize international work on human rights, conflict prevention, and the protection of civilians.

An Agency for War Victims

For frustrated humanitarian institutional reformers, I return to a long-standing yet orphaned innovation, namely, to set aside perennial institutional rivalries and create a consolidated UN agency to assist and protect war victims. This would entail pulling together the current capacities for assisting and protecting refugees and others in refugee-like situations (mainly IDPs) located in the Office of UNHCR and the major humanitarian operational capacities of the World Food Programme (WFP), UNICEF, and the UN Development Programme (UNDP), along with the UN Secretariat's Office for the Coordination of Humanitarian Affairs (OCHA). Such a consolidation would have the advantage not only of addressing squarely the problems of IDPs, who have no legal or institutional home, but also of reducing the legendary waste and turf battles within the UN system. Such a reform would involve the consolidation of parts of the United Nations organization proper; it would thus not require constitutional changes.

Ironically, it almost came about in 1997, shortly after Kofi Annan took over from Boutros Boutros-Ghali as secretary-general. Annan ordered a systemwide review of the world organization with especial attention to humanitarian and human rights operations. He put in charge Maurice Strong, the Canadian businessman and old UN hand who had first made his mark as secretary-general of the 1972 Stockholm Conference on the Human Environment. Strong's penultimate draft of proposals for reform recommended handing responsibility for internally displaced persons over to UNHCR, and an appendix even fleshed out the possibility of creating over the longer run a consolidated UN humanitarian agency along the lines that I have indicated.

Other UN agencies—especially UNICEF and WFP—as well as NGOs in the guise of their U.S. consortium, InterAction, sensed a threat to their territory. They feared that UNHCR would come to loom over them in size and authority, and that their increasingly important, in budgetary and personnel terms, humanitarian capacities would dwindle and even be subsumed in a new consolidated agency. Annan backed off in light of the fierce opposition led by donors who preached coherence and consolidation but had their own agendas as well—including protecting the territory and budget allocations of their favorite intergovernmental and nongovernmental organizations in quintessential patron–client relationships. The final version of his 1997 reorganization was largely a repackaging of the former Department of Humanitarian Affairs as OCHA.[43] The quintessential old-wine-in-a-new-bottle routine meant that largely meaningless cooperation was reaffirmed as the UN's mechanism of choice for dealing with crises of forced displacement. Ironically, the final group of eminent persons organized during the Annan era was the High-level Panel on UN System-wide Coherence on Development, Humanitarian Assistance, and the Environment. Its recommendations for consolidation, or "delivering as one," have met the same inglorious fate as earlier calls, including Robert Jackson's 1969 *Capacity Study*—namely, no action.[44] The UN's default setting is more coordination, the mere mention of which makes eyes glaze over because there is no power of the purse to compel working together. The result is a low level of actual collaboration, which Antonio Donini dubbed "coordination by default."[45] Prospects for successful coordination for R2P or anything else depend on getting the main UN operational agencies that play a role for refugees and internally displaced persons (UNHCR, UNICEF, UNDP, and WFP) and those outside the UN framework (International

Committee of the Red Cross, IOM, and the largest international NGOs) to pull together. Wherever the United Nations orchestrates an overall humanitarian response, there is no structural explanation for well-coordinated efforts when they happen; rather, they depend on good faith, luck, and personalities.

The IDP situation is especially problematic, not only because no agency is responsible, but also because no legal statute guides state or agency behavior. Susan Martin has argued in favor of a new agency for IDPs because "accountability is the bottom-line. And no one is accountable."[46] Starting in 2005 the Inter-agency Standing Committee (IASC) initiated the so-called cluster approach as the latest experiment in coordination, first to address the needs of IDPs but then expanding more generally to other chronic and sudden-onset emergencies. The most generous and positive assessment to date was written by independent consultants for OCHA. Its conclusion is underwhelming: "the weight of evidence points to the conclusion that the costs and drawbacks of the new approach are exceeded by its benefits."[47]

Not one of the bevy of organizations that flock to emergencies has the ability to meet the needs of IDPs. But my argument here is that decentralization hardly serves refugees either, so yet another UN agency for IDPs is not the answer. Coordination lite works on occasion because of serendipity. As numerous NGO and UN officials lament, "Everyone is for coordination but nobody wants to be coordinated." It is time, certainly within the context of an international responsibility to protect civilians from mass atrocities, to consolidate the various moving parts of the core UN system rather than just hoping that the current provider of last resort will manage to provide what are essential services.

Non–U.S. Military Capacity

Downsizing the armed forces over the last twenty years has meant an insufficient supply of equipment and manpower to meet the demands for military intervention for human protection purposes. There are bottlenecks in the U.S. logistics chain—especially in airlift capacity—that make improbable a rapid international response to a fast-moving, Rwanda-like genocide.[48] Using the conventional military logic that it takes four units to sustain one in the field, about half of the U.S. Army is tied down in Afghanistan and Iraq and a quarter of its reserves overseas, while about a third of the National Guard is committed to the war on terror.[49] Questions are being raised even about the capacity to respond to a serious national security threat or a natural disaster like Hurricane Katrina, let alone minor distractions like Haiti or major ones like the Democratic Republic of Congo. Moreover, too little doctrinal rethinking about R2P has taken place within Western militaries.[50]

Nonetheless, the change in the normative approach should not be minimized and is one on which the new Barack Obama administration could and should build, starting with a report from a bipartisan Genocide Prevention Task Force led by Madeleine Albright and William Cohen.[51] We have witnessed a values breakthrough of sorts: the responsibility to protect qualifies as emerging customary law after centuries of more or less passive and mindless acceptance of the proposition that state sovereignty was a license to kill.[52] And Susan Rice, having been part of the lamentable Clinton administration's decision that kept the United States out of Rwanda, has expressed clearly the need for Washington not to repeat that mistake and to take the lead in conscience-shocking situations. Along with Hillary Clinton and James Jones, there is what could be called a dream team to prevent genocide, according to John Prendergast of the "Enough" project.[53]

Mass starvation, rape, and suffering will continue in the post-9/11 world, and we will know about them rapidly. For at least some conscience-shocking cases of mass suffering, there simply will be no viable alternative to military coercion for human protection purposes. There is some flexibility for action in minor crises. For instance, the prediction that major powers other than the United States would not respond at all with military force to a new humanitarian emergency after 9/11 proved too pessimistic. France's leading a European Union (EU) force into Ituri in the Democratic Republic of Congo in the summer of 2003 temporarily halted an upsurge of ethnic violence and demonstrated to Washington that the EU could act outside of the continent independently of NATO. This possibility was strengthened by Europe's takeover from the North Atlantic Treaty Organization (NATO) of the Bosnia operation in December 2004 as well as ongoing efforts in Chad and the possibilities for a European addition to the UN force deployed in the eastern DRC.

While there is little evidence that European or Canadian populations or governments are willing to invest more public resources on their militaries, a faint hope remains that at least an EU security identity could underpin a more operational responsibility to protect in modest crises. *A Secure Europe in a Better World*, formulated in 2003, lacks the crispness of U.S. national security strategies.[54] While spending on hardware falls considerably short of targets, nonetheless the number of European troops deployed abroad has doubled over the last decade and approaches the so-called Headline Goals, which set targets for the European Union in terms of military and civilian crisis management. As two Europeans have noted, "This incremental approach may move some way further yet, but it will come up against budgetary ceilings, against the unwillingness of some governments to invest in the weapon and support systems needed, and against the resistance of uninformed national publics."[55]

Europeans should share the burden of boots on the ground better even if U.S. airlift capacity, military muscle, and technology are required for larger and longer-duration deployments. For better or worse, the United States in the Security Council and elsewhere is what former U.S. secretary of state Dean Rusk called the fat boy in the canoe: "When we roll, everyone rolls with us."[56] With Washington's focus elsewhere, the danger is not too much but rather too little military intervention for human protection purposes. Unless European and other populations support higher expenditures on the military, there is little alternative to the overworked global policeman.

Rebuilding State Capacity

Unlike humanitarian intervention, the responsibility to protect seeks to place less emphasis on reaction (that is, coercion under Chapter VII) and more on less intrusive policy measures, what some have called "upstream R2P."[57] The importance of preventive measures was very much in evidence in the reactions to forestall Kenya's postelection violence from becoming even more horrific. Both former secretary-general Kofi Annan, who was the chief mediator, and current secretary-general Ban Ki-moon have described the collective efforts in early 2008 as an effective application of R2P prevention logic.[58]

As indicated earlier, one political innovation of the responsibility to protect is to help potential failed states to build capacity to protect their citizens. One of the major changes in emphasis is on rebuilding states. What is described as the "second pillar" of the World Summit's agreement on R2P is the international commitment to help states to help themselves. The United Nations and its intergovernmental and nongovernmental partners should seek to help states succeed, and not simply react once weak ones have failed to meet their prevention and protection requirements or actually have been responsible for mass atrocities.

The innovation here is to identify the value that is added by looking through an R2P lens in order to help identify additional efforts and potential synergies among the host of ongoing projects and programs of the UN system and international NGOs. Efforts, so often frustrated in the past, to encourage interagency collaboration and cross-sectoral efforts could and should receive additional impetus with the motivation to avoid R2P situations. More broadly, the wide-ranging efforts to rebuild and reconstruct countries like Burundi and Sierra Leone—the first pilot projects of the Peacebuilding Commission that began operations in 2006—are helped by referring to R2P. Such efforts are valuable in and of themselves, but also they can be justified because they reduce the risk of a recurrence of armed conflict and boost a state's resilience to face future crises. Part of the innovation required here is within the UN system itself, to ensure better collaboration between New York and the field.

Conclusion

While the political innovations just described are the central purpose of this essay, it is important in conclusion to indicate the three ways that the ICISS's work on R2P pushed the ethical and normative envelope so that vocabulary and values have changed at UN headquarters in New York as well as in other settings. The first is in the report's opening sentences, which insist that sovereignty encompasses a state's responsibility to protect populations within its borders. That is, sovereignty entails responsibilities and not merely privileges. An important spillover from the R2P norm is that even committed advocates of human rights and robust intervention now see state authority as elementary to enduring peace and reconciliation, and they recommend fortifying failed or fragile states. This realization does not reflect nostalgia for any national security state of the past, but a realistic appraisal of a new bottom line: it is neither NGOs nor UN human rights monitors, as important as they are, but rather reconstituted, functioning, and responsible states that will guarantee human rights.

The second ICISS ethical and normative contribution consists of moving away from the rights of outsiders to intervene toward a framing that spotlights the rights of those suffering from war and violence to assistance and protection. Abandoning the picturesque vocabulary of the French Doctors Movement shifts the fulcrum away from the rights of interveners toward the rights of affected populations and the responsibilities (if not legal obligations) of outsiders to come to the rescue. The new perspective thus prioritizes the rights of those suffering from murder, starvation, or systematic rape and the duty of states and international institutions to respond. Rather than looking for a legalistic trigger to authorize states to intervene—that is, legal hairsplitting about whether there is really genocide according to the 1948 convention—R2P specifies that it is shameful to do nothing when conscience-shocking events cry out for action.[59] The norm thus attempts to mobilize responsibility based on embarrassment in front of peers, but not yet on a sense of legal obligation.

The third ethical and normative contribution is a straightforward recognition that the responsibility to halt mass atrocities may be too much too late. The responsibility to react is preceded by responsibility to prevent. Indeed, ICISS said "prevention is the single most important dimension of the responsibility to protect," a sentiment reinforced by the World Summit.[60] This cannot be said too frequently, because a limited number of third world spoilers frequently get substantial diplomatic resonance from claiming that humanitarian intervention is a synonym for Western imperialism.

The R2P norm has moved quickly, but the concept is in its infancy. The secretary-general's special adviser, Edward Luck, provides a note of caution: "Like most infants, R2P will need to walk before it can run."[61] Nonetheless, many victims will suffer and die if R2P's adolescence is postponed. Vigilance is required to keep up the pressure to better provide this public good for displaced populations. The early 2009 report by the secretary-general was discussed by the General Assembly in July, which afforded civil society and supportive governments the occasion to push skeptical countries and the UN bureaucracy to take seriously Secretary-General Ban Ki-moon's earlier words: "R2P speaks to the things that are most noble and most enduring in the human condition. We will not always succeed in this cardinal enterprise, and we are taking but the first steps in a long journey. But our first responsibility is to try."[62]

R2P is an idea, and we should remind ourselves that ideas matter, for good and for ill. Political theorist Daniel Philpott's study of revolutions in sovereignty demonstrates that they are driven primarily by the power of ideas, and we are in the midst of a revolution in which state sovereignty is becoming more contingent on upholding basic human rights values.[63] Gareth Evans encourages us in his new book on the subject: "And for all the difficulties of acceptance and application that lie ahead, there are—I have come optimistically, but firmly, to believe—not many ideas that have the potential to matter more for good, not only in theory but in practice, than that of the responsibility to protect."[64]

Patience may be a virtue, but so too is impatience in that the normative and operational potential of R2P is enormous and the political bar is not impossibly high. We are, after all, speaking of halting mass atrocities. The ICISS triggers for an international responsibility were massive loss of life and ethnic cleansing. And the World Summit identified genocide, war crimes, ethnic cleansing, and crimes against humanity as triggers. We are thus starting with the morally, legally, and politically easy cases. We are not talking about dampening the seventy-five smoldering conflicts that the International Crisis Group is monitoring this month that could turn deadly, we are not trying to establish peace on earth, and we are not attempting to rid the planet of all human rights abuses. Surely it's not quixotic to say no more Holocausts, Cambodias, and Rwandas—and to mean it.

Notes

1. International Commission on Intervention and State Sovereignty, *The Responsibility to Protect* (Ottawa: International Development Research Centre, 2001). See also Thomas G. Weiss and Don Hubert, *The Responsibility to Protect: Research, Bibliography, Background* (Ottawa: International Development Research Centre, 2001). For the interpretations of one of the co-chairs, see Gareth Evans, *The Responsibility to Protect: Ending Mass Atrocity Crimes Once and for All* (Washington, DC: Brookings Institution Press, 2008). For the perspective of one of the commissioners, Ramesh Thakur, see *The United Nations, Peace, and Security: From Collective Security to the Responsibility to Protect* (Cambridge: Cambridge University Press, 2006). The author's own version of this itinerary can be found in Thomas G. Weiss, *Humanitarian Intervention: Ideas in Action* (Cambridge: Polity Press, 2007). See also Alex J. Bellamy, *Responsibility to Protect: The Global Effort to End Mass Atrocities* (Cambridge: Polity Press, 2009).

2. Gary J. Bass, *Freedom's Battle: The Origins of Humanitarian Intervention* (New York: Knopf, 2008), 382.

3. David Rieff, "A False Compatibility: Humanitarian Action and Human Rights," *Humanitarian Stakes Number 1*, MSF Switzerland, September 2008, 41.

4. Stanley Foundation, *Actualizing the Responsibility to Protect* (Muscatine, IA: Stanley Foundation, 2008).

5. Hugo Slim, "Dithering over Darfur? A Preliminary Review of the International Response," *International Affairs* 80, no. 5 (2004): 811–33. See also Cheryl O. Igiri and Princeton N. Lyman, *Giving Meaning to "Never Again": Seeking an Effective Response to the Crisis in Darfur and Beyond* (New York: Council on Foreign Relations, 2004), CFR no. 5.

6. Roméo Dallaire, "Looking at Darfur, Seeing Rwanda," *New York Times*, October 4, 2004. See also Roméo Dallaire, *Shake Hands with the Devil: The Failure of Humanity in Rwanda* (Toronto: Brent Beardsley, 2004).

7. See Ramesh Thakur, "Humanitarian Intervention," in *The Oxford Handbook of the United Nations*, ed. Thomas G. Weiss and Sam Daws (Oxford: Oxford University Press, 2007), 387–403. For other views, see Christopher Bickerton, Philip Cunliffe, and Alexander Gourevitch, eds., *Politics without Sovereignty* (New York: Routledge, 2007); Simon Chesterman, *Just War? Just Peace? Humanitarian Intervention and International Law* (Oxford: Oxford University Press,

2001); Martha Finnemore, *The Purpose of Intervention: Changing Beliefs about the Use of Force* (Ithaca, NY: Cornell University Press, 2003); and Fernando Tesón, *Humanitarian Intervention: An Inquiry into Law and Morality*, 3rd ed. (Ardsley, NY: Transaction Publishers, 2005).

8. Norwegian Refugee Council, *Internal Displacement: Global Overview of Trends and Developments in 2007* (Geneva: Internal Displacement Monitoring Centre, 2008), 6–21. This is not to say that existing statistics are uncontested because of disputes as to who counts. These statistics reflect the usual practice of referring only to persons uprooted by conflict, but some observers press for much broader notions to encompass millions more uprooted by natural disasters and development. Moreover, there is also no consensus about when displacement ends, thereby inflating figures in some cases. For a discussion, see Erin D. Mooney, "The Concept of Internal Displacement and the Case for IDPs as a Category of Concern," *Refugee Survey Quarterly* 24, no. 3 (2005): 9–26; the title of the entire issue is "Internally Displaced Persons: The Challenges of International Protection," and its sections are titled "Articles," "Documents," and "Literature Survey."

9. See David A. Korn, *Exodus within Borders* (Washington, DC: Brookings Institution, 1999).

10. This story is told by Thomas G. Weiss and David A. Korn, *Internal Displacement: Conceptualization and Its Consequences* (London: Routledge, 2006).

11. David Hollenbach, "Internally Displaced People, Sovereignty, and the Responsibility to Protect," in *Refugee Rights: Ethics, Advocacy, and Africa*, ed. David Hollenbach (Washington, DC: Georgetown University Press, 2008), 179.

12. ICISS, *Responsibility to Protect*, xi.

13. Pope Benedict XVI, "Address to the General Assembly of the United Nations" (Vatican City: Holy See Press Office, April 18, 2008).

14. Anthony Lewis, "The Challenge of Global Justice Now," *Dædalus* 132, no. 1 (2003): 8; and Mohammed Ayoob, "Humanitarian Intervention and International Society," *International Journal of Human Rights* 6, no. 1 (2002): 84. For the context that drives Ayoob's skepticism, see Simon Chesterman, Michael Ignatieff, and Ramesh Thakur, eds., *State Failure and the Crisis of Governance: Making States Work* (Tokyo: UN University Press, 2005).

15. See Bertrand G. Ramcharan, *Contemporary Human Rights Ideas* (London: Routledge, 2008); Julie A. Mertus, *The United Nations and Human Rights*, 2nd ed. (London: Routledge, 2009); and Roger Normand and Sarah Zaidi, *Human Rights at the UN: The Political History of Universal Justice* (Bloomington: Indiana University Press, 2007).

16. Quoted by William Korey, *NGOs and the Universal Declaration of Human Rights: "A Curious Grapevine"* (New York: St. Martin's Press, 1998), 9.

17. Kofi A. Annan, *The Question of Intervention: Statements by the Secretary-General* (New York: UN, 1999).

18. See, for example, Frances M. Deng et al., *Sovereignty as Responsibility: Conflict Management in Africa* (Washington, DC: Brookings Institution Press, 1996); Francis M. Deng, "Frontiers of Sovereignty," *Leiden Journal of International Law* 8, no. 2 (1995): 249–86; Roberta Cohen and Francis M. Deng, *Masses in Flight: The Global Crisis of Internal Displacement* (Washington, DC: Brookings Institution Press, 1998); Roberta Cohen and Francis M. Deng, eds., *The Forsaken People: Case Studies of the Internally Displaced* (Washington, DC: Brookings Institution Press, 1998); Francis M. Deng, *Protecting the Dispossessed: A Challenge for the International Community* (Washington, DC: Brookings Institution Press, 1993); and Francis M. Deng, "Dealing with the Displaced: A Challenge to the International Community," *Global Governance* 1, no. 1 (1995): 45–57.

19. *2005 World Summit Outcome*, UN document A/60/1, October 24, 2005. Paragraphs

138–40 concern the R2P but human rights also are sprinkled throughout the text and are especially prominent in "Section IV. Human Rights and the Rule of Law," paras. 119–45.

20. International Council on Human Rights Policy, *Catching the Wind—Human Rights* (Geneva: International Council on Human Rights Policy, 2007), 7.

21. See Michael Barnett and Thomas G. Weiss, eds., *Humanitarianism in Question: Politics, Power, Ethics* (Ithaca, NY: Cornell University Press, 2008).

22. Richard N. Haass, *The Opportunity: America's Moment to Alter History's Course* (New York: Public Affairs, 2005), 41.

23. See Mary Kaldor, *New and Old Wars: Organized Violence in a Global Era* (Stanford, CA: Stanford University Press, 1999). For a discussion of the nature of humanitarian action in these armed conflicts, see Peter J. Hoffman and Thomas G. Weiss, *Sword & Salve: Confronting New Wars and Humanitarian Crises* (Lanham, MD: Rowman & Littlefield, 2006); and David Keen, *Complex Emergencies* (Cambridge: Polity Press, 2008).

24. Thomas G. Weiss, *Military-Civilian Interactions: Humanitarian Crises and the Responsibility to Protect*, 2nd ed. (Lanham, MD: Rowman & Littlefield, 2005).

25. See, for example, Mohammed Ayoob, "Humanitarian Intervention and International Society," *Global Governance* 7, no. 3 (2001): 225–30; and Robert Jackson, *The Global Covenant: Human Conduct in a World of States* (Oxford: Oxford University Press, 2000).

26. Hugo Slim, *Killing Civilians: Method, Madness, and Morality in War* (New York: Columbia University Press, 2008).

27. Robert J. Rummel, *Death by Government* (New Brunswick, NJ: Transaction Publishers, 1994), chap. 1.

28. Mario Bettati and Bernard Kouchner, eds., *Le Devoir d'ingérence: Peut-on les laisser mourir?* (Paris: Denoël, 1987); and Mario Bettati, *Le Droit d'ingérence: Mutation de l'ordre international* (Paris: Odile Jacob, 1987).

29. Evans, *Responsibility to Protect*, 28.

30. Martha Finnemore and Kathryn Sikkink, "International Norm Dynamics and Political Change," *International Organization* 52, no. 4 (1998): 887–917.

31. Michael Barnett, "Humanitarianism Transformed," *Perspectives on Politics* 3, no. 4 (2005): 723–40.

32. Thomas G. Weiss, "Collective Spinelessness: U.N. Actions in the Former Yugoslavia," in *The World and Yugoslavia's Wars*, ed. Richard H. Ullman (New York: Council on Foreign Relations, 1996), 59–96.

33. Thomas G. Weiss, "The Sunset of Humanitarian Intervention? The Responsibility to Protect in a Unipolar World," *Security Dialogue* 35, no. 2 (2004): 135–53.

34. "Speech Given by the Prime Minister in Sedgefield, Justifying Military Action in Iraq and Warning of the Continued Threat of Global Terrorism," March 5, 2004, www.guardian.co .uk/politics/2004/mar/05/iraq.iraq (accessed May 10, 2009).

35. See, for example, Gareth Evans, "Uneasy Bedfellows: 'The Responsibility to Protect' and Feinstein-Slaughter's 'Duty to Prevent,'" speech at the American Society of International Law Conference, Washington, DC, April 1, 2004, www.crisisweb.org/home/index.cfm?id =2560&l=1 (accessed May 10, 2009).

36. J. Martin Rochester, *Between Peril and Promise: The Politics of International Law* (Washington, DC: CQ Press, 2006), 95.

37. António Guterres, "Millions Uprooted: Saving Refugees and the Displaced," *Foreign Affairs* 87, no. 5 (2008): 93.

38. Thomas G. Weiss and Ramesh Thakur, *The UN and Global Governance: An Unfinished Journey* (Bloomington: Indiana University Press, 2010), esp. chapter 10.

39. Adele Brown, *Reinventing Humanitarian Intervention: Two Cheers for the Responsibility to Protect?* (London: House of Commons Library, 2008), 18.

40. I acknowledge here insights from Don Hubert's private paper developed for the Global Centre for the Responsibility to Protect, August 2008.

41. Ban Ki-moon, *Implementing the Responsibility to Protect, A Report from the Secretary-General,* UN document A/63/67, January 12, 2009.

42. Global Centre for the Responsibility to Protect, *The 2009 General Assembly Debate: An Assessment* (New York: GCR2P, 2009), 1. The four states were the usual suspects: Venezuela, Cuba, Sudan, and Nicaragua.

43. Kofi Annan, *Renewing the United Nations: A Programme for Reform* (New York: UN, 1997). For the details of this story, see Thomas G. Weiss, "Humanitarian Shell Games: Whither UN Reform?" *Security Dialogue* 29, no.1 (1998): 9–23.

44. High-level Panel on UN System-wide Coherence on Development, Humanitarian Assistance, and the Environment, *Delivering as One* (New York: UN, 2006); and United Nations, *A Capacity Study of the United Nations Development System,* 2 vols. (Geneva: United Nations, 1969), document DP/5. The importance of changing the excessively decentralized UN system is a major theme in Thomas G. Weiss, *What's Wrong with the United Nations and How to Fix It* (Cambridge: Polity Press, 2009), chaps. 3 and 7.

45. See, for example, Antonio Donini, *The Policies of Mercy: UN Coordination in Afghanistan, Mozambique, and Rwanda* (Providence, RI: Watson Institute, 1996), occasional paper #22.

46. Interview with the author, October 11, 2005.

47. Abby Stoddard, Adele Harmer, Katherinie Haver, Dirk Salomons, and Victoria Wheeler, *Cluster Approach Evaluation: Final Draft* (New York: OCHA Evaluation and Studies Section, 2007), 1.

48. See Alan J. Kuperman, *The Limits of Humanitarian Intervention: Genocide in Rwanda* (Washington, DC: Brookings Institution Press, 2001).

49. See Patrice C. McMahon and Andrew Wedeman, "Sustaining American Power in a Globalized World," in *American Foreign Policy in a Globalized World,* ed. David P. Forsythe, Patrice C. McMahon, and Andrew Wedeman (New York: Routledge, 2006), 12–14.

50. See Victoria K. Holt and Tobias C. Berkman, *The Impossible Mandate? Military Preparedness, the Responsibility to Protect, and Modern Peace Operations* (Washington, DC: Stimson Center, 2006).

51. Genocide Prevention Task Force, *Preventing Genocide: A Blueprint for U.S. Policymakers* (Washington, DC: American Academy of Diplomacy, United States Holocaust Memorial Museum, and the U.S. Institute of Peace, 2008).

52. For a brief discussion, see Thomas G. Weiss, "The Ultimate UN and Human Value: Making 'Never Again' More than a Slogan," in *The United Nations and the Evolution of Global Values,* ed. J. J. G. van der Bruggen and Nico J. Schrijver (The Hague: Kluwer, forthcoming).

53. Quoted in *The Economist,* December 13, 2008, 43.

54. *A Secure Europe in a Better World,* http://ue.eu.int/pressData/en/reports/78367.pdf (accessed May 14, 2009).

55. See Bastian Giegrich and William Wallace, "Not Such a Soft Power: The External Deployment of European Forces," *Survival* 46, no. 2 (2004): 163–82, quote 179.

56. Quoted by Lincoln Palmer Bloomfield, *Accidental Encounters with History (and Some Lessons Learned)* (Cohasset, MA: Hot House Press, 2005), 14.

57. Edward C. Luck, "The United Nations and the Responsibility to Protect," *Policy Analysis Brief* (Muscatine, IA: Stanley Foundation, 2008), 6.

58. Roger Cohen, "How Kofi Annan Rescued Kenya," *New York Review of Books,* August 14,

2008. www.nybooks.com/articles/21719. See also Desmond Tutu, "Taking the Responsibility to Protect," *International Herald Tribune,* February 19, 2008.

59. See Scott Straus, "Darfur and the Genocide Debate," *Foreign Affairs* 84, no. 1 (2005): 123–33.

60. ICISS, *Responsibilty to Protect*, xi.

61. Luck, "The United Nations and the Responsibility to Protect," 8.

62. Ban Ki-moon, "Address of the Secretary-General, Berlin, July 15, 2008," UN document SG/SM/11701.

63. Daniel Philpott, *Revolutions in Sovereignty: How Ideas Shaped Modern International Relations* (Princeton, NJ: Princeton University Press, 2001).

64. Evans, *Responsibility to Protect*, 7.

Part V

Protection in Response to Economic Need and Environmental Crises

11

Economic and Environmental Displacement

Implications for Durable Solutions

Mary M. DeLorey

Large-scale migration is a reality of our times, and there is every indication that new factors, such as climate change, have the potential to increase dramatically both the number and needs of the displaced. To more effectively respond to current migration flows, we need to expand our understanding of the multiplicity of factors driving people to migrate, the significance of defining distinct categories of migrants, and the implications of narrowing or expanding the concept of what "forced migration" and the need for protection means today.

This chapter focuses on the economic factors that may result in forced migration. These include the severity of poverty; economic factors that lead to violent conflict, subsequently resulting in the traditionally recognized forms of forced displacement; and environmental conditions that compel new forms of necessity-driven migration. Identifying legitimate distinctions between various forms of migration and displacement is necessary to ensure that hard-won and internationally recognized protections for refugees, asylum seekers, and internally displaced populations are maintained and strengthened.

In recent discussions with the United Nations High Commissioner for Refugees (UNHCR) on improving the international response to mixed migration flows, great emphasis has been placed on the protection system as currently defined in reference to refugees and asylum seekers. This should not be surprising, as the need to promote and defend protection rights for these endangered individuals and groups is central to the UNHCR mandate. What is problematic is that these discussions fluctuate between recognition of the gaps in international protection for other vulnerable migrating populations on the one hand, and on the other, efforts that appear to preserve the rights of one vulnerable group (refugees) potentially at the cost of minimizing or denying the pressing needs of others.

This is of even greater concern when a large proportion of the migration occurring globally is categorized as "voluntary" and treated as if it were a relatively frivolous act of improving one's lot in life, even when the conditions that led to migration afforded few viable options to remain in communities of origin. The lack of internationally recognized rights to minimum standards of development or of a right to basic protections in migratory processes creates an environment in which exploitation and abuse flourish before, during, and after migration.

The litany of suffering and abuse experienced throughout the world by migrants, particularly those without legal status, is extensive. Information on the extreme conditions under which migrants travel or are transported by smugglers is abundant, including drowning and suffocation in overcrowded and dangerous cargo holds, mutilations from falling or being pushed from trains, deaths from exposure or dehydration at border crossings, high rates of physical and sexual violence in transit, and detention under terrible conditions. All of these abuses occur under conditions where there is little or no recourse to adequate protection, legal representation, or services.

In this context, the factors compelling so many to take great risks with their lives and their futures deserve serious analysis and response. The legitimacy of the "voluntary migration" concept should be called into question for people facing severe economic deprivation, the symbiotic relationship between economic inequalities and protracted conflicts, and emerging impacts of climate change and environmental degradation. From the perspective of the Catholic Church and many of its social service and international development organizations, the movement of "those who flee economic conditions that threaten their lives and physical safety, the so-called 'economic migrants' . . . is obviously more forced than voluntary."[1]

The need for an improved overall response was well articulated in a statement of nongovernmental organizations to the UNHCR Standing Committee on the asylum-migration nexus:

> While we agree with UNHCR and States that it is essential to continue to distinguish those who have and raise claims to asylum, that should not end the conversation, or the need for a protection response regarding the others. But, because the risk is so high for so many, because the rates of death are being propelled steadily higher by a mix of human smugglers, traffickers, and enforcement-induced channelling of migrants into ever more dangerous routes, the international conversation—and response—cannot end simply by calling the rest of the travellers "economic migrants." . . . If not asylum-seekers, *many* are victims of human trafficking or other international crimes. Literally countless others are victims of extortion, assault, rape, and murder on the high seas, and in other border areas. Protection is not just for asylum-seekers and refugees. . . . We believe that at the core of international mandates for protection is recognition that it is mortal risk that compels protection, not status.[2]

The severity of abuses, mounting death rates, and minimal protection of the most basic rights of this larger body of migrants cannot be ignored. An emerging recognition of what has become a diffuse humanitarian crisis in some regions makes an increasingly strong case for the development of greater protection coverage and greater implementation of currently existing migrant rights provisions.

Before we can consider what might be the right answers to such complex challenges, we need to examine whether we are asking the right questions. When it comes to current migration from areas that may simultaneously suffer from some combination of poverty, conflict, poor governance, corruption, environmental degradation, and so on, who defines the choice in migration and who does the choosing? How severe do conditions need to become to reach a tipping point where migration can no longer be considered a choice? If the alternative is starvation? Or is malnutrition the acceptable dividing line? Or is the lack of access to health care, basic education, or minimal standards of employment to meet the needs of one's family a sufficient criterion?

A Few Definitions

We can begin by considering some basic definitions that will be used throughout this chapter. In any discussion of migration or its management and impact, we need to clarify how broadly or narrowly we are defining the terminology employed.

Refugees

The word "refugees" here will not be used loosely; that is, it will not include other forms of involuntary or forced migration as has become rhetorically commonplace, but rather will refer to the 1951 United Nations (UN) Convention Relating to the Status of Refugees definition and subsequent expansion under regional legal instruments and jurisprudence. Hence, I refer here to people outside their country of origin who are unable or unwilling to return there because of a well-founded fear of persecution.[3] After the establishment of the 1951 UN Convention, the refugee notion broadened to also include those who have fled the indiscriminate effects of generalized violence or serious public disorder.[4]

Internally Displaced Persons (IDPs)

The internally displaced are often similar to refugees in their reasons for displacement and in hardships experienced, but they remain within their own country of origin, and those displaced by natural disasters and large-scale development projects are often recognized as involuntarily internally displaced persons as well. IDPs may be particularly vulnerable, as they often remain in close proximity to armed conflicts and groups that caused their displacement, and there are few international legal or institutional systems in place to respond to their protection needs. States have primary responsibility for responding to the needs of the internally displaced (rather than the international protection regime), though in many cases the state is unwilling or unable to respond adequately or is actively involved in causing or at least tolerating significant displacement of its own citizens. More precisely, based on the UNHCR's *Guiding Principles on Internal Displacement*, "Internally displaced persons are persons or groups of persons who have been forced or obliged to flee or to leave their homes or places of habitual residence, in particular as a result of or in order to avoid the effects of armed conflict, situations of generalized violence, violations of human rights or natural or human-made disasters, and who have not crossed an internationally recognized State border."[5]

Economic Migrants

There are currently close to 200 million persons living outside of their country of origin. The majority of these persons would be considered economic migrants, or persons who migrate for reasons of family reunification, education, improved employment options, and so on. In this essay the focus will not be on those for whom migration is clearly a personal choice or opportunity, but on the significant number of vulnerable migrants leaving situations of poverty, marginalization, environmental degradation, and/or a combination of economic and conflict conditions, though the conflict itself may not be the primary motivation for migration. For these economic migrants, or perhaps more accurately, these economically displaced, the concept of "choice" is questionable.

Although much of migration in all its forms still occurs within the boundaries of people's own countries, it is the cross-border movement that has garnered much attention, alarm, and resistance in official and unofficial policy and practice. Current avenues for legal and safe migration throughout the world are quite limited and more reflective of social fears and political sensitivities than the economic realities of countries of destination or origin. This disconnect has given rise to restrictive migration policies and increasingly harsh enforcement measures as well as large-scale, irregular migration, a condition under which all manner of exploitation has been documented.

The limitations of the most basic protections for economic migrants are perhaps unintentionally underlined in one of the instruments designed to increase their protection, the International Convention on the Protection of the Rights of All Migrant Workers and the Members of Their Families, which entered into force in 2003 (though adopted by General Assembly resolution in 1990).[6] It is telling that those who drafted the Convention felt it necessary to explicitly include Article 9, which states that "the right to life of migrant workers and members of their families shall be protected by law."

Environmental Migrants

It is worth noting a category projected to expand dramatically into the future, given what is known about global climate change and its current and future impact on the environment and livelihoods of some of the poorest nations and their people. Currently, according to the International Organization on Migration, "Environmental migrants are persons or groups of persons who, for compelling reasons of sudden or progressive changes in the environment that adversely affect their lives or living conditions, are obliged to leave their habitual homes, or choose to do so, either temporarily or permanently, and who move either within their country or abroad."[7]

Environmental degradation has led to past and current displacement and migration, but the scale of what we may be facing in the not distant future deserves particular attention. Currently, environmental migrants generally have moved or been displaced within their own countries of origin on a temporary, seasonal, or permanent basis. When they have crossed borders, they have generally been considered economic migrants. However, if the projections for climate change impact come to pass, the justification for classifying such displacement as voluntary is likely to be erased.

Trafficking in Persons

Finally, migrants and displaced persons are a disproportionate percentage of the victims of human trafficking. By trafficking in persons we refer to

> the recruitment, transportation, transfer, harboring or receipt of persons, by means of the threat or use of force or other forms of coercion, of abduction, of fraud, of deception, of the abuse of power or of a position of vulnerability or of the giving or receiving of payments or benefits to achieve the consent of a person having control over another person, for the purpose of exploitation. Exploitation includes, at a minimum, the exploitation of the prostitution of others or other forms of sexual exploitation, forced labor or services, slavery or practices similar to slavery, servitude or the removal of organs.[8]

In contexts where safe, legal, and timely options for migration or resettlement are limited or do not exist, migrants, displaced persons, and refugees are at considerable risk of becoming victims of human trafficking as they make desperate decisions to get out of harm's way or are deceived by what they believe to be legitimate job offers by employment contractors, acquaintances, or even friends and relatives.

Economic Drivers and Conflict Displacement

There is a substantial body of research and analysis on the relationship between violent conflict and economic factors such as wealth creation and distribution, resource scarcity and control, economic profiteering from conflict by armed actors and others within society, and so on. Several key ways economic factors lead to conflict will briefly be summarized here, although it must be clearly stated that these factors are generally only part of a more complex toxic mix of elements creating violent conflict today. Just as it is a truism that healthy families tend to exhibit very similar characteristics whereas dysfunctional families manifest their own unique set of dysfunctions, so too the unique set of the historical, economic, social, and political features that lead to violent conflict in poorly functioning societies should not be underestimated.

The nature of violent conflict continues to evolve over time, altering some aspects of the relationship between conflict and displacement. This brief overview will look at the relationships between income levels, their distribution, and conflict; access and control of natural resources; and the impact of conflict itself on subsequent economic vulnerability of those directly displaced by conflict, but also more broadly on their societies.

The majority of violent conflicts since World War II that have generated forced displacement have been within rather than between nation states. In general they are longer and have more directly targeted civilians than has been the case in interstate conflicts. Most of today's violent conflicts are also disproportionately occurring in some of the poorest nations, though a simple causal relationship between high rates of poverty and conflict should not be assumed. Factors that have been associated with the prevalence or likelihood of violent conflict (poor governance, environmental stressors, population growth, lack of democratic structures) are also correlated with high rates of poverty, whether violent expressions of conflict exist or not.

Most economic studies of violent conflicts have indicated that increased levels of wealth within a society reduce the likelihood of civil war. According to World Bank figures, a country with a gross domestic product (GDP) of $250 per capita has a 15 percent probability of war at some time in the next five years. This probability is reduced by half in countries with a GDP of $600 per person and continues to decrease to 4 percent for a country with a per person income of $1,250.[9] A number of studies assert that there is little empirical evidence to demonstrate a strong relationship between overall inequality in a society and the likelihood of violent conflict. However, when income disparity accrues along ethnic or regional lines, a situation that Macartan Humphreys refers to as "horizontal inequality," there is a much stronger case for the combination of economic inequality and such social factors resulting in violent conflict.[10]

It should also be noted that internal conflicts impel nonstate armed actors to become economic actors in order to generate funding to sustain their basic needs as well as to promote their military, political, and economic agendas. Where insurgents or rebels receive general support from the local population, there may be options for them to carry out activities on a part-time basis and maintain some form of regular employment to meet basic needs. This was the case with Chechnya rebels and the Irish Republican Army (IRA), for example.[11] But this is not the norm. Most insurgent groups maintain their activities through either the support or sponsorship of external actors (third parties that could include other governments, diaspora communities or corporations, and entities with vested interest in the conflict and its outcome), or through some form of control of natural resources (such as conflict diamonds), geographic control of agricultural production, and/or a variety of illicit activities such as looting, drug production, and kidnapping for ransom (or "miracle fishing," as the Revolutionary Armed Forces of Colombia [FARC] guerrillas referred to their kidnapping strategy).

Although not a new phenomenon, the role natural resources and particularly extractive industries play in the creation or sustainability of current conflicts has received much-needed attention in recent years. Research such as that conducted by Paul Collier and Anke Hoeffler at the World Bank has led to the assertion that economies largely dependent on the sale of primary commodities, whether extracted natural resources or agricultural products, are particularly prone to civil violence.[12]

The tremendous resources generated by extractive industries have too often done little to reduce the poverty of the many and much to enrich the coffers of the few, while exacerbating or generating conflict—an outcome frequently cited as the "paradox of plenty." There are many ways this relationship manifests itself beyond the financing of armed actors who may gain control of such resources. For example, extraction wealth can be more unjustly distributed across geographic and societal fault lines than more dispersed sources of wealth. Wealth generated from extractive industries may be particularly lucrative, and has had a history of limited transparency and accountability in terms of profits generated, whether these profits are destined to go to state or nonstate actors. Such factors create a ripe playing field for corruption to flourish, with the potential to further undermine governability and simultaneously provide substantial additional resources that can be applied to armed conflict.

Even removing the element of the abuse of resources for personal enrichment, it has been demonstrated that governments which rely on natural resources rather than taxation tend to be characterized by weak institutional structures and to have limited motivation to respond to needs of their citizens, who in this context are less likely to be seen as stakeholders in sustaining governmental functions. In addition, either the existence of violent conflict or the fear of its occurring can in and of itself create greater dependency on extractive industries or primary commodities, as other economic resources, including tourism, manufacturing, foreign investment, and agricultural production, decline in a situation of instability.

A vicious circle can be further established as increased military expenditures on the part of the state generally go hand in hand with decreased social expenditures. A decline in social spending can impact the very factors that determine whether or not conditions are viable for people to remain in their communities or lead to increased levels of displacement.

Finally, it should also be noted that there are often long-term economic ramifications for people who have been forcibly displaced, whether they remain within their own country or cross borders in their flight. Returning refugees and IDPs often find homes and land destroyed or occupied by others, as has been the case in Guatemala, the Balkans, and Sudan's Darfur region. In many cases the option for return will never occur, nor will any form of compensation be made available comparable to what has been lost in terms of homes, property, belongings, and livelihoods. Indeed, even when peace agreements include acknowledgment of economic losses and ostensibly provide some form of redress, such provisions—if implemented at all—are slow in coming and minimal in coverage. Peace agreements in Guatemala, Mexico, and Peru and a demobilization accord with paramilitaries in Colombia all included some combination of provisions intended to address the issue of the return or distribution of land, resettlement options for the displaced, and various forms of compensation. In large measure these provisions have not been implemented. Collective ownership and customary tenure of land, most closely associated with indigenous populations and with Afro-Colombians in the case of Colombia, have often been lost as a shared community asset, with accompanying losses of cultural identity and survival. Such unresolved aspects of violent conflict deepen and expand impoverishment, with the potential to stimulate subsequent migration.

The seeds of large-scale migration may be sown by the fallout from earlier conflicts that leave unaddressed the economic and social underpinnings that caused the conflict in the first place, and by the added burden of the uncompensated victims of such conflict. El Salvador is a case in point. Although its peace accord is often referenced as a success story, issues of land and income distribution, access to rural credit, and reinsertion of armed actors were not well addressed, and murder rates (attributed to disenfranchised youth gangs and more generalized crime) are higher now than during the conflict itself. Migration patterns that took off during the war and established themselves in its problematic aftermath have fueled high rates of continuing migration. Between 20 and 25 percent of the Salvadoran population now lives outside the country.

The Economics of Involuntary Migration

The current controversy over forced versus voluntary migration primarily focuses on people who are migrating or have been displaced for reasons other than violent conflict, generalized violence, or direct forms of persecution. As stated earlier, such migration is generally referred to as voluntary in nature, even as those migrating confront conditions that present few viable alternatives to remain and meet their basic needs. Highlighting the conditions confronted in many countries that produce mass migration today, economist Jeffery Sachs has become a notable spokesman for the necessity of addressing the widespread poverty that maintains its grip on much of the world's population. He states the stark reality that "more than 8 million people around the world die each year because they are too poor to stay alive." Every morning our newspapers could report, "More than 20,000 people perished yesterday of extreme poverty."[13]

Nearly half of the six billion people in the world today are living in poverty, with poverty subdivided into extreme, moderate, and relative. This terminology, though technically accepted and recognized, nonetheless has a surprisingly cavalier tone, considering the seriousness of poverty's consequences. Extreme poverty refers to people who survive, just barely, on less than one dollar a day. They are largely unable to meet basic needs, as demonstrated by the harrowing death rates noted above. Amazingly, the poor who survive on one to two dollars a day are considered to be at a moderate poverty level. It is hard to imagine that anyone surviving on two dollars a day would themselves believe their poverty is moderate. However, it should also be noted that in large measure, particularly when it comes to cross-border migration, it is not the very poorest who are most likely to migrate. The resources of the very poorest are limited to such a degree that it hinders their ability to relocate altogether.

Adding to these conditions, one of the most recent developments of concern for poor countries and communities is the global food crisis that came rapidly to the fore in 2008. The price of wheat doubled in less than a year, rice—the staple food of three billion people worldwide—tripled in cost in eighteen months, and there were increases in the cost of other staples. The result was widespread hunger, and many poor families had to utilize 75 percent of their income for food. According to the World Bank, these elevated prices are expected to continue at least through 2009, and though they may balance out over time, they will continue through 2015 to be higher than levels in 2004. As of yet the food crisis has not created large-scale migration across borders, but combined with other current crises (in economic markets, in environmental change, etc.) the cumulative impact remains to be seen.

Current migration trends can also be analyzed in the context of globalization processes that have created both substantial opportunities and inequalities in an increasingly interconnected system of economic and social relations. Inequalities between and within countries have accelerated in recent years. In 1900 the ratio of the average income in terms of purchasing power of the five richest countries to the five to ten poorest was 9 to 1; by 1960 it was 30 to 1; today it is 100 to 1.[14]

Although countries and regions can attest to a diversity of driving factors for migration, the example of Latin America (a region producing one of the highest rates of migration) is illustrative. The basic economic framework that has been promoted within Latin America since the 1980s has not produced the hoped for positive results for a large percentage of the population, particularly for the poor. This model has been characterized by a radical modification of economic structures and primary actors, including the reduction of the role of the national government in the economy, which has resulted in a limited number of winners and many losers. Priority is given to foreign trade over economic development within countries, and traditional agricultural production and small and medium enterprises have been reduced in favor of agricultural concentration and large-scale manufacturing.

The model has resulted in a reduction in social welfare protections, expectations for employment, and real wages. For example, in the last twenty years the Mexican minimum wage has decreased by 70 percent in real terms. Given the rapid onset of widespread and now global economic crisis in 2009, it remains to be seen what the implications will be for developing countries and the most vulnerable in their societies. The economic prescriptions promoted until recently as normative for growth, fiscal responsibility and participation in neoliberal financial practices are now called into serious question if not disrepute by poorer nations that have not experienced the economic benefits anticipated.

In addition, the current design of many multilateral trade agreements and economic integration processes—accompanied by exaggerated promises of economic growth for the benefit of all, reduction of migration, and creation of viable employment alternatives—have not lived up to public relations claims.

Although positive macro level growth rates have been documented, little has been achieved and in fact much lost in terms of poverty reduction and improved economic distribution. In the period following the approval of the North American Free Trade Agreement (NAFTA), for example, Mexico lost over 2 million agricultural jobs, with 1.7 million small farmers forced from their land and into urban areas or across borders. Mexican migration to the United States increased by 1.5 million from 2000 to 2005, alone with an estimated five hundred thousand undocumented Mexicans entering annually by 2005. NAFTA, of course, is not the only economic factor implicated in this case, but its impact on poverty reduction is far from encouraging. Even before the recent large-scale increases in migration in the Americas, the International Confederation of Free Trade Unions and the *Organizacion*

Regional Interamericana de Trajabadores (ICFTU/ORIT) was sounding an alarm. González Alvarado and Hilda Sanchez have noted that an ICFTU/ORIT resolution was concerned about "the marked increase in migration in the Americas. . . . Most migrant workers left countries because of recurrent economic crisis or serious political conflicts." Hence the top priority for the international community should be "to help create situations where people were not forced to leave their family, their community, or their country." Furthermore, the resolution urged the international bodies, especially UNHCR, "to review the criteria for the recognition of . . . refugee status in order to establish protective mechanisms for those who leave their countries fleeing from extreme hardship."[15]

As a side note, it should also be mentioned that some of these proposed "cures" for displacement can be as bad as, if not worse, than the problems they seek to resolve. Large-scale development projects, designed eventually to improve living conditions within countries, have long been cited for causing large-scale displacement. The World Bank has estimated that every year since 1990, 10 million people are displaced by infrastructure development projects. In the last fifty years, 25 million have been displaced in India in this manner and 40 million in China. Little sympathy is garnered for those displaced in this manner, even as they confront many of the same issues as those displaced for other reasons, with particularly negative impacts for populations that were historically marginalized prior to displacement. According to a World Commission on Dams study, increased impoverishment has generally been the end result for resettled people, with unemployment, hunger, debt bondage, and cultural disintegration characterizing their displacement experience.

Thus, large-scale and high-risk migration is likely to continue to be a hallmark of the coming years if more serious attention, commitment, and resources are not directed toward the factors that eliminate the right not to migrate or be displaced. UNHCR documents explicitly concur with the Global Commission on International Migration report when the latter states that "women, men, and children should be able to realize their potential, meet their needs, exercise their human rights, and fulfil their aspirations in their country of origin, and hence migrate out of choice, rather than necessity."[16] Such an affirmation of the right not to migrate similarly is a core principal in Catholic social teaching on migration.

Environmental Migrants: Climate Change and Environmental Degradation

The issues of environmental degradation and climate change and their relation to forced displacement are included here because this form of displacement is expected to expand considerably in the coming years. It is impacted by a variety of economic conditions and policies and currently confronts many of the same limitations on protection as the broad category of economic migration. In fact, the current level of slow-onset environmental migration is generally considered economic rather than environmental in motivation and is responded to as such.

Certainly not all environmental drivers of displacement can be attributed to climate change, but it is the issue that has captured much attention in the past decade, although harbingers of this growing crisis have been cited for a longer period of time. It is still unclear how large and how rapidly it will cause or expand displacement, and projections vary widely. According to the UN International Strategy for Disaster Reduction (ISDR), over the past thirty years disasters—storms, floods, and droughts—have increased threefold.[17] As early as 1990, the Intergovernmental Panel on Climate Change argued that the greatest single impact of climate change would be on migration/displacement.

More recently John Holmes, UN undersecretary-general for humanitarian affairs and emergency relief coordinator, stated that "Nine of out of every ten disasters are now climate-related." In 2007 his office at the UN issued an unprecedented fifteen funding appeals for sudden natural disasters, five more than the previous annual record. Fourteen of them were climate-related.[18] Additionally, according to World Bank reports, if sea levels increase by a single meter as a result of melting ice fields, 56 million people will be displaced in eighty-four countries.[19]

Elizabeth Ferris of the Brookings-Bern Project on Internal Displacement outlined the primary conceptual models currently applied to project climate change impacts on future displacement.[20] She highlighted four key focus areas. The first area in which climate change impacts displacement is the likely increase in sudden-onset natural disasters (hurricanes, flooding, etc). These climatic phenomena are expected to become more prevalent and cause increasing damage. As with current natural disasters, most of those displaced by such future disasters are likely to remain within the borders of their country, and those who cross international borders will generally be considered voluntary migrants.

Displacement as a result of the sudden onset of disasters is often temporary, although it may have long-term economic impacts for people already living at or below subsistence levels. For an example of the disproportionate impact of natural disasters on the poor with preexisting vulnerabilities, we can look to the example of the impact of Hurricane Mitch—a natural disaster that caused devastating damage in Central America in 1998. The devastation of the hurricane was followed by increases in subsequent cross-border migration. Household economies without any form of insurance against such disasters (loss of homes and income, increased health costs) were hard hit, and agricultural capacity and infrastructure needed to be rebuilt. The destruction was particularly widespread and long-term for those least able to recover, namely, poor families and communities who, due to their earlier marginalization, often lived in substandard housing in precarious, risk-sensitive geographic areas.

Although temporary displacement begins in anticipation of or upon impact of natural disasters, the longer-term displacement or associated migration generally occurs some months later, as families are not able to sufficiently recoup what can be devastating economic losses. This delayed response generates disaster/environmental-related migration that is often simply categorized as voluntary economic migration.

The second model for climate change impact on displacement is slow-onset environmental change (desertification and agricultural decline, increased water-related stressors, whether in terms of access to water or its overabundance, and other changes in weather patterns that make former livelihoods unsustainable). People displaced through these longer-term processes will generally also be considered primarily economic or voluntary migrants.

Environmental degradation, whether directly related to climate change or an overlapping reality, can be a gradual process over a number of years that contributes to migratory patterns within and between countries. When the initial migration flow is ignored and factors promoting voluntary movement continue to deteriorate, increasing migration levels can exacerbate preexisting conflicts. Based on the illustrative example of Darfur and how this process has played out in other contexts, the rather common sense assessment has been made that "it is easier to integrate hundreds of people displaced as a result of environmental degradation than it is to resettle, return, or integrate hundreds of thousands as a result of violent conflict created by inadequate responses to the initial migration."[21]

A third area concerns how climate change may lead to greater conflict over scarce essential resources (water, adequate food production) and thus to subsequent displacement. Although the displacement has multiple causes and may begin with the environmental factors, those displaced by subsequent conflict are likely to be characterized as traditionally recognized internally displaced and refugees based on the conflict motivator, rather than as environmentally displaced. They may also continue to be considered economic migrants if the conflict itself is not seen as the primary reason for their movement.

Researchers such as Tad Homer-Dixon have examined environmental changes and their impact on conflict-based theories of scarcity. His research has largely focused on the impact of the scarcity of water and arable land, primarily in Africa, on patterns of population movement. With climate change, such impact is likely to increase as the amount of arable land in the world decreases, fresh water sources decline, water tables in general are lowered, and aquifers dry up.[22]

The fourth area that Ferris cites is the interaction of climate change impact and poor governmental response, resulting ultimately in eventual forced migration. Famine is an example of an end result of conditions that usually involve some combination of poor environmental conditions, inappropriate or inadequate government response, and societal fissures that drive or sustain inequalities or conflict. One of the concerns in this area is the speed at which environmental change is occurring—a rate that can outstrip the ability of even willing and able governments and communities to adapt quickly enough to address increase food security challenges.

Environmental change, even when not the principal driver of displacement, is likely to have a multiplier effect on other factors contributing to the need to migrate. Discussions are already under way on how the international system should (and will be able to) respond to people displaced by climate change who will simply not be able to return to areas that are no longer habitable. This produces a new challenge to the concept of durable solutions and how it will be applied in the future. In this context it must be asked what protection norms currently exist or should be developed for people who will never have the option to return home?

An area of particular concern is the expectation of an increase in statelessness, most immediately in relation to the situation of small island nations that may be inundated and cease to exist. Several island nations in the Pacific are already nego-tiating contingency plans with other countries for resettlement of their populations should the need to abandon their land become imminent.

Conclusion

There remains a need for continued recognition and strengthening of the unique protection rights of refugees and asylum seekers as defined by the 1951 UN Conven-tion, as well as subsequent recognition of those endangered by widespread violence and conflict, as the UNHCR has consistently maintained. The larger issue of our time is how to ensure more appropriate and humane responses to a broader range of vulnerable displaced and migrating populations and to protect their most basic of rights. Concurrently, we are confronted with the necessity to support more effective responses to address the economic, conflict, and environmental factors that have undermined the possibility of a safe and dignified life in many areas experiencing high rates of emigration.

There are no simple answers or quick fixes to such needs for large-scale change, but some initial steps can be taken to begin to address aspects of the current protec-tion gaps. For Catholic Church organizations, our starting point in conceptualizing a just and humane response to migration is based in principles contained in Catho-lic social teaching on migration.[23] Given the concerns outlined in this chapter, the recommendations that follow grow out these principles, which largely summarize approaches elaborated by Church as well as by civil society advocates and the UN special rapporteur on the human rights of migrants.[24]

Principle 1. Everyone has a right to find opportunities within one's own homeland or the right not to migrate.

This principle is drawn from Catholic social teaching and more general human rights perspectives and it emphasizes that all people have the right to find in their own countries the economic, political, and social opportunities to live in dignity and not be compelled to migrate. Although addressing the economic drivers of mi-gration and displacement is likely to be a far greater challenge than establishing and implementing protection mechanisms, responding to this challenge must remain a priority for states and the international community. Thus, we can recommend initiatives in the following areas:

Reducing poverty and social exclusion. One significant step in the right direction was the development of the Millennium Development Goals (MDGs), which arguably represent an international consensus on commitments and measurable standards by which poverty and marginalization can be reduced. Greater commitment to and promotion of these goals must continue as vigorously as possible, even given current global economic concerns. As Archbishop Celestino Migliore of the Holy See's Delegation to the United Nations recently stated, "A failure in attaining the MDGs in the LDCs [Least Developed Countries] and other poor countries would mean a moral failure of the whole international community and have political and economic consequences even beyond the geographic boundaries of [these countries]."[25]

Climate change. Additionally, as outlined in this chapter, the time to prepare for emerging displacement caused by environmental degradation and climate change is now, not when it reaches crisis proportions. In situations where the population that will be impacted is small and the threat is imminent (such as Pacific Island nations), proactive planning is under way. The greater challenge will be in areas where large-scale population movement is already occurring and more recent environmental push factors are not sufficiently understood.

Environmental displacement research. More research should be dedicated to understanding the relationship between climate change, migration, and forced displacement. That would make possible adequate planning and response to anticipated needs can occur prior to displacement.

Mitigation and adaptation initiatives. Significant resources should be dedicated to initiatives to mitigate and adapt to environmental change, as well as to more general disaster risk reduction. That is particularly the case where impact on poor and marginal communities is most likely to be severe.

Principle 2. Where conditions do not exist to meet the basic needs of people, they have the right to migrate to support themselves and their families.

This, too, is a principle of Church teaching: "When persons cannot find employment in their country of origin to support themselves and their families, they have a right to find work elsewhere in order to survive. Sovereign nations should provide ways to accommodate this right."[26] These concerns lead to several recommendations.

Increase legal migration options. Every effort should be made to promote legal migratory channels that more adequately respond to the mutual economic, labor, security, and human rights needs of countries of origin and destination. The existence of realistic levels of safe, legal, and regulated migration options has the potential to reduce many of the extremes of exploitation currently experienced by migrants in transit.

Incorporate a human rights framework into migration policy and multilateral agreements. "States should incorporate the applicable human rights framework into their bilateral and regional arrangements for managing migration flows. Specific attention should be paid to detainees, smuggled migrants, and victims of trafficking, children, women, asylum-seekers and other vulnerable groups."[27]

Principle 3. The Catholic Church recognizes that sovereign nations have the right to control their borders in ways that respect the human dignity of migrants.

The Church has not promoted an "open border" policy, but rather safe, legal, orderly policies that are as generous as possible and that take into account the needs of both migrant families and the communities/countries of destination. Enforcement and border control practices need to be applied in a humane manner that respects the human dignity of migrants. This will require:

Incorporate the principles of the International Convention on the protection of the rights of all migrant workers and members of their families into national migration policies. An international legal framework for the protection of migrant workers exists and came into force in 1990 (in the form of the UN Convention on the Rights of Migrant Workers and Their Families). It has not, however, been ratified by any of the major industrialized destination countries and lacks effective implementation or enforcement. Though it may be unlikely for the major destination countries to sign or ratify the Convention in the foreseeable future, states should be encouraged to, at a minimum, incorporate guidance provided in the Convention to ensure that migration takes place in humane and equitable conditions and with comprehensive protection for nonnationals in expulsion procedures.[28]

Principle 4. The human dignity and human rights of all migrants should be respected.

Regardless of their legal status, migrants, like all persons, possess inherent human dignity that should be respected. This will require the following initiatives:

Expand national and international human rights protections for migrants regardless of status. It must be recognized and affirmed that even in the absence of migrant-specific protection coverage, "States have the responsibility and the obligation to respect and protect the human rights of all those within its territory, nationals and non-nationals alike, regardless of mode of entry or migratory status."[29] Migrants, as with all persons, have inherent human rights that must be respected.

Recognize humanitarian imperatives. There should be recognition of humanitarian imperatives and the need to create international standards for humanitarian response to vulnerable, injured, and traumatized migrants.[30] Existing guiding principles on the rights of the internally displaced and on human rights in disaster response should serve as a starting point.

Migration is not only an economic, social, and legal issue; it is also a humanitarian and, ultimately, a moral one. The status quo is morally unacceptable; we can and we must create better solutions.

Notes

1. Cardinal Stephen Fumio Hamao (address, Commission for the Pastoral Care of Migration and Tourism, Sri Lanka, March 7, 2003).

2. UNHCR, Standing Committee 39th Meeting, *NGO Statement on UNHCR's Activities in Relation to the Asylum-migration Nexus*, Agenda Item 3 (ii), June 25–27, 2007.

3. See 1951 Convention Relating to the Status of Refugees, Article I, A (2), www.UNHCR.org/ protect/PROTECTION/3b66c2aa10.pdf (accessed April 13, 2009).

4. This expansion refers to the development of regional legal instruments (1969 OAU Refugee Creation, 1984 Cartagena Declaration), legal recognition in a large number of states, and practice of both states and UNHCR.

5. *UN Guiding Principles on Internal Displacement: Introduction, Scope, and Purpose* (New York: OCHA, 1998).

6. *International Convention on the Protection of the Rights of All Migrant Workers and the Members of Their Families,* UN General Assembly resolution 45/158, December 18, 1990.

7. International Organization for Migration (IOM), Discussion Note: Migration and the Environment, IOM Council 94th session, (November 2007).

8. In 2000, when the upsurge of this trade in human beings gained greater attention, this internationally agreed upon and expanded definition of trafficking was developed as part of the *UN Convention against Transnational Organized Crime,* and more specifically its *Protocol to Prevent, Suppress, and Punish Trafficking in Persons, Especially Women and Children.*

9. Macartan Humphreys, "Economics and Violent Conflict" (2003), www.preventconflict .org/portal/economics (accessed April 28, 2009).

10. Ibid.

11. Ibid.

12. Paul Collier and Anke Hoeffler, "Greed and Grievance in Civil War," Policy Research Working Paper, *World Bank Development Research Group* (May 2000). www-wds.worldbank .org/servlet/WDSContentServer/WDSP/IB/2000/06/17/000094946_00060205420011/ Rendered/PDF/multi_page.pdf.

13. Jeffrey D. Sachs, *The End of Poverty: Economic Possibilities for Our Time* (New York: Penguin, 2005).

14. Nancy Birdsall, speech, Symposium on Global Demographic Change: Economic Impacts and Policy Challenges, Jackson Hole, Wyoming, August 2004, www.kc.frb.org/Publicat/ sympos/2004/pdf/Birdsall2004.pdf (accessed April 30, 2009).

15. Iván González Alvarado and Hilda Sánchez,"Migration in Latin America and the Caribbean: A View from the ICFTU/ORIT," 8th Congress, Toronto, April 1993, 105, www.ilo.org/ public/english/dialogue/actrav/publ/129/19.pdf (accessed April 5, 2009).

16. Global Commission on International Migration (GCIM), *Migration in an Interconnected World: New Directions for Action,* report, October 5, 2005, 4, UNHCR Refworld, www .UNHCR.org/refworld/docid/435f81814.html (accessed May 1, 2009).

17. Elizabeth Ferris, "Making Sense of Climate Change, Natural Disasters, and Displacement: A Work in Progress" (lecture, Brookings-Bern Project on Internal Displacement, Calcutta Research Group, Winter Course, December 14, 2007), www.brookings.edu/speeches/2007/

~/media/Files/rc/speeches/2007/1214_climate_change_ferris/1214_climate_change.pdf (accessed April 28, 2009).

18. John Holmes, "The Need for Collaboration," *Forced Migration Review* 31 (October 2008): 4.

19. World Bank, "Climate Changes and Impact on Coastal Countries," http://econ.world bank.org.

20. Ferris, "Making Sense of Climate Change."

21. Scott Edwards, "Social Breakdown in Darfur," *Forced Migration Review* 31 (October 2008): 24.

22. Daisy Francis, "Shifting Context for Humanitarian Action: Implications for the Protection of Refugees and Internally Displaced Persons (IDPs)," Working Paper, Catholic Relief Services, Baltimore, MD (2007).

23. Catholic Bishops of Mexico and the United States, *Strangers No Longer: Together on the Journey of Hope*, A Pastoral Letter Concerning Migration, January 22, 2003, www.usccb.org/mrs/stranger.shtml (accessed May 1, 2009).

24. Notably, the International Catholic Migration Commission.

25. Celestino Migliore, Statement to the 63rd Session of the General Assembly of the United Nations, proceedings of High-level Event on the Millennium Development Goals, New York, September 25, 2008, www.holyseemission.org/25Sep2008.html (accessed April 5, 2009).

26. Catholic Bishops, *Strangers No Longer*.

27. Jorge Bustamante, "Promotion and Protection of All Human Rights, Civil, Political, Economic, Social, and Cultural Rights, Including the Right to Development," report, special rapporteur on the human rights of migrants, Human Rights Council, 7th session, A/HRC/7/12, 61, February 25, 2008.

28. Bustamante, "Promotion and Protection of All Human Rights," 62.

29. Article 16 of the International Covenant on Civil and Political Rights, as well as article 24 of the International Convention on the Protection of All Migrant Workers and Members of Their Families, grant in very broad terms the right to recognition everywhere as a person before the law, which pertains to all people in any territory, regardless of status.

30. John Bingham, "Call for the Development of Humanitarian Standards of Response to Migrant Victims of Violence and Trauma Crossing Borders," submitted to the International Organization for Migration at the 94th session of the IOM Council by the International Catholic Migration Commission, November 29, 2007.

12

Refugees or Economic Migrants

Catholic Thought on the Moral Roots of the Distinction

Christopher Llanos

This chapter outlines one moral framework for questioning the normative force of the sharp distinction between so-called refugees and economic migrants, namely, that of Catholic social thought (CST).[1] The ethical framework presented pays special attention to understanding the moral roots of the claim that refugees make on the international community.

The legal distinction between refugees and economic migrants is officially sustained through a single, well-known international legal yardstick for refugees defined by the United Nations (UN) Convention and Protocol Relating to the Status of Refugees.[2] CST, through the Pontifical Council for the Care of Migrants and Itinerant Peoples, on the other hand, has expressed a moral intuition that those who flee "armed conflicts, erroneous economic policies, and natural disasters" can be thought of as de facto refugees.[3] Perhaps as a result of their long, direct work with refugees, organizations like Jesuit Refugee Service (JRS) also have proposed that many persons, other than those that neatly fit the UN Convention definition, are in need of similar protections to those accorded Convention refugees.[4] In fact, JRS also adds an additional overlapping category when it includes those who migrate due to "social collapse consequent on conflicts and human rights abuse." In this way, JRS and some Catholic moral theologians echo the Pontifical Council's moral intuition.[5] However, while questioning the distinction between the economic and the political, they do not automatically call for a revision of the UN Refugee Convention.[6]

We will first briefly visit the contexts in which the defensibility of a sharp distinction between refugees and economic migrants arises. Second, we will investigate and construct a possible explanation of CST's moral intuition regarding who actually has a moral claim to refuge among the varied types of migrant cases. This process will lead us to articulate a general moral (not legal) definition of a refugee; that is, of a migrant who has a moral claim to protection on the international community.[7] Third, I will briefly illustrate the approach using an example of the collapse of socioeconomic rights guarantees, though not treating cases where economic factors are connected with unambiguous UN Refugee Convention criteria.[8] Finally, we will very briefly address how this moral analysis fits with some possible directions for dealing with migrants or those who have been displaced.

The Contexts

The moral question about distinguishing refugees and economic migrants is more easily understood when placed in the specific contexts in which it has surfaced. First, therefore, we will review the historical international context of refugee regimes.[9] We will then explore how the nature of today's migratory movements and politics has brought the question into focus.

The Precursors of the UN Refugee Convention

The first high commissioner for refugees was established by the League of Nations to deal with very specific migrant emergencies.[10] The commissioner initially concentrated on Russian migrant groups but later the focus expanded to include other specific groups such as Turks and Greeks.[11] Following a similar pattern, when large flows of migrants began to leave Nazi Germany, the League of Nations established another high commissioner to deal with these flows. Given this pattern, we can easily see that in the beginning, international action on behalf of refugees was designed to meet the needs of very specific migrant emergencies rather than the needs of all refugees anywhere in the world.

The UN Refugee Convention

Although the 1951 UN Refugee Convention we have today appears to be of a more stable pedigree than its predecessors in the League of Nations, it also began in order to address some quite specific emergencies. The millions displaced by World War II continued to be a major problem years after the end of the war. In addition, the Cold War also emerged as an important migratory context for those displaced by the world war. The UN Refugee Convention, with its legal definition of a refugee, emerged as an international instrument for addressing this specific refugee problem. The restriction of the definition of refugees to persons displaced by events prior to 1951 highlights the Convention's specificity.[12] The definition was tailored for particular displaced populations to avoid inadvertently committing signatory states beyond the target migrant flows. Given the nature of the circumstances that gave rise to these flows, it was to be expected that the definition would emphasize "political" circumstances.

In addition, the UN Refugee Convention was negotiated by communities zealous to maintain their sovereign prerogatives over migration. This was especially true in the case of the United States. This zeal moved in the direction of trying to keep a great deal of control over who could enter a country at the national level.[13] Thus, there was opposition to a definition that tried to include all refugees; rather, the definition ran in favor of the specific refugee flows that the negotiating countries had an interest in regulating. The resulting definition would have in theory tied signatory countries to receive the particular refugees that were of interest, while leaving their hands free to respond as they wished to other refugees.

Of course, the UN Refugee Convention was amended with the 1967 Protocol, but the definition was left largely unchanged. In 1967 the Cold War was in full swing and the amendments, while clearly opening the Convention to worldwide refugee flows, did not change the essentials of the definition; it merely counted as refugees those displaced because of events after 1951.[14] As a result, even after 1967 the world was left with one international legal regime for refugees—the UN Refugee Convention— whose definition was crafted to limit obligations of countries to particular refugees and leave as much room as possible for national discretion.

It is not surprising, therefore, that the Convention definition would become a touchstone for defining all refugees. In addition, given the origins of the UN Refugee Convention and the interests that were probably incorporated into its definition, it would not be surprising if it only encompassed a subset of all those who actually needed protection. CST suggests that migrants fleeing severe socioeconomic deprivations are among those needing protection.

The Prominence of Irregular Migratory Movements

The question of definition also arises in relation to irregular flows of migrants. Such flows have gained prominence in the public mind in recent years.[15] They have also become a political liability for many national governments. Prior to World War I, many nations did not exercise much sovereign control over the movement of persons across their borders.[16] Therefore, irregular flows are really a phenomenon of recent times. Given increased border controls and the fact that people who migrate do not always have the capacity to get all the necessary papers, these irregular flows are also a conduit for refugees. Unfortunately, they are also a conduit for many other types of flows, including some less desirable criminal elements, and therefore such flows are sometimes designated "mixed migratory movements."[17]

Given the nature of these flows, the question of how best to categorize migrants has become a concern from several angles. The mixed nature of the flows makes urgent the creation of tools that help identify who really needs the protection of a political community, who does not need protection but would make a desirable addition to the community, and those whom the community does not want within its borders.[18] However, even with better tools, making distinctions among migrants may be fraught with difficulties.

In this volume Mary DeLorey discusses the ways in which economics, politics, and other social factors often interact. She points out the systemic relationship between economics and civil conflict. For example, a World Bank study maintains that countries with per capita incomes around $1,250 are four times less likely to experience civil war within five years than countries with per capita incomes around $250.[19] Of equal importance, certain types of economies show a tendency to weak state structures and weak governments. Such governments may be less able or motivated to address the needs of their populations. Also, quite telling, DeLorey explains how populations displaced by conflict often end up suffering serious economic deprivation that, in turn, prompts further migration. Thus political, economic, and other social structures interact in almost seamless ways. Economic and political considerations can be active within a single migrant flow, or even within a single migrant. This can make distinguishing political and economic migrants a rather surreal endeavor. Nevertheless, distinctions among migrants must be made.

First, political communities that are on the receiving end of these irregular flows are pressured to distinguish among migrants due to concerns about the effects on the community of undocumented migrants. Their governments are likely to work for restrictive ways to distinguish refugees from other migrants. Anxieties can create political liabilities for the national governments, especially if those governments are seen as not really being in control of the situation.[20] Such anxieties may not work to the benefit of those who really need protection.

Second, pressure to distinguish refugees from other types of migrants also arises in the context of the work of the United Nations High Commissioner for Refugees (UNHCR). From the point of view of the UNHCR, clarity about who qualifies as a refugee, on both a conceptual and procedural level, is a high priority in the midst of receiving country jitters. In such pressured circumstances the UNHCR may not always work to the advantage of all who truly need protection.

Third, organizations like JRS and Amnesty International, with long histories of direct work with refugees and forcibly displaced persons, hold that the UN Refugee Convention does not encompass all who are in need of protection.[21] Their concern in the midst of mixed migration flows is to make sure that those who need protection get it.

Thus we see that this discussion is surrounded by thorny political realities. The history of international refugee regimes has suggested the single definition for refugees of the UN Refugee Convention. Although it is a legal definition, its singularity on the international scene, combined with its endurance over time, may have created a presumption that it corresponds to the moral definition of a refugee. However, the current nature of migrant flows does not fit the legal institutional frameworks established by the UN Refugee Convention and other migrant instruments. These flows are a political liability for countries' governments and put pressure on international and national legal instruments. Thinking about the moral understanding of a refugee is one possible step toward clarifying the distinction between economic and political migrants. This, in turn, can help illuminate what we want to accomplish on the human, advocacy, legal, and institutional levels.

Toward an Articulation of the Moral Intuition: Defining Refugee

As stated at the outset, we will work toward articulating the moral intuition by drawing on the resources of Catholic moral thought. To limit this discussion, we will set our sights on the types of situations that are mentioned by the Pontifical Council and JRS. We will build a moral definition of refugee that can explain CST's claim regarding those who should count as de facto refugees. Even though the moral definition ends up differing from the legal definition of the UN Refugee Convention, one need not conclude that the Convention refugee definition ought to change. The moral definition speaks to the question of who makes a moral claim on the international community for protection; the UN Refugee Convention is but one avenue of response.

The Contributions of Catholic Social Thought

The Human Person, Community, and State. Understanding how human persons, community, human rights, and the state are related in CST is a key to understanding the intuition that basic socioeconomic deprivation is just as important for a valid refugee claim as other types of basic deprivations. First, according to CST, the human being is social by nature. Human beings can only develop as persons within human communities. This social reality is an unchosen starting point as well as being a choice. A choice against this sociality is a choice for the destruction of the human person, whether that choice is made by the person or the communities in which the person is located.[22]

This personal sociality manifests and realizes itself by the formation of, and participation in, communities. It is an active exchange of receiving and contributing in all dimensions and capacities of the person. All persons are unique, and their participative contribution to others and the community will be distinctive. As such, impeding or destroying this participation is not only destructive to the person—a violation of human dignity—but ultimately a loss to the whole community.[23]

Second, the political community is the encompassing community in which all persons ought to find what they need to be fully participating members of society. In today's world these political communities tend to be thought of as corresponding to the community of citizens and residents of a country.[24] These countries are interdependent for the goods their citizens and residents need and want. Accordingly, it is the job of the political institutions of these countries to secure for all their residents and citizens access to what is necessary for them to participate, and thus flourish as social beings. Outside of these political communities, human beings cannot become full persons because they will not have what is necessary, and because they will not have the community in which their social being can be realized.

Third, CST has defined human rights as "the minimum conditions for life in community." Socioeconomic rights are just as important as what traditionally has been known as political rights.[25] If human beings are to realize their personhood, they must have access to certain socioeconomic minimums like basic education, basic health services, and ways of earning a living. This does not mean that the political community directly supplies these goods, but that the institutional structures of that political community are such that every person can participate in the political community, access these goods, and contribute to the community. In this process the human being develops as a person.[26] Participation becomes difficult without some guarantee of socioeconomic minimums through the political communities' informal or formal institutions.[27]

If a political community fails to secure access to "the minimum conditions for life in community" for some of its members, then those members are not able to make their contribution and grow as persons. This is a grievous offence against the person because of the sociality of human beings. We are speaking not of luxuries, but of human rights like basic education, basic health care, and some basic material securities. Without such things, persons are for all practical purposes left without a political community in which they can participate.[28]

This then is probably why the Pontifical Council refers to the right of membership in a community, or right to a country, as a core right born of the "basic requirement of the very nature of human beings."[29] The Council sees this foundational right to membership as the center of the moral claim to asylum. Since human dignity is intrinsically social, we all have a basic right to membership in a political community where the minimum conditions for life in community are reasonably guaranteed.[30] This right is at the center of the claim to asylum because, given our social reality, without a community to which to belong, we cannot start to become fully a person.

It is worth noting two things about this basic right to a community. One, this is a right to one political community, and not a right to a country of our choice. Most of us are born into a country, and by birthright this community is obligated to institutionally secure the minimum conditions for life in that community.[31] We usually do not choose the country and the country usually does not choose us, but we are loosely stuck with each other.[32] Two, the conditions that must be guaranteed are the minimum requirements for life in the community in which we find ourselves to be members. Therefore, the minimum conditions are partially relative to the particular political community we are talking about. For example, in a fairly wealthy political community, participation may be very difficult for someone who is much more materially poor than anyone else. This would be so because the affluence of everyone else may have resulted in the common use of means of communication that are just not accessible to someone who is much poorer than the average. However, in a far less affluent political community, that same level of poverty would not be as great a hindrance to participation. Nevertheless, the relative nature of some of these minimums does not necessarily rule out the existence of absolute minimums that are valid for all human beings no matter where they live. Catholic thought does tend to speak of a universal human community, and human nature, that could be the basis for absolute minimums.[33] The relative character of some of these minimums may be important when we begin thinking about what it takes for one's relationship with a political community to be ruptured.

Fourth, the state is but one organization within the political community; it is not the political community in its fullness. Persons need the political community, not the state per se, and it is estrangement from the political community that leaves one helpless, not problems with the state in isolation.[34] However, within the political community the state has a particular function in support of the common good that has sometimes been referred to as the public order function. The state's role is to make sure that the relations among organizations, associations, communities, and persons are ordered in such a way that they provide for the common good of all members of the larger community—thus the term "public order."[35] One might say that the state is the guarantor of basic human rights. It makes sure that through the political community, all members can reasonably access the minimums should they so desire.

In addition, the state, for better or worse, is often accorded a public symbolic role within the political community. That is, when the state acts or speaks, it can often claim to speak or act for the political community, or be understood to be doing so.[36] Similarly, when it fails to act or speak, it can also be seen to be communicating publicly on behalf of the political community. This is especially important when the state fails to act where basic human rights are being systematically obstructed within the political community. Here the state's failure to act can turn those systematic obstructions into acts of the political community rather than just the acts of a wayward few. Thus, people can become estranged from the political community without being directly acted upon by the state.

These contributions from CST regarding the relationship of human persons, communities, states, and basic human rights suggest that persons may begin to need the protection of a political community other than their own when the political community in which they find themselves systematically fails to meet their "minimum conditions needed for life." In such a situation the affected citizens are effectively denied the necessary participation in a community that is a vital part of being human. Thus, they desperately need to remedy this situation or to find a community where such participation can begin to be established. Thus, we might say that it is not simply the lack of political and economic minimums but the absence of community that is the root of the moral claim to asylum.

The Universal Human Community. CST also has a universalist emphasis that is important for this discussion. CST identifies a larger, universal human community in which we all share responsibility for each other.[37] Political communities can be understood as realizing such responsibilities on a local level. However, when that realization fails, the responsibility is once again felt by the universal human community. Given today's social organization, responsibility to the person lacking community support can only be answered by effective participative reincorporation into a political community. If the estrangement is such that this cannot be done with a person's home community, then other political communities must respond as part of the larger human community.

Toward Articulating a Definition in Harmony with the Moral Intuition

The majority of us have a country with an associated political community by birth.[38] The Catholic contribution suggests that when some members of a country are effectively not able to participate in their home political community and are without reasonable channels for correcting it, these persons' basic human rights are being denied. This cuts to the core of who we are as human persons by virtue of our intrinsic sociality.[39] When this strain culminates in final alienation from the political community, the "unprotected vulnerability" of persons' dignity makes a claim on the international community.[40]

In the following I will explain this situation more precisely in a moral definition of refugee. The criteria that follow, from which the definition will be constructed, are not new. The turn toward understanding refugees in terms of rights violations has been going on for many years.[41] Normative human rights criteria for a person to be a refugee have been put forward by persons like Andrew E. Shacknove as early as 1985.[42] In fact, the criteria I synthesize below are similar to those of Shacknove, even though he comes at them from a different moral anthropology and political philosophy.

Basic Human Rights Failures. As stated above, Catholic social thought has argued that socioeconomic rights can be just as basic as political rights. When we see basic rights as protecting participation in community, it is not difficult to understand that certain levels of education, access to health aids, and subsistence would be just as necessary as guarantees against things like reprisals by government for one's political opinions. Whether or not intended by the government, if these basics are not secured, persons are not able to participate, and the relationship with the community is upset. This necessary participation in the political community is multileveled; it is religious, social, familial, economic, and so on.[43] Therefore socioeconomic rights must be part of the basic package for life in community. In fact, given the link between socioeconomic rights and participation in the political community, we might say that failure to protect basic socioeconomic rights is a political failure.

CST suggests at least one necessary condition for someone to be in need of the help or protection of a country other than the home country: the failure to secure some basic human rights, regardless of whether those rights are political, religious, social, or economic.[44] A person needs transnational protection when the home country has failed to safeguard the minimum conditions for participation in community for that person.

We should note that sometimes people lose access to certain basic rights protections, like freedom of movement, because of being involved in criminal activities. Therefore, this first point should be qualified by the assertion that certain limitations on basic rights may be acceptable when they are legitimate punishments for illegal activities, for example, kidnapping or murder.

The Current Exhaustion of Possibilities for Redress. When we participate in communities, even in well-functioning ones, give and take is often needed. Unintended, and sometimes intended, errors will always occur. As a result, every community needs institutionalized mechanisms for healing the breaches that occur when mistakes happen. An error in which people get hurt does not automatically mean that the relationship is irreparably damaged.

Similarly, rights violations occur in many countries, and many countries have mechanisms for bringing these issues to the attention of the state for correction. In such cases rights violations do not have to become something that ends in a rupture between the political community and the offended persons. Therefore we come to a second necessary condition: that the person has made all reasonable efforts, given the situation, to have the basic rights failures addressed by the political community, and it appears that nothing else can reasonably be done to make the community rectify the situation.

The Person Wants the Help of Another Country. People have multileveled and heterogeneous relationships with their political community, which is made up of many persons, associations, and institutions, including the state.[45] Because people are themselves part of these relationships, their moral claim as refugees does not emerge until they themselves have given up on their political community, whether or not they preserve hope for the future. Therefore, though we see repeated basic human rights violations and note that persons have exhausted all reasonable means of redress, they have not yet made the claim that characterizes a refugee in the international community until they temporarily, or permanently, give up on the political community. For that reason, we encounter the paradox of people who seem to have been forced to leave their home, yet have also taken the decision to do so.[46] This situation underscores that even if the basic human rights violations fall into the camp of socioeconomic rights, the root rupture is ultimately a political one.

From this point of view, the first two conditions specify what can lead to the rupture of the all-important relationship, but it is the actual final rupture of that relationship with the political community that gives rise to the moral claim; that rupture involves both the migrants themselves and the political community. A final judgment that the relationship with the political community is broken is a necessary part of a valid moral claim to refuge in another political community. Therefore, we might add a third necessary clause: persons who are refugees have reached a point where they have given up on their relationship with their home political community and seek the help of another political community to regain this necessary dimension of being human.[47]

Persecution and Its Reasons

Since much is made of both the requirement of a "well-founded fear of persecution" and the reasons for that persecution, it is worth saying at least a brief word about this requirement. There has been recent work on the relation of persecution to human rights violations, including socioeconomic rights violations. This work deals with the types of cases that occur today. Michelle Foster has published one of the most complete treatments of the human rights interpretation of persecution from a legal perspective.[48]

In some ways, her interpretation of what constitutes persecution under the Convention looks a lot like what we have described as conditions one and two, above. However, her interpretation of valid reasons tends to limit conditions one and two by a third condition, and that is a sort of discriminatory clause. Therefore, socioeconomic claims would matter because particular persons, for identifiable but illegitimate reasons, are the subjects of discrimination regarding their core socioeconomic rights.[49] This is reasonable given the ordinary understanding of persecution as being singled out because of "race, religion, nationality, membership of a particular social group or political opinion," which could be construed as a basic rights violation.[50]

However, within the context of CST, persecution, or being singled out, is not the root of the moral claim to refuge in a political community. The moral claim arises because of the foundational assault on a person's dignity that becomes evident when a person's relationship with the political community is irreparably broken. It is this, not the persecution, that makes the moral claim. Persecution is a basic rights violation that may or may not result in an irreparable break with the political community.

In defense of the discrimination-based approach, perhaps one could say a person's relationship with the political community cannot be irreparably broken unless the rights violations are limited to an otherwise identifiable sector of a political community. That is, if the basic human rights violations are indiscriminate and those whose rights are violated do not constitute a unique sector of the population, except by virtue of the rights violation, then they can still participate meaningfully in the political community. In other words, the core rights violations must take place in such a way that it also constitutes the basic rights violation of discrimination.

However, it is not clear to me why this follows. In specific political communities, there will be certain political and socioeconomic rights that are so central that when they are not respected, persons will usually not be capable of participating in the community in any meaningful way. Being singled out or discriminated against sometimes may constitute one such basic rights violation that is made manifest through targeted rights violations or failures, but it will not be the only one. If a whole set of political and socioeconomic basic rights are violated, whether or not the violations occur against members of an identifiable sector, such persons remain without what is usually necessary for communal participation. The refugee claim arises ultimately from the rupture of persons' relationship with their political community, not the persecution per se. The root problem, from a Catholic perspective, remains the same. That being said, even if not tenable in CST as a moral explanation of what makes for a refugee, the expansion of the understanding of persecution may be politically useful for getting help to those who need it.

Determining the Depth of Socioeconomic Rights Violations

When socioeconomic rights are added to a mix, the question arises of where one ought to draw the line between violations that matter and economic circumstances that may be regrettable but do not make a claim on others for help.[51] That is, when does migration move from bettering one's economic circumstances to being a moral claim for refuge? How bad do the socioeconomic circumstances have to get for migrating to be more than merely improving one's economic and social lot?

These questions connect to larger discussions surrounding the determination of what constitutes a basic need or a basic right. This is a very large historical conversation that cannot be embarked upon here. However, it is worth making at least three observations.

First, the refugee claim does not arise directly out of socioeconomic deprivation or political rights violations. Rather, the claim is rooted in the reality of failures of the political community to guarantee effectively the basic rights of some of its members. In other words, when a political community fails to secure the basic political or economic rights of some of its members, the community has failed in its obligations as a political community to some of its members. This failure to guarantee is at a different level than the actual deprivation or personally experienced violations. The source is the failure to provide the security or guarantee that a political community owes its members. Therefore, the fundamental question for the moral claim is what counts as a serious failure to guarantee or secure rights on the part of the political community, not how deadly was the actual attack or how seriously has the person been deprived of socioeconomic goods. This brings us to the second observation.

The inclusion of socioeconomic rights is sometimes critiqued because of the seeming impossibility of determining where to draw the line between basic socioeconomic rights violations and nonbasic ones. However, first, this critique misses the fact that rights violations that fall under the traditionally political spectrum of rights are also subject to gradations. Many who have reason to fear for their lives, and would be covered by the UN Refugee Convention, do not face immediate and targeted danger. In fact, they may not have ever been direct targets of violence but still have good reason to fear violence. Their observation of a pattern of violence and killings within their country may have given them good reason to fear becoming a victim. Such conclusions require judgments about what levels of violence, what rates of killings, and so on constitute a failure to secure rights and what do not. A reasoned conclusion that the political community is failing to guarantee their basic rights would be based on patterns and statistics that indicate systematic failures to protect by the political community and its state. In both the political and economic dimensions, unless persons have been actual, repeated victims of violence, judgments have to be made about what constitutes a political community's failure.

Michelle Foster points out that drawing these lines in the realm of political rights has been made possible through the buildup of case law and the production of country reports regarding human rights. These materials are also available for socioeconomic rights in such a form that it is possible to make graded distinctions as to what might constitute basic socioeconomic failures in different countries.[52] Thus, not only are there aids for drawing those lines, but these standards can be made relevant to particular national circumstances.

Third, a further objection is raised that socioeconomic rights are inherently different from political rights as they are progressive.[53] That is, socioeconomic rights are progressively realized over time as resources become available. However, while there is a certain relative-to-resources aspect of socioeconomic rights, this relativity is arguably present with political rights as well. Henry Shue's watershed work pointed out the economic dependency of political rights.[54] In addition, the relationship between politics and economics brought forward in Mary DeLorey's essay in this volume suggests that there is a strong tie between the resource base and the guaranteeing of political rights. Therefore, it would seem quite likely that political rights suffer from the very same pitfall as socioeconomic rights in being resource dependent. In addition, as Michelle Foster points out, the progressive nature of rights does not rule out actual obligations. For example, the gradual realization of rights to health care does not mean that citizens of a poor country have no right to any minimum level of health care.[55]

Perhaps the real problem is not that we can never be sure where to draw the line with socioeconomic rights violations; this can also be a problem for political rights. The predicament is once we can no longer exclude people on the basis that the political community has failed to guarantee socioeconomic rights, we acknowledge the possibility of a vastly increased number of claims on the international community by migrants.[56] Nevertheless, the moral claim stands despite our fear of what would happen if we acknowledged that many more had legitimate claims to refuge than currently admitted under the UN Refugee Convention.

A Definition

The contributions from CST would suggest that the Pontifical Council's moral intuition is based on an understanding that human persons have an intrinsic need to participate in communities. When we are faced with persons (a) whose political communities have failed to secure their basic human rights, including socioeconomic rights, for reasons other than involvement in an internationally accepted understanding of criminal behavior; (b) who have little reasonable hope left that their home political communities will address this situation; and (c) who have themselves given up on their home community, our moral intuitions tell us that we owe these persons the support of another political community. A moral definition of a refugee constructed from this articulation of the moral intuition might be any persons who are the victims of ongoing basic human rights failures in their home political community for reasons other than involvement in criminal behavior, for whom there is no reasonable recourse left to that political community for redress of these failures, and who have given up on their relationship with the home community, whether or not hope is retained for future restoration. Such persons make a moral claim characteristic of refugees on the international community.

An Illustrative Case

The Pontifical Council claims that victims of armed conflicts, erroneous economic policies, and natural disasters do not fit the current UN Refugee Convention definition but that we owe them protection. JRS seems to add one more case: mass displacements resulting from social collapse. This additional category sounds like it refers to failed states or nearly failed states. Failed states correspond to political communities in which the institutional structures, including the state, have collapsed such that the political community has more or less fallen into anarchy. In such situations we really cannot speak of there being any institutional or systematic protection of basic human rights, nor of there being any real political community.

To illustrate how a moral claim arises in such circumstances, we will look at a situation that appears close to social collapse.

Haiti

The 2008 Failed State Index ranks Haiti as the fourteenth weakest state in the world. Daniel P. Erikson refers to Haiti as "the closest example of a failed state this side of the Atlantic."[57] In 2008 its score was 99.3 (higher is more unstable) and in 2005, when Erikson wrote his article, it was 99.2.[58] Although some controversy surrounds the Failed State Index, Haiti's recent history does suggest that there is truth to the classification. Therefore, the Haitian situation may come close to describing perhaps what JRS is referring to when it speaks of "mass displacements due to social collapse."

Haiti has produced many migrants in recent years. Although the arrival and interdiction of boats carrying Haitians traveling to the United States has received much international publicity, the mass movements of Haitians to the Dominican Republic (DR) have not received as much coverage. The number of Haitians living in the DR has been estimated to be from five hundred thousand to one million, even though the government of the DR claims that only four thousand have legal documentation.[59]

It has been debated whether the flows of Haitian migrants into the DR and toward the United States consist of refugees or economic migrants.[60] In the United States this issue has especially come to the fore regarding the differential treatment of Cubans and Haitians. Cubans almost automatically have been given asylum, whereas most Haitian applications have been rejected. Poverty continues to be seen as the primary driving force behind Haitian migration into the DR and toward the United States, even under the present failing state situation that threatens all human rights, both political and economic.[61] The World Bank estimates that 54 percent of Haitians live below the one dollar a day abject poverty line.[62]

We can look at this from the point of view of our definition. When we speak of Haiti as a failed state, we are actually speaking of a situation where the political community is fragmented and, as a result, is usually unable to guarantee even the absolute minimums for basic human rights. The poverty statistics suggest that the majority of Haitians not only live in a state of socioeconomic rights failures, but lack even the absolute minimums on a socioeconomic level. While we can speak of some relativity as regards socioeconomic rights for the purposes of participation in a political community, when we are below the equivalent of one dollar a day, we have reached a level that is prohibitive for healthy participation in any political community in today's world. Therefore we can say that the first and second conditions in our moral definition of a refugee are clearly met for the majority of Haitians.

This situation is not new, although since the end of the Duvalier regime we might say the instability of the state structures and the political community has increased. Nevertheless, the inability of the political community to provide the minimum requirements for participation in community has been ongoing. There have been many serious attempts to address these issues from the side of the Haitian community. Therefore, it is not unreasonable for individual Haitians to conclude that there is little hope for redress of these failures to guarantee rights. Given this situation, many individual Haitians may reasonably conclude that their basic human rights, both of subsistence and of security, are not being protected and are not likely to be protected in the near future. Consequently, individual Haitians who give up on the Haitian political community and seek entry into another political community would seem to have a legitimate moral claim on the international community.

Making One Change to the Haitian Scenario.   Let us suppose that Haiti was different. Assume it has reasonably functioning informal and formal institutions and a moderately stable state structure. Assume the poverty is largely a result of a history of bad policies but that now the country is institutionally capable of doing better.

In this case we could argue that the current failure to secure rights probably does not in most cases create the situation necessary for rupturing the bond with the political community. Members now have channels through which they can deal with rights violations. In addition, we presume that Haiti also now has an institutional structure by which it could make better use of technical and material international aid. Therefore, the shift away from a weak or failed state situation works against fulfilling the second condition of the loss of any reasonable hope that the home community will address the situation. A stronger state provides more reason to continue hoping in the efficacy of one's relationships within the political community. Nevertheless, members can continue to lack basic necessities.

The migrant from a Haiti with a stronger state may have a moral claim to aid, but not a moral claim for a new political community. In this situation it is less likely that the relationship with the political community will be ruptured. The difference between this scenario and the actual Haitian situation is the institutional functionality of the political community that still allows for constructive participation of its citizens. In the real Haiti, those institutional structures have largely broken down, and there is little current hope of effective restructuring in the near future.

On Whom Does the Claim Fall?   We now consider the actual scenario facing Haiti's neighbor, the DR, where there could already be upward of a million undocumented Haitians. The consequences of granting documented entry, especially with the implications this would have for future flows from Haiti, are politically overwhelming. Sometimes, in moments of natural disaster, economic collapse, or outbreaks of terrible human rights violations like genocide, the nearest neighbor is not the most prepared or capable country for receiving thousands of refugees. Are they required to do so from this moral perspective?

The moral claim in CST rests on a shared universal responsibility for one another. Therefore, the claim is made on the whole international community, though it is quite clear that sometimes it can only be satisfied when particular political communities step up and receive refugees. It is also clear, given the nature of current international institutions, that the claim is likely to be placed before a particular political community, not an organ of the international community itself. Therefore, the example of Haiti and the DR suggests that a serious effort to realize our responsibilities requires alternative approaches to resolving the problem of absent political communities. Simply receiving refugees into a new country might be just one among many methods for restoring people's communal life. In addition, the acknowledgment of these moral claims on the international community may also require a restructuring of international institutions.

A Final Addendum Regarding Practical Implications of This Moral Definition of a Refugee

Given the approach taken in this essay—constructing a moral definition of a refugee—one naturally might ask about the implications of this moral framework and definition for the UN Refugee Convention. One might ask whether the UN Refugee Convention definition of refugee should be revised at some point. However, there is more than one way of tackling the UN Refugee Convention.

As indicated earlier, the current international political climate does not favor a formal expansion of international obligations. Nevertheless, without changing the actual UN definition, individual countries, within their own case law, have de facto interpreted the definition of refugees to include those suffering from socioeconomic rights violations. These national precedents have sometimes had the effect of expanding obligation either by extending the meaning of "persecution" or by recognizing socioeconomic rights violations as supporting refugee status.[63] These precedents suggest that a country-by-country approach may produce better results than trying to legally bind signatory countries to a wider international definition of refugee. Some progress might be made with those countries that have already shown a tendency toward a more expansive socioeconomic understanding of the Convention definition of a refugee.

Conversely, Mary DeLorey, in this volume, suggests taking a different tack. She seems to favor adding institutional frameworks to deal with socioeconomic failures rather than expanding the UN Refugee Convention. Rather than legally defining such migrants as refugees, she prefers some type of humanitarian categorization. Perhaps DeLorey thinks that this direction might be more successful at meeting the needs of these migrants while safeguarding international commitments to the UN Refugee Convention. If this approach were more successful at garnering international support for all those who fit CST's moral definition of a refugee, it would seem to be a good approach. However, if this approach were meant to make sure that, in today's unfavorable climate, at least the most urgent cases were handled by the UN Refugee Convention, then there is a problem. This approach simply shifts the issue to which cases are most urgent.

Political cases are not necessarily more urgent than socioeconomic cases. While some political cases face immediate danger if not granted refugee status, many do not. Many fear rights violations but might, even if they were to stay in their own country for the rest of their lives, escape any actual direct violation of their freedoms. On the other hand, some of those who suffer socioeconomic rights violations (such as children deprived of proper nutrition, health care, or schooling) can face immediate and lifelong consequences for these rights violations. The urgency can be quite real. It is a mistake to presume that socioeconomic rights failures are necessarily less urgent than political ones. Therefore, DeLorey's approach would seem reasonable (1) as long as it is the most fruitful, (2) as long as it is not simply a means of securing continued international commitment to the UN Refugee Convention in a critical moment, and (3) as long as it is not trying to say that those who are legally defined Convention refugees are the most critical cases.

Finally, another approach is that of Susan Martin, who proposes a new international regime for forced migrants based on four quadrants that are meant to cover all types of basic rights insecurities: (1) migrants who come from countries that are willing and able to protect their members, (2) migrants who come from countries that are willing but unable, (3) migrants who come from countries that are unwilling but able, and (4) migrants who come from countries that are unwilling and unable. She sidesteps the issue of who is a refugee by speaking of "forced migrants," which itself may produce a problematic tendency to obscure the migrants' capacity for agency. (This component of agency is understood by the third condition of the moral definition we have constructed earlier; that is, persons do not become refugees until they have given up on the home community and seek the help of another country.) However, this schema has the advantage of giving a general sense of who needs help while at the same time intuitively suggesting alternative types of responses. For example, building a country's capacity to secure basic human rights might be better than simply receiving migrants when the migrant-producing country in question is willing to secure these rights but simply unable. This possibility becomes obvious within Martin's schema. Her schema is very general and a long way from taking concrete institutional form, but it suggests an interesting alternative approach that might produce an institutional framework which allows the international community to respond to the moral claim of all refugees without necessarily opening the specter of hugely expanded migratory obligations. In addition, it implicitly directs our attention to the root of the moral claim: the state of the relationship of the migrant with the political community.

Notes

My thanks to Joanne Whitaker's insightful response to my first draft and to David Hollenbach for his helpful and practical suggestions. I also very much appreciated the comments, suggestions, and questions from other participants in the conference, "The Deeper Causes of Forced Migration and Systemic Responses," which have spurred much further thought on this difficult and urgent situation.

1. See Pontifical Council Cor Unum and Pontifical Council for the Pastoral Care of Migrants and Itinerant People, *Refugees: A Challenge to Solidarity* (Vatican City: Pontifical Council for the Pastoral Care of Migrants and Itinerant People, 1992), no. 4; William R. O'Neill and William C. Spohn, "Rights of Passage: The Ethics of Immigration and Refugee Policy," *Theological Studies* 59, no. 1 (1998): 85; and Jesuit Refugee Service, "What Is the JRS? Refugee Statistics," Jesuit Refugee Services, www.jrs.net/about/index.php?lang=en&abId=what4 (accessed May 14, 2009).

2. I use the word "international" to distinguish instruments that are used in all geographic areas from regional ones like that of the Organization of African Unity (African Union), *Convention Covering Specific Aspects of Refugee Problems in Africa* (Addis Ababa, Ethiopia: African Union, 1969), and national instruments that may define refugees differently from the United Nations; United Nations, *Convention and Protocol Relating to the Status of Refugees* (Geneva: United Nations High Commissioner for Refugees, 2007). See also United Nations, *UN Refugee Convention*, Art. I, A(2). Amended in Protocol Art. I, 2 and 3.

3. Pontifical Council, Cor Unum, *Refugees*, no. 4.

4. JRS has published a book that gives accounts of its twenty-five years of experience working directly with refugees: Amaya Valcarcel, ed., *The Wound of the Border: 25 Years with the Refugees* (Rome: Jesuit Refugee Service, 2005).

5. See, for example, Jesuit Refugee Service, "What Is the JRS?"; O'Neill and Spohn, "Rights of Passage," 85.

6. Moral claims do not necessarily have to be enshrined in law. The moral and the legal are not coterminous.

7. Even though the moral definition of a refugee may include more migrants than the legal definition, one cannot simply conclude that the legal definition ought to be broadened.

8. Michelle Foster, in her *International Refugee Law and Socio-Economic Rights: Refuge from Deprivation*, Cambridge Studies in International and Comparative Law (Cambridge and New York: Cambridge University Press, 2007), clearly and convincingly shows how economic factors and UN Refugee Convention factors can often go hand in hand in actual cases.

9. Susan Martin's discussion of this history, in this volume, is particularly helpful for understanding why the UN Refugee Convention may not encompass all who have a moral claim to refuge.

10. For other discussions of the development of UN's international regime for refugees, see James C. Hathaway, "A Reconsideration of the Underlying Premise of Refugee Law," *Harvard International Law Journal* 31, no. 1 (1990): 129–47; Hathaway, "Why Refugee Law Still Matters," *Melbourne Journal of International Law* 8, no. 1 (2007): 89–103; and Rieko Karatani, "How History Separated Refugee and Migrant Regimes: In Search of Their Institutional Origins," *International Journal of Refugee Law* 17, no. 3 (2005), www.lexisnexis.com/libdb.fairfield.edu/us/Inacademic/.

11. According to Reiko Karatani, this first high commissioner established by the League of Nations initially dealt with Russians, then took on groups of Greeks, Turks, Bulgarians, and Armenians. Unlike today, they were helped as groups rather than being considered on a case-by-case basis. In 1933 a second commissioner, the high commissioner for refugees coming from Germany, was also established to deal with the flows of migrants out of Germany. Karatani, "How History."

12. The 1951 definition was, "As a result of events occurring before 1 January 1951 and owing to well-founded fear of being persecuted for reasons of race, religion, nationality, membership of a particular social group, or political opinion, is outside the country of his nationality and is unable or, owing to such fear, is unwilling to avail himself of the protection of that country; or who, not having a nationality and being outside the country of his former habitual residence as a result of such events, is unable or, owing to such fear, is unwilling to return to it." United Nations, *UN Refugee Convention*, Art. I, A(2).

13. This point is specifically made in Hathaway, "A Reconsideration," 133.

14. United Nations, *UN Refugee Convention*, amended in Protocol Art. I, 2 and 3.

15. By "irregular" I mean flows that do not go through the legally established channels. For example, irregular flows would refer to flows of migrants who arrive without the proper documentation, i.e., without any documentation when visas are necessary, with forged documents,

with visitors' visas when they plan on working or staying in the country, etc. Irregular also can refer to flows of migrants that do not go through an established port of entry, but bypass the immigration and customs post of the receiving country. See Amnistía Internacional, *Vivir en las sombras: Una introducción a los derechos humanos de las personas migrantes* (Madrid: Editorial Amnestía Internacional, 2006), 15ff.

16. Karatani, "How History."

17. "Refugee or Migrant? Why It Matters," *Refugees* 148, no. 4 (2007): 8.

18. I am using "political community" similarly to the way CST uses it. CST employs the term in many of its major universal social documents. In particular, see Catholic Church, "Gaudium et Spes: Pastoral Constitution on the Church in the Modern World," in *Church Documents Reference Suite* (1965; Boston: Pauline Books & Media, 2000), nos. 73–76; Pope John XXIII, "Mater et magistra," in *Church Documents Reference Suite* (1961; Boston: Pauline Books & Media, 2000), nos. 122, 150, 152, 168, 194. This is also similar to the way the term is used by Michael Walzer, who sees the political community as underlying the state. See Michael Walzer, "The Moral Standing of States: A Response to Four Critics," *Philosophy & Public Affairs* 9, no. 3 (1980): 210; and Michael Walzer, *Spheres of Justice: A Defense of Pluralism and Equality* (New York: Basic Books, 1983), 31. It is more or less the equivalent of the concept "political society" used by John Rawls in his book, *Political Liberalism*. There he imagines the political society as a self-contained and complete social system in which all members find what they need. However, he refuses to call the political society a community because he thinks of communities as united by a common, comprehensive doctrine. The use of community has no such implication in this essay. Nor do we presume that political communities are completely self-contained and complete. Rawls's use of language clearly indicates that there is a sort of equivalence between his concept of "political society" and the common use of the word "country." The political society is the society whose borders more or less correspond with a country and its citizens. John Rawls, *Political Liberalism*, The John Dewey Essays in Philosophy, no. 4 (New York: Columbia University Press, 1996), esp. 40–43, 51, 69, 222, 297, 338, 350, 354ff. The term "political society" is also used as an equivalent to "political community" in CST's major social documents. See, for example, Pope John Paul II, "Centesimus annus," in *Church Documents Reference Suite*, ed. Pauline Books & Media (1991; Boston: Pauline Books & Media, 2000), nos. 7, 25.

19. Mary DeLorey is citing a study by Macartan Humphreys, "Economics and Violent Conflict" (Cambridge, MA: preventconflict.org [now under International Association for Humanitarian Policy and Conflict Research], February 2003), www.preventconflict.org/portal/economics/Essay.pdf, 2 (accessed May 14, 2009).

20. This point is brought home in "Refugee or Migrant? Why It Matters," 9; and Stephen Castles, "Confronting the Realities of Forced Migration," Migration Policy Institute, www.migrationinformation.org/Feature/display.cfm?id=222 (accessed May 14, 2009).

21. Jesuit Refugee Service, "What Is the JRS?" Amnesty International says that there are many more who are forced from their homes than those covered by the Convention refugee. They suggest that it is better to think of migration on a continuum between forced and voluntary migration. See Amnistía Internacional, *Vivir en las sombras*, 11f.

22. The universal social teachings of the Church contain numerous affirmations of the intrinsic and basic sociality of the human person and the various ramifications of that sociality and its relation to participation in the political community. See Catholic Church, "Gaudium et Spes: Pastoral Constitution on the Church in the Modern World," in *Vatican Council II, the Conciliar and Post Conciliar Documents*, ed. Austin Flannery, Vatican Collection (Northport, NY; Dublin: Costello Publishing; Dominican, 1966), nos. 12, 25; Pope Pius XI, "Quadragesimo Anno," in *Church Documents Reference Suite*, ed. Pauline Books & Media (1931; Boston:

Pauline Books & Media, 2000), nos. 42, 118; Pope John XXIII, "Pacem in terris," in *Church Documents Reference Suite*, ed. Pauline Books & Media (1963; Boston, MA: Pauline Books & Media, 2000), nos. 31, 46; Catholic Church, "Dignitatis Humanae: Declaration on Religious Freedom," in *Church Documents Reference Suite*, ed. Pauline Books & Media (1965; Boston: Pauline Books & Media, 2000), no. 4; Pope Paul VI, "Octogesima Adveniens," in *Catholic Social Thought: The Documentary Heritage*, ed. David J. O'Brien and Thomas A. Shannon (1971; Maryknoll, NY: Orbis Books, 1992), no. 24; and Pope John Paul II, "Centesimus annus," no. 13; Pope John XXIII, "Mater et magistra," no. 219.

23. In addition to the references already given in note 22, see United States National Conference of Catholic Bishops, "Economic Justice for All," in *Catholic Social Thought: The Documentary Heritage*, ed. David J. O'Brien and Thomas A. Shannon (1986; Maryknoll, NY: Orbis Books, 1992), esp. nos. 77–78; and Pope John XXIII, "Pacem in terris," nos. 46–69.

24. See references in note 18.

25. One of the major claims of the United States National Conference of Catholic Bishops economic pastoral of 1986 was that socioeconomic rights were just as basic and political as other basic rights and therefore required the same guarantees as other basic rights. United States National Conference of Catholic Bishops, "Economic Justice," nos. 17, 79–84. The essential and basic nature of socioeconomic rights has also been successfully argued in a watershed work by philosopher Henry Shue, *Basic Rights: Subsistence, Affluence, and U.S. Foreign Policy*, 2nd ed. (Princeton, NJ: Princeton University Press, 1996). His work was first published in 1980 and updated in 1996. The argument remained basically unchanged in the second edition.

26. Catholic Church, "Gaudium et Spes," no. 25.

27. Thomas W. Pogge has argued that human rights need not be secured by formal legal edict, for a legal edict is not a guarantee. Rather, institutional arrangements and structures within and among communities, whether formal or informal, are what ultimately secure the enjoyment of human rights. Thomas W. Pogge, "Human Rights and Human Responsibilities," in *Global Responsibilities: Who Must Deliver on Human Rights?* ed. Andrew Kuper (New York: Routledge, 2005), 14–17.

28. United States National Conference of Catholic Bishops, "Economic Justice," nos. 77–84.

29. Pontifical Council Cor Unum, *Refugees*, no. 9.

30. Catholic thought is consonant with some political thinkers who have communitarian leanings. For example see Walzer, *Spheres of Justice*, 31. Michael Walzer considers himself to be a liberal that sees the need for a communitarian correction in liberalism.

31. Of course, there are political communities that have traditionally accorded membership by bloodline rather than birthright.

32. Walzer speaks of the political community as a sort of a Burkean contract in which we find ourselves without being able to identify an exact agreement. Walzer, "Moral Standing," 211.

33. Catholic thinking is both communitarian and universal. We are bonded both in specific communities and in a shared universal community of human persons. As such it is conceivable that the minimums for communal participation can differ from community to community, but there are certain fundamental core minimums that are necessary for all human beings, no matter where they are. Philosopher Martha Nussbaum has worked many years on developing and justifying a core set of human capabilities that are related to basic human rights that apply in all communities. See Martha C. Nussbaum, "Capabilities and Human Rights," *Fordham Law Review* 66, no. 2 (1997): 273–300.

34. CST is insistent on the socially heterogeneous nature of the political community and the

state as one component with a specific role within the political community. Catholic Church, "Gaudium et Spes," nos. 73–75; Pope John Paul II, "Centesimus annus," nos. 7, 13; Pope Pius XI, "Quadragesimo anno," no. 78; and Pope Paul VI, "Octogesima Adveniens," no. 24.

35. See Catholic Church, "Dignitatis Humanae," no. 7; and Pope John XXIII, "Pacem in terris," nos. 46–69. See also David Hollenbach, "Afterword: A Community of Freedom," in *Catholicism and Liberalism: Contributions to American Public Philosophy*, ed. R. Bruce Douglass and David Hollenbach, Cambridge Studies in Religion and American Public Life (Cambridge and New York: Cambridge University Press, 1994), 325–26.

36. While CST would prefer that the state was not seen always to speak for the entire political community, it is de facto treated as the political community's spokesperson in many forums. See Joel S. Migdal and Klaus Schlichte, "Rethinking the State," in *The Dynamics of States: The Formation and Crises of State Domination*, ed. Klaus Schlichte (Aldershot, UK, and Burlington, VT: Ashgate, 2005), 28.

37. This universal community is both a reality and something to be accomplished. See Catholic Church, "Gaudium et Spes: Pastoral Constitution on the Church in the Modern World," nos. 26, 29, 38.

38. We should recognize that there are many persons who are born outside the country of their ancestors, in locations like refugee camps, who have never enjoyed formal explicit membership in any country.

39. Catholic Church, "Gaudium et Spes," no. 25.

40. I create the term "unprotected vulnerability" by borrowing from Michael Walzer's use of related terms in his discussion of the primary nature of membership in a political community. See Walzer, *Spheres of Justice*, 31.

41. See Foster, *International Refugee Law*, 27–35.

42. The three conditions that will be outlined below, though emerging from a different political understanding of human society and the person, are similar to that proposed in 1985 by Andrew Shacknove. Although his political anthropology is different from CST's as expounded in this essay, and his three criteria for being a refugee do not completely match the three in this essay, his criteria and the ones presented here might have similar practical moral outcomes as to who gets identified as having a valid moral claim to being a refugee. His article can be a help in clarifying the particular Catholic moral position developed in this essay. See Andrew E. Shacknove, "Who Is a Refugee?" *Ethics* 95, no. 2 (1985): 274–84.

43. Pope John XXIII, "Mater et magistra," nos. 59–61.

44. Shacknove puts this failure to guarantee basic human rights, or failure on the level of "basic needs," as a "necessary but not sufficient" element for being a refugee. See Shacknove, "Who Is a Refugee?" 281.

45. See Pope John XXIII, "Mater et magistra," nos. 59–61.

46. This element of the possibility of a refugee's agency is reflected in the UN Refugee Convention definition when it uses the word "unwilling" in stating that the refugee "is unwilling to avail himself of the protection of that country." United Nations, *UN Refugee Convention*, Art. I, A(2). Michelle Foster convincingly argues that many traditional convention refugees are refugees because of choices they have made—having or not having made a choice is not crucial for one's status as a refugee. See Foster, *International Refugee Law*, 8.

47. Andrew E. Shacknove suggests that one must suffer basic human rights violations in one's home state, there must be no possibility of recourse to the home state, and one must actually access international help. The relationship is specifically with the state, not the political community. Shacknove, "Who Is a Refugee?" 274–84.

48. Foster, *International Refugee Law*.

49. Foster uses the term "core elements" of rights to indicate the depth of rights failure

that is necessary to establish persecution. So the mere fact of discrimination does not qualify as persecution, but when discrimination involves "core elements" of rights, it does amount to persecution. Unfortunately she does not describe the meaning of "core elements" in much practical detail. See Foster, *International Refugee Law*, 94–98, 196–200, 213, 228–29.

50. See Articles 2, 7, and 14 in United Nations, "Universal Declaration of Human Rights," Office of the High Commissioner for Human Rights, www.unhchr.ch/udhr/lang/eng.htm (accessed May 14, 2009).

51. Foster speaks about this problem. See Foster, *International Refugee Law*, esp. 152–54.

52. Ibid., esp. 152–54.

53. See Foster, *International Refugee Law*, 137.

54. Shue, *Basic Rights*.

55. Foster, *International Refugee Law*, 137–41.

56. Foster directly takes up this question and deals with it as the "floodgates" issue. Ibid., 344–48.

57. Daniel P. Erikson, "Haiti after Aristide: Still on the Brink." *Current History* 104, no. 679 (2005): 83.

58. "The Failed States Index: About 2 Billion People Live in Countries That Are in Danger of Collapse. In the First Annual Failed States Index, Foreign Policy and the Fund for Peace Rank the Countries about to Go over the Brink," *Foreign Policy*, no. 149 (2005): 59; and "The Failed States Index 2008: Whether It Is an Unexpected Food Crisis or a Devastating Hurricane, the World's Weakest States Are the Most Exposed When Crisis Strikes. In the Fourth Annual Failed States Index, Foreign Policy and the Fund for Peace Rank the Countries Where State Collapse May Be Just One Disaster Away," *Foreign Policy*, no. 167 (2008): 67.

59. James Ferguson, *Migration in the Caribbean: Haiti, the Dominican Republic, and Beyond*, Minority Rights Group International Report (London: Minority Rights Group International, 2003), 8.

60. See the discussions of Carolle Charles, "Political Refugees or Economic Immigrants? A New 'Old Debate' within the Haitian Immigrant Communities but with Contestations and Division," *Journal of American Ethnic History* 25, nos. 2–3 (2006): 190–208; Azadeh Dastyari, "Refugees on Guantanamo Bay: A Blue Print for Australia's 'Pacific Solution?'" *AQ—Australian Quarterly* 79, no. 1 (2007): 4–8; Henry J. Reske, "Courts Wrangle over Haitians: Federal Judge Who Stopped Repatriation Overruled by Divided Appellate Panel," *ABA Journal* 78 (1992): 30; and Chinta. Strausberg, "'Unequal Justice': Haiti vs. Cuba," *Chicago Defender*, April 24 2000.

61. Erikson, "Haiti after Aristide," 83–84; Ferguson, *Migration in the Caribbean*, 8ff.

62. World Bank, "Haiti Country Brief," World Bank, www.worldbank.org/ht (accessed May 14, 2009).

63. Michelle Foster's book is littered throughout with examples of cases and countries that have accepted socioeconomic-based definitions of persecution. Foster, *International Refugee Law*. For work-related rights, see the text and footnotes on pp. 91–98. See p. 102 for an especially interesting South African decision regarding work.

Contributors

Arash Abizadeh is associate professor of political theory at McGill University. His research focuses on democratic theory and questions of identity, nationalism, and cosmopolitanism; immigration and border control; Habermas and discourse ethics; and seventeenth- and eighteenth-century philosophy, particularly Hobbes and Rousseau. His publications have appeared in journals including *American Political Science Review, History of Political Thought, Journal of Political Philosophy, Nations and Nationalism, Philosophical Studies, Philosophy & Public Affairs, Political Theory,* and *Review of Metaphysics.*

Frank Brennan, SJ, is a Jesuit priest and professor of law at Australian Catholic University. His books with the University of Queensland Press include *Legislating Liberty* (1998), *Tampering with Asylum* (2003), and *Acting on Conscience* (2007). In 2002 he was awarded the Humanitarian Overseas Service Medal for his work in East Timor and was a recipient of the Australian Centenary Medal in 2003 for his service with refugees and for human rights work in the Asia-Pacific region.

Mary M. DeLorey is strategic issues advisor for Catholic Relief Services (CRS), where she has worked for the last ten years. Her primary policy focus is on Latin American regional policy concerns, including the impact of migration and internal displacement in the region. She also has responsibility for policy coverage on trafficking in persons more globally for CRS. Prior to CRS, DeLorey worked with research, advocacy, and policy organizations on initiatives addressing migration and foreign policy.

J. Bryan Hehir is the Parker Gilbert Montgomery Professor of the Practice of Religion and Public Life at Harvard University's Kennedy School of Government. He also serves as the secretary for health and social services in the Archdiocese of Boston. His teaching and writing focus on ethics and international relations and the role of religion in politics. His essays include "The Moral Measurement of War," "Military Intervention and National Sovereignty," and "Catholicism and Democracy."

David Hollenbach, SJ, holds the University Chair in Human Rights and International Justice and is director of the Center for Human Rights and International Justice at Boston College, where he teaches theological ethics and Christian social ethics. His research interests are in the foundations of Christian social ethics, particularly human rights, the role of the religion in political life, and issues facing refugees. With Georgetown University Press he has published *Advocating Refugee Rights: Ethics, Advocacy, and Africa* (2008) and *The Global Face of Public Faith* (2003). He is also a frequent visiting professor at Hekima College in Nairobi, Kenya.

Daniel Kanstroom is the director of the International Human Rights Program and a law professor at Boston College Law School. Together with his students, he has provided counsel for hundreds of clients and argued major cases in many courts. His latest book is *Deportation Nation: Outsiders in American History* (Harvard University Press, 2007). His articles have appeared in the *Harvard Law Review*, the *Yale Journal of International Law*, the *Stanford Journal of Civil Rights and Civil Liberties*, and the French *Gazette du Palais*.

Christopher Llanos, SJ, obtained his doctorate in religion and society from Harvard University. As a Jesuit he has worked with Jesuit Refugee and Migration Services while holding other jobs. He currently lectures in theological ethics at two associate colleges of the University of the West Indies—St. Michael's Theological College in Jamaica and the Regional Seminary, St. John Vianney and the Ugandan Martyrs, in Trinidad.

Maryanne Loughry, RSM, is a Sister of Mercy, a psychologist, and an academic with research affiliations at Oxford University, Boston College, and Flinders University of South Australia. She is currently the associate director of Jesuit Refugee Service Australia, where she is researching the social effects of climate change on Pacific Islanders. Her publications have appeared in several locations, including the *Journal of Refugee Studies* and *Journal of Humanitarian Assistance*.

M. Brinton Lykes is professor of community-cultural psychology and associate director of the Center for Human Rights and International Justice at Boston College. She works with survivors of war and gross violations of human rights using the creative arts and activist scholarship to analyze the causes and effects of violence and to develop programs to rethread social relations and transform social inequalities. Her work is widely published; she is coeditor of three books and coauthor of *Voices and Images: Maya Ixil Women of Chajul* (MagnaTerra, 2000).

Susan F. Martin holds the Donald G. Herzberg Chair in International Migration and is director of the Institute for the Study of International Migration at Georgetown University. Previously she served as the executive director of the United States Commission on Immigration Reform. Her publications include *Refugee Women* (2003), *The Uprooted: Improving Humanitarian Responses to Forced Migration* (2005), and *Managing Migration: The Promise of Cooperation* (2006), all with Lexington Books.

Agbonkhianmeghe Orobator, SJ, is the Provincial of Eastern Africa Province of the Society of Jesus and lecturer in theology at Hekima College Jesuit School of Theology in Nairobi, Kenya. His areas of special interest include ecclesiology and ethical issues facing the Christian community. He has recently published two monographs: *Theology Brewed in an African Pot* (Orbis, 2008), and with Elias O. Opongo, *Faith Doing Justice: A Manual for Social Analysis, Catholic Social Teachings, and Social Justice* (Paulines Publications Africa, 2007).

Archbishop Silvano M. Tomasi, CS, is the Holy See's permanent observer to the United Nations and other international organizations in Geneva. He holds a doctorate in sociology from Fordham University. A member of the Congregation of the Missionaries of St. Charles-Scalabrinians, he has worked in and written on the area of migration. He has served as director of the Center for Migration Studies in New York; director of pastoral care of migrants and refugees at the U.S. Conference of Catholic Bishops; secretary of the Pontifical Council for Migrants and Itinerant People in Rome; nuncio of the Holy See in Ethiopia, Eritrea, and Djibouti; and observer to the African Union.

Thomas G. Weiss is Presidential Professor at The City University of New York Graduate Center and director of the Ralph Bunche Institute for International Studies. He is president of the International Studies Association and chair of the Academic Council on the United Nations System. He has written extensively about multilateral approaches to international peace and security, humanitarian action, and sustainable development. His latest book is *What's Wrong with the United Nations and How to Fix It* (Polity, 2009).

Index

Abizadeh, Arash, 6, 48, 147–66, 271
Adelman, Howard, 28
Afghanistan, 101, 171, 193–94
African National Congress, 124
Albright, Madeleine, 219
Aleinikoff, Alex, 134n27
All Africa Conference of Churches, 39
American Bar Association Commission on Immigration Policy, Practice & Pro Bono, 120
Amnesty International, 132n10, 173, 210, 252, 266n21
Annan, Kofi: and R2P, 212, 214, 218, 221; on sovereignty, 210–212
Appleby, Scott, 190
Aquinas, Thomas, 186
Aron, Raymond, 192
Ashcroft, John, 119–20
asylum and refugee law, U.S., 6, 115–45; applications for asylum, 117, 119, 130, 135n32, 135nn34–35; applications for refugee status, 119, 134n31, 135nn32–33; asylum adjudication disparities, 118–21; asylum bar for persecutors, 124–25, 140n92, 140n95; and BIA, 115, 119–20, 122–23, 124–25, 135n37; BIA "streamlining" and reorganization, 115, 119–20, 137n62; Bush administration, 115, 117, 124; definition of refugee, 127, 134n31; determinations of eligibility and special cases, 119, 135nn32–33; and DHS, 117, 123, 124; differentiating asylum and withholding, 135n34; differentiating legitimate/illegitimate versions of the political, 128–30, 131, 144n143; discretionary calculations, 126, 141n118; and Displaced Persons Act, 124,

128, 140n92; dissonance and ambivalence in, 115–16, 131n5; DOJ appointments/hirings, 115, 119, 131n2, 135n38; evolution of asylum and its political considerations, 126–27, 142n122; exceptions/executive discretion, 123, 128, 138n78, 138nn81–82, 139n85; exclusions from protection, 121–25, 128; executive and legislative power/decisions, 129, 144n143; impact of the IIRIRA and asylum restrictions (1990s), 130; judicial criticism, 120–21, 136n51, 136n56; material support bar, 122–24, 138nn70–71, 138nn77–78, 138nn81–82; national security discourse and restrictive immigration policies, 116, 132n9; Obama administration, 117; parole power, 129; partisan refugee law, 129–30; presidential consults with Congress, 119, 135n33; and Refugee Act (1980), 124, 127, 129, 134n31, 142–43n130; and Refugee Convention, 116, 117, 124, 128, 129, 131nn6–7, 132n10, 139n89; and serious nonpolitical crimes, 125, 140n105, 141n113, 141nn106–8; and "seventh preference" category, 129; specific protective mechanisms for certain populations, 118, 133–34n24, 134n26; statistics on admission and resettlement, 116–17, 132n17; and Supreme Court, 124, 125, 140n92, 141n107; and term "political asylum," 127–28; USA Patriot Act and the REAL ID Act, 117, 122, 133n20
asylum seekers/refugees and national exclusion policies, 5–6, 97–114, 115, 121–25; the Australian Pacific Solution and border protection policy, 98–103, 111–12; Cambodia's exclusion of Montagnards, 99, 103–11;

275

asylum-seekers (*continued*)
exceptions/executive discretion in U.S. asylum law, 123, 128, 138n78, 138nn81–82, 139n85; and human rights NGOs, 98, 105, 108, 109–10; and Kew Gardens Principle, 97–98, 112; material support bar in U.S. asylum law, 122–24, 138nn70–71, 138nn77–78, 138nn81–82; persecutors in U.S. asylum and refugee law, 124–25, 140n92, 140nn94–95; problem of using human rights paradigm to critique government choices, 98, 111–12; "push" factors/"pull" factors, 101; and Refugee Convention, 97, 116, 121, 124, 131n7, 137n65; serious nonpolitical crimes, 125, 140n105, 141n113, 141nn106–8; and UNHCR compromises on refoulement, 110, 111. *See also* asylum and refugee law, U.S.

Augustine of Hippo, 186, 195
Australian border protection policy excluding asylum seekers, 98–103, 111–12; detention centers, 102; new human rights provisions, 102–3; Pacific Solution and government deterrence strategy, 101–2; the 2001 *Tampa* incident and asylum seekers, 99–101
Australian Human Rights Commission, 103
Australian Maritime Safety Authority, Rescue Coordination Centre, 99–100
Ayoob, Mohammed, 209

Bader, Veit, 154
Bagheritari, Manilee, 83
Balkans: conflict-driven refugees, 193; and just war ethic, 200–201; Kosovo, 193, 200–201, 211; returning refugees and economic vulnerability, 237; R2P and UN failures, 211, 213
Bass, Gary, 207
Benedict XVI, Pope: address to UN General Assembly on human rights and the state, 61, 64, 65, 66n3, 208–9; and R2P, 208–9
Bethe, Hans, 188
biblical ethics and theological understanding of displacement, 39–41, 45–47, 49
Blair, Tony, 214
Blake, Michael, 151, 153
Board of Immigration Appeals (BIA): and asylum adjudication disparities, 115, 119–20, 135n37; and exclusions from asylum protection, 122–23, 124–25; "streamlining" and reorganization, 115, 119–20, 137n62
Bolshevik Revolution, 19

borders and boundary laws. *See* state sovereignty and boundary laws/borders
Boutros-Ghali, Boutros, 218
Brennan, Frank, 5–6, 97–114, 271
Brodie, Bernard, 188
Brookings-Bern Project on Internal Displacement, 28, 241
Bruce, Tricia C., 50n5
Burma, 115, 131n3
Bush, George W. (administration): Iraq war and abuse of R2P, 213–14, 215; and political consideration in asylum law, 115, 117, 124
Butchart, Alex, 84

Cambodian national policies and Montagnard asylum seekers: agreements with/limitations on UNHCR, 104–5, 106; forced removal/deportations, 103–4, 106–8, 109–11; and history of Montagnard influxes from Vietnam, 104–6; and human rights NGOs, 105, 107, 108, 109–10; the 2005 memorandum of understanding (MOU), 103–4, 106–8, 110; tripartite agreements, 99, 103–11; UNHCR and repatriation agreements, 103–4, 105–8, 110, 111; UNHCR's failures, 99, 103–11
Canada: Guatemalan migration to, 85; immigration rates, 165n50; and R2P, 220; and U.S. compliance with nonrefoulement obligations, 116, 132n10
Canadian Council for Refugees, 132n10
Canadian Council of Churches, 132n10
Carens, Joseph, 151
Cartagena Declaration on Refugees (1984), 23, 56
Catechism of the Catholic Church, 61, 62
Catholic rationalism and just war ethic, 187
Catholic social thought (CST), 61–63, 249–69; distinction between refugees and economic migrants, 162n10, 252–60; and economic migration, 243–46, 252–60; and just war ethic, 191, 195; and "minimum conditions for life in community," 253–55, 261–62, 267n33; moral intuition and moral definition of refugee, 252–60; and "peace building," 191; and personal sociality, 253, 266n22; and the "political community," 251–55, 261–62, 266n18, 266n22, 267n27, 267nn33–34, 268n36; and R2P, 63, 208–9; on socioeconomic rights, 253, 256, 258–60, 267n25; theological framework for Christian response to

suffering of refugees/IDPs, 43–45, 46–47, 49, 52nn28–29; and the universal human community, 63, 69n30, 254, 255, 267n33, 268n37. *See also* Catholic tradition of human rights advocacy on behalf of the displaced; Christian theological/ethical tradition and justice for the displaced

Catholic tradition of human rights advocacy on behalf of the displaced, 4–5, 55–69; the affirmation of human rights as source of action, 64–65; Benedict XVI's address to General Assembly, 61, 64, 65, 66n3, 208–9; and common good of the receiving state, 61–62; and cultural rights, 63; and human rights in relation to human mobility, 68n22; and illegal migrants, 62–63; and immigrants' duties of respect toward country of adoption, 62; and international refugee regime, 56–59; John Paul II, 60, 61, 62–63, 68n22, 69n26; John XXIII and the Vatican II, 59, 67n15; Leo XIII's *Rerum novarum*, 59; and membership in the state/universal human family, 63, 66n3, 69n30; Paul VI, 59–60, 67n15, 68n18, 69n29; perspective of integral humanism, 59; Pius XII and *Exsul Familia*, 37, 40, 59, 67n14, 68n18; post-World War II advocacy on behalf of the war-displaced, 59, 67n11; the principle of subsidiarity, 64; and responsibilities of the state, 61, 66n3; and rights to move, leave country of origin, and enter another country, 61, 68n22, 69n26; and right to return, 63; and R2P, 63, 208–9; the social doctrine of the Church, 61–63; and sovereign nations' control of borders, 245; theology of the Church and ecclesiological approach to displacement, 41–43, 46, 49, 52n23; Vatican II and the church community, 42–43. *See also* Catholic social thought (CST); Christian theological/ethical tradition and justice for the displaced

Central American Free Trade Agreement, 79

The Century of Total War (Aron), 192

Chang, Howard, 154

Chechnya rebels, 236

Chertoff, Michael, 123, 138n82

Childress, James, 187

China, 27, 240

Christiansen, Drew, 44, 47

Christian theological/ethical tradition and justice for the displaced, 4, 37–53; biblical ethics, 39–41, 45–47, 49; and Catholic social teaching, 43–45, 46–47, 49, 52nn28–29; complementarity of humanitarian and structural responses, 45; contributions of other religious traditions, 49–50; ethical prescriptions based on, 47–49; faith-based organizations in camps and detention centers, 38, 50nn4–5; forced migration and global ethical framework, 44–45; and Gospel accounts of Jesus' birth and infancy, 40–41; historical relationship between theology, religion, and refugees, 37–39; hospitality and ethical responsibilities of prosperous states, 39–40, 48, 49; and multiple causes of displacement, 44–45, 52n32; and a new refugee regime of ethically generated systemic response, 47–48; and New Testament accounts of the Holy Family, 40–41; Old Testament ethical injunctions, 39–40, 49; persecution/displacement of early Christians, 42; and positive contributions of religion, 48–49; religion and displacement (links between), 38–39, 48, 49, 51n9; "shepherding ecclesiology" and the Church in Africa, 52n23; structural implications of ethical norms, 45–49; theology of the Church/ecclesiological approach to displacement, 41–43, 46, 49, 52n23; three overlapping elements of the theological framework, 39–49; Vatican II and the church community, 42–43. *See also* Catholic tradition of human rights advocacy on behalf of the displaced

citizenship: and democratic self-determination, 158–59; social rights/obligations in, 155–56, 164n39; state sovereignty and distinction between citizen and foreigner, 148–49, 158–59; the state's protection of culture, 156, 164n42

Clark, Lance, 82

climate change, 29, 241, 242, 244. *See also* environmental migrants and forced displacement

Climate Change, Natural Disasters, and Human Displacement: A UNHCR Perspective, 29

Clinton, Bill (administration), 130

Clinton, Hillary, 220

cluster approach, 26–28, 172, 219

Cockburn, Cynthia, 81

Coghlan, Denise, 109

Cohen, Roberta, 24, 28, 208, 211

Cohen, William, 219

Cole, Philip, 151
Collier, Paul, 236
Colombia, 115, 237
Commission for Historical Clarification (CEH) in Guatemala, 71, 77
community-based development and participatory engagement processes, 80–83. *See also* gender and forced displacement; "political community"
Compendium of the Social Doctrine of the Church, 59
conflict-driven displacement, 7–8, 169–83; and economic drivers, 235–38, 251–52; end of Cold War, 193; and gender-specific violence, 71; and IDPs, 1–2, 170–71, 172, 173–74, 179; intrastate conflicts, 192–93; Iraqi refugees, 173–80; and just war ethic, 191–94; national positive duties in sharing the burden of asylum, 97–98, 174–76, 180; new challenges of mixed populations, 55–56, 169, 170, 251–52; protracted refugee settings, 171–72, 179, 183; return and resettlement issues, 171, 178, 179, 237–38, 251–52; urban refugee settings, 7–8, 172–73, 176–78, 179; Weiner's five types of war and the refugees produced, 192–93. *See also* just war ethic (JWE)
Convention against Torture (CAT), 118, 133–34n24
Convention for the Prevention of Internal Displacement and the Protection of and Assistance to Internally Displaced Persons in Africa, 56
Convention Governing the Specific Aspects of the Refugee Problems in Africa (1969), 56
Convention on the Elimination of All Forms of Discrimination against Women (CEDAW), 83
Cornwall, Andrea, 82
Cuba, 130, 261
Currie, Dawn, 82–83
Cyclone Nargis, 17, 27
Cyprus, 25

Dallaire, Roméo, 207
DeLorey, Mary M., 9, 231–47, 251–52, 259, 263–64, 271
Democratic Republic of Congo (DRC), 193, 207, 220
democratic theory of popular sovereignty, 148, 156–59
Deng, Francis, 24, 208, 210, 211

Department of Homeland Security (DHS), 117, 123, 124
Department of Justice (DOJ), U.S.: asylum law and politicized appointments/hirings, 115, 119, 131n2, 135n38; Executive Office of Immigration Review (EOIR), 117, 119; Office of Professional Responsibility (OPR) and inspector general (IG), 119; and refugee status/asylum applications, 117, 119, 129, 144n150
Displaced Persons Act (1948), 124, 128, 140n92
Dominican Republic (DR), 261, 262–63
Donini, Antonio, 218
Dostoevsky, Fyodor, 64, 131n1
Dummett, Michael, 156
Dworkin, Ronald, 126

East Timor, 211
Ecclesia in American (John Paul II), 69n26
economic migrants and forced displacement, 2, 9, 231–47; and access/control of natural resources (extractive industries), 236–37; and Catholic social thought, 243–46, 252–60; and cross-border movements, 234; definitions, 128, 143n132, 233–35, 250–52, 263–64; distinctions between refugees and economic migrants, 128, 162n10, 250–52; economic drivers and conflict displacement, 235–38, 251–52; the economics of involuntary migration, 238–40; and global food crisis, 238–39; Haitian case, 260–63; and human rights framework in migration policy, 244–45; the ICFTU/ORIT resolution on increased migration in the Americas, 239–40; and International Convention on the Protection of Migrant Workers, 234, 245; legal migration options, 244; long-term impact on subsequent economic vulnerability, 237–38, 251–52; and multilateral trade agreements, 239; open borders and labor immigration, 154, 163n31; and the problems created by proposed cures, 240; recommendations for overcoming protection gaps, 243–46, 263; and rights protections regardless of status, 245, 247n29, 263; and the "voluntary migration" concept, 231–32, 234; and widespread extreme poverty, 2, 238, 243–44. *See also* environmental migrants and forced displacement
El Salvador, 124–25, 130, 238
empowerment, 80–81, 85
environmental migrants and forced

displacement, 2, 9, 18–19, 28–30, 234–35, 240–43; and access/control of natural resources (extractive industries), 236–37; and climate change, 29, 241, 242, 244; definitions, 234–35; environmental displacement research, 244; and expected increase in statelessness, 243; natural disasters, 17–18, 27, 28–30, 172, 241; slow-onset environmental change/degradation, 242. *See also* economic migrants and forced displacement

Erikson, Daniel P., 261

European Union (EU): open borders and fears of labor migration, 163n31; resettlement and Iraqi refugees, 178; and R2P, 220

Evans, Chris, 103

Evans, Gareth, 213, 222–23

Evian conference (1938), 20

exclusion. *See* asylum seekers/refugees and national exclusion policies

Executive Office of Immigration Review (EOIR) in the U.S. Department of Justice, 117, 119

Exsul Familia (Apostolic Constitution) (Pius XIII), 37, 40, 59, 67n14, 68n18

Failed Responsibility: Iraqi Refugees in Syria, Jordan, and Lebanon (International Crisis Group), 173

faith-based organizations, 38, 50nn4–5

Fakhouri, Jean-Marie, 106

Falla, Ricardo, 77, 78

Familiaris Consortio (John Paul II), 61

Federal Immigration Cases and Agency Decisions database, 127

Federation for American Immigration Reform (FAIR), 116, 132n9

Feller, Erika, 27

feminist scholarship: and community-based development and participatory engagement processes, 81–83; on forced migration and development, 72–73. *See also* gender and forced displacement

Ferguson, Niall, 192

Ferris, Elizabeth G., 64, 241–42

Finnis, John, 186

Firestone, Shulamith, 83

forced displacement/migration, 1–11, 169, 170–73, 178–80; calls for a "new humanitarian-protection compact," 2–3, 19; categorizations of displaced people, 16–19, 29–30, 56, 264; and Catholic social thought, 45–45; and

cluster approach, 26–28, 172; designation based on causes of the forced movement, 16–17; designation based on geography, 16; designation based on time/phase of displacement, 17; gaps in basic protection and assistance, 1–2, 18, 24–26, 74–76, 88n17, 169, 208, 231–32, 252; gender-based and sexual violence, 71, 73–76; global ethical challenges, 45; governments' willingness/abilities to provide protection, 29–30, 264; migration patterns and ideological construct of community, 85, 93n89; new challenges of mixed populations, 55–56, 169, 170, 251–52; newly emerging categories, 26–30; new questions about scope of responsibilities, 1–3; protracted refugee settings, 73, 74–76, 171–72, 179, 183; religion and displacement, 38–39, 48, 49, 51n9; statistics, 15–16, 31nn1–2, 73–74, 73–76; urban refugee settings, 172–73, 176–78, 179. *See also* conflict-driven displacement; economic migrants and forced displacement; environmental migrants and forced displacement; gender and forced displacement; internally displaced persons (IDPs); international refugee regime; just war ethic (JWE); return, resettlement, and repatriation

Foster, Michelle, 257–58, 259, 260, 268n46, 268–69n49

Fourth World Congress on the Pastoral Care of Migrants and Refugees (1998), 60

Franken, Mark, 52n29

Freedman, Lawrence, 187

freedom of movement, 150–52

Freeman, Samuel, 153

Freire, Paulo, 81

French Episcopal Committee on Migration, 39

French Revolution, 149

From Exile to Peril at Home (Human Rights Watch), 173

"gender and development" (GAD) model, 72–73, 76

gender and forced displacement, 5, 71–93; and Australian detention centers for asylum seekers, 102; and barriers to women's participation in decision-making and development, 82–83; and "community," 84–85; community-based development and participatory engagement, 80–83; critical interrogation of masculinities, 84, 93n87; and

gender (*continued*)
"empowerment," 80–81, 85; and ethical challenges of activist scholarship, 85–86; feminist scholarship on, 72–73, 81–83; and gaps in basic protection/assistance, 74–76, 88n17; "gender and development" (GAD) model, 72–73, 76; gender-based violence and asylum, 88n17; Guatemalan alternative and gender-based refugee policy, 76–79, 86; Guatemalan women refugees in Mexican refugee camps, 78–79, 86, 90n49; and IDPs, 73; refugee and returnee children, 91n65; refugee camps and gender-based violence, 73, 74–76; refugee camps and women's participatory processes/projects, 78–79, 80, 82; refugee data, 73–74; and structural violence, 77, 90n42; UNHCR responsibility, 73–76; wider social conditions of gendered inequality and poverty, 84; "women and de-velopment" (WAD) discourse, 72, 75–76, 79; "women in development" (WID) discourse, 72, 75–76
Geneva Conventions, 24–25, 209
Genocide Prevention Task Force, 219
Gibney, Matthew, 121
Gladkova, Inna, 109
Global Commission on International Migra-tion (2005), 57–58, 240
Global Forum on Migration and Develop-ment, 58
The Global Migration Crisis (Weiner), 193
Global Migration Group (GMG), 57, 65–66n2, 74, 84
Gonzales, Alberto, 121, 137nn62–63
Goodling, Monica, 119
Goodwin-Gill, Guy, 110
Great Lakes area of Africa, 193
Great Lakes Pact and the Rights of Displaced People: A Guide for Civil Society (2008), 56
Groody, Daniel, 39, 46
Guatemala: asylum applications, 130; civil war and human rights violations, 76–77; Com-mission for Historical Clarification (CEH), 71, 77; "community" and migration patterns, 85, 93n89; gender-based refugee policy and practices, 76–79, 86; returnees, 79, 237; vio-lence against Mayans in rural communities, 77–78, 90n42; women refugees in Mexican refugee camps, 78–79, 86, 90n49
Guidelines on the Protection of Refugee Women (UNHCR, 1991), 74

Guiding Principles on Internal Displacement (2001), 16–17, 18, 24–25, 28, 56, 171, 179, 180n5, 233–34
Guijt, Irene, 81
Gulf War (1990–91), 93
Gustafson, James, 191
Guterres, António, 2–3, 18–19, 27, 169, 171, 176, 214

Haass, Richard, 211
Habermas, Jürgen, 166n60
Hagan, Jacqueline, 43–44
Haiti, 130, 211, 260–63
Harrell-Bond, Barbara, 81
Hathaway, James, 28
Heath, Joseph, 155–56, 164n39
Hehir, J. Bryan, 8, 47, 185–205, 271
Helton, Arthur, 127, 129
Henkin, Louis, 142n121
Himes, Kenneth, 187
Hiroshima and Nagasaki bombings, 187, 188
Hobbes, Thomas, 161n2
Hoeffler, Anke, 236
Hoffmann, Stanley, 187
Hollenbach, David, 1–11, 97–98, 187, 208, 272
Holmes, John, 241
Homer-Dixon, Tad, 242
hospitality, 48, 49
Howard, John, 100–101, 111–12
Howard, Michael, 187
humanitarian intervention: just intervention and cases overriding nonintervention prin-ciple, 189–90; and just war ethic, 189–90, 202–3; northern Iraq (1991), 24, 211, 213; and R2P, 212–13, 215–16, 217, 222; and state sov-ereignty issues, 189–90, 196–97
Human Rights Council, 58
Human Rights First, 115, 116
Human Rights Watch, 210; and Iraqi refugees, 173, 179; and Montagnard asylum seekers, 105, 108, 109, 110
Humphreys, Macartan, 236
Hurricane Mitch (1998), 241

IDPs. *See* internally displaced persons (IDPs)
Illegal Immigration Reform and Immigrant Responsibility Act (IIRIRA), 130
Immigration and Nationality Act (1952), 124, 134n31, 143n137
Immigration and Naturalization Service (INS), 130

India, 240

Indonesia: asylum seekers and 2001 *Tampa* incident, 99–101; and 2004 tsunami, 17, 27

Indra, Dorren, 81

infrastructure development projects, 17, 240

Institute of Development Studies (IDS), University of Sussex's Pathways of Women's Empowerment project, 85

INS v. Aguirre-Aguirre (1999), 125

InterAction, 218

Inter-Agency Standing Committee (IASC), 26, 219

Intergovernmental Panel on Climate Change (IPCC), 241

Internal Displacement Monitoring Centre, 171, 174

internally displaced persons (IDPs): changing ratio of refugees to, 28, 208; and cluster leadership approach, 26–28, 172, 219; and conflict-driven displacement, 1–2, 170–71, 172, 173–74, 179; data/statistics on, 15–16, 31nn1–2, 73, 171, 180n5, 208, 224n8; definitions, 180n5, 233–34; gaps in rights protection, 1–2, 24–26, 208; Guiding Principles (2001), 16–17, 18, 24–25, 28, 56, 171, 179, 180n5, 233–34; Iraqi refugees, 7, 24, 173–74, 179; and just war ethic, 194–202; and refugee regime, 24–28; and R2P, 208; and states' responsibilities, 233; UNHCR programs and policies, 25–28, 73

Internal Security Act (1950), 128

International Association for the Study of Forced Migration, 28

International Commission on Intervention and State Sovereignty (ICISS) and 2001 R2P report, 190, 204n26, 207, 211–13, 221–23

International Committee of the Red Cross, 218–19

International Committee on Refugees, 20

International Confederation of Free Trade Unions (ICFTU), 239–40

International Convention on the Protection of the Rights of All Migrant Workers and Members of Their Families (1990), 56, 234, 245

International Council on Human Rights Policy, 210

International Crisis Group, 173, 223

International Labour Organization (ILO), 56, 65–66n2

International Migration and Human Rights (Global Migration Group report), 74, 84

International Organization for Migration (IOM), 29, 65–66n2, 219, 234

International Refugee Organization, 20, 67n11

international refugee regime, 15–33, 56–59; barriers to refugee participation in, 82–83; categorizations of displaced people, 16–19, 28–30, 56, 264; Christian theological framework for, 47–48; and Cold War conflicts, 23; distinction between refugees and economic migrants, 128, 162n10, 250–52; evolution of, 19–28, 31; expansion and good offices of the UNHCR, 22–24, 27–28; first High Commissioner for Refugees, 19, 250, 265n11; and focus on IDPs, 28, 208; formal instruments of protection, 56; gaps in the system, 1–2, 18, 24–26, 74–76, 88n17, 169, 208, 231–32, 252; and global humanitarianism, 58; and IDPs, 16, 18, 24–28, 56, 179, 208; and irregular migrations, 251–52; and League of Nations, 19–20, 250; and national positive duties in sharing the burden of asylum, 97–98, 174–76, 180; and national protectionism, 58; post-1990, 23–24; post-World War II, 20; and Refugee Convention, 21–22, 23, 56; rethinking in light of human rights and the global common good, 3–4, 15–33, 264; two tracks in addressing displacement, 57; and UDHR, 20, 57, 209. *See also* forced displacement/migration; refugee definition; return, resettlement, and repatriation; United Nations High Commissioner for Refugees (UNHCR)

International Rescue Committee's Post-Conflict Development Initiative, 80

International Security (journal), 192

Iraq: humanitarian intervention in (1991), 24, 211, 213; the 2001 *Tampa* incident and asylum seekers from, 101; U.S-led war in, 169, 173, 193–94, 213–14, 215

Iraqi refugees, 7–8, 173–80; asylum in industrial countries, 174; IDPs, 7, 24, 173–74, 179; and Iraq war, 169, 173, 193–94; to Jordan, 174, 175–77, 179, 182n36; to Lebanon, 174, 175–76; reports of human rights groups and research organizations, 173, 181n18; return and resettlement issues, 178, 179; to Syria, 174, 175–78, 179, 182n36; UNHCR response to, 174–76; urban refugee settings, 7–8, 176–78, 179, 182n36; women and girls, 177

Iraq Rhetoric and Reality: The Iraqi Refugee Crisis (Amnesty International), 173

Irish Republican Army (IRA), 236
irregular migrations. *See* mixed/irregular mi-
grator movements

Jackson, Robert, 218
Jesuit Refugee Service (JRS), 50n4, 98; and
Cambodia's deportation of Montagnard asylum seekers, 109, 110; and moral definition of
refugee, 249, 252, 260
John Paul II, Pope, 60, 61, 62–63, 68n22, 69n26
Johnson, James Turner, 186, 187
Jones, James, 220
Jordan, 174, 175–77, 179, 182n36
"Jubilee Charter of Rights of Displaced People,"
68n19
just war ethic (JWE), 8, 185–205; and change,
194–95; and Christian realist anthropology, 195; and conflict-driven displacement,
191–94; and the consensual view of world
politics, 195–96; and consideration of cause,
196–99; and consideration of "last resort,"
199–200; and consideration of proportionality, 199–200; and deterrence, 188–89;
development within/beyond the tradition,
188–91; the historical argument, 196; and
humanitarian intervention, 189–90, 196–97,
202–3; *jus ad bellum* (just cause), 186, 187,
189–90, 196–200; just means (*jus in bello*),
186, 187, 190, 195, 200–201; and Kosovo, 193,
200–201; and military intervention, 189–90,
196–97, 200–203; and Niebuhr, 187, 188; and
nuclear age bombings, 187, 188; paradoxical
role in political conflicts, 202; and "peace
building," 190–91; postbellum issues (*jus
postbellum*), 191, 201–2; and post-9/11 wars
in Afghanistan and Iraq, 193–94; prebellum
issues, 190–91; and prospective casualties/
refugees of war, 197–99; rethinking in light
of obligations to refugees/IDPs, 194–202;
and R2P, 190, 197; and state sovereignty,
186–87, 189–90, 195, 196–97; testing by
questioning the central premise, 195–96;
three intellectual conclusions grounding
justifications for force, 195–96; and Walzer,
187–88, 191, 199
just war ethic (the historical model), 185–88,
195; Aquinas and the means questions, 186;
Augustine and just cause/right intention,
186; and Catholic rationalism, 187; just cause
(*jus ad bellum*), 186, 187, 189–90; just means
(*jus in bello*), 186, 187, 190, 195, 200–201;

medieval period, 186; and Natural Law
ethics, 187; renewal (late 1950s to 1970s),
187–88; World War II, 187, 188

Kalin, Walter, 179
Kanstroom, Daniel, 5–6, 115–45, 272
Karatani, Reiko, 265n11
Keely, Charles, 21
Kenya, 221
Kerwin, Donald, 122
Kew Gardens Principle, 97–98, 112
Ki-moon, Ban, 214, 221, 222
Kolvenbach, Peter-Hans, 43
Kosovo, 193, 200–201, 211
Krulfeld, Ruth, 85
Kymlicka, Will, 156, 165n50

Langan, John, 187
Latin America and economics of involuntary
migration, 239–40
League of Nations, 19–20, 250, 265n11
Lebanon, 174, 175–76
Legomsky, Stephen, 120
Leo XIII, Pope, 59
Leuprecht, Peter, 107, 109
Lewis, Anthony, 209
liberal egalitarianism and borders: arguments
for closed borders, 153–56, 159; arguments
for open borders, 149–53, 159; and civil
rights, 149; classical liberalism, 149, 150–52;
and doctrine of human rights, 150, 160,
166n59; and moral duties of humanitarian
assistance, 150; social liberalism, 149, 150,
152–56; and socioeconomic rights, 149; and
state sovereignty, 147–50, 160, 166n59. *See
also* state sovereignty and boundary laws/
borders
Liberia, 115, 193
Limón, Lavinia, 130
Llanos, Christopher, 9–10, 162n10, 249–69, 272
Loughry, Maryanne, 7–8, 76, 169–83, 272
Lubbers, Ruud, 106
Luck, Edward, 222
Lykes, M. Brinton, 5, 71–93, 160, 272

MacDonald, Jeffrey, 85
Macedo, Stephen, 154–55
Majawa, Clement, 45, 52n23
Mama Maquín (Guatemalan women's organi-
zation), 78
Mandela, Nelson, 86–87

Marshall Plan, 191
Martin, Susan F., 3–4, 10, 15–33, 50n2, 76, 219, 264, 272
Masses in Flight (Cohen and Deng), 24
McGrath, Susan, 28
Merry, Sally Engle, 83
Messer, Ellen, 78
Mexico, 78–79, 86, 90n49, 239–40
Migliore, Celestino, 244
Migrant and Refugee Day (Catholic Church), 61, 68n22
Millennium Development Goals (MDGs), 243–44
Millennium Summit, 28
Miller, David, 152
mixed/irregular migratory movements, 251–52; defining, 251, 265n15; new challenges of, 55–56, 169, 170, 251–52
Moghadam, Valentine, 83
Montagnards: forced deportation of asylum seekers, 104, 109–11; history of migratory influxes from Vietnam, 104–6; refugees granted permanent residence in the U.S., 105; tripartite agreements concerning asylum seekers, 99, 103–11; and voluntary repatriation, 105–6
Montevideo Convention (1934), 212
Mooney, Margarita, 53n38
The Morality of War (Orend), 191
Morgenthau, Hans, 188
Mukasey, Michael, 135
Murray, John Courtney, 187, 188, 191
The Myth of Community: Gender Issues in Participatory Development (Guijt and Shah), 81

Nagel, Thomas, 118, 131n1
Nansen, Fridjoft, 19
Nansen International Office for Refugees, 19–20
Natural Law ethics, 187
Nawyn, Stephanie J., 38
New International Economic Order (NIEO), 214
New Testament, 40–41
Niebuhr, Reinhold, 187, 188
Ninth Circuit Court of Appeals, 120, 140, 141n108
Nolin, Catherine, 85
Non-Aligned Movement (NAM), 217
nongovernmental organizations (NGOs): and the asylum-migration nexus, 232; and

national policies that exclude refugees, 98; and protection needs of the forcibly displaced, 172; and R2P, 218–19
nonrefoulement: and Refugee Convention, 21, 116, 132n10, 142n121; UNHCR compromises, 110, 111; and U.S. asylum and refugee law, 116, 132n10, 142n121
North American Free Trade Agreement (NAFTA), 239–40
North Atlantic Treaty Organization (NATO), 220
Nussbaum, Martha, 267n33
Nye, Joseph, 187

Obama, Barack, 117, 219
Ogata, Sadako, 33
Old Testament, 39–40, 49
On the Pastoral Care of Migrants (1968), 68n18
Oppenheimer, Robert, 188
Orend, Brian, 191
Organizacion Regional Interamericana de Trabajadores (ORIT), 239–40
Organization of African Unity (OAU) Refugee Convention, 16, 22–23
Organization of American States, 23
Orobator, Agbonkhianmeghe E., 4, 37–53, 273

Pacem in terris (John XXIII), 61, 68n22, 69n30
Pagonis, Jennifer, 109
Patai, Daphne, 86
Paul VI, Pope, 59–60, 67n15, 68n18, 69n29
"peace building," 190–91
Peace of Westphalia (1648), 4–5
Perry, Stephen, 152
Phelan, Michael, 132n10
Philpott, Daniel, 222
Pius XII, 37, 40, 59, 67n14, 68n18
Plan Panama, 79
Pogge, Thomas W., 267n27
"political community": association by birth, 255, 268n38; and Catholic social thought, 251–55, 261–62, 266n18, 266n22, 267n27, 267nn33–34, 268n36; and distinctions among irregular/mixed flows of migrants, 252; and foundational right of membership, 254; and Haiti as failed state, 261–62; and "minimum conditions for life in community," 253–55, 261–62, 267n33; the state's role in, 254–55, 267n34, 268n36; and Walzer, 266n18, 267n32, 268n40

Pontifical Council for the Pastoral Care of Migrants and Itinerant People, 68n19, 249, 254, 260
Populorum progressio (Paul VI), 69n29
Posen, Barry, 200–201
Posner, Richard, 136n51
Potter, Ralph, 187
poverty, global, 2, 238, 243–44; and gendered inequality, 84; Haiti, 261; and liberal egalitarian arguments for open borders, 152; and urban refugee settings, 176. *See also* economic migrants and forced migration
Prendergast, John, 220

Ramsey, Paul, 187, 188
Rawls, John, 153, 266n18
REAL ID Act (2005), 117, 122, 133n20, 135n32
Refugee Act (1980), 124, 127, 129, 134n31, 142–43n130
refugee camps, 73, 74–76, 171–72; and Cold War conflicts, 23; domestic and gender-based violence in, 74–75; faith-based organizations in, 38, 50n4; Guatemalan women refugees in Mexico, 78–79, 86, 90n49; mainstreaming of women, 76; structural design/physical layout and health services, 75; and women's engagement in participatory processes/projects, 78–79, 80, 82; women-specific programmatic responses, 75–76
Refugee Convention. *See* UN Convention Relating to the Status of Refugees (1951)
refugee definition: and the Cold War migratory context, 250, 251; and conditions for protection, 256–57, 268n44, 268nn46–47; distinction between refugees and economic migrants, 128, 162n10, 250–52; expanded, 22–23, 263; gaps in Refugee Convention definition, 1–2, 8, 252, 266n21; and irregular migratory movements, 251–52, 265n15; and issue of choice/agency, 257, 264, 268n46; moral definition and Catholic social teaching, 249–69, 265nn6–7; OAU Refugee Convention, 22–23; and obligations of sovereign signatories to particular refugee flows, 250–51; and persecution, 257–58, 268–69n49; and "political community," 251–52, 253–55, 266n18; Refugee Convention, 1, 3, 18, 21, 162n10, 170, 180n4, 233, 249–51, 252, 253, 265n12, 268n46; and socioeconomic rights, 253, 256, 258–60, 263–64, 267n25; and U.S. asylum and refugee law, 127, 134n31

refugee regime. *See* international refugee regime
Refugee Rights: Ethics, Advocacy, and Africa (ed. Hollenbach), 97–98
religion and displacement, 38–39, 48, 49, 51n9
remittances, 152
Rerum novarum (Leo XIII), 59
responsibility to protect (R2P), 8–9, 28, 207–27; and Bush administration's justifications for Iraq war, 213–14, 215; and Catholic social thought, 63, 208–9; and changing ratio of refugees to IDPs, 208; and civil society's norms entrepreneurs, 213, 217; and conceptual clarity, 215–16, 217; and creation of UN agency for war victims, 217–19; current diplomatic atmosphere in General Assembly debates, 214; defining, 207–9; and earlier UN failures, 207, 211; and the EU, 220; evolution of the norm, 211–14; five political innovations, 215–21; and historical backdrop of human rights, 209–11; and humanitarian intervention, 212–13, 215–16, 217, 222; the ICISS's 2001 report, 190, 204n26, 207, 212–13, 221–23; and international human rights law, 209–10; and longer-term strategy, 216–17; and military interventions in new wars of the 1990s, 211, 213; and non-U.S. military capacity, 219–20; and prevention/the responsibility to prevent, 8–9, 213, 216, 221, 222; and rebuilding state capacity, 213, 222; and Refugee Convention, 207; and the Rwandan genocide, 202, 207, 212, 220; "sovereignty as responsibility," 8, 190, 197, 207–11, 221–22; strength of diplomatic opposition to, 216–17; and UN General Assembly's 2005 World Summit, 8, 209, 211, 213, 215, 216–17, 221
return, resettlement, and repatriation, 23–24, 171, 178–79; and Catholic social thought, 63; Guatemalan refugees, 79, 237; and long-term impact of economic displacement, 237–38, 251–52; Montagnards and UNHCR agreements, 103–4, 106–8, 110, 111; and politicization, 79; and UNHCR, 22, 23–24, 103–4, 105–8, 110, 111; U.S. statistics, 116–17, 132n17
Revolutionary Armed Forces of Colombia (FARC), 236
Rice, Susan, 220
Richards, Michael, 77
Rieff, David, 207

Rinnan, Arne, 99–101
Roosevelt, Eleanor, 20, 209
R2P. *See* responsibility to protect (R2P)
Rummel, Robert J., 212
Rusk, Dean, 220
Russett, Bruce, 187
Rwanda, 193, 202, 207, 212, 220

Sachs, Jeffrey, 238
Scheffler, Samuel, 155
Schirmer, Jennifer, 78
Schrag, Phillip, 127
Second Circuit Court of Appeals, 120
A Secure Europe in a Better World (2003), 220
Seedat, Mohammed, 84
self-determination, 157–59
Senior, Donald, 40, 42
September 11, 2001, attacks, 116–17, 193–94
Seventh Circuit Court of Appeals, 120, 136n51
Sexual Violence against Refugees: Guidelines on Prevention and Response (UNHCR, 1995), 74
Shacknove, Andrew E., 143n132, 256, 268n42, 268n44, 268n47
Shah, Meera, 81
"shepherding ecclesiology," 52n23
Shue, Henry, 259, 267n25
Sierra Leone, 193
Sihanouk, Prince (Cambodia), 106
Slim, Hugo, 212
Smith, Dorothy, 85
Somalia, 193, 210, 211, 213
Sri Lanka, 17, 27
Stackhouse, Max, 187
Stanley Foundation report on the responsibility to protect (2008), 207
State of the World's Refugees (UNHCR, 2006), 27
state sovereignty: and citizenship, 148–49, 158–59; and humanitarian intervention, 189–90, 196–97; and just war ethic, 186–87, 189–90, 195, 196–97; liberal egalitarian challenge to, 147–48, 149; R2P and "sovereignty as responsibility," 8, 190, 197, 207–11, 221–22; and the systemic character of war, 192
state sovereignty and boundary laws/borders, 6–7, 147–66; Catholic recognition of, 245; citizenship status and fusion of social rights/obligations, 155–56, 164n39; classical liberalism, 149, 150–52; closed border arguments, 153–56, 157–59; democratic principle of legitimation, 158–59, 160–61; democratic

procedural-political arguments, 148, 156–60; and democratic self-determination, 157–59; democratic theory of popular sovereignty, 148, 156–59; distinction between citizen and foreigner, 148–49, 158–59; and fears of labor immigration, 154, 163n31; and freedom of movement, 150–52; human rights and moral duties of humanitarian assistance, 150; human rights and popular sovereignty, 150, 160, 166n59; instrumental argument, 157, 165n48, 165n50; liberal egalitarian arguments, 147–56, 159; open border arguments, 149–54, 156–60, 159; principle of differentiated participatory rights, 160, 166n60; and putative harms to the domestic poor, 154–55; and "social cooperation," 153; social liberalism, 149, 150, 152–56; the state's protection of citizens' culture, 156, 164n42; and values of equality and justice, 150, 152–53; and welfare state considerations, 153–54
Stockholm Conference on the Human Environment (1972), 218
Stone, Sharman, 103
Strong, Maurice, 218
Suárez-Orozco, Marcelo, 77–78
subsidiarity principle, 64
Sudan: Darfur and R2P failures, 207; moral question of *jus in bello* and military force, 200–201; religion as instrument of displacement, 38; returning refugees and IDPs, 237; UNHCR's programs for IDPs, 25
Syria, 174, 175–78, 179, 182n36

Temporary Protection Status (TPS), 118, 133–34n24
terrorism, material support for, 122–24, 138nn70–71, 138nn77–78, 138nn81–82
Thakur, Ramesh, 215
Third Circuit Court of Appeals, 120, 124, 136n56
Tomasi, Silvano M., 4–5, 38, 44–45, 46–48, 55–69, 273
trafficking in persons: and the Catholic Church, 65; definitions, 235, 246n8; U and T visas, 118, 133n24
tsunami (2004), 17, 27, 172
Tucker, Robert, 187

Ubud Writers Festival (Indonesia), 97
U (crime victims) and T (trafficking victims) visas, 118, 133n24

UN Charter, 189, 192, 196–97
UN Conference on Trade and Development
(UNCTAD), 65–66n2
UN Convention against Transnational Organized Crime, 246n8
UN Convention Relating to the Status of
Refugees (1951), 18, 56, 162n10, 170, 250–51;
and Cambodia, 104; and Catholic moral
definitions, 10, 263–64; drafting, 59, 67n11;
and evolution of refugee regime, 21–22, 23;
exclusion clauses, 21, 116, 121, 124, 131n7,
137n65, 139–40n89; gaps and populations
not covered, 1–2, 8, 252, 266n21; and issue of
choice/agency, 268n46; the 1967 Protocol,
18, 56, 124, 128, 129, 139–40n89, 162n10, 251;
nonrefoulement obligations, 21, 116, 132n10,
142n121; obligations of sovereign signatories
to particular refugee flows, 250–51; official
definition of refugee, 1, 3, 18, 21, 162n10,
170, 180n4, 233, 249–51, 252, 253, 265n12,
268n46; and persecution, 16, 74, 257–58,
268–69n49; political cases, 263–64; precur-
sors, 250, 265n11; and rights of IDPs, 73; and
right to asylum, 97; and R2P, 207; socioeconomic cases, 263–64; and U.S. refugee and
asylum law, 116, 121, 124, 128, 129, 131nn6–7,
132n10, 139n89
UN Department of Economic and Social Affairs (UNDESA), 65–66n2
UN Development Programme (UNDP),
65–66n2, 218–19
UN Economic and Social Council, 67n11
UN Emergency Relief Coordinator, 172
UN High Level Dialogue on Migration and
Development (HLD) (2006), 58
UN High-level Panel on System-wide Coherence on Development, Humanitarian Assistance, and the Environment, 26, 218
UN High-level Panel on Threats, Challenges,
and Change, 214
UNICEF, 218–19
UN International Strategy for Disaster Reduction (ISDR), 241
United Nations High Commissioner for Refugees (UNHCR), 65–66n2; and Cambodia's
exclusion of Montagnards, 99, 103–11;
cluster leadership approach, 26–28, 172,
219; and Cold War-era large-scale refugee
movements, 23; compromises on refoule-
ments, 110, 111; creation of, 170; definitions of
refugees, 22–23; exclusions from protection

(serious nonpolitical crimes), 125, 141n106;
expansions of refugee regime and good
offices, 22–24; gaps in protection and assistance, 18, 169, 231–32, 252; and IDPs, 25–28,
73, 172; and Iraqi refugees, 173–80, 182n36;
and newly emerging categories of forced migrants, 26–30; and participatory processes
in refugee camps, 78–79; and protection/
assistance to displaced women and children,
73–76; and repatriation issues, 22, 23–24,
103–4, 105–8, 110, 111; R2P and war victims,
218–19; statistics on forced migrants, 1,
15–16, 31nn1–2, 180n5; the 2008 Note on
International Protection, 18; urban refugee
policy, 173, 176–78, 179
United States asylum law. *See* asylum and refugee law, U.S.
Universal Declaration of Cultural Rights, 83
Universal Declaration of Human Rights
(UDHR), 57, 209; and forced displacement,
57; and international refugee regime, 20,
57, 209; and right to leave and return to any
country, 20, 150, 161n9; and right to seek
asylum, 20, 127; and R2P, 197
University of Sussex's Pathways of Women's
Empowerment project at the Institute of
Development Studies (IDS), 85
UN Office on Drugs and Crime (UNODC),
65–66n2
UN Peacebuilding Commission, 221
UN Population Fund (UNPFA), 65–66n2
UN Relief and Rehabilitation Administration
(UNRRA), 20
UN Relief and Work Administration for Pales-
tinian Refugees, 20
UN Relief and Works Agency (UNRWA), 15, 73
UN Secretariat's Office for the Coordination of
Humanitarian Affairs (OCHA), 218
UN Transitional Authority in Cambodia, 105
urban refugee settings: Iraqi refugees, 7–8,
176–78, 179, 182n36; poverty and rental ac-
commodations, 176; and prostitution/sex
work, 177; registration problems, 176–78;
UNHCR's policy, 173, 176–78, 179
U.S. Committee for Refugees and Immigrants
(USCRI), 171–72
U.S. Conference of Catholic Bishops, 39,
53n38, 267n25
U.S. Courts of Appeals: asylum exclusion and
definition of "persecutor," 124, 140nn94–95;
asylum exclusion and definitions of serious